"*Two Feet Back* is captivating and hugely ins[...] [...]ant Korgan is the most positive, engaging individual I have ever encountered, and is certainly an inspirational hero to carry the banner for spinal cord injury awareness."
—*James J. Lynch, MD, FRCSI, FAANS, Board-certified Neurosurgeon, Fellowship-Trained Spinal Neurosurgeon*

"I've been lucky to have an incredible support system of positive thinkers in my life. Meeting Grant was more proof that when you put out those positive vibrations they will come back to you. Grant and Shawna are true magnets of positivity. Training with Grant has reminded me of the baby steps needed to make champions win, and spinal cord injuries walk."
—*Julia Mancuso, Olympic Gold Medalist*

"As we became friends with Grant, we were constantly blown away by his badassness and positive attitude. He was just NOT going to take no for an answer. He was determined to get on his feet again."
—*The Glitch Mob*

"There is only one word that can describe Grant: unbreakable. It is impossible to stop him. He is a real-life Superman that brings positivity to every situation."
—*Roy Tuscany, Co-founder and President, High Fives Foundation*

"Grant Korgan could whip his former self in an arm-wrestling match."
—*Sylas Wright*, North Lake Tahoe Bonanza

TWO FEET BACK

GRANT KORGAN

Two Feet Back
Copyright 2012 Grant Korgan

Cover Photo © Jeff Ross
Cover Design: © Ronnie Parker

Published by
Lucky Bat Books
luckybatbooks.com
10 9 8 7 6 5 4 3 2

Interior Photos: Jesse Adams, Angelo Anastassatos, Jamie Cooper, Eliot Drake, Lizzy English, Ken Evans, Keoki Flagg, Chris Hansen, Doug Hansen, Jasmine Hasi, Jesse Hon, Shaun Kegel, Pam Korgan, Duncan Lee, Jessi LeMay, Steven Malekos, Liz Margerum, Brooks McMullen, Jason Mead, Ryan Oddo, Justin Patt, Jeff Punya, Reno Gazette-Journal, Andrew Ryan, Jamie Schmidt, Nik Sullivan, Matt Theilen, Bret Valle, Fairlane Vicente, Whitney Waldroup

ISBN: 978-0-9849154-9-1

*This book is dedicated to a woman who stood by her man
in a time when her man could not stand for himself.
To the queen of my universe, my true north.
To my Shawna*

CONTENTS

PART THREE
CHOOSE POSITIVITY

PROLOGUE

Namaste (pronounced namahstay): *A Sanskrit greeting to express, "I honor the place in you where Spirit lives. I honor the place in you which is of Love, of Truth, of Light, of Peace: when you are in that place in you, and I am in that place in me, then we are One."*

On March 5, 2010, I broke my back.

But that's not why I wrote this book. If all I had to offer was a blueprint to how to recover the use of broken parts, that would be a pretty sad commentary on who I am and who those who love me reminded me to be.

You're going to get plenty of pretty gnarly details about my body here. (Maybe more than you want.) But I promise I wouldn't bother telling you about pee bags and bone shards and wheelchairs if that was all there was.

From an early age, I wanted to make an impact on the world. I worked hard in school, got good grades, started a nanotechnology firm with real-world applications. The work I did proved to be the enabling technology in some high-level research campaigns: potentially reducing cancerous tumors, improving homeland security, and even working toward fusion energy—an unlimited alternative power source. I met my dream girl, got married, had money, and that was great. I made scientific contributions, and I'm proud of that. But it turns out that was all the easy stuff.

Many people think all those things were what I was getting back to—job, money, romance. But let me tell you, when I was lying there in the hospital bed, watching my wife, Shawna, keeping a bubble of hope and positivity around me, as we slept in our van to afford physical therapy, as we used every last cent we had or could get on medical bills, I learned to accept the gifts of time and effort (and money) that people—even strangers—offered. I found there were better parts of myself to get back to. And, more importantly, better parts of other people to love.

I think we come into this world beautiful and whole. But life is a lesson in forgetting. It is so easy to lose track of that better self in the chaos and competition of everyday life. I wasn't even aware that something vital was slipping away.

My journey through recovery has been an exercise in remembering—remembering who I am, what's important in the world, and what love is. It hasn't changed me, because that person was always there. Rather, being broken down to the core of who I am gave me the gift of being able to build back up on a much stronger foundation.

We are all survivors of something. If you take out "let me compare mine to yours," we all have pain in common. There are plenty of people with much worse medical conditions than mine, conditions without recovery, and there are plenty of people with much better circumstances than my own. But we all know about suffering.

My dad says, "It's not IF shit is going to happen, but when. And the difference is how you deal with it." We've all been through the shit.

But I've never bought into the idea of good or bad events. My world is made up of cause and effect. Pain is a unitless quantity. It is or it isn't, and it IS for *all of us*. When we take out any kind of rating scale, any kind of comparison, it's easy to see that whether it's a broken back, bankruptcy, or love on the rocks, one is not worse than the other but for how we deal with it.

Pain is so often a solitary state, but we can all learn from each other's collective experience. How you handled a fire that took all your belongings can help me when facing a physical therapy session that seems impossible. How my buddy got through his divorce helps me see how to get through hopelessness and back into my true self.

Breaking my back wasn't the first accident I had. It wasn't even the first catastrophic accident. But because I had Shawna and was able to accept help from others, it offered a much bigger set of lessons for me. While I've always healed in the past, I didn't bring my memories of a better self through those recoveries.

So no, this wasn't my first major injury. I'm an independent athlete. I like sports that pit my skill and endurance against the natural world. Some people call them "extreme" sports, but I'm not a fan of that moniker. Independent sports, adventure sports, fine. But the only thing extreme about my sports was, is, and always will be the training.

My grandma always thought I had just plain lost my mind. The way she saw it, I'd be out kayaking one day down a perfectly good river when I saw a waterfall and thought, "Oh my God, there's a waterfall," and just fell off. Like the first time I was on that river, I just tipped off a waterfall by accident. But my grandmother, she didn't even drive. Hated the freeway. The simple act of driving was an adrenaline overload for her. But consider this: You can probably drive and eat a snack; you turn on blinkers, use the gas and brake and don't even think about it. No adrenaline to go junkie on. But you put my grandma on the road and she's going to spike adrenaline and probably crash—and take people with her. "Extreme" sports are my driving. I work hard to teach myself how to drive before I get on the freeway.

People call me an adrenaline junkie. But that label ignores not only what I do but who I am. The idea of an adrenaline junkie is that somehow adrenaline allows people to step out of who they are. And while I'm sure there are people who use adrenaline to take them out of their lives, who use being way outside their skill sets to push them into a fear-based high, that's not what I do. It's not what the other athletes I know do. We don't do the things we do as a way to escape; we do it to find ourselves.

There's nothing like a life-altering injury to help you appreciate how small the gears that keep a life going are. When a good day is measured in inches, not miles, the smallest decisions, the smallest shifts in intent, make all the difference.

The day I broke my back, I took a snowmobile off a jump and into a beautiful spring afternoon sky. Though I overshot where I wanted to land by nearly one hundred feet, I would've been fine but for that last two feet. It wasn't that I overshot my mark; it was that I overshot it by a mere two feet too much. If I'd only gone ninety-eight feet farther than I had planned, I would've been just fine. If I had landed a mere two feet back, I would've gone home that night to my new wife and gotten ready for a new chapter in my life, just as I'd planned. We'd had it all mapped out.

As it happened, that extra two feet changed my life in ways I never could've planned for, but I've found I was training for it my entire life. Everything Shawna and I have done since that day has been in service of getting *my* two feet back. I've regained much of what the doctors were sure I had lost. But my feet, the two feet that took me into back woods and rivers' edges, down the aisle and into meetings, the feet I hadn't even thought about in years, they became the world. The day my feet turn from burning lumps of pain into functioning appendages, I will be back. But I will never go back to the road I'd been traveling before. I don't want to.

I don't know where my feet are taking me these days, and that's just fine with me. I'm just happy to be along for the travels.

Writing this book has been about finding that place in me that lives in others as well. It is that place where we all find spirit, love, and light. It was hard at times, not just emotionally, but simply tracking down the facts, asking people about those weeks where I was slipping in and out of consciousness, talking for hours with Shawna about what that time had been like for her. It also meant endless decisions. Which people would I include by name? Whose identity should I change or hide? Would it change my truth if I combined people or compressed timelines? Would it matter if I got the color of the hospital floors wrong? How much detail would people really need to know about the truth of my recovery? How much was I comfortable sharing?

In the end, I made every decision with the end in mind. I want people to understand the reality of spinal cord injuries—the ugly and the sublime. I want people to understand what it's like for the person to whom the injury happens, but always with an eye toward what it's like for those around him or her. When in doubt, I chose what made me uncomfortable because that's the edge truth dances on.

Thanks for taking time to follow my journey. I hope it helps you undo the forgetting of life and remember the good you know. I needed a broken back to get me standing in my truth. You don't.

Namaste.

Grant and Shawna Korgan in Hawaii (Photo courtesy of Grant and Shawna Korgan)

INTRODUCTION

By Shawna Korgan

As I watched Grant write this book, I was once again inspired by this man, inspired by his true desire to simply give, to empower, and to share his heart so that others might be empowered to live their dreams, live their best lives. This is who my husband is, and I knew that from the moment I met him. I was always in awe of his power to dream big, his determination to make those dreams a reality, his pure passion for life, his unwavering positivity, and his genuine desire and ability to support the dreams of those around him. He infused my spirit with strength when I needed it, and my heart with love every moment of every day.

So when I found myself holding the face of my beloved, looking into his eyes as he told me that he couldn't feel or move anything from the belly button down, I knew that I could not, and would not, give him anything less than my highest version that he had always empowered me to be. I would draw upon the love and the promises I had made to him just five months prior, and the vision of our future that we had so beautifully created together. The situation, the accident, the experience was so intense, and one that I could have never seen coming and could have never prepared for. And yet, I felt a strength rise up in me that I knew was always there. It also came with a level of calm, focus, and an almost "mother bear" level of protection. This mode allowed me to almost disconnect from the emotions, so that I could stay more deeply connected to Grant, the situation, and what needed to be done.

As odd as it may sound, I never saw the injury. I have always seen, and always will see, my husband as whole, complete, and perfect.

As we found ourselves on this new journey, I had an opportunity to find gratitude, to seek the silver linings. I believe that one of the greatest gifts we can ever receive as human beings is to be of service to others. I found myself receiving this beautiful gift—the gift of not just being of service to *any* human being, but a human being that is the essence of my heart, the shining light in my life, my husband, my True North. And yet, every day, I am given an even more profound gift. I get to be the witness of greatness and inspiration. I am filled with awe and wonder that even though he wakes up every day with the reality of burning pain in his feet, and the inability to experience the bliss of throwing on his running shoes to take our dog for a run or to enjoy the simple pleasure of wiggling his toes, he has not wavered in his power to dream, his desire to give, his ability to empower, and his decision to always choose positivity.

I am honored to be his wife, his teammate, and I will forever walk by his side.

Shawna Korgan (a.k.a. "The Naa")

PART ONE
DECIDE WHAT YOU WANT

Grant on Mt. Whitney, 2006 (Photo by Eliot Drake)

I CLIMB

My bag of tricks is a quiver of survival tools essential to achieving the goal. Tools made of high-end, beautifully anodized, CNC-machined, 7075 and 6061-T6 aircraft-grade aluminum, Polypropylene, Dyneema, nylon, and Kevlar make up the ever-evolving risk-reduction gear strategy constantly in play as I problem-solve my way from the bottom of the rock to the top of the goal. Climbing the vertical face of a mountain wall requires agility, stamina, and a crystal clear definition of what success looks like for me.

The plan is always the same: I decide what I want out of my climb, strategize my resources at hand to constantly minimize exposure, execute without hesitation, and manage the often-overwhelming mental game to stay on track regardless of circumstances.

I visualize myself at the top of the climb, moving with precision through the many crux moves of the pitch, and then, feet firmly planted on horizontal ground at the bottom, I begin the work to achieve the vertical. I lay my gear out on my ground tarp and select the needed sizes of cam protection (spring-loaded camming devices), my passive protection (nuts, hexes, tricams), various locking and non-locking carabiners, slings, aiders, quick draws, a haul bag, a wall hauler, shoes, approach shoes, daisy chains, jumars, climbing rope, haul rope, helmet, knee pads, the belay device, water, and more snacks than I can carry—all of it thought through down to the fifi hook on my harness.

I love to climb. And because my mind loves to widget and loves gear, aid climbing completely fills the present with its constant kinematic equations re-

quired to safely continue upward. Aid climbing fills my bandwidth and quiets the noise.

With the perfectly sized cam in hand for my first placement, I compress the opposing-faced lobes—which are designed to maintain a constant camming angle with the rock, ensuring the normal force provided by the cam pressing against the rock face will supply enough resistive force (friction plus resultant vector) to hold a cam in equilibrium with the rock—with my hand, place the device in the crack of rock in front of me, and clip one of the two matching carabiners fixed to my harness with a daisy chain and an aider (a six-foot webbing ladder to climb).

I walk my feet as high up the aider as I can, being mindful to connect my fifi hook as high in the daisy chain as possible and to minimize the amount of rope slack between my belay partner and me and again go about the work of setting my next piece of protection as high as I can possibly reach. I focus on my breathing, as I am in the most probable place for a fall; in this mental space, there is only presence.

Once my next piece is fixed, I attach the other matching carabiner setup (with the second aider and daisy chain attached to my harness) to that cam's carabiner, set to and climb the new webbing ladder, fix myself to the highest point on the daisy, and repeat this process of gear selection, upward movement, and mind/body strategy until I reach the top of that particular pitch.

My hands become swollen and bloody with the constant interface of skin and rock and the repetitive placement of gear. My vision is consumed with rock, though I am beautifully aware of the expansive void that grows bigger behind me with each further-committed move I make.

I will climb, I will aid, and after some number of pitches, I will top out, and stand triumphant at the top of my goal.

March 5, 2010

"BREATHE, MAN, JUST BREATHE." Duncan's face looks down at me, exhaling white puffs. "Come on, Bro, focus right here."

I stare, because my life depends on it, into his watery blue eyes. My own fill with tears.

"Here, focus here, stay with me, Grant. Stay with me, Bro."

My microscopic inhalations, squeaky, whimpering "uh?" sounds, take monumental effort. Four, five, six seconds pass between each tiny "uh? ... uh? ... uh?" It would be easier, less painful, just to stop breathing, and sometimes I do.

"Come on buddy. Breathe for me," Duncan, my friend since first grade, is firm, insistent, even a little annoyed. "*Breathe*, man."

I do what he says, because I have no choice. I realize once again what lies in store for me. I can't do anything but lie here and deal. Just wait here in the snow for that helicopter they promise me is coming, and breathe.

"Just...keep...talking," I exhale. Shit. Gotta inhale. Open the abdomen, push more shards of bone into muscle. "Uh? ... uh?"

How long has it been since they said the chopper was coming...twenty minutes? Thirty?

I *know* my feet are where they should be; I mean I saw them through my helmet's face shield as Ryan laid me here in the snow. Logically, I know my legs are down there, but I can't move my neck to look down from inside this helmet, and what I feel there is...nothing. Nothing at all below my belly button except this odd sensation of a warm sack of metal BBs strapped to my waist. That's all. Just a sort of warm, eerily comfortable sloshing just below my belly button. Below that, I feel nothing, can move nothing.

Above my belly button, though, it's Armageddon. My back is more than broken—it has exploded, and it feels like there are particles of bone shooting through every fiber in my torso. Just wedging and cutting all the surrounding muscle like serrated knives in all directions, and as my body shivers uncontrollably, seizure-like, on its plunge into hypothermia, the knives push deeper and deeper.

I have to keep telling myself where my feet are, because my brain thinks that my whole lower body has rolled underneath my torso. I feel like I'm actually lying on my pelvis and thighs, cartoonishly bent in half, like, if I could turn my head to the side, I'd see my calf, or could reach up with my hand and grab my heels.

I'm vaguely aware of the sound of Ryan's snowmobile in the distance, carving away at the makeshift helipad designed to help the chopper that must come, absolutely must come, and carry me to safety.

How long has it been? If it's possible, my breath is even more labored, now becoming a faint, "huh… huh… huh…," like a scared puppy.

In my head, a different battle wages: *Fuck I don't know how much longer I can do this. Fuck I can't hold on can't hold on.* And then, *Yes, you can. Keep breathing, don't freak out, stay strong, keep breathing, don't freak out, stay strong, keep breathing, don't freak out, stay strong.*

I keep thinking the pain will crescendo and level off, because how can it keep intensifying without end? Yet it does, it just keeps building and building and building. Searing hot razors in my back, my abdomen, my chest. I'm crying, a deep, internal cry, not just a weepy cry but crying in my bones and muscles and cells. And there are tears rolling down my face, and I wish I could just take off this fucking helmet and wipe the tears off my face, but I can't even do that, and I can't say anything or do anything about it, and if we even try to move my helmet the damage could escalate.

"Hang in there, buddy. Doin' okay? Stay with me, okay? Heli's coming," Duncan says. Ryan has the camera in my face. Hiding his worry, I know.

I need Duncan to keep it together. I try to think of something to say, something funny, to keep it light. I just keep smiling, like, "It's just a bump in the road, guys. We're okay." *I'm sorry I fucked up this perfect day.*

Fuck, how much longer? The clouds are turning a darker shade of gray, the shadows getting longer. All around me there's not a sound, just a snowy silence.

Okay, helicopter. I need you now. You coming?

It was the best day of sledding . . . and the worst (Photo by Duncan Lee)

CHAPTER 1
THE ACCIDENT

That morning I woke in the blue-black of early morning, feeling surprisingly well rested.

Too well rested. Shit, had I missed it?

I shot up to look over Shawna's shoulder at the alarm clock, which I'd set to go off at an ungodly 5:30 in the morning.

I exhaled deeply and rolled back onto my elbows. 4:57 a.m.

But I was too stoked for the day ahead to go back to sleep. It was way too early to wake Shawna up, so I slowly, gingerly pulled myself up to sit and leaned against our headboard, rubbing the sleep from my face.

I looked over at the dreaming blond slumbering beside me, the neighbor's outdoor floodlight sending a shaft of white light across her shoulder. Almost five months I'd been married to Shawna, and still, every morning, I woke up in near disbelief that I was lucky enough to awake and find this supermodel laying next to me. I sat there for a few moments and listened to her soft puffs of breath and stroked her hair, tousled now from sleep.

Warm, relishing the sensation of the sheet against my bare legs, and overcome with desire for my sleeping bride, I considered lying back down and spooning the morning away. But the siren call of snowmobiling in Sonora's fresh powder was too strong to ignore, and it had been far too long a wait for me. So I planted my feet on the floor, carefully removing the covers so as not to wake Shawna, and stood. I reached my hands high into the air, inhaled, and stretched my entire body, from my fingers to my toes. Then I tiptoed out of the room in my boxers, with our big brown dog, Obie, trailing behind me. I opened the back door to let him out, and then ambled down the hall to make the coffee.

The cozy perfume of freshly brewed coffee wafted gently through the air and woke Shawna, who wanted to be sure to see me off on this, my first day back on a sled all season. I returned to the bedroom, coffees in hand, to find her sitting up in bed.

"Morning, babe," she said, yawning and rubbing her eyes as she sat under the covers in her impossibly small, white cotton t-shirt.

"Good morning," I said, handing her a warm mug of creamy coffee and kissing the top of her head.

Ryan Oddo planned to arrive right at 6:00, so we could get an early start on the 120-mile drive to Sonora, where we'd meet up with our buddies Duncan and Ken. I didn't want to keep him waiting, so without sitting to drink my coffee, I began turning circles in the room, mentally ticking off the things I needed to do. By now I was wound up. I headed to my closet, grabbed a duffel, and threw in my go-to clothes for starting a day of snowmobiling—a quilted blue, fire-proof Carhartt jacket and tan Carhartt pants, both of which were covered with patches and grease stains from years of dirt bike, truck, and snowmobile maintenance. Then I went back to the kitchen, grabbed a handful of protein bars, ripped one open and shoved it down my throat as I moved through the house collecting gear.

I opened the garage door at 6:00 sharp to find Ryan's enormous truck idling on the driveway. He pulled in, and after a solid round of brotherly hugs and high fives, we began loading my sled, duffel, and other gear into the back of the truck, neither of us speaking, just two snow junkies moving on automatic pilot.

Shawna, now wearing leopard-print fleece pajama pants and an over-sized sweater over her t-shirt, stepped into the garage in her black shearling boots, carrying her coffee with one hand and restraining Obie with the other.

"Hey, Ryan," she said, holding Obie by the collar to keep him from jumping on Ryan.

"Hey, Naa!" he said, hugging her and then rubbing Obie's head.

The gear was loaded quickly. The sun was coming up to reveal a perfect bluebird day, crisp and cold, with not a cloud in the sky. A shiver of excitement ran through me, and Shawna could read it from across the garage. She smiled, watching me approach her.

"Go big today, babe," she said, putting her hands on my face to kiss me goodbye.

"I love you," I said, quietly. Then I turned to Ryan and shouted, "Let's go, dude; it's on!"

We hopped in the truck, backed out, and I waved to Shawna. I had butterflies in my stomach. It was going to be one of The Great Days. It was gorgeous out, we were high on anticipation, the music was cranked, and we were rolling with $30,000 worth of toys in Ryan's big, beautiful, dialed-to-the-hilt Chevy Duramax truck, high-fiving each other, singing songs, and fist-pumping the sky as we rode south, paralleling the eastern Sierra, on the way to go big at Sonora.

March 5th was on pace to be one of the greatest days on record. Not just because it was shaping up to be one of the best days for snowmobiling, but also because this Friday was the culmination of months of hard work that had drained my energy, cut into my personal time, and deprived me of the bliss of being a newlywed. Just this week, I had reached the end of that long, difficult path, and come Monday, I'd take my first steps along a brand new one.

My business partner and best friend, Steven Malekos, and I had spent the past two months working at Stanford, our heads buried in a six-figure nanotechnology project that we knew could potentially, literally, *change the world*. With a two-pronged end-game potential, we were talking about applied laser physics research that, if successful, had the ability to make headway in proton acceleration (which has implications in potential cures and advanced therapies for cancer). It could also have legs in the area of fusion research, which, if successful, could provide unlimited alternative power, using the simple model of our sun, with the only by-product being *clean water*. This was technological development in a realm that many brilliant people had spent their entire lives studying. The stakes were incredibly high and the science so promising that we'd ultimately put our finances, our relationships, and our bodies on the line, working ninety hours a week in a windowless lab at Stanford for the first two months of 2010.

Once our portion of this project was finished, it signaled an end to the active role I had played as president of NanoLabz, the nanotechnology firm I had co-founded six years prior. Since marrying in October 2009, Shawna and I, both business owners, had barely seen each other, and had been so focused on work that we'd even held off taking our honeymoon until this project was complete. For the last two months, I had only seen Shawna on the occasional, brief weekend visit at home in Reno.

And despite many unforeseen challenges, Steven and I did finish. I left Stanford with a plan to spend a relaxing week at home with my wife, getting in some long-overdue snowmobiling after a winter of total recreational deprivation, and maybe even taking a quick weekend road trip with Shawna. Then, first thing Monday, I'd begin the next chapter: moving into an advisory position at NanoLabz and beginning my training to be a helicopter pilot, the career I had wanted since childhood and known for years was my true calling, what everything I had been doing all my life had led me toward. I drove I-80 east through Donner Pass with my windows down, exhilarated by the notion that this was a prophetic week, a fulcrum upon which my life would turn. Beginning next week, I'd get what I had told Steven I wanted as we cleaned up the lab the day before: "I just want to have a simpler life, and more time with my wife."

The work portion of the pivotal week upon which my whole life turned passed rather unremarkably. Monday, March 1 was Shawna's birthday, which we really didn't intend to celebrate until the following weekend when we could get away for a few days. On Tuesday, the primary activity of the day was cleaning my van for that trip and taking Obie, the dog we'd only had for a few weeks and which I'd barely seen, for a long walk. On Wednesday (Oh, how the paperwork eats up valuable time!), Steven and I spent the entire day prepping the necessary documentation for delivery of our finished project, the last bit of the NanoLabz job. And Thursday, I

Sonora Pass, 2010 (Photo by Ryan Oddo)

joined Shawna's Crunch Cardio class at The Sanctuary, a wellness retreat/
fitness club/spa, of which she was co-creator and co-owner.

The Sanctuary had been Shawna's dream and guiding passion since
age thirteen. Her education had been in anatomy and physiology, and her
professional aspirations had been in the field of holistic wellness. She threw
her heart, soul, and body into every class or client session. Which might
explain why that class had made me feel so whipped.

That, in itself, was remarkable. I was a professional athlete, and, with
the exception of the previous two months, I had spent nearly every day
of my life engaged in some kind of outdoor sport. I'd worked my way up
from Class 1 kayaker to Class 5 over ten years' time, had spent twenty years
riding bicycles, and since putting on skis at age two, I had dedicated entire
seasons to my development as a skier. The changes from sport to sport
with the seasons had kept my body cross-trained to the point where it was
ready to go the minute the call came. I had always taken immense pride in
the fact that my lifetime of training had created muscle memory, so that
I knew I could do pretty much anything right off the couch and fire on
all cylinders. We called them "Off-the-Couch Productions," me and my
buddies from Incline Village, Nevada, the little town on the shore of Lake

Tahoe where I'd spent most of my life. Like, I'd get a call in the middle of a workweek, and I could say, "Sure! I'll jump in on that ridiculously hard kayak run I've never done before. It'll be my first time kayaking all season, and we're kayaking that? Game on!" Sure, I knew lots of kayakers had been boating every day for months to prep for that same run I'd just shown up for, but I knew I could rely on my innate athletic ability and years of training enough to just show up. I loved off-the-couching, having the body primed at all times and ready for anything.

But after two months hunched over lab equipment, I felt run down after a one-hour Crunch Cardio class. Yet at the same time, I thought, with all confidence in my body's ability to rebound, "Isn't it so great that my body works the way it does?"

And I needed it to, because six feet of snow had dumped in the Sierra that week, and the call did come. My childhood friend, Duncan Lee, along with our friends Ryan Oddo and Ken Evans, were ready to go snowmobiling. "Green light! I'm there!" I said, even though I was whipped from a Crunch Cardio class. I'd been so deprived, so desperate to get out there into that powder. It had to be that Friday. It wouldn't have occurred to me to say no. I'd rally.

Sonora, just about an hour and a half south of Reno, was hands down our favorite place in the world to snowmobile. Not to short-change the other areas popular to local snow enthusiasts—Castle Peak, Mount Rose, Little Truckee Summit, Jackson Meadow—which in their own ways are all amazing, full of great terrain and offering lots of possibility for riders deep in their backcountry woods. But not a one, not a single one, is on the scale or magnitude of Sonora. This area of roughly 200 square miles, depending on that year's access laws, off the Sonora Pass Road, is the second-highest-elevation pass through the Sierra Nevada range, where you'll find peaks 10,000-plus feet high that are completely open to climbing, jumping, skiing…anything. And there's a sense of lawlessness there, a rush that comes from feeling about a million miles from anyone, that just can't be replicated on snow anywhere near the Tahoe basin.

Grant touching the void, Sonora Pass, 2010 (Photo by Shaun Kegel)

Any day you go to Sonora is a big day. The terrain challenges every skill and forces talent progression without asking. Every time you go to Sonora it's the biggest jump you've ever done, the biggest chute you ever climbed, the biggest drop you've ever descended, the closest brush you ever had with an avalanche—at least, that had been the case with me.

Back in 2004, thanks to being in the right place at the right time, I had narrowly missed an avalanche on another Great Sonora Day. I was riding a 2000 Summit 700 ZX Chassis, a gorgeous yellow snowmobile that looked to me like a pissed-off bumblebee. Being in my late twenties, I was still early on in my development as a snowmobiler, but I had learned enough about snow science to understand how avalanches worked. I knew that when you have dissimilar layers of snow, all coming in at different times, and in different temperatures, conditions were ripe for avalanches. Being from Tahoe, what we call the "Banana Belt" for its warm, placid, almost benign winter weather, we didn't get much of this. But I knew enough to be terrified of skiing in the Pacific Northwest, the Canadian Rockies, or Utah. Shit, I'm scared to death of Utah, the Death Zone, where every season there are reports of avalanche deaths. Places like that, with those lake wind advisories that freeze moisture in the air then force a snow dump of four feet so you're skiing on ice floe, an entire mountain can cut loose in a second.

Bottom line, you never go out into the avalanche-prone zones the day after it snows—especially in a place like Sonora. Every single day you wait after a snow, it gets exponentially safer, until about a week, when that advantage begins to exponentially diminish. So there was always a calculation rolling in my head.

On that day in 2004, another perfect day, we were just barely inside that window of safety, probably taking too much of a chance, but everyone was vibrating at such a high level. And we never had a day there that wasn't through-the-roof amazing, so this day was irresistible.

We had arrived at a big, long series of hills, covered in the lushest powder. We threw pow turns, boondocking through the trees, and then my buddies, the same three guys, headed up that hill. I was squeamish about avalanche danger, and though we hadn't tested the snow by digging avy pits to check the snow layers, I knew there were some slick under-layers of ice from past storms. I veered left to the flat to watch them go up and note their locations in case we needed to dig them out later. It's what you do.

I watched without breathing, expecting the snow to slide. It didn't. Over and over they went up and nothing slid. We felt safe.

We headed off to one of our favorite zones at Sonora, a saddle between two mountains. But because of the breadth of the mountains, this low point became a gully, a channel between about a thousand feet of mountain on both sides, so that snowmobiling inside it was like traveling between two walls of snow. I liked putting the sled on its side, carving into those walls with the upper side of the snowmobile, interfacing with the mountain.

Which is what I was doing when I heard the unmistakable crackle of splitting ice. A sort of thumping settling, then a fracture zipping from behind me across the wall I was carving, shooting across the entire 1,500-foot long, 500-foot tall wall of snow at hundreds of miles an hour. Like lightning slicing the snow ten feet above where I rode.

My brain kicked into calculation mode. If I could shoot up the wall, get on top of the slide, it wouldn't pull me down with it. But as I pinned the throttle and tore upward, the snow began pulling me upstream, like a river. I knew I couldn't make that move, or I'd be flipped upstream and pulled underneath.

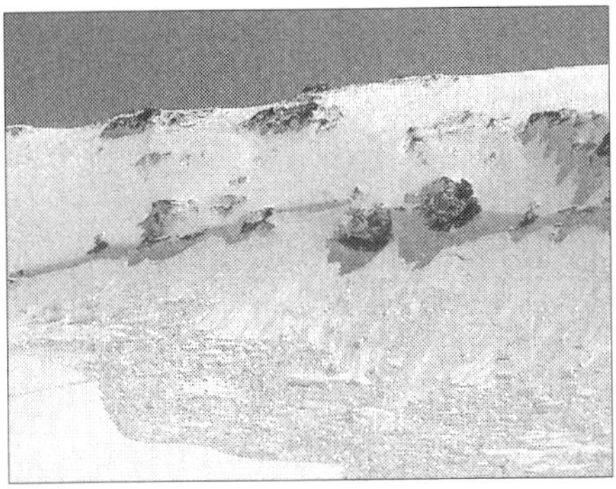

Avalanche at Sonora Pass (Photo by Ryan Oddo)

But if the snow was going to act like a river, I could kayak. So I did. Drawing on my years of river training, I shifted my weight to the downhill side, turned the sled to ride the sheet of snow like a waterfall, and pinned the throttle as far as it could go, maxing out the sled at about ninety miles an hour. With the snow moving at about twenty and increasing in velocity by the second, I could outrun it at this speed. The snow started breaking into chunks, turning into a boulder field that could easily wrap me up inside it, but unbelievably, I was skipping off the chunks, outrunning them.

I risked a glance over my shoulder and saw the snow growing more distant behind me. Exhilarated, I fist-pumped the air with my left arm. "YEEEAAAAH!" came my war cry, my veins raging with adrenaline.

I pulled into the meadow where Duncan, Ryan, and Ken had been watching me, their machines ready to go after me had I been pulled under, and saw that the slide had stopped. Amped to the gills, I lunged off the sled directly onto Oddo, tackling him to the ground and screaming, "DUDE! Holy shit! Fuck yeah, that was *too* close!"

March 5, 2010 was again a spectacularly perfect day at Sonora. It had snowed for the last two days, and the conditions were epic, one for the books. The snow had all come in at the same temperature, meaning there would be no slick under-layers of ice for new powder to slide on—avalanche danger today would be extremely low.

Deep pow turns with Truckee, California in the background (Photo by Duncan Lee)

The plan was to spend a whole day on the sleds, filming for our snow-mobile company, Alpine Assassins, which was a company Duncan, Ken, Randy, and I had founded to support backcountry enthusiasts across the board, no matter their sports. Founding member Randy Sugihara once said, "It doesn't matter how big you go, as long as you go." His words became the cornerstone of the AA organization, which aimed to unify the broad range of backcountry users (from BC skiers to the hardcore hill climbers to the ramp jumpers to the mellow trail crews). Alpine Assassins promoted inclusion, which it did by selling gear, conducting safety clinics, and making sports films, all of which would lead up to, eventually, the full-length, feature film we were shooting that day.

Right away we set up our tripods and began rolling cameras on the sleds coming off the truck, the morning's first, quick runs. Savoring every moment, deliberate in our filming plans, we took our time getting all our gear on, planning the shots we knew we wanted to get—three big jumps were the bill for the day. Trucks locked, helmets on, sleds revving, we banged bars all the way out into the open snow, our ritual. Roads became trails, which became huge, open expanses of cliffs and mountains, speed clicking up—forty miles per hour, fifty, sixty, seventy—egging each other on, boys being boys.

I threw pow turns because I could, around and around, playing with the throttle, my balance, the fresh snow.

I got into snowmobiling from watching Ewoks in *Star Wars: Return of the Jedi*. After seeing those speeder bikes tearing through the trees, I wanted a speeder bike more than anything. That sense of flying above the ground. Sledding through powder—that, more than anything else—is like that. The pow turn is smooth, flowing, a dance, more like flying through the air than plunging through snow. The machine and rider become one, and the duo goes from being a clunky, loud machine to a light, nimble, beautiful translation of balance, throttle, and physics.

Finally it was time to build and hit the first big jump of the day.

We wanted to start by hitting a jump I'd nailed the previous year. It was pretty big—a rock outcrop so large and round a rider could spend long seconds in mid-air. Flying. Like good snowmobilers, in our avalanche safety kit, we always carried shovels (along with probes, beacons, overnight gear, emergency medical supplies, etc.), and set to scooping the snow, building and shaping a giant cheese wedge jump set back roughly twenty feet from the rocky ledge we planned to fly over. We'd built it every year, but this year we were working a different angle, setting it back farther than previous years, changing the flight path, packing out a longer in-run, and starting

Two jumps before Grant broke his back (Photo by Duncan Lee)

the day with what would be one of the biggest jumps of the year. This one was five or six feet high, about twelve feet long, and if all went as planned, would send me more than a hundred feet through the air.

Ken was feeling this jump, itching for it. "I got it," he said, and we knew he wanted to hit it first. We set up all the cameras, positioned at three different angles, synced up our radio communication, and Duncan gave the green light.

"Okay, Ken's rolling," Duncan's voice said through my radio, and I knew I had about three seconds before I'd see him.

Ken's sled left the ground and traveled for *days.* Yes! A hundred feet? One-fifty? I was high, intoxicated, literally vibrating, I wanted that jump so badly. Ached for it.

My body positioned itself on the 2008 SkiDoo XP 800cc, 2-stroke, 146-inch track, ultra sled to take the jump next, while my engineer brain took over. I examined the jump from all angles. *Okay, given the trajectory that I want, I want about this much speed. Given I want to go this far with this trajectory, and this angle, I want to get to this height and I want to land there.* I did equations, some easy math to determine that I needed to be going roughly 15.5 miles per hour when I came off the lip. Visualizing my

Life-long friend Duncan Lee giving Grant the look-down
(Photo by Ryan Oddo)

run has always been critical to me in these "go versus no-go" scenarios. I ran film of it in my head, saw myself clipping along at precisely 15.5. My mental game was strong; my head was where it needed to be. It was time. I turned on my GoPro helmet camera, and to later let Shawna know I was thinking about her, held my wedding ring up to the lens. I hit the throttle, feeling like I'd hit 15.5 exactly. I came in it at the angle I wanted, and nailed it—an amazing flight with a bone-jarring impact. Absolutely beautiful. My landing, just a few feet to the left of where Ken's had been, was gorgeous, exactly as I'd seen it in my head. All was right and perfect in the universe.

Next it was Ryan's turn, then Duncan's. By now, I was filming from the rock outcrop. Duncan, my brother from another mother, seemed to be doing his jump just for me. He leaned off his sled, stared right at me the whole way down, and even though I couldn't see his face through his helmet, I knew he was grinning the whole way down.

I'd met Duncan on the playground at Incline Elementary School, both of us first-graders. I'd spotted him building a model airplane on the concrete during recess. I had walked up and asked what he was doing.

Without looking up, he had responded, "Building an F-111." And when I had insisted there was no such thing, his clever reply had been, "Yes-huh!"

"Nu-uh," I said, and then, "Well… can I help you build it?"

He agreed, and we'd been brothers ever since.

After Duncan's jump, I became seized with a retroactive pang of winter deprivation. "I have to hit that one again," I said. I'd missed all the other film shoots they'd done this year, had been in a lab for two months. I had to soak up every moment, hit every jump, make up for lost time. My boys agreed, and I was off, not a moment to lose.

This time, I wanted a new approach. Once again, the calculations began: *Veering right this time instead of left, I can catch the lip just right, get a little more height. A solid fifteen ought to do it.* I turned the throttle, pulling right, then hit the air.

I sailed a little bit higher. Too high. I was flying, flying…I knew I was going to hit hard, but by now there was nothing I could do. Although I nailed the landing, it was ugly, too hard. My head fogged, my sight blurred.

After bringing the sled to a stop, I sat for a moment, dazed, my head ringing. I checked my limbs, moved my head from side to side, and made sure I hadn't broken anything. The jump had rung my bell, but I was okay.

I sat up, feeling slightly dizzy, wondered fleetingly if I'd given myself a concussion, and decided it didn't matter. I had no plans to stop, despite the fact that, in my mind, a sort of post-nap, waking-dream-like conversation was happening in my head that went something like this: "Hey, look, I'm snowmobiling! Right on!"

I know. At this point I should have stopped, right? Forget it. I'd simply waited too long for this. Shit, I was at Sonora. I had planned to go hard all day, and that didn't involve stopping after two jumps. I dug in, shook it off. I rallied through the woods, threw more pow turns, goofed off, and watched, as if from a distance, my friends packing up gear to head off to the next location. I watched them dig the next jump while I sat there doing nothing—in and of itself a complete taboo in our world. I was aware of that, too, aware that I was sitting on my sled and just watching the other three dig my jump, as if to say, "Hey, thanks for building that, bro; I appre-

Grant loves to fly (Photo by Ken Evans)

ciate it!" I knew it was shitty, and yet there I sat. I knew I needed to take a minute, which I took, but told the others nothing.

I stood up on the side of the snowmobile and took a piss—as it turns out, the last time I'd stand to piss for a very long time, and it fills me with longing, now, to think about how cavalierly I did it. I ate a Clif bar, pounded a Sugar-Free Red Bull. Shook off the hard hit, and I was back.

My mental clarity and situational awareness came back just in time to finish building the jump. I visualized the successful trajectory, pulled my starter cord, then sent it full throttle on my sled to the sky. Another picture-perfect jump. High-fives went all around, energy was at its highest, and we were off to our next jump.

For four years we'd all romanticized this jump. We'd longed to hit it, pulled up to it every year to consider for a moment, "Maybe this time?" and then, reluctantly, moved on every time. It was designed and built each year by a snowboarding film company, and, though the jump looked enticing as

The second jump of the day, before Grant ends up on his back
(Photo by Ken Evans)

hell, each year it had been rebuilt a little wrong, at least for a snowmobile. Following the steep take-off ramp came forty feet of flat ground, with a tree in the way, and a sharp knuckle that had to be flown over. (The knuckle is the area where the ground goes from flat to the safety of a steep landing zone.) The steep fall-away transition zone in the jump was about eighty vertical feet. It would make for a perfect landing. Beyond the steep transition slope was no man's land—the flats. After about a hundred horizontal feet of flats, the line closed out into a perpendicular wall of trees.

For snowboards, of course, it was perfect—on a board you could land on that transition, manage the flat, turn tightly. But on a snowmobile, you'd have to go big enough to clear both the tree and the knuckle, but small enough to get down on the transition before it flattened out, and avoid landing on flat ground. Land on flat ground and you would probably break your back.

But this year, it was a thing of beauty. The boarders had gotten it just right. We pulled up on our sleds, the four of us, sitting behind and to the side of the ramp, staring beyond the lip of the jump, knowing that on this, the greatest day of sledding we could ever remember having, we'd also, finally, have this. I was driven by a compelling force that I didn't quite understand. It was deep, loud, and clear within me. I felt calm, clear, and powerful in saying these words: "Green light. This one's for me."

"Bro, the light's changing," said Duncan as we walked up the ramp jump. "I don't know … day's almost over. Snow's firming up. We probably won't get a good shot, man."

I could see myself going off this jump and landing perfectly. My brain was already ticking off calculations, running film of it. The jump spoke to me, the challenge of its steep, tight, technical pocket-landing a siren call for me. The four years of mystique and two months of sitting in a hole at Stanford and this perfect day, this perfect weekend that was meant to change my life, all had to mean something, right? Clouds be damned, now was the time.

"This one isn't about the camera," I said. "This one is for me."

But the clouds *were* changing, becoming darker, grayscale, ominous. In earnest, I approached my calculations with precision, figured the trajectories and speed I needed. I spotted the tree I'd use as my check tree, which would allow me to gauge and calibrate my takeoff speed. And it was all about speed—get rolling, make it happen, seize the moment, gotta go, getting darker, squeeze this jump in, everyone's waiting.

I gave the thumbs up to my crew, each of whom had a camera and a unique angle on the jump, because it was worth trying to capture it. Ryan was down below, waiting at my finish line. Duncan was off to the side and Ken up top, shooting the jump. I let my sled take me up the hill, killed the engine, and carefully considered my plan. I exhaled. I needed to take a minute, check in with myself, to find out what my little voice was saying. "How do you feel about this? Why are you doing it? Who are you doing it for?" It was common practice for me.

My little voice said, "Go for it." I didn't just want it. I *needed* it. It was meant for me.

I fired up my sled and waved my arm wide in a circle above my head. "I'm going!"

"Grant's going," I heard Duncan's voice on the radio in my pocket.

"Dropping," I said.

As I began my approach, I caught sight of my check tree, fifty feet or so from the lip of the jump. I kept my eyes on it, because I knew exactly how quickly I should be going when I passed that tree. Instantly, I knew I was moving too slowly.

Any other day, I would have stopped, circled back, and begun again. My engineer brain operated this way: recalibrate, create the perfect conditions, nothing out of place. But as I said, I was deprived. More than that. I was *depraved*, frantic to take this jump, on this perfect day. I didn't have time to circle back—*now, do it now*, I told myself. Darkening clouds pushed me on, "Hurry up, everyone's waiting on you." So, if I was going too slowly, I'd just give it a little more gas and BRAAAAAP! Off the lip I went.

The second I left the ground I knew I'd overshot the jump. I would miss the mountain entirely, go at least one hundred feet beyond my touchdown point, land completely on flat ground, just barely beyond the safety of the transition slope. Going eighteen miles an hour, when I should have been doing seventeen. Still climbing when I should have been cresting, rounding the backside of the tree. There went the mountain, the knuckle, the transition … I was still climbing. I was now looking at more than one hundred feet of free fall to flat ground.

You're breaking bones, I said to myself, completely lucid and methodically calculating, seeing everything moving in slow motion, without a sound. Time slowed down to frames. I had maybe three seconds. But it felt like minutes of internal conversation and cognitive thought. *What bones am I breaking? Do I jump off the sled or stay on?* Weather had changed throughout the day, the warmth of the sun melting the snow, then sunset freezing it up to ice again.

If I jump off, I'll break my back, I thought. The last thing I wanted was paralysis, but I could handle some broken bones. If I stayed on, though, I'd have a foot or more of surface area that could dissipate the pressure, plus the cushion of the seat. I'd keep my butt off the seat and lean to the left to break the right leg. *No, wait! If I break my femur, we're too far into the backcountry; I could die in two hours from blood poisoning.* No, I'd take the right foot out of the cup, break the left leg when I land on it. *That's it.*

Seconds before Grant's spine bursts (Photo by Duncan Lee)

Second angle of Grant's back-breaking jump (Photo by Ken Evans)

I pulled my right foot out of the foot cup, saw ground approaching fast, and revved the engine, the idea being that I would keep it moving forward to lessen the impact.

I hit the ground and *snap*. I brought the sled to a stop before I hit the trees. But the damage was done. When I'd hit, like a light switch, everything from my belly button down had turned off. Gone.

Completely running on adrenaline now, I struggled to bring the sled to a stop before hitting the tree line—*brake brake brake brake brake* and stop, just as I had begun to slide between the trees.

Ryan, watching from his post at the bottom of the jump, knew the landing had been bad, but just how bad it had been wasn't obvious to any of them. Ryan was at the tree line, at my side, by the time I cut my engine and sat slumped, hanging to the left of the sled.

"Are you okay?" he shouted.

"My back is broken, I can't feel my legs," I said. "I need a helicopter." By now, I was in gripping agony, chopped in two and folded in half.

Years of riding together, years of training in wilderness first-aid and rescue courses, years of living in the mountains, years of safety clinics, filming, and know-how clicked into gear.

A break in any of the twenty-four differently shaped vertebrae of the spine leaves the extraordinarily delicate spinal cord exposed and vulnerable. One wrong move could sever it, resulting in permanent paralysis. Getting me from the sled to the ground meant playing Rochambeau with my chance of ever walking again; a mere twinge could sever the cord.

With zero hesitation, Ryan tore off his helmet and gloves, and gingerly slid behind me on the seat to execute our hastily made plan to get me off the sled. He would become a human backboard.

Duncan was there with us in seconds, having seen the strange landing but not really knowing ... fuck, we'd all had strange landings before that didn't result in broken backs. It hadn't been obvious just how wrong things had gone from where he'd been.

"Grant broke his back. We gotta get him off the sled," Ryan began explaining his plan to Duncan. "Get Ken down here."

"Ken, Ken, Grant broke his back, not good, need medevac now. Get down here," Duncan radioed up to Ken, then took his helmet off and went to my feet.

Ryan's muscles tightened. He grabbed me around the chest, and made himself as stiff as humanly possible. As gently, as slowly as he possibly could—more slowly than I thought I could bear—he pulled me onto him, transferring my weight to his own back. Duncan went to work, maneuvering our legs up over the sled, sliding Ryan off, keeping his own body perfectly straight, now responsible for the weight of both of us, sliding us both into the snow. Once in the snow, the plan was to gradually replace Ryan, as he slowly slid out from under me, with packed snow.

Now I had a decision to make. Did we risk severing my spine to get me in a space blanket, a dry environment that might help me avoid hypothermia, should we, God forbid, be forced to spend the night here? Or did I remain in the snow, risking hypothermia yet preventing further spine movement, in the hope that a helicopter could come rescue me? It was all or nothing. The weather was changing, a storm was clearly moving in.

Even an inch of movement could destroy my life. I'd either die of hypothermia here or get a shot at recovery if a chopper came. My odds improved if I stayed where I was.

Thoughts of Shawna filled my mind. Just five months ago, I had promised so many things to her, so many amazing things—a life of adventures, of dancing, running, traveling, being her complete source of happiness. By fucking God, I would have that. I'd pull the sword out and start swinging it at people, fight until my last breath to get back to being the man she married. We had too many plans, and a wheelchair was not in them. I'd lie here in the snow and take my chances. I chose hope over warmth.

By now, Ken had arrived on his sled. "Ken, helicopter..." Duncan said, and, like that, it was decided. All our hopes were pinned on that ride, and Ken, the fastest of the four, was gone.

Grant in the first ten minutes of this journey
(Photo by Ryan Oddo)

CHAPTER 2
RESCUE

R isky though it may have been, the pivotal decision I made in a split second that I would remain in the snow turns out to have been more fortuitous than I had believed it would be. The extreme cold cut down on swelling, thereby potentially reducing further pressure on my spinal cord. I've since learned that when an NFL player suffers a spinal cord injury, the current protocol is ice—to actually produce a state of hypothermia to slow the blood and reduce pressure.

Still, there was the pain. And it just kept getting worse. Breaking my back was painful enough, but then there was the shivering that only exacerbated it. The impulses of the muscles contracting and releasing for at least an hour and a half, the shivering signalling my descent into hypothermia, was all absolutely blinding. It took all of my energy, every ounce of it, to manage my pitiful, wincing, high-pitched "huh? ... huh? ... huh?" breaths. Each puff of air was a dagger, wedging bone fragments more deeply into muscle, so that the daggers spread further throughout my upper body with every breath. So I held my breath, as much as I could, until Duncan or

Ryan, whoever's turn it was to keep me going while the other drove mad circles on his snowmobile to carve the helipad, popped into the left of my rapidly clouding view of darkening sky to say, "Grant, breathe, keep breathing."

All I wanted to do was unfold. The sensation that my calves were behind my head was so real, so unsettling, that I almost believed I could simply unbend my body and alleviate the pain. I even made small attempts to do so, but was prevented each time by Duncan and Ryan, who by turns kept me down.

In my delusional state, I searched frantically for something to focus on. I noticed how remarkably blue Duncan's eyes were, even through my helmet face shield. Why had I never noticed before? "Your wife... She's a lucky girl," I wheezed. "You have... beautiful eyes." Those eyes, I knew, wanted to cry but would never do so in front of me.

Then another thought occurred to me: my camera! The helmet camera we'd received the night before from a sponsor—was it still rolling?

"Hey, I got footage...of the jump," I said in a whisper to Duncan. It was arduous, talking.

"With what?" he asked.

"GoPro, helmet."

"There's nothing there, man."

"Must have...ripped off during impact," I said, disappointed.

The thought, *I want to completely document this injury,* had never consciously entered into any of our minds. We never really thought, *Golly gee, this next year's gonna be a rough one. Let's make a movie about it.*

Still, though, Alpine Assassins had been born with that mindset in place, the idea of capturing all the moments that make professional snowmobiling so intense for us. So we never powered down; in fact, we were always aware of the cameras, thinking about how this footage would turn out later. That point-of-view helmet cam, we knew, would be something we'd all want to see later.

Duncan, who had been director of photography and principal cinematographer on our film, left me with Ryan and hiked up to where I'd landed.

He began pacing in circles, examining the tracks in the snow. There was an odd hole... He reached inside and pulled out the GoPro camera.

The footage contained my jump, from start to finish, the impact, and twenty minutes of white that followed the camera being ripped from my head. Then, movement, and Duncan's face peering into the lens.

What had driven us to Sonora was precisely the thing that made rescue so difficult. We were hours from our home in Reno, hours from anywhere—even from the nearest ski resort, Mammoth Mountain. We were a good twenty miles, in the snow, from any trucks, any method of conveyance out of the snow.

Ken left the scene at a race pace, knowing time was against us. This meant holding the throttle all the way to the rev-limiter, pushing the snowmobile as fast and hard as it would possibly go without blowing up, doing up to eighty miles an hour through trees, in and around deep, twisting mountain passes for roughly seven miles until, finally, he reached the road that took him thirteen miles to the military base and, hopefully, a helicopter.

No doubt that his ride meant life or death for me, but it meant the same for him. As I was later able to piece together from talking with Ken, Duncan and Ryan, he rode at an average of seventy miles per hour, over rough terrain and rollercoaster-like whoops of at least three feet that were created by other riders, the pressure on his own back, the extraordinary fatigue imposed on his body from continuous impact, beginning to cause numbness in his extremities. But he never slowed, just cranked the throttle, waaaAAAHHH, taking hairpin turns, then hitting a bounce and losing contact with his sled. Then *bounce*, another one, brought the sled back under him enough to take hold of the handle again and regain control of his savage machine. On three separate occasions, Ken very nearly needed his own helicopter.

Upon exiting the Sonora Pass, another crucial decision: Turn toward the trucks that were now visible—a choice that might have meant an hour's drive to a place with cell service, risking a backcountry overnight due to the deteriorating sky conditions, or keep riding the five minutes to the Sonora military base, hoping against hope there was a helicopter there. He rode away, pinned the throttle at full speed, through the dry dirt, mud puddles, sagebrush, and rocks, for the base's runway and fire station.

He rode right past the large "Do Not Enter" signs, heading straight for the on-base helipad. He was intercepted by a uniformed and armed Marine in a white Ford Explorer. Not knowing whether the man would shoot him and not having time to care, he sped toward the Explorer, screaming for help for his broken friend. Upon learning of the situation, he told Ken to get in, and then raced to the fire station, radioing ahead that they needed a helicopter. The station operator radioed the CALSTAR Care Flight helicopter. Ken, who could now hear the conversation with the pilot, learned that not only was this the one and only helicopter in the area, but it was at that moment on approach at South Lake Tahoe, on its way in from a routine training trip in Placerville. They were approximately one minute from landing, the runway was in sight, and the weather was deteriorating. On board were the pilot, two nurses, and a trainee. The chopper was supposed to gas up—a process that would likely have taken thirty minutes or more—and call it quits for the day.

"This guy's going hypothermic any time now—can you do it?" asked the operator.

Pause. Calculations of fuel, weather, time…

"Yes. We can do it. We're on our way."

After Ken pointed to our location on a topo map, the station sent coordinates to the heli. The chopper pulled up, began its rescue trip to Sonora. The truck escorted Ken to his sled, and he began the long ride back.

A word about the universe: It provides. I'm not going to sit here and say that I was lucky to have broken my back. But the universe provided for me in more ways than I can count that day. Of course, the fact that we caught the one and only helicopter in proximity to Sonora, the remotest patch of wilderness in that region of the Sierra; that it had been a minute or less from touching down for the night; and that these three men were able to secure my rescue are, in my mind, the primary reasons I'm alive today. But think about it—in order for that to happen, my three Alpine Assassins brothers had to do everything perfectly, be synchronized like fine watches.

And for four guys out in the woods, who never expected an incident like this, to have the precise survival training we needed that day, to get me off the sled perfectly, and to make the call (the right call) to lay me in the snow, risking hypothermia, and then send the one perfect person at the exact right time on that heroic ride to get the heli, to beat the changing weather and the sunset and dangerous roads and hypothermia, all to get me that rescue... Well, all I can say is that I believe we were guided, in a way.

Those guys, they didn't make a single mistake. They each acted instantly and autonomously. They just knew what to do. And while I felt their love, and their worry, we didn't stop to freak out. None of us. Instead, it was, "You, do this. You, over there, you do that. This is what's happening."

But in terms of the universe, there's something else I've been thinking: Maybe the universe is trying to tell me something. I mean, I had closed the book on one life, was about to embark on another. There were so many other decisions I had made that week, that month, that, as I'd discover later, made this a pivotal day in many more ways than this injury.

Plus, I'd overshot that jump because of a one-mile-an-hour speed differential. I had landed *two feet* beyond the buttercup, beyond the transition I'd been aiming for, hitting flat ground instead. I'd only gone a hundred vertical feet to flat ground. This wasn't from 300 feet up, me way out in midair, showboating on my sled, drunk. This wasn't just me being an idiot or making bad choices. This was a professional athlete filming in a well-contained, rehearsed situation, one I'd considered dozens of times, one that wasn't unlike dozens of other jumps I'd done. This was years of preparation and experience that included thousands of jumps.

This was by no means the biggest or hardest jump I'd ever done. This wasn't pushing the limits of my abilities. This was well within my wheelhouse. This was the culmination of twenty years of experience, going out five days a week on a dirt bike, a mountain bike, a snowmobile, or a kayak, free falling fifty feet a day or more.

Ryan Oddo, with Grant's entire recovery in his hands
(Photo by Duncan Lee)

So, yeah, I blew it; but on the other hand, did I, really? *ONE mile an hour* too fast? *Two feet* too far? Doesn't all this irony, serendipity, whatever you want to call it—doesn't this near-miss stuff have to *mean something*?

Because if it doesn't—if there's no point to all this, if there's no lesson at all that the universe was trying teach me, and if no one learns anything and nothing changes, then this accident is just a tragedy. No, not even that. It's just a donation.

There was always somebody with me. While Ken was on his terrifying race to save my life, Duncan and Ryan had what, in my opinion, might have been a tougher job: staying with me. This period, which lasted a little more than two hours (but felt like days), between the moment I broke my back and the arrival of the helicopter, was the most intense experience any of us had ever had. And what made it harder for them was that neither of them wanted me to know just how sad and frightening it was to see their buddy laid out, whimpering, experiencing the worst pain of his life. So they switched off, relieved each other often. In their eyes I read, "Holy shit, man. Holy shit."

And on their breaks from dealing with me, they did something just as critical, which was to prepare the helipad Duncan had selected, in the meadow roughly one hundred feet below us. With their snowmobiles, they groomed the pad, smoothed it out enough to lay out the branches they had cut down into an X that would mark the spot for the heli. Then they'd groomed the trail between it and us, back and forth, getting it as smooth as possible to create a navigable path for nurses and a gurney.

Duncan did a lot of "Remember whens." He told me the story of when we BMX-biked the Burnt Cedar Pool back at home in Incline Village when we were in high school. I had been a lifeguard and knew when they drained that pool, so one day after it had been drained, I called Duncan, and the two of us seized the opportunity to ride our bikes in the pool. I like thinking it's the only time in history that it was ever done.

But, as you'd expect, someone called security on us. When they arrived, Duncan and I hid in the pool, waiting. And just when we thought the cop was gone, we jumped out. One caught sight of us and tailed us as we rallied our bikes, jumped the benches, threw our bikes over the gate on the other side of the pool, scaled the rocks below, and narrowly evaded capture. Duncan went one way, I went another, and about four hours later, we met up at my house and laughed at how awesome we were.

It was a sweet, sweet story, one of many he told me that day: "Remember the time we…? Remember how…?"

And me saying, "uh? ... uh? ... uh?"

And it just kept getting colder and darker.

And then, Ken. Oh, thank God for Ken. "It's coming! The heli's coming!" he called to us.

When Ken rode over to us and explained his ride, who he'd talked to, and what had transpired, we knew we'd have to wait a little while for the helicopter. But we knew, thanks to Ken's training, that he had conveyed the right latitudinal and longitudinal position to the pilot, that they had been coming from South Lake Tahoe, and that the pad was all ready for it, so it could be any minute.

Yet there was all this waiting, this interminable waiting. This horrible time where Duncan and Ryan still needed to come up with things to say to me, still had to keep me breathing while Ken rode back and forth on the high ridge top nearby, keeping an eye out for the helicopter, prepared to wave his arms in his bright red full-body suit and snowmobile, so the pilot could see us.

What was happening in my mind was this: "I can't believe I'm here again." I thought I had paid this price ten years ago, after ramming my knee into my chin during a ski jump in Colorado and breaking my face. I had been down this road. I had lain in the snow with a shattered face, knowing I would have years of recovery ahead of me, and multiple surgeries. And I had told myself, "Never again. Ever." And here I was, lying in the snow and thinking, "More years of recovery. More years of my life in doctors' offices. More people cutting me open, putting their hands inside my body." I was *fucking pissed off.*

There it was, really—much more than the pain, which was in and of itself completely overwhelming, I was mad as hell. And oh, the guilt. What would I be dragging Shawna through?

And my parents? My friends? After what I'd done to them already, breaking my face? "Again, really?" they'd say. Look at all I'd just created for myself, and for my family, and for my friends, and for my wife, a change in all of their paths, three years or more of difficulty. I knew the road ahead, and it *sucked.*

My mind went round and round the full spectrum of guilt. I had screwed up everyone's day. It was my fault they wouldn't get to jump the canyon gap that day. I'd really screwed up the filming. And there went the plan to pick up our wives, get dressed up, and attend the movie premiere for our friend Jamie, a filmmaker whose own debut film would be launching that night. Fucked that up, too.

And sorry, guys, no more fun Facebook posts saying, "Hey, look, I'm in a foreign country, having a great time jumping this eighty-foot cliff!" No, now it would be, "Bro, I cried all morning. I love you. Fuck."

Even through the pain I wanted to tell them, "Hey guys, don't worry, keep having fun, sorry this looks fucked up, but it's not that bad, don't worry about me. As soon as the heli gets here, someone else is going to deal with this, okay?"

Ryan Oddo, the human backboard (Photo by Duncan Lee)

And there was hope, always hope. Hope the helicopter would get me to the hospital just in time to catch the surgeon who would fix the problem, sew me up, like, "Whew! That was a close one!" and I could wiggle my toes again.

On top of all that, as I was lying there, desperate for that chopper, I was also arriving at a sort of epiphany: It started to hit home that I was beginning a new journey. I mean, I knew I'd come to a fork in the road that week. But I had thought I'd be taking one route, the one in which I had enough funding pulled together to begin my helicopter licensing, in which my soul mate and I could settle into our happy marriage, even take that honeymoon we'd postponed for the time when we wouldn't be so busy and the timing would be perfect.

As an engineer, I craved optimization, symmetry. Any straying from the path was completely uncomfortable. And here I was, *so completely* off the path I had taken years to build and just *four days* to stray from. It was unbelievably maddening.

But now, it looked like I'd be taking this other route instead. So even then, even with all the drama and pain, I said to myself: "Well, I wanted a simpler life and more time with my wife. I guess this is how that's going to happen."

Of all the emotions I felt, though, I didn't really feel scared, not right away. After all, I was intimately in tune with how Care Flight worked. And I knew, in these situations, how possible it was to get a helicopter out here. And I felt in my heart that things would be okay. That I'd make it out, that Shawna would be there for me 100 percent, and that I'd get through this to the other side.

But then Ken had gotten back and ten minutes passed, then twenty, then thirty, and still no helicopter. Had they gotten lost? Was it too late? Had they run out of fuel? Would I have to stay out here all night? It was getting darker and darker, and I was closer and closer to the edge of complete insanity from the pain with every passing second.

And hypothermia was beginning to settle in.

"I'm not shivering anymore," I told Ryan. And we exchanged glances; the clock was starting. We knew that, once the shivering stopped, my body was too cold to protect itself. In hours, maybe five, maybe only two, organ failure would set in. So yes, my fear was becoming more real by the minute. And yes, we were still filming, because I'd told them to. I knew I'd want to see this.

And it was, "Keep breathing, Grant. It'll be here any minute; just hang on, buddy. You okay?"

In a way, yes, I was, because my pain began to level out without the shivering, I was getting numb from the cold, and for that I was thankful.

In the air were the words, "Anytime now. Anytime..." *And me, thinking, I don't know how much longer I can deal with the pain. I want out of here I want out of here I want out of here, get me out of here, OH MY GOD GET ME OUT OF HERE.*

And then, the sweetest sound I've ever heard in my entire life. The *chuh-chuh-chuh-chuh* sound of rotor blades in the air.

Ken, from his ridge top, waved the helicopter in, led it right to me on his miracle sled. I saw trees and sky and then this beautiful, beautiful copter banked a turn over my head, this beautiful CALSTAR helicopter breathed its heat onto my face.

FUCK YES!

Care Flight crew doing it, and doing it well
(Photo by Duncan Lee)

CHAPTER 3
THE RING

I just love helicopters. I mean, yeah, sure, I wanted to be a helicopter pilot because, through Care Flight, I could help people in a real, hands-on way. But to be honest, much of the appeal of it is that helicopters are just flat out really *fucking cool*.

Just four days earlier, I had come home from a long stint in Silicon Valley, chomping at the bit to get started on my career as a Care Flight pilot. I had plans to sell my snowmobile deck, had lined up a buyer for my beautiful truck, and planned to use all that money to pay for my helicopter ratings. Now, here I was, watching a Care Flight pilot coming for me.

Although Duncan and Ryan had done their best to groom the landing pad, all those feet of snow that had dumped the previous week were still uneven and difficult to maneuver through. Although the heli's skids were touching the snow, the pilot opted to keep the blades spinning with just enough gyroscopic stability to keep the bird from settling at an awkward angle. The nurses hopped out, one male and one female, and Duncan and Ryan rode them out on their sleds, via their nicely groomed trail, right to me. Then they quickly set about their work.

Within seconds I was on a hard, extraordinarily painful backboard, so unlike the snow I had melted into and that had conformed to my every contour. Now I could feel something like knives sliding into my back, as my body was smashed into the board and a cervical neck brace and forehead strap bound me to the gurney. With two people on either side of me and one above my head, I was placed perpendicularly atop Ryan's sled, eventually bending his tunnel gear rack, and delicately, slowly, at something like a half a mile per hour, carried to the helicopter.

Under the tail boom I went, blades spinning what felt like inches above my face, *CHUH-CHUH-CHUH-CHUH*, then hot exhaust, *SSSHHHHH*, blasting me in the face. My mind occupied itself with the workings of the helicopter, the genius of the pilot in sustaining some collective by barely hovering over the snow and maintaining cyclic, never letting the chopper fully settle into the snow but instead using a very small amount of thrust to generate stability.

Every microscopic bump or tilt of the sled sent stabbing pain through me. Snow flew everywhere—the last I'd see it for a long time—then a low door that was a mere four inches above my face opened. A twinge of claustrophobia that I'd never felt before rushed through me, then I was inside. Warmth, the cockpit, the pilot's voice, a door slamming. Duncan and Ryan and Ken were gone, and it was all gray sky and clouds through the small windows, as the violent, comforting shaking inherent in a heli takeoff gave way to familiar smoothness, and we were off.

Then frantic action set in on board.

"Call my wife, please!" I said to the compassionate eyes of the female nurse, who told me she would, took her number and, in the unending duties involved in stabilizing my condition, never seemed to be doing so.

Scissors sliced through expensive gear. Another nurse began hunting for a vein to get some morphine in me, take that horrible pain away, but my God, he just stabbed and stabbed my arm, finding nothing, just stabbed and stabbed. I was hypothermic, my veins were closed, but he just kept slapping, then stabbing ("Nope"), then slapping and stabbing ("Not there"). Now arm pain, too, on top of all this? Slap number five, then nothing, and I grabbed his arm. "Stop!"

Care Flight en route to the Reno, Nevada hospital (Photo by Duncan Lee)

I've gotta do something here, I thought. The little bit of aviation experience I'd had gave me an intimate awareness of the intercom systems on these helicopters. With my right arm, the one that hadn't just withstood a barrage of failed injections, I grabbed the boom on the helmet of the female flight nurse, who was leaning over me, hard at work. With my left arm, I reached up to the intercom switch attached to her flight jacket. Into the boom mic hovering right in front of my face, I said, over the intercom, "Hey! I can pump up my right arm so you can get a vein!"

The pilot turned around, "What the hell?" And the nurses exchanged brief looks. I pumped and pumped my right fist, then *THUNK*, sweet, sweet morphine into my vein on the very first try.

"That should start to ease the pain," she said. "Tell me when you feel that."

Nothing. I waited a beat.

"You should be feeling that, are you feeling that?"

"Not at all." I really wasn't, not at all.

Another injection, double the amount. "Are you feeling that?"

Yes, I was. "No, I don't feel anything." I'm not usually big on pain medication, but God, bring it, please bring on the meds.

Another injection. *Maybe I've overdone it,* I thought.

"How about now?" she asked.

"Uh, no, no, I'm not," I slurred.

"Okay, man," the other nurse chuckled.

Then *GGGRRrrrrChuck*, a grinding noise—the helicopter had landed on the roof of the hospital in Reno. That was it.

Again, people scrambling, under the door, then tail boom, rotor blades, *CHUH-CHUH-CHUH*, and even more people. There was a gurney and the dark, cold night, wind blowing, then inside an express elevator, with what felt like dozens of people moving at hyperspeed, calling strange words to each other and marking on clipboards.

"Call my wife! Somebody call my wife!" I kept saying to anyone who paid any attention. I was a piece of meat on a slab, couldn't even be heard or seen. There were just orders barking across the room and clipboards.

"Do you have insurance?" someone asked me.

"Yeah," I moaned.

"Where's your card? Is it in your wallet?" she pressed.

"Yeah."

The elevator door opened, then white fluorescent lights flew past me overhead. I was suddenly in what seemed like a garage—triage—a huge warehouse of a room in which I was the only patient, and I began asking questions: "Tell me what's happening! Am I going to be okay? What are you doing? Can you call my wife?" No one would answer; no one would look at me. Was I dead? Was I dreaming this? Why wouldn't anyone talk to me? *Look at me!* People scurried and scurried, machines blinked and beeped. Finally, a woman approached.

"Sir, do you have insurance?"

"Yeah," I repeated, looking around the room. Who had I told this to before?

"Is your card in your wallet?"

"Yeah, I already told somebody, my card's in my wallet."

"Can you tell me where?" she asked, poking around in my pockets.

"Seriously, I promise, I have insurance!" I waved her away. "I have rad insurance! The cards in my wallet, in my gear bag. My friend Ryan has it. Can we move on?"

More writing and writing on the clipboard.

"Please, can somebody call my wife?"

I began feeling relief from the pain—aching instead of stabbing. I could breathe. The morphine was doing my talking. Was I cracking jokes, trying to lighten the mood?

"Hey, I can't feel my feet!" I said in a joking way, but only sort of, because I was also saying, "Please tell me those things are going to work again." Here I was in ICU, a terrifying place after a terrible few hours, and all I wanted was a kind person to tell me, "It's a sprain. You're in shock, bro, but don't worry, you're gonna go into surgery and it'll all be fine." Like a reporter, I was asking the hard questions, and they were all giving me no comment. I thought maybe I could joke, make them laugh enough to like me, loosen up, tell me the truth.

"Did anyone call my wife? Shawna, my wife is Shawna. Somebody call my wife, please!"

"I'll call your wife," said a man's voice. Finally, a face was looking at me. He could see me! "I'm your case worker, I'm here to help you. Give me your wife's number and I'll make sure to call her for you, okay? We'll get her here to you."

Someone, a human being to talk to! I asked, "Will my feet work? Will I be able to walk? Do you think I'll be able to walk again?"

But then it was just more clipboarding, more scurrying, still no answers. And more cutting of clothes, thousands of dollars' worth of gear... there goes $500, and there, that pressure suit's $500, and there's my one-piece suit that's $500, and there go my $500 boots and $50 socks, and hundreds of dollars in poly-based underlayers, and just cutting and cutting, *right next to the zippers.* "There's a zipper *right there,* you could just unzip that!" I told the man who was cutting and not even acknowledging me, just cutting.

Then I lay naked on the gurney, and then it was, "Okay, guys, you ready? On one!"

"Whoa, what are you doing?!" I called.

Then "Two!"

"What are you doing? Tell me what you're doing before you do it!"

"Three!"

The sheet on which I lay was yanked, more excruciating pain, and more of me, a piece of meat, being placed on another slab. In the chaos of their focused efforts to help me, direct communication remained minimal.

And now I was on a new bed, under a sheet, then in a new room. My head was strapped to a board, and over me lay a sheet.

"All right, we're going to need you to take off your wedding ring," came a nurse's voice from my left. I looked toward the voice and found her scribbling away on her clipboard, not looking at me. Surely I'd heard her wrong? I just looked at her, blinking. She stopped writing, looked at me, and held her hand out.

"Can you remove that ring, please," she repeated abruptly, without a note of questioning in her voice.

I pulled my left hand away from her. "No, I'm sorry, I just got married five months ago and this is the most important thing in the world to me," I said, by now my voice trembling. Certainly I wouldn't lose this, too, would I? I scanned the room, hoping to identify someone among the dozen or so people milling about that might have heard this exchange, who might come to my rescue and save me from having to remove my ring.

"Give me your wedding ring now, sir," she repeated, reaching for it.

Up until now, I'd been polite, working to restrain the panic, to make sure I thanked everyone who helped me, tried to make sure everyone else was comfortable. But now the fighter in me was coming out, and I was ready to drop her.

"No, no way; it's not coming off," I said firmly, holding my hands together. What was she thinking? I might never see it again in all this chaos! I didn't know who she was, where she was going, what she planned to do with it. Fuck her, my ring would be staying right here with me, thank you very much. I crossed my arms in defiance.

"Look," she said, now grabbing for it as she said, through gritted teeth, "you can either give it to me, or I can forcibly remove it from your hand. So I'd suggest you stop fighting me and just take it off now."

Now it was on. If she wanted to take from me the one tether to my life that I now had, she'd have a serious fight on her hands.

Clearly hesitant to demonstrate force in a room of her peers, she eventually muttered an exasperated "hmmph" under her breath and retreated out the door when she realized I wouldn't give an inch.

I lay there with my arms still folded, certain this was some trick of hers designed to catch me off guard and steal my ring. But when there was movement at my door a few minutes later, I was surprised to find, instead, a different, younger, friendlier face smiling down at me. This woman with the round face, stocky build, and sparkling eyes seemed, at last, to *see* me and to care about what she saw.

"Grant Korgan?" she asked, calmly and sweetly.

"Yeah?"

"Hi, there, Grant, my name's Tiffany? I'm a nurse here?" Her voice made every statement a question. "I understand you hurt your back snowmobiling?"

"Yeah… I went off this jump," I said, too exhausted to recount the day.

"I'm a snowmobiler, too!" she said, approaching my bed. "My family and I ride out near Little Truckee Summit."

"That's cool," I said, calmer, resting a little now.

"Yeah, my husband and I ride together a lot," she said, smiling faintly. "How long have you been married?"

"Five months. October 8," I said, holding up my hand to show her my ring. "Best day of my life."

"Yeah, I know the feeling," she said and turned her eyes to the floor. "Listen, I know how hard it is to take that ring off, but we really need you to, because we need to do a CT scan on you. If you don't take it off, it'll fluoresce through the whole thing and ruin the scan, and we won't get a good picture."

I looked at her and down at my ring.

She looked at it, too, then at my face. "I know it would mean the world to me to know how safe my wedding ring was, if I were in your situation." She took my hand in hers. "I promise you," she said, looking me right in the eye, "if you give me your ring, I'll make sure it gets to your wife. I promise you that. Okay?"

I looked down at my ring, looked back at her, then slowly eased the ring off my finger.

"Thank you," she said. "See, I'm going to put it right in here." She dropped the ring into a small plastic pill container and snapped it shut. "I'll keep it right here in my pocket, and I'll be sure to put it right in your wife's hands. Okay?"

I nodded my head, a tear trickling out the corner of my eye. I watched her leave the room and then called out, again, to no one and anyone, "Has anyone talked to my wife yet?"

Someone had. Because moments later, the most glorious sight in the universe appeared in my doorway: Shawna.

My blood pressure, which had been climbing since my helicopter ride, dropped noticeably. Shawna swept into the ICU, reached my side, and put her hands on either side of my face, her hazel eyes looking me square in mine.

"I'm sorry. I am sooooo, so sorry," I wept.

"Baby," she said, stoic, brave, and comforting, "we'll get through this. No matter what happens, we'll get through this. Okay? We'll get through this walking and kayaking and traveling the world and doing all the things we want to do. We'll get through this. We're all here; we're behind you."

We. It was then I realized my parents were behind her.

I was crying uncontrollably now, finally able to let down my guard.

"I'm here, baby, I'm right here with you, and I am not going anywhere. Okay? So don't you change a single goal; we'll fight through it together. We'll do whatever it takes to get through this."

And I realized that, maybe for the first time this whole day, I finally did know it would be okay.

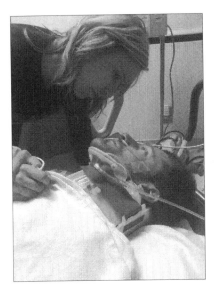

Grant and Shawna in the
ICU (Photo by Pam Korgan)

CHAPTER 4
TRUE NORTH

I knew that things like this could slowly rip people apart, destroy a re-lationship's foundation. While I knew without a doubt, as I laid in the snow that day, that Shawna would still love me no matter what, our love hadn't been tested like this. Fear and doubt had crept in; would she be over-whelmed, terrified, run screaming when she saw me? Because that would be a whole different injury. Forget my back, my heart would have exploded.

So for her to arrive and assuage every fear, to tell me that not only did she love me but that nothing, not a single one of our plans, nothing about our relationship, would change, that no one was leaving, that no way was I a different man in her eyes... well, there was no surgery in the world that could do more healing for me.

Our connection had been rare and unbreakable from the beginning. We'd been like satellites revolving around each other, reliant upon each other instantly for the very air we breathed.

We had met in February 2007. I had just returned home from a month-long kayaking trip in the Patagonia region of South America. My room-mate, Eliot, picked me up at the airport, and in the car announced, "Dude, there's a party tomorrow night and I want you to go, will you go with me?"

He'd just done me the favor of picking me up at the airport, so I said, "Sure!" But after unpacking a month's worth of stinky kayak gear, not to mention coping with the jet lag and time difference, I was wiped out. So when Eliot came to my room the next day and said, "All right, are you ready? It's party time," I wavered.

"Man, I'm sorry, I've still got a bunch of stuff I'm dealing with here, and I'm beat. I think I'm gonna pass."

Eliot, a fellow scientist and the pride of MIT, is a lot like me: He sees things in black and white. If you say you're going to do something, you're doing it. He put his hand on my shoulder, looked me dead in the eye, and said, "Bro, you said you'd come." And with raised eyebrows he said, "You *need* to come to this party."

I knew he was right, and I knew, from the look in his eye, the smile on his face, that there was something about this party that I wouldn't want to miss. I sighed. "Okay, let me throw on some clothes."

The party was at the home of a county commissioner—a gorgeous, contemporary home full of concrete flooring, modern art pieces, an enormous fireplace, and a huge, sweeping view of a small lake that could be seen from the living room and a large balcony.

As soon as the door opened, Eliot and I were swept into the warm room and greeted by a series of old friends and parents of friends and colleagues, just hug after hug after hug. And it was after a hug and pat on the back from my friend, Ralph, that I looked up and saw, through a sea of people roughly forty-feet deep, the eyes of a woman I instantly sensed I knew.

She was standing against the far wall near the dinner table, holding a drink, and was deeply engaged in a conversation with someone I barely noticed. All I saw was her, a blonde in a long-sleeved black shirt, jeans, and heels.

Dancing through life (Photo by Matt Theilen)

I exhaled. *Ahh*, I thought, almost relieved. *THERE you are.*

I moved toward her, parting the sea of people, ignoring the enormous table that was home to the evening's feast, a hot, garlicky cauldron of *bagna cauda*, and pushing past old friends I hadn't seen in years and on any other day would be bowled over to see again. Because all I saw were those eyes that were now locked with mine. Those eyes and mine were having a long, in-depth, soul-baring conversation that played out in the mere seconds it took me to reach her.

I've gone over waterfalls in a kayak. I've hiked Half Dome eight times. I've backflipped on skis and paraglided into the clouds. But rarely had I ever felt my heart beating the way it did as I crossed the room to meet Shawna that night—although the closer I drew toward her, the more re-laxed I began to feel.

What I wanted to say (and still regret that I didn't) when I arrived at her side was, "Hi, I'm Grant, and I love you." But what I actually said was a shaky, deep sort of "Hiiiiiii…"

"Hi," she smiled. And there we stood, gazing at each other like two people reunited after a lifetime of familiarity.

Friends and conversations came and went, and she and I drifted through the party, never getting too far apart, always within sight of the other in the periphery, tethered as if by an invisible string, maintaining a constant connection, with barely a word exchanged.

At the end of the night, we'd barely done more than say hello and exchange some light, friendly small talk. Still, there was no desperate rush to make my move, get her phone number, make a date. Our connection was so assured in my mind that to do any of this would almost ruin it. The calm that had now settled on me, knowing I'd found a piece of me I didn't even know had been missing, was all I needed.

Eliot and I stepped out into the silent, cold night air and pulled the door closed behind us. We walked slowly to the car, me wearing a smile on my face. *I finally understand why people get married,* I thought. Then, more to myself than to Eliot, I quietly said, "I can't believe it. I'm getting married!"

As it turns out, both the flight nurse and the case worker had called Shawna, on separate occasions.

And of course, *of course,* I should have realized that she would know, she'd have some inkling that something was wrong even without a phone call, and she did. That day at work at The Sanctuary had been a crazy one for her, yet she'd had trouble focusing on any of it. She'd spent much of the day gazing out the window in her office. And while she knew in her bones I was okay, intact, she also knew something was off. She became even more unsettled when the light outside began dimming and she had heard nothing from me.

Usually, when I spent a day at Sonora with my buddies, I would take a while to get in touch with her, and it would generally be well after dark when I did. But on this particular day, because we had dinner plans and the movie premiere, I had said I would be calling around three or four o'clock. When it was growing dark, and we should have been planning dinner, there was still no word from me.

Shawna and I craved each other's company, always, and while we reveled in our own and each other's independence, we usually touched base

Engaged at last
(Photo by Matt Theilen)

regularly, exchanged *I love you*'s and *Can't wait to see you*'s, made some kind of connection, not because we felt obligated but because, since we'd been together, we didn't feel whole otherwise. Something was off now, and she knew it. So she dialed and redialed my phone, all the while thinking, "Why am I calling him? He won't get service in Sonora." Yet still calling, seeking reassurance.

She drove home from work, unsettled but getting dressed for dinner, expecting the best. She put her phone down, stepped away, then felt a twinge. She turned back around and checked the phone. A call had come from a 530 phone number—California—and somehow she'd missed it. Normally, she'd ignore a number she didn't recognize, but something told her to pick up and call it back.

The flight nurse answered, identified himself. "Your husband, Grant, is with us in a helicopter. He's been in an accident and hurt his back, and we need you to get to the hospital and meet us there as quickly and as safely as possible."

Not "broken." *Hurt my back.*

Still, she knew what that meant. It had to be gnarly, had to be, for me to a) be in a helicopter, and b) have a flight nurse, not me, calling her.

Shawna raced to the hospital, pushing her Mini Cooper over one hundred miles an hour on the highway, gunning it all the way to the ER, leaving the car running at the front door without so much as a backward glance to look for a valet, just tearing through the emergency room, to the nurse at the front desk, only to come to a grinding halt when she was told, "You'll have to wait here."

So she waited, and waited, for probably ten minutes, although it felt like thirty or more. People left, others entered. One young woman blew into the room in a panic about her own husband, who had also apparently been in an accident. Yet Shawna remained calm, a rock in a swirling stream of chaos, relying on her ability to focus in high-pressure situations that would throw most people into hysteria.

Soon my parents arrived and met her there, and they all waited, tuning out the noise as best they could but growing more anxious by the second.

"Can you tell me how much longer it's going to be? My husband was helicoptered in; a flight nurse called me... " Shawna tried again.

"Hmm, let's see," said the unbelievably slow-moving nurse who showed absolutely no urgency in the situation as she almost comically pushed key after key on her computer.

"Can you call someone?" urged Shawna, thinking, *How is it that all of you don't know exactly who Grant is? He's the guy that flew in on a helicopter, for God's sake!*

"He's in triage," reported the slow nurse.

"Okay, where's triage? Take me to him."

"We can't take you to triage."

Okay, let's try this a different way. "Look, I know you guys have stuff you need to do, but I need to see my husband right now, I need to see that he's okay. I got a call from a flight nurse, and then a case worker!"

"I'm sorry, you'll have to wait; you can't go back there."

It pays to have friends in high places—doctors, medics, administrators. We had friends that worked here. Shawna began scrolling through her phone's contact list, dialing anyone we knew who might work at the hospital, and asking, "Can you help me? I need to see Grant."

By the time she found someone to help her, the caseworker arrived. But first, before anything else, he said, "Did you bring an insurance card?"

When Shawna first saw me in the ICU, I was still on the backboard, wearing a C-collar. And while I didn't appear *broken* in an obvious way, the most disturbing part of the sight was that I was alone in the room. Aside from a few staff members milling about, not seeing or acknowledging me in any way, it was just me, in a lonely corner, waiting.

It seems odd to say this, considering what I'd been through, what I looked like, and the situation we were in, but Shawna never, ever seemed to see my injury. She didn't break down; she didn't cry—at least, not in front of me. Mourning a loss wasn't productive in this situation, and it made no sense, so it didn't happen. It's one of my very favorite things about her: She's the strongest person I know. So she was the rock, while I cried.

I looked into her eyes, mine full of tears, and said, "Babe, I can't feel my legs. I can't move my legs; I can't feel *anything* below my waist."

"I know, baby," she said, with tears beginning to well up in her eyes. She took a deep breath, and said with steady calm, "It's going to be okay."

But they'd still told her nothing. She had no idea what had happened. All around her talk of needing a surgeon was in the air, but she didn't know why. Could it be a simple matter of spinal shock? Temporary paralysis? Did they really need to start cutting me open without first telling us a diagnosis, explaining our options? They weren't just ignoring me now, they were ignoring her, too, and she wasn't having it.

"I need to know what's happening," she told an aide. "We're not just going to start cutting my husband open; tell me what's going on. Where's the doctor?"

Shawna was a fearsome sight to behold, and the confidence it inspired in me was tremendous. It was this insistence of hers that finally, FINALLY, brought a surgeon to us to tell us what the hell was going on.

The closest thing I got to an actual diagnosis was this: I had a burst fracture of my first lumbar vertebra (L1)—literally smashed between the vertebrae above (T12) and below it (L2), shattered into thousands of pieces that lodged into my muscles and tissues. At the site of this collision, my spinal cord was compressed 60 percent, which was what had caused that horrific sensation of being folded in half.

(I remain convinced that my second jump of the day, the one that had first rattled and dazed me, had cracked or weakened my vertebrae, priming me for the vertebral explosion that happened later. And while there's never going to be any way to know for sure, the doctors believed this was plausible.)

One of the most confusing, frustrating things about any spinal injury is that, unlike most diseases or injuries, there's no way at all to provide a definitive prognosis. So while Shawna desperately tried to get a handle on this thing and figure out exactly what we could expect, she was rapidly coming to grips with the fact that there was no way to know such a thing. Everyone was different. Nerves are tricky little suckers; they're completely unpredictable. For good reason, no one at the hospital was going to extend any reason at all to hope for a full recovery.

Surgeons are often regarded as having a slice-and-dice approach, with bedside manner sometimes being secondary to the tools and the table. And I couldn't have cared less at that point about the surgeon's bedside manner. I just wanted him to put me back together again.

But then again, there was Shawna, who was frustrated and looking for answers, and my surgeon, with his cold abruptness, was giving her nothing.

"Do we really need surgery? Is this the only option?" she asked, interrupting his terse description of his plan to open me up. She had repeatedly asked to see X-rays, some kind of picture of what was going on, to understand why surgery was necessary, but had gotten nowhere. Her training and experience as a physical trainer had made her cautious about the idea of surgery for surgery's sake.

He folded his arms, pursed his lips, sighed, and regarded her with a sarcastic, condescending look that said, *Yeah, dummy, of course he needs surgery!* And what came out of his mouth, so curt and matter-of-fact, wasn't any less disdainful.

"His L1 vertebra exploded," he told her, smirking, as if explaining something obvious to a very small child. "He has bone fragments throughout the injury site. Those have to come out. And we have to decompress his spinal cord. The sooner we do it, the better. There's really no other option." He recrossed his arms, looked down at her, and smirked, clearly content that he'd said all that was necessary.

Looking at him and mustering all her confidence, she asked, "Can I ask … have you done surgeries like this before? I mean," she stammered, afraid to offend him, "Do you … specialize in this?"

"Look," he said, impatiently shaking his head, "I'm an orthopedic spine surgeon, and I've been doing this kind of thing for years. But look, if you want to keep thinking about it and researching my credentials, I have a line of surgeries I can put in front of him while you waste time deciding."

Taken aback and realizing this was out of her hands, Shawna said, "I'm sorry, I just… It's just a lot to take in."

"In order to achieve the greatest level of decompression, this surgery needs to happen within twenty-four hours."

"Right. I'm sorry. Let's do it," Shawna said with a nod, realizing I was in the best possible hands, and that prolonging the conversation could put me in further danger. "Thank you."

"All right," said my surgeon, closing his chart. "Surgery is scheduled for noon tomorrow."

With that, he gave her a parting smirk and was gone.

I slipped gratefully into unconsciousness.

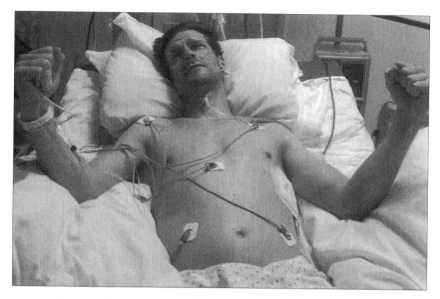

Electrode Korg, determined to rise (Photo by Steven Malekos)

CHAPTER 5
THE BUBBLE

The next thing I remember is Randy Sugihara and mind-blowing, explosive, gut-wrenching pain.

I awoke, immediately confronted by the outrageous hurt and the awareness that I was squeezing something in my hand. The harder I squeezed, the better I felt. At 185 pounds of solid muscle and soaked in adrenaline, I gave it everything I had, which was a lot.

"GUHRR! GUHRR! GUHRR!" I yelled, panting and squeezing the life out of that thing in my hand, because I felt that if I didn't, I might lose control of the pain. And all the while my howls of pain came out as a deep, guttural "RAAAAAAAHHHHHRRR!"

I looked up, traced with my eyes the hand I was squeezing and likely breaking, up, up, up, to my friend, Sugi. How did he get here?

Randy Sugihara, or Sugi, is the fourth owner of Alpine Assassins, with Ken, Duncan, and me. Because he lives in Ogden, Utah, where he owns an auto dealership, he had missed this day of filming. But when the call came telling him I'd been hurt, Sugi jumped in his monster truck, without hesitation, and drove the ten hours to Reno to see me. Then, upon being turned away at the hospital door, much like Shawna had nearly been, he covertly sneaked behind another family, into the ICU and into my room. I needed, at that precise moment, his hand to squeeze.

"I'm going to break your hand," I grunted, still squeezing, my eyes tearing up with the pain.

"Dude, squeeze," he said. "It's okay. Just keep squeezing."

Which I did for roughly forty-five minutes more.

Later, long after this night, Sugi, who has himself experienced compound fractures from snow sports, witnessed the birth of his own two children, and been busted up by years of racing, would tell me, "Bro, I've never seen a human in that much pain."

Hours later, I awoke again, this time in an elevator. I was headed to surgery. Shawna was there, of course, but also many other people. Like my mind was going through a yearbook, showing me everyone I'd ever known. Because here was Kelly! *And lookit, Steven, oh my best friend, Steven, you're here in my dream, too? And Ryan, look, Ryan Oddo's here, what's up, Ryan?*

Stoned out of my mind on morphine, I was slap-happy, finding it hilarious that an episode of *This is Your Life* was rolling before my eyes in this hospital elevator. "And you, too? Of *course* you're here!" I said over and over. "What's up, man?"

Oh, and I'd never been funnier. Here I was strapped to a bed with a broken back and I was doing a stand-up comedy routine that had my friends roaring. I thought, *I can't wait to wake up and tell Shawna about this dream.*

The elevator doors opened. White lights. Unconsciousness again.

Pre-op procedures had begun promptly at 10:00 a.m. for the noon surgery. It was explained to us that, if luck was on our side today and I could rely heavily on my own blood and not transfusions, there would be two surgeries taking place. The first would involve entering from the side of my body and replacing the burst L1 vertebra with a metal "cage." The second was to connect the vertebra above and below with a titanium rod that went through and thereby stabilized the cage. If my body was too reliant on transfused blood, I likely wouldn't be able to have both procedures done at once. That would mean opening me up again the following day—an option that we knew was extremely dangerous, and to which my body would very likely not respond well. Our mantra, which became the mantra of the approximately fifty or so people that came and went from the ICU waiting room to show their support during the nine or so hours I was in surgery, became *two surgeries, two surgeries, two surgeries.*

While I knew that surgery, particularly this surgery, would be a dangerous thing, I also knew it was the first step to ending this nightmare. It was my best chance of turning things around, getting up from this hospital bed and out into the world where I belonged. So I wasn't scared; I was pumped. Surrounded by the calming, loving energy of the dozens of friends I knew were nearby, I was as much at ease as I could be about all that would unfold.

Shawna and I were given a moment alone, just a moment, and we didn't linger.

"I love you," she said, squeezing my hand. "I'll see you when you wake up."

"I love you, too," I said. We looked at each other, our eyes saying all we needed to say.

These were my last moments of real consciousness for eight days.

Shawna barely remembers the walk to the waiting room. But somehow she found herself there, surrounded by twenty-five or thirty people, and more kept filing in all the time.

Reassuring nurses promised her they'd bring updates, but with the long day of surgery ahead, she knew they'd be few and far between. Kids were screaming, people were bustling—chaos reigned all around her, and, amid this chaos, there was so much support and love in the room for Shawna.

First hours of marriage, Yosemite, October 2009 (Photo by Matt Theilen)

Many people brought many things to help pass the time. Among them, Ken's wife, Bridget, had brought headphones.

"Shawna, why don't you just lie down, put these on, and rest," she said. Shawna hadn't so much as closed her eyes in twenty-four hours.

Shawna gave her a grateful look and said, "Thanks, B, that would be good." She put the headphones on, lay back on a couch, closed her eyes, and listened to calming music. Shawna wanted to connect with me, and she knew she could do that by connecting with the most significant moment she and I had shared. She focused on becoming my anchor, connecting through the memory of the most powerful moment of all—our wedding.

As Bridget lightly brushed her hair with her fingertips and another friend of ours, Sam, a fellow kayaker and seven-day adventurist, rubbed her feet, Shawna closed her eyes and thought back to that day just five months ago, when we stood in the dappled sunlight on the lawn of the Ahwahnee Hotel at Yosemite, surrounded by friends and family, each of whom had written a sentiment of love or a wish for us on a river rock. Those rocks formed the circle in which we stood and exchanged our vows.

*Wedding ceremony on
the lawn at Yosemite's
Ahwahnee Lodge (Photo
by Matt Theilen)*

We held hands and gazed at each other, in awe of this astonishing love that we now knew existed in the universe, were fully awe-struck to find, and which sometimes overwhelmed us with its force.

Standing in the circle, drinking each other in, we read from our own rocks, upon which Shawna and I had written our promises to each other.

I promise to forever pursue our love, nurture our incredible realities, and honor the never-ending depth of every heartfelt moment we share on this small planet.

I promise to always encourage you to trust and follow your awe-inspiring heart, to continue to live on life's skinny branches, knowing that my undying love surrounds, supports, and fills your untamed spirit with the ability to fly.

I promise to embrace the wonder, allow your beauty to flow through me and immerse my soul in the exploding passions that are the unstoppable waves of the ocean crashing on my shores until the end of time.

I promise to always say yes…Yes to the life we dream, Yes to the goals and realities of our blissful union, and Yes to the fulfillment of your perfect destiny.

I promise to know your truth, honoring the very essence of who you are, inspiring you to continue to live big, to be present in the moment, and to forever follow the truth that overflows the cup of your spirit.

Those vows—to protect me, support me, surround me with love—became a guiding blueprint for the days to come. She would uphold them, no matter what.

With her eyes closed in the waiting room, we were together again, back on that early fall day five months before, standing in the perfect circle of our never-ending love. Whole and complete.

The first update, a vague but reassuring one, came a few hours later. Things were going "just fine."

More hours passed.

By now, Duncan had made it back to town and had come prepared to document on film the goings-on in the waiting room while I was in surgery. He captured dozens of people, various circles of friends that in some cases I hadn't seen in years. Kayaking friends, dirt bike friends, paragliding friends, wakeboarding friends, snowmobile friends, party friends, the Burning Man crowd, high school buddies, college friends... all standing there showing Shawna and me support, getting to know each other, swapping stories, sending good thoughts. By the time they left that room, they were all one: a unified circle of support for my recovery. More than that—they had become family. It was our first glimpse of the remarkable humanity, generosity, and love that the universe would provide to us in our hours of need.

Our friends Steve and Naomi arrived with stacks of pizzas for everyone, and another couple, Jamie and Cary, made phone calls that Shawna didn't have the heart or energy to make. People made coffee and soda runs and laughed at hilarious childhood stories. Time and again, Shawna met someone new and wondered, *How did you even know to come here?* And eventually she came to the realization that whoever was there was supposed to be there. Their energy was clearly now a part of the process.

Shawna was overwhelmed with gratitude for all the people who came to offer support in the waiting room. However, because of the intensity of my situation and the fact that sympathy is sometimes more natural than optimism, she had begun to create a Bubble of Positivity that no one— not even doctors—could pierce with negative energy. Kindly but firmly, Shawna insisted that there be no crying, no hysterics, nobody losing their shit over worry for me, no "This really sucks."

Consequently, the Bubble was formed.

Having her degree in Health Ecology and being a certified fitness trainer, Shawna was knowledgeable about, and fascinated by, the human body. She was always seeking facts from doctors, nurses—anyone who would talk to her. She spent hours online while I was in surgery, researching spinal cord injuries, tracking down medical professionals who would reveal any detail, absorbing all she could about neurology and the workings of the spine. One technician whose job was to monitor nerves during surgery provided a few useful details. Her reports of, "Well, I'm not getting a strong signal from these right now, but that's normal, there's a lot of shock going on," and later, after surgery, "There seem to be more nerve impulses now," fed Shawna's hunger for information, implanting ideas about nerve regeneration, physical therapy, recovery.

While I was in surgery, she was already forming a plan for my recovery. The fact that surgeons, doctors, and therapists, despite the extraordinary body of collective medical knowledge they possessed, weren't offering much reason to be hopeful for a full recovery, or that they had already begun using words like "wheelchair," was frustrating. But Shawna knew that was their job, focusing on the physical work of fixing my body, and that they were reluctant to sell hope that, based on the statistics, could be misguided.

Hearing, after six hours, that they would be able to do the second surgery after all, and that, after nine hours, I was still doing well, was fantastic, but she certainly didn't need to start asking for a prognosis. She knew that any responses they provided would be based merely on their collection of professional experiences, and would always be tempered with the fear of offering too much promise and risking litigation. They didn't *know me*. They didn't know what Shawna and I were capable of together.

In Shawna's mind, there was no doubt that I'd have a full recovery, but she knew it would be achieved by having a successful surgery, talented and dedicated therapists, relentless positivity and determination, and lots of hard work.

It was because of this mindset that Shawna feared leaving the room for any period of time at all. She hated to miss the rare updates about the progress of my surgery, but also because doing so might allow the Bubble to be

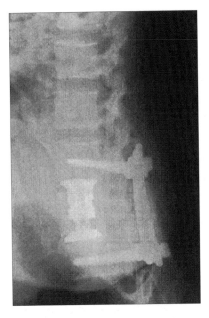 

Side view of Grant's new   *Rear view of Grant's new L1*
L1 vertebra   *vertebra (Photos courtesy of Grant*
                                  Korgan)

burst. Of course, when nature's call finally became too strong to ignore, she left for a brief trip to the bathroom, only to discover that a report from the surgeon had come while she'd been gone. The report had been good: Everything was going well, but surgery would take another three hours.

By 10:00 p.m., I was returned to my room in ICU with a tube in my chest to drain my lungs. The nurses called for Shawna and brought her to me.

The surgeon's work had been pitch-perfect. Although he was still smirking even after nine hours of surgery, his explanation that no transfusions had been necessary and that both surgeries had been completed was a huge relief to both the surgical team and Shawna. But he also acknowledged that I would be in a lot of pain when I awoke. I had been given a morphine drip, and a button was placed in my hand so that I could control it a bit when I awoke.

The surgeon's manner was cold, his smirk somewhat puzzling, considering the circumstances, but Shawna saw it as a small price to pay. Because of him, I had successfully come out the other side of a long, difficult surgery and was placed firmly on the road to recovery.

Shawna rarely slept in those first couple of days. This was mostly because, aside from my bed, there was nothing but a hard, straight-backed chair in the room to accommodate her. She tried for three days to grab moments of sleep, sitting on a chair with her head face down on my bed as I lay unconscious. But after three straight days with her feet on the ground, never reclining or sleeping deeply, the pressure and swelling in her feet and ankles became too much to bear. When my best friend, Steven, came in to check on her and offer help, my loving wife held up a sore leg: "Look," she said, in a mock pout. "I have cankles."

When my dad arrived later that day and got the report from Steven, he seized the task. Finally, he could contribute something concrete to this situation. Dad headed straight for the nurses' station to demand a decent reclining chair for her. The nurses, who had by now befriended Shawna and appreciated her willingness to contribute to my care, were mortified to realize that they had neglected her comfort. They scoured the hospital floor by floor until they finally secured a reclining chair, then pushed it theatrically into my room.

The nurses were as helpful and compassionate as they could possibly be. Shawna quizzed them regularly about spinal cord injury, what they had seen over the years, and recovery. In those brief conversations, she focused only on facts: What, exactly, happened to my spinal cord? Was there still compression? Was it severed? Could she see an X-ray? She knew they couldn't offer a prediction, and she didn't ask for one. Their focus was on keeping me alive. They were guarded about sharing too much, and their information was limited by legalities. The crumbs she received gave her nothing that she could piece together to satisfactorily arrive at a plan for our next steps.

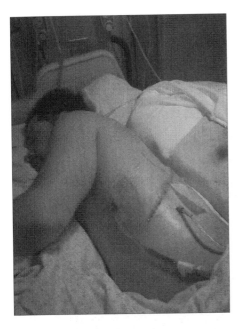

Grant in the ICU with
two chest tubes (Photo by
Steven Malekos)

Somewhere around day four after my surgery, my surgeon returned to provide a bit more information. No, the cord had not been severed, only bruised. Obviously, there was nerve damage, and a physiatrist would be in to see me shortly. She would be monitoring my rehabilitation.

To finally get some substantial information was a relief to Shawna, but it was cold comfort, considering the surgeon's expression. She'd been willing to disregard it in the chaos of my injury and surgery, and felt an enormous debt of gratitude to him for the fine work he'd done. But now, exhausted and overwhelmed, she was weary of the smirk. It wasn't a smiley, "everything's great" kind of smirk, but a shitty, pompous, simpering grin that implied he was talking to an idiot.

When he'd finished his brief explanation, she cocked her head and studied his face, waiting for more. Nothing came.

He met her gaze and asked, "Is there something else?"

"No, I'm sorry. I just, I feel like…" she stumbled, unsure of how to proceed without offending. "The look on your face… You looked like you were smiling, like maybe you were about to tell me something funny. Did I miss something? I mean, it doesn't seem funny."

"Not a thing," he said, looking chastened for a moment into a more contrite expression. He tucked his clipboard under his arm in a gesture of finality. "I'll check in later." The smirk reappeared, and remained until he was gone.

The physiatrist, a rehabilitation physician who led the hospital's team of physical therapists, arrived within the hour to perform a few tests to check my progress.

She asked Shawna to wake me. "Grant, baby, you need to wake up," she said, gently rousing me.

My eyes opened, closed, fluttered, opened, closed.

"He's going to need to be awake while I do this," the doctor said, preparing her tests.

The first highly scientific and technical test involved poking me in various places with a safety pin and asking, "Do you feel that?" Each attempt took a few tries as Shawna worked to get me lucid enough to pay attention.

"Okay, Grant?" said the doctor. "I'm gonna need you to try to contract your thigh muscles, okay? We need to check the impulses in your quads. Can you do that for me? Try to contract your thighs for me."

With all my might, everything I had in me at the time, which wasn't much, I was able to muster the tiniest flicker of muscle contraction in my upper thigh.

"Great!" she reported. "That gives us something to work with. These might be walking legs."

Well, of course they are, thought Shawna, protecting the Bubble, even within herself. *But it's sweet of you to say so. Thanks for being on board.*

According to the physiatrist, one of the first orders of business was to get me fitted for a back brace so I could begin moving safely and start my recovery therapy. She indicated we had a few hours before the technicians would be by. And here, for the second time, Shawna's bladder demonstrated very unfortunate timing. Thinking she had plenty of time to spare, she dashed out the door to pee, only seconds before two strange men in hospital garb arrived. I later discovered one worked for the orthotics company and the other was a hospital tech. All I knew at the time was that they looked like hospital staff, and they were manhandling me, roughly scooting me onto a gurney without a moment's glance for a nurse or even a relative to assist.

Shawna's phone rang as she walked back to my room; it was an ICU nurse. "Shawna, we need you to come back," the woman said. "They've taken Grant already. I'm sorry, we didn't even know they were here."

I woke briefly, disoriented and frightened to find myself and the apparatus connected to my chest tubes being wheeled by two strange men down a hallway and into a large, empty room. It was here that, in an extraordinarily painful and inexcusably coarse forty-five minutes or so, a cast was made of my torso, which was then used to mold the unforgiving, triple-strap, "turtle's shell" of a brace I would wear every moment in which my spine exceeded thirty degrees beyond flat for the next three months. It would support my spinal column while the new hardware connecting my upper and lower vertebrae took its permanent residency.

The casting process required that I be placed on time-sensitive plaster sheets (top and bottom), which would harden to create a perfect mold of my torso. This process was to take place directly on top of the chest tubes and on top of the stitches and the thirty or so huge metal staples running the length of my spine and across my side, holding me together.

When we stopped moving, I realized that I knew one of the guys in the room with us—I loosely knew him from kayaking. Ted was a brand-new employee of the brace-making company, and after prepping the room, was hanging around to observe the process for the first time. "Hey, man," I croaked.

"Hey, buddy. We're gonna fit you for a brace, okay? It won't take long, just lie still."

It quickly became clear to me that I was separated from Shawna, separated from any gentle hands sympathetic to my brutally vulnerable state. There were now three men in the room: Ted at the foot of the bed and the two large men who wheeled me in on either side. The cold and seemingly careless prep work began with the two other men rolling me back and forth, lifting my whole body in a fresh bed sheet to move me from my ICU bed to the cold casting material, then back to the bed, tugging aside my chest tubes repeatedly, apparently racing the clock to get my torso wrapped in the plaster sheets before the forms prematurely set up. If the sheets set up too quickly, this would cost the dynamic duo time, a nearly negligible material cost, and the inconvenience of doing the process twice. Rather than start over with fresh materials and taking the time necessary to act with care and consideration for my broken and delicate physical state, the decision was silently made to get the job done with the current materials.

The situation was clearly stressful as this team went at me like a dirt bike on race day, all the while engaged in casual conversation with each other as if I weren't in the room. There was little attempt at being gentle, and my cries of "Aarrhh! FUCK!" didn't yield much sympathy. They were more like landscapers on a job site than professionals charged with human care.

I looked repeatedly to Ted, who watched worriedly but said next to nothing. I was hoping for some protection but found none. The hospital tech on my right was going too far. Realizing that I was being handled in an inappropriate way, I called out to Ted to come to my aid. He was obviously uncomfortable with my treatment, his hands visibly shaking, but he was new to the procedure and deferred to the "experts."

I began to realize the full gravity of my situation when the guy on my left, Ted's boss, irritated by Ted's anxiety, sent Ted out of the room, leaving me alone to deal with the pain of their progress. In my semi-conscious, drugged state, it crossed my mind that I was hallucinating some sort of *Clockwork Orange* scenario and alternately moaned and whimpered in both pain and terror.

"Look man," said the asshole hospital tech on my right. "The sooner you stop complaining, the sooner we get this done. Now, stop being a bitch."

My therapy began on my first day out of surgery. Into one ear, an iPod delivered healing, calming music. Into the other, Shawna whispered affirmations: "The surgery was successful. Your body is healing. We're sending healing energy into your back. We're in your nerves, moving down into

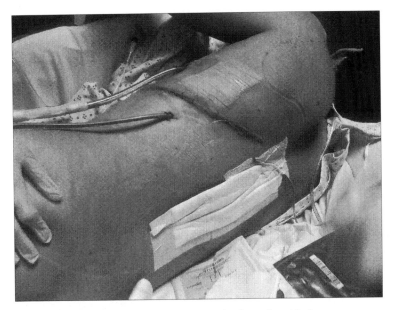

Grant in the ICU, tubed, stitched, and stapled
(Photo by Shawna Korgan)

your hips, your butt, your upper thighs." She verbally sent healing throughout my body. She sent me on athletic adventures, things she knew my body
would remember. "Okay, babe, today we're going mountain-biking. It's a
beautiful day. The air is cool; the sky is blue. You smell the pine trees on the
breeze. We're headed down a rough trail. For this, you need those strong
core muscles to keep you balanced. Use those thigh muscles to push uphill,
think about the balls of your feet. Focus on those legs; think about all those
nerves mending, sending impulses all the way down to your toes. You feel
that, babe?"

My waking moments were fleeting and contained mere snippets of
scenes that made little coherent sense to me. In one of those moments, my
eyes opened to find Shawna leaning over me, tucking sheets around me. I
could smell her, that natural, sweet, soapy scent she has that is a miracle of
science, simply indescribable in its ability to mean home to me. And dangling before my eyes was a ring—my wedding ring, I eventually compre-
hended after a few moments—from a long chain around her neck. I smiled
and said, sleepily, "Hey, my ring!"

A part of me relaxed seeing it. It was the first time I'd seen Shawna holding my ring since our wedding day, when I had sworn it would never again leave my finger.

I dozed off, comforted by the knowledge that our marriage, figuratively and now quite literally was in Shawna's possession, where I knew she'd keep it safe until I was well enough to carry my half of it once again.

For eight days, I experienced these rare moments, glimmers really, of just enough lucidity to be aware of a new visitor or a new exam or of my briefly contributing nonsense to ongoing conversations. Then I'd push the morphine button and fall back out of consciousness.

Meanwhile, Shawna was struggling to sleep at all in her tireless efforts to preserve the Bubble. Well-meaning friends suggested she leave me in the capable hands of the nurses for a while, to take a break, take a nap, even go to a spa. "There's nothing you can do for him right now," they'd say. "You need a break, take care of yourself. He'll be fine; we'll stay with him."

No, she'd insist, it wasn't that she didn't trust them or the nurses, but truly, there wasn't another place in the world she would rather be. It took days of prodding to get her to go home, but finally, on day four, when she was forced to leave the room anyway while the doctor did rounds, with her dad and my mom just outside my door, Shawna went home to clean up and pack some clothes. There, alone in the shower, she finally let grief overtake her. She sobbed hard, hot tears, let all the fear and worry and anger flow through her. Then she turned off the water, dried her tears along with the rest of her, dressed, threw some clothes in a bag, and was back by my side in a mere forty-five minutes.

She hated ever to leave, regardless of who was with me, because without her in the room, anyone, a doctor, a nurse, anyone could come in and influence my recovery. What if she missed some crucial information about my care, something she'd need to know later? What if I awoke and found her gone? What if it caused me (or anyone else) to doubt, for even a second, her willingness to see me through every single moment of this recovery, no matter what it involved? What if I awoke and overheard a practitioner's

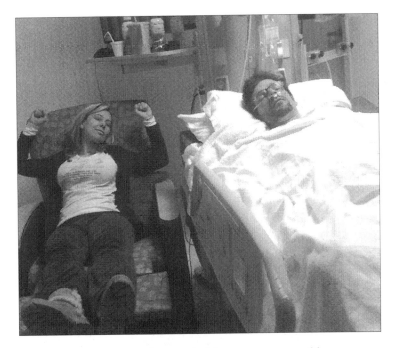

Shawna smiles in relief from no more cankles
(Photo by Pam Korgan)

dire predictions of long-term paraplegia? What if, in my vulnerable state, my recovery was actually set back by such discouraging news? What if, without a voice of my own, something was done to me that neither she nor I would approve?

"The Naa," as we always called my spa-owning, independent, Zen wife, became extremely protective, ready to take down anyone who didn't contribute to my recovery in a healthy way. The idea that I might awake and wonder, "Did Shawna leave me?" was enough to keep her firmly planted to my bedside round the clock.

And rightly so, because in my doped-up state, my mind was certainly beginning to wander into bizarre territory. For three days, I woke up convinced that I had been discarded and left for dead in the hospital's basement.

"Babe, why are we in the basement?" I asked Shawna the first time this happened. "This bed is plastic, why am I on a plastic bed? We're in the basement!"

News had circulated throughout Reno over the last year about this hospital's multimillion-dollar remodel. So if that was the case, why was I here, in a basement, on a plastic bed? Why no flat-screen TV? Why no remote-controlled curtains, million-dollar equipment? From my vantage point, this looked like one of the back rooms at the Stanford labs where the broken equipment was cannibalized to make other things work. The room felt enormous but poorly lit, with décor that reeked of the 1970s. And, as far as I could tell, I was the only patient here. The TV, a small, outdated model, sat silently in a corner.

Maybe the surgery had gone horribly wrong? Had I been put down here to hide a mistake? My semiconscious, hallucinatory mind had me convinced they were stashing my body here, keeping me alive only so I could become an organ donor.

Frantically, I scanned the room for Shawna, and, after stretching my neck as far as I could, I saw the top of her head as she tried to grab a few minutes of shut-eye, with her head face-down near my hip.

Oh no! I thought in a horrifying moment. *She thinks I'm dead! No! Baby, I'm alive, I'm here!*

My terror persisted for days, until Shawna, now curious herself, finally tracked down a nurse to find out why on earth this portion of the hospital had obviously not been remodeled yet. What she learned was comforting. It had actually been a practical focus on patient care that kept us in this old room. Here, because of the layout, the nurses, in their station just outside each room, could keep close watch over ICU patients. It took some convincing on Shawna's part, especially considering my state of mind, but I finally believed her when she said all was well.

On day five, I woke in a hallucinatory state, completely confused by the nurse at the foot of my bed who was writing on a chart and the inexplicable presence of someone else next to her on the floor. "Babe! What's that guy doing down there?" I asked Shawna. "It looks like he's doing a cool tattoo. How come she's getting a tattoo in here? Let me know how it goes." Shawna laughed, her first real laugh in five very long days. And then I was asleep again.

Another day, when I woke up surrounded by faces I couldn't recall, I was convinced we were living in a hippie commune.

Other times, I'd just express gratitude—to the nurses who seemed to always be checking in on me and offering support to Shawna; to Shawna's dad, Doug, for rubbing my feet; to my Mom for being willing to help in any way she could, to Shawna for whatever amazing thing she'd be doing at the time; to strangers in the hallway. Even while semi-conscious, I was aware of the effort it took to attend to my many needs, and all I could offer was my deep gratitude, which I offered in buckets at every opportunity.

These small waking moments were often funny in their strangeness, but they were also frequently terrifying for me, so that even for the one-hour block of time when Shawna was forced to leave my room as doctors did their rounds, she waited until the last possible moment, until she was kicked out, to leave, and then paced the floor in anxiety until she was allowed back in. There was nothing, not a medicine dispensation, a sponge bath, a wound cleaning, that Shawna didn't approve of or take on.

Because of my fragile state and the energy any visits at all would sap from us, the nurses were more than happy to help protect the Bubble in any way they could. On their suggestion, Shawna instituted a password that only our parents, Steven, and Duncan were given. The nurses acted as security guards to relieve Shawna of the additional burden of turning people away when she simply couldn't deal with another visitor.

Shawna kept her own emotions in check, realizing that the few visitors I had were constantly looking to her, gauging her reactions in order to determine their own. She knew my recovery could be affected if someone came in and lost their shit, crying or expressing worry over my condition, so she appeared stalwart for nearly everyone who came to see us.

But one night, I awoke to a mostly dark room. A bit of light from the corridor peeked through the gap where the curtains had been left slightly parted. The usual hospital sounds hummed at their nighttime pace. By this time, the quiet dimness was familiar, but I still noticed when Shawna was not by my side. I squinted to look through the doorway to where the nurses occasionally passed by with trays and carts and the odd gurney. But the hallway was empty except for two people. Shawna, in her gray yoga pants and a long-sleeved yellow t-shirt, was standing on her slippered toes to hug her dad tightly around his neck. Her face was pressed against his chest, his chin resting on top of her head. His arms encircled her. From where I squinted in my hospital bed, I could see her wipe an escapee tear from her cheek with the back of her hand.

During most of her days, while I was unconscious, Shawna spent her time doing research on recovery techniques, various therapies, practitioners around the country, and experimental treatments they were developing. And with the nurses' patient guidance, she quickly, efficiently, took control of my day-to-day care. It eased my mind tremendously to have my well-being in her capable hands.

On day seven, when a doctor arrived and announced to Shawna that one of the two tubes in her sleeping husband's chest was to be removed that day, she was very disconcerted.

"Is this going to hurt him?" she asked, getting antsy.

"Well, it's going to seem kind of brutal, but I have to do it really quickly so I get the tube completely out," he explained. Then he leaned down and grabbed the tube with two hands.

"One... two..." and he yanked, ripping the tube violently from my chest in a move Shawna swore might tear my lung out.

"Hmmmm," I said, and drifted back into deep sleep.

Eight days after my surgery, I awoke from a vivid dream. My best friend and business partner, Steven, was standing by my bedside. With inexplicable speed, my arm rocketed out to grab Steven's hand.

"Steven!" I cried urgently in my very first moment of cognitive awareness. "I solved it! I've got it all figured out!"

"Whoa-kay, buddy!" he replied, startled. "Solved what?" He and Shawna exchanged startled, amused glances.

"I created it! It's a robot." I then proceeded to detail for him the extraordinary functions of the XP-3000 ultra-robot.

"Okay, cool," he urged, thrilled just to see me awake but utterly confused. "What problem does it solve?"

"The problem is…" I said, lapsing again into sleep, "it sucks."

Minutes later, I awoke again.

"Steven! I finished it! I finished the design!"

"Okay," he said, cautious now. "What was the problem?"

"It needed D batteries!"

Asleep again.

Then, finally, on day nine, I awoke for real. No more hallucinations. I found myself in the most conscious state I had experienced since surgery, and immediately had my second chest tube removed. And for the first time since I'd arrived at the hospital, it seemed that I might just be on the mend.

I awoke feeling much as I would first thing in the morning. The pain was there, but in the background. For this moment, I felt completely lucid, if very rough and a bit confused, and ready to enter the day.

My first words, the first words of the week that I remember as being unencumbered by hallucinations, were, "I need some coffee."

Following that came my questions: How did the surgery go? Am I moving my toes? What's happening? Am I going to recover?

Shawna patiently answered as much as she could, explaining that my spine was still in shock, telling me what little she knew from conversations with nurses, doctors, the physiatrist.

I didn't really feel like a beaten, injured man. Instead, I had the frustrating, maddening feeling that my hips and legs weighed a million pounds or had been bolted to the ground. It was as if the lower half of my body had been crushed to the earth, anchoring the parts I could move, which consisted of my shoulders and head. My back and abdominal muscles were absolutely useless.

I had only been awake ten minutes. As my new reality began to fully dawn on me, my friend Eliot's father, Daryl, whom I respect deeply and hadn't seen in months, opened the door. It only took one look at the lovely flowers in his hands to reduce me to a gut-bursting storm of tears so violent I could barely breathe.

Daryl laid the flowers on the chair by the door and, with his hands up as if to stop my crying, backed away slowly. He turned to Shawna and said, "I'll come back later." And he quietly closed the door, leaving us alone in the room.

Grant on the South Branch of California's Feather River
(Photo by Lizzy English)

CHAPTER 6
ENTER AND DEAL

My awakening had set things at the hospital into motion. Shawna and I quickly came to understand that the plan was to *get me out*. Like, immediately. I was being kicked out of the hospital. By tomorrow at 1:00 p.m., I would be transferred, via ambulance, to the inpatient rehabilitation center across the street. So much for taking time to mentally adjust to my situation—there was no more time.

But before I could go, they had to make sure I could sit up. The process, which began on my last day in ICU, had taken several people—Shawna, nurses, the physical and occupational therapists. First, a pillow was placed between my legs to keep them straight. Then several people, some toward my head and some at my feet, rolled my body onto its side.

I don't think I can adequately describe the pain of moving, for the first time, a body that has endured a broken back, the surgical reattachment of

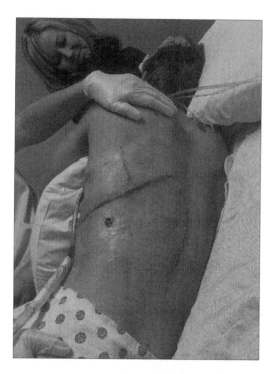

*Grant being rolled on his
side in the ICU (Photo by
Pam Korgan)*

that back with a titanium cage and rod, thousands of bone shards penetrat-
ing, and then being removed from, muscles and tissues, then lain motion-
less in a hospital bed for over a week. There certainly wasn't a place in
my body that wasn't experiencing pain of some sort. There were the acute,
piercing, knife points of pain that terrorized the muscles throughout my
torso. There was the whole-body soreness of long-dormant muscles forced
to awaken before they were ready. And there was the dull, throbbing ache
of my head, thrumming away as it swam in days' worth of morphine and
other drugs. And then there was the bone-tiredness I experienced after the
slightest movement, and which I had to push my way through as more and
more was asked of me.

Rolling was just the beginning—then there was sitting up. Without a
brace yet, with nothing to support the weight of my body but the bed that
lifted me to a slight incline and a few hands that gradually turned me to sit
with my legs off the edge of my bed and then let go, I had to use my own
depleted core strength and determination to maintain a balanced, seated
position at the edge of my bed.

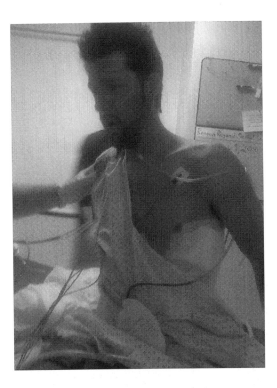

Grant's first time sitting up (Photo by Shawna Korgan)

Prompted by my pale, sweaty face and pained grimace, Shawna stood at the ready, arms out, ready to hold me and lay my aching body down again.

"Are we sure about this?" she asked, fidgeting uncomfortably. "Shouldn't he have his brace before we do something like this?"

"He needs to get moving in order to start the healing process, and before we can release him," said a nurse, clearly much more accustomed to and comfortable with placing such demands on fragile patients.

"It just seems like we could be doing some damage here," said Shawna.

The nurses looked at her, then looked at the physical therapist, waiting for a final verdict. The physical therapist chose to ignore this comment.

"Okay, Grant, how about we get you started with some basic occupational therapy?" she said. "Think you could brush your teeth for us?"

Nurses bustled about, securing for me a clean toothbrush, some toothpaste, and a glass of water.

While the idea of brushing my teeth after more than a week appealed to me, I blanched at the idea of taking on even this simple task. Certainly it would be more than I could handle.

Outwardly, I said nothing. I was simply too exhausted, too overwhelmed with pain to do more than balance on the edge of the bed, with an expression of misery on my face.

With a few strokes of my toothbrush, the most movement I could muster from my muscles, I was thankfully relieved of the brush, wiped dry, and returned to my reclined position on my bed. I fell fast asleep.

My good friend from Incline High School, Trent Marietta, now worked as a paramedic, and had spied me going into surgery the previous week. Despite the fact that we hadn't seen or talked to each other in about a decade, he had found Shawna in the waiting room that day, introduced himself, and assured her that he would be her "inside man" and get regular status updates for her. Since then, he had managed to check in on me every day following my surgery, to keep track of my progress and imminent transfer to inpatient rehab. He told my doctors, my nurses, anyone who would listen, "I'm helping Grant, and I will be transporting him to inpatient," just so there was no mistake.

My transfer was scheduled for 1:00 the next afternoon—a ridiculously short turnaround time, in my opinion. But at 8:00 that morning, Shawna was just beginning to gather our nine days' worth of accumulated belongings and to fill out the tons of paperwork that had just been thrust at her when Trent poked his head in the door. He was a thin man who wore an enormous smile full of white teeth and a "Paramedic" cap and jacket that seemed too large for him. "We're all set out here. You ready?"

"What? You're kidding," Shawna said. "I thought we had until 1:00?"

"We have someone waiting on this bed," said the attendant who was now bustling through the room, making ready for the next patient.

"Hold on," said Trent, and disappeared out the door. Shawna scrambled to pull our stuff together. Fifteen minutes later, Trent returned. "Okay, you guys have a few more hours. Eleven o'clock."

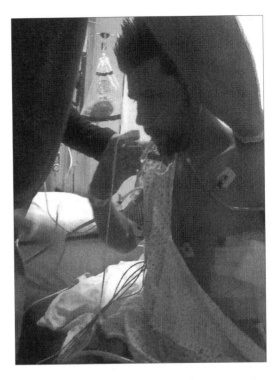

Grant brushing his teeth
for the first time since
the injury (Photo by
Shawna Korgan)

Though grateful for Trent's efforts and connections, Shawna's frustration over feeling kicked out subsided little. With tears in her eyes that she didn't want me to see, she began throwing the last of our things into a bag, while I lay there helpless and frightened about our too-rushed move.

When the time came, Trent escorted us as I was quickly transferred from my hospital bed to a mobile bed, to which I was then strapped. Shawna walked with me as I was wheeled gently onto the waiting ambulance, which would drive us approximately a thousand feet to inpatient rehab. It was my first breath of the cold, fresh air since the day of my injury.

Everything was moving so fast, I was being foisted off to another strange place, and I was completely unable to move or respond. Every movement hurt. My situation was completely uncontrollable. Fresh air or not, I was utterly traumatized. Tears filled my eyes, finally spilling down my cheeks. I could say nothing over the enormous lump that sat in my throat. Shawna, who now sat composed beside me in the ambulance, squeezed my hand. Trent, on my other side, squeezed the other.

"It's okay, man, just a little bit farther now," he said, while Shawna discreetly wiped my tears.

Within minutes, we arrived at the inpatient rehab center, where Shawna's parents and my mom were there to greet us. I let out an audible sigh of relief. Still holding my hands, Shawna and Trent wheeled me inside, and I found myself at one end of a long hallway, which would lead me to my room.

The group of us entered the small room, where a TV was forcefully blaring unwanted outside stimuli at us. Directly in front of us was an empty bed—my bed. At the far end of the room was another bed, and on it sat a guy who looked to be about my age.

"Hey, what's up?" I said, and looked worriedly at Shawna. The overseeing physiatrist had assured us that I would have a single room; she had called ahead to secure a space that Shawna could share with me.

Shawna saw hesitation in my eyes as I looked anxiously from my roommate to her. "I'll go check, babe, I'll be right back," she said discretely, placing her hand on my shoulder before leaving the room with Trent to track down someone who could right the situation.

Fearing an awkward silence and anxious not to let my would-be roommate feel responsible for my dismay over this room, I immediately introduced myself and explained my situation.

His name was Greg. And in a bizarre twist of fate, Greg not only had the same type of spinal injury as I'd had—he had burst fracture at T11, just two vertebrae higher than my L1—but he had also done it while snowmobiling. And it had happened just two hours after my accident.

In fact, his injury had taken place at Mammoth Mountain, a few hours south of Sonora. Because I had scored the last helicopter, Greg had been forced to wait through six hours of pain I could now well imagine as being a kind of torture, until Search and Rescue crews got him out of the woods. They dragged him through the snow on a snowmobile to an ambulance, which took forever to drive him to an airplane, which then flew him to the same hospital where I'd been.

Fortunately, his injury had been less severe, with far less compression. Greg was already moving his toes, while I could still move nothing.

No two spinal injuries are the same. But if he could move his toes already, who was to say I couldn't?

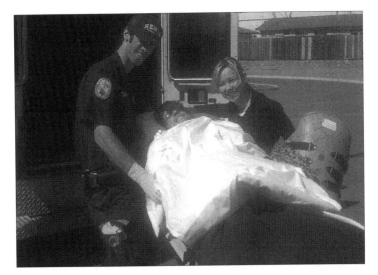

Trent Murrieta transferring Grant to inpatient
(Photo by Pam Korgan)

When Shawna and Trent returned with news that a new, single room had been found for me, Greg and I had already become friends. And I knew meeting him had been exactly what I'd needed at that moment.

Just then his wife entered the room—she was the same woman who had been hysterical in the hospital waiting room when Shawna had first arrived the night of my injury. Clearly, Shawna and I decided later, all of us had been meant to meet.

"So I'll be seeing you in therapy," Greg said. "Take care 'til then, man."

"Hey, you too," I said. "We're gonna crush this thing!"

They wheeled me to the very end of the hallway, to the largest hospital room I had ever seen in my life. Situated in a corner, at the end of the hall, this room that was often host to traumatic-brain-injury patients was lined on one side with windows, giving it a bright, open feeling—as much as could be found in such a clinical setting. A peaceful, calming silence settled on us. There wasn't a TV in sight.

Trent gently wheeled my bed into the room, turned it to place the headboard against the wall, and stood with his hands on his hips, obviously pleased that his friend had managed to land in what was clearly an enviable room. But all I could see was the image through the window directly to my right, a hospital-room view that seemed imbued with a sort of universal significance: a Care Flight helicopter touching down on the helipad on the roof of the hospital across the street.

The irony of my situation slapped me in the face. Here I lay with a broken back, forced to see my own stalled life dream play out before my eyes across the street. That dream now comingled with memories of my last helicopter view—that lifesaving thirty-minute ride from Sonora. The horror of that situation, the gratitude I felt for the pilot and crew and technology, the loss of the dream I'd thought would become reality just two weeks ago, overwhelmed me.

The reminders of what I couldn't do seemed to be everywhere, and it felt cruel. Here was Greg, with the same injury, already experiencing movement in his feet. There were helicopters outside my window, reminding me that if I weren't lying here in this hospital bed, I'd be flying one of those. While I was aware that I should be seeing all these things as inspiration, as visions of what lay ahead for me if I kept focused on my goal and worked hard, I still fought with my own resentment, feeling the weight of everything that had been taken from me. For the second time that day, I cried bitter tears.

Trent soundlessly backed out of the room, tipping his hat slightly at Shawna as they exchanged glances. I lay, mystified, with my head turned to stare out that window for what seemed like an hour. Then, the chopper's propeller blades gathered speed, its body lifted slowly, gently, up, and then away, ready now to save someone else's life.

In another bit of cruel irony, it turns out that my lifesaving helicopter ride had actually cost us less than my 1,000-foot ambulance ride across the street.

The exorbitant costs of my injury were beginning to confront us in full. When I was first transferred to inpatient rehab, hospital staff had been referring to "months" of rehab, but within only a day or so of my arrival, case workers began filing in to explain my benefits and to politely, apologetically, yet firmly insist that a stay of thirty days was the maximum length of time allowable by my insurer. Beyond that, we were free to remain here and pay, out-of-pocket, the $5,000-per-day fee.

I repeatedly argued, "But my insurance is *rad*. It's the *best money can buy!* Are you sure you've got that right? You'd better check again. I mean, I got the highest health rating, an A-plus, you can check! I've never missed a payment!"

The very nice case workers just smiled their sympathetic, knowing smiles, patted me on the shoulder, and gently assured me, "I know, I know. I'm sorry. But you only have thirty days."

It was just one more great reason to have Shawna as an integral part of my daily care. Pretty soon, the staff got into the habit of including Shawna in any and all areas of my care. They began leaving a tray of supplies by my bedside and saying, "Shawna, you got that?" If a nurse who was unfamiliar with me came into the room to attend to me, I'd have to respectfully insist, "No, no, my wife's got that. I want my wife to do that." And then he or she would back off, hands in the air.

Shawna took on any job she could, from helping the nurses to put on my new back brace and roll me—a once-every-hour event around the clock—to overseeing the administration of the approximately twenty medications I took on a daily basis to changing the bandages at my surgery site. All this she did with brisk, upbeat efficiency, never so much as wrinkling her nose, not even when catheterizing me with the seventeen-inch tube that made it possible for me to urinate every four hours. When finished, she removed her gloves, patted my clothes back into place, and sat down beside me, unfazed, my own dignity utterly unperturbed.

Once, I awakened to find Shawna standing over me, wiping my bare butt with sterile wipes—I had shit myself. She was quietly, calmly cleaning me. I just stared in disbelief. Had she always done this? Had Shawna always been assisting me with this business of having no control over my bowels? Would this be a normal occurrence for us from now on?

"What are you doing? What happened?" I asked, mortified, instinctively reaching to push her away and attend to it myself, yet quickly realizing I could do nothing of the sort.

"Nothing, babe, it's fine. I'm almost done," she said, smiling at me sweetly.

"Oh my God," I said, half laughing, half crying. "I love you. I love so much."

"Grant, everything is okay. I love you, too; don't worry about it. You're my everything."

She tossed the wipes in the trash, quickly washed her hands, then returned to me to pull my clothes back on and give me a kiss. She leaned down, hugged me, stroked my head as I wept over the traumatic thing I'd just seen, over the silent beauty of her heart. The depth of my love for Shawna—even more, my *awe* of her—could find no limits.

"It's okay, baby. It's okay," she whispered, just stroking my head until I fell asleep.

While I hated for Shawna to be burdened with these tasks, I hated it more when the medical staff did it. While the nurses seemed to accept Shawna's lead role in my care just fine, the overseeing physiatrist seemed resentful of what she perceived as my over-dependence on my wife. She often made comments to Shawna like, "He needs to learn how to do that himself, because when you get home..."

But that was just it. At home, it would be only Shawna and me. No hiring of nurses, no Shawna going back to work and leaving me alone. This was our life now. My recovery was our entire focus. If she couldn't take on these tasks, who would? I had more than I could handle.

Shawna's part in my recovery by now was much more than keeping me safely inside the Bubble. From a practical standpoint, it only made sense to understand how to treat a pressure sore or how to insert a catheter. So when the physiatrist piped up with objections, Shawna politely but firmly insisted, "When he can do this, he'll tell me. We want him to be independent, too. But right now, I'm just preserving his dignity. He's got enough on his plate."

Once I was established in my rehab room and comfortable enough to be left alone for minimal stretches of time, Shawna decided it was time to make the room, which would be ours for the next month, into a home. Family, friends, and even the director of the facility made sure we had whatever we needed to be comfortable—from a portable fridge to milk for coffee, and even fresh flowers.

One day, Shawna went out to pick up more clothes from home, some groceries to keep in our room, and some medicated hand cream that the nurses had recommended when her dry, overworked hands began to crack and bleed.

She returned a few hours later with a duffel bag full of clean clothes, a shopping bag, and a bright smile.

"I got you some things!" she said, clearly excited and beaming with pride. "I got you..." She reached into the bag dramatically and said, "bananas!" She produced the perfect fruit with a flourish.

"Great, babe, thank you," I said, subdued but smiling at her charming routine.

"And..." she said, reaching in once again, "coffee!"

"Thanks!" I was amused and could tell this was building to something.

"And..." again she reached into the bottom of the bag, "Ta-da! I got you a gift!"

"No way!" I said, impressed by her thoughtfulness.

She produced a small, square package, perfectly wrapped in white paper with a red bow. "Open it!" she said with the eagerness of a child.

My fingers moved slowly, clearly too slowly for Shawna, who was so proud of the gift she'd bought me that I could see she was dying to grab it out of my hands and open it herself.

"This is just something to keep you focused on your goal," she said, beaming.

Finally I was able to read the box. She had bought me a remote-controlled helicopter.

"Look, now you can fly in your room!" she said with a huge, expectant smile, clearly believing I would be thrilled.

I wasn't. As was becoming my standard M.O., I once again burst into tears. Violent, shaking sobs. Shawna went into a panic.

"Shit! Oh, shit, I'm sorry!" She snatched the toy away from me, threw it in the bag and tossed it across the room as if it were dynamite. "Oh my God, I'm so sorry!"

Grant paddles over California's Fantasy Falls
(Photo by Lizzy English)

She crawled into bed with me, cuddled me, and said, "It's okay; I'm sorry. I'm sorry."

When would this stop? At what point would I stop measuring time in "Before Injury" and "After Injury"? When would I stop saying things like, "Just ten days ago, I could stand up and take a piss by myself," or "Two weeks ago, I could bathe myself"? And now, in the arms of the most amazing woman I'd ever known, a woman who'd done something so thoughtful as buy me a toy to remind me of my life's dream, and while I knew I was surrounded by people who loved me and would do anything to assist in my recovery, I was still focused on what could have been, what I couldn't have now. How could all this be real, how could I really be paralyzed from the waist down when just a few weeks ago I could do anything I wanted with my body?

I knew there was no way I could recover until I stopped looking back and started looking forward. I had a month in this place, with hard work ahead of me, and I had nowhere to go but forward.

We kayakers abide by the law of "Enter and Deal." In a lot of sports, you get "do-overs." Don't like your bike trail? You can hop off and walk. Skis not feeling right? Stop, reassess, and side-step if you absolutely have to. With a lot of things, you can take a break, call a timeout, re-strategize, regroup. But kayaking, my favorite sport, is beautiful in its relentlessness. It forces you to move forward. There are no breaks. Water's constantly moving ahead; you can't change the current. You can't get to the top of a rapid, then back up because it doesn't feel right and say, "You know, this one's gnarly, guys; let me turn around and try again some other time." Tough. You have no choice, you have to enter the rapid and deal with what comes your way.

You're committed once you're at the top of that rapid, whether you want to be there or not. It's Enter and Deal time. You have no choice but to deal with whatever comes your way.

Now my back was broken. There was no calling "time out," no looking back and saying, "Gee, that was a dumb idea, let's put that on hold for a bit, come back later, and try it again." Whether or not I was ready for the tough times ahead made no difference—they were coming. Lying here with a titanium cage in my spine and legs that didn't work, I had to deal with what would come. I was fully committed. No time for negativity, for fear, for anger. I had to enter and deal.

Free as a bird to explore all of Europe
(Photo by Pam Korgan)

CHAPTER 7
(MY) BACK STORY

Having been born in Edmond, Oklahoma, it wasn't a given that I'd become avid for any kind of extreme sport. Though I had inherited my mother's natural adventure-seeking tendencies, Oklahoma isn't exactly the natural place to foster them. My dad wasn't thrilled with the place either. When I was just sixteen months old and my older sister just three, he became so interested in making a change for the better in our family's lives that he decided to take a road trip to search for the best place in the country to raise a family, with the intention of finding us a new home. A determined man with unswerving, single-minded focus (a trait I inherited), he knew that my sister and I were at ideal ages to relocate, and being that his developer/mortgage banking business was scalable for any locale, it was the best possible time to make the change he so strongly desired. So he hopped in his chocolate-brown 1977 J-10 Jeep truck (with special Levi-buttoned, tan-stitched upholstery), intent on the idea that he would not return until he had found our new home.

He had been on the road for months before he called my mom from the Hyatt in Incline Village, and said, "I found it. Get on a plane and come check this place out."

Resistant to the idea of moving from the dream home and good life she and our dad had built, my mom was less than thrilled with his report. But she rarely argued with him on such matters, so she packed us up and the three of us flew to Nevada.

In 1978, Incline Village was an obscure, pseudo-hippie mountain town where housing was fairly cheap. And as an outdoor enthusiast to the core (another trait I inherited), my mom was sold the minute she saw Lake Tahoe. Before long, we were residents.

We were happy there. My sister and I thrived at Tahoe, playing amid rocks and trees, splashing in streams, climbing up mountains and skiing down them. By the time I was in sixth grade, I was racing on skis as part of a downhill racing team, and I was a 24/7, hard-core adventure-seeker.

I'm pretty sure I got the idea of doing a backflip into my head after watching the movie *Ski Patrol* or something. But once the idea had entered my mind when I was fourteen, I couldn't let it go. I became convinced that I could do it, that I simply *had* to do it.

I analyzed the jump in my head, thought about it from all angles to determine exactly what I would need and where I'd need to be in order to do it. I decided that the bottom of Golden Eagle Bowl at the Diamond Peak Ski Resort in North Lake Tahoe was the perfect spot. And I got so excited once I'd made that decision that I went ahead and claimed it. I told one of my buddies, "Bro, today, after school, I'm going to do a back-flip on skis."

I'd innocently announced it out of sheer enthusiasm and a desire to impress, but now I'd actually made myself accountable. Word spread quickly through the school's small population, and by the time I arrived at Diamond Peak to do my jump, I found an audience of a half-dozen or so kids waiting for me. My heart sank for an instant as I realized there was no backing out. I gathered my wits and headed up the hill.

I took a deep breath and started down the hill. I tucked, tucked, tucked, pulling in more speed, until I came into the flat. Then momentum had me climbing the other side of the canyon, up the steep jump. And up, up, up I went. I turned and turned, my legs kicking wildly at about fifteen feet in the air, and I looked frantically at the ground, desperate not to land on my head. But I couldn't keep the spin going, so down I came, painfully, head-first, on the flat ground. I lay there for a quick moment, my head aching and my ego bruised.

Fortunately, at fourteen, my bones were rubber and my ego's need for redemption wouldn't allow me to stop. Now that I had an audience, there was no way I'd quit until I'd successfully completed my backflip.

In the movie *Rad*, a 1980s film about BMX racing that I had watched hundreds of times over the previous five years, my childhood hero, Cru Jones, explains the technicalities involved in doing a backflip on a BMX bike. The basic principle, I knew, was the same regardless of the sport—lead with your head, and your body will follow. You have to look where you want to go, and your body does the rest. Likewise, don't look where you *don't* want to go—which is what I'd done.

After my first disastrous attempt at a backflip, while I was lying there in the snow, I thought about my mistake, concentrated on a correction in my head *(look where you want to go, look where you want to go),* and headed straight back up the hill while my friends down below had a good laugh about how bad I was at this.

And down I went again. During that trip down the hill, I thought to myself, *Okay, if I focus on the obstacle, if I focus on what I don't want, that's where I'm going to go.* Down I came into the canyon, mounted the jump, all was going smoothly, and then, in mid-air, my ski ejected itself from my foot. And once again, I began flailing wildly in the air. At least, though, I got a full rotation, had kept my head in the right spot, and managed to do a full flip. I hit the ground with only my right ski and immediately fell to the left, rag-dolled forward, and tumbled through the snow to an ugly stop.

I knew the third time would be the charm. I raced up the hill, already tasting the success of what I knew would be a perfect backflip.

And it was—everything from the downhill speed to the climb up the jump into the air, to the spot-on rotation, to landing right on my feet and skiing away like a pro. At that point, I had the jump. I was a master. I couldn't *not* land one now.

I came home early that night to have dinner with my family, buzzing with eagerness to share the news of my accomplishment. My mom put dinner on the table and sat down, and I leaned across the table and announced to my family, "Guys, I did my first backflip on skis today!"

Skiing in California, 2000 (Photo by Eliot Drake)

Mom was stoked. "No way!" she said, living vicariously through me, a childlike smile on her face. "I can't believe it; that's awesome! Tell me all about it!"

But before I could, my dad leaned across the table and, between mouthfuls, said, "You're an idiot,"

Plenty of people might call these risks I've taken stupid. My dad just can't for the life of him understand why I would want to go upside down through the air and land on skis. Not that he hadn't once taken risks himself in his youth. But that all changed the day he watched his sixteen-year-old best friend die on a motorcycle. Since then, not a logical, pragmatic cell in my dad's body thinks that such risks are cool. For him, for lots of people, the ratio of risk to return seems absolutely ridiculous. But my mom, who grew up waterskiing, pulling off tricks until the boat ran out of gas without ever truly experiencing disaster, was just as pumped as I was when I pulled off stunts like my backflip.

But don't misunderstand me; I am not an adrenaline junkie. It's an important distinction. I've always been this way. When I was a toddler, my mom caught me sitting at the top of the refrigerator. I had pulled out drawers to make myself a staircase up to the counter, then worked my way over to stand on jars and climb onto the fridge. This wasn't learned behavior, a toddler seeking a rush from danger. This was curiosity, a natural drive to push myself further and higher because it just felt like I was supposed to do it.

The shortest answer for why I do these things is this: Because that's how I am completely true to myself. It's how I'm wired. It's where I experience complete presence, complete solace, complete freedom. When I'm in mid-air, doing a backflip on skis, going over a waterfall, or jumping a hundred feet on a snowmobile, all the noise, all the scattered odds and ends racing around in my mind, consuming my energy, competing for my attention, all fall away. There's no multitasking, no bills, no calls to make, clients to please or appointments to keep. Because now there's no room on my bandwidth for anything but the stillness, the presence of being right here, right now. And those moments of freefall are the only places where I find that presence, a sense of complete and utter calm.

Not that there aren't adrenaline junkies out there doing these same things, constantly looking for that sweet rush, always pushing the boundaries of what's safe in order to continue feeling it. And if that's what drives them, great. I'm not here to judge.

But for me, it's like when other people do yoga or go running or take bubble baths or write novels or drive cars really fast. Focusing on just that one thing is a way to quiet the noise. It's an opportunity to ground myself, to connect completely to the universe because there's only the present moment, being completely aware and in tune with every part of my body and its movements, and nothing else matters or even exists.

It's not adrenaline I'm hooked on. It's peace and quiet.

When I was eighteen, I moved to Gunnison, Colorado, to attend Western State College. With a music scholarship that paid for most of my education, I was a business major with a music minor, so I was basically learn-

Grant dropping into a favorite line, Sonora backcountry, 2010
(Photo by Shaun Kegel)

ing how to party really well. At this point in my life, skiing was everything to me, and my only goal was to become a pro skier. I did plenty of racing and took part in the Crested Butte extreme freeskiing competitions. And although I never stood on top of the podium in the world of professional skiing, I didn't race to participate; I raced to win, every time.

Though I heavily participated and competed in freeskiing, most of the backcountry skiing I did was with my best friend, Casey.

Casey was my backcountry guide, my outdoor adventure guru, my Jedi knight. He taught me everything he knew about backcountry terrain, avalanche safety, and climbing. He single-handedly taught me how to rock climb.

Being from Tahoe, I thought I knew snow, but the first time I went skiing with Casey in my freshman year of college, and showed up wearing cotton long johns, I realized just how little I knew. "Dude, don't you know cotton kills?" he asked, incredulous. "You never, ever, *ever* wear cotton out here. What happens when you sweat, huh? Cotton won't wick the moisture off of you—that's just hypothermia waiting to happen."

Our plan for that day was to hike up and ski down Red Lady. I lusted after the sheer, 3,000-foot vertical face. I was insane thinking I could ski that face, Casey told me, insisting it was completely unsafe.

"It's cool, bro, I know what I'm doing," I dismissed him, teasing him a little for being overly cautious. "I'll be careful."

Casey chuckled and shook his head, then put his hand on my shoulder. "Bro, let's do this the right way..."

He guided me up a safer face, and showed me how to test snow for avalanches, which he explained was all about the study of how snow falls and what each accumulating layer of snow looks like. Choosing a spot of snow representative of the face we'd be skiing, Casey pulled the shovel out of his pack and dug an avy pit, a cut straight down through the vertical face of snow, exposing layer after layer of snow down to the ice cap closest to the stable base layers. Like tree rings, the layers reveal everything one needs to know about the history of what lies beneath—was it a big snow dump; did it come in warm and then cool to a different type of snow?

"We're stylin'. This looks good to go," Casey said, pointing to our avy pit like a science teacher. "No dissimilar layers here. You want adhesion and symmetry, not difference. Mass times gravity with minimal friction or proper loading—that's an avalanche."

There were only two things that terrified me in life: Paralysis and avalanches.

It was the first time I realized the difference between snow in Colorado and the snow I knew at Tahoe. It's wind-loading that seems to kill people at Tahoe. The tremendous winds we get there pile up powder on the leeward side, building up a false mountain side that, once it gets too heavy, can break off in chunks and take skiers with it. Sometimes there's point loading, in which it takes nothing but a sudden movement—the wind or the slightest shifting in the snow, for instance—and, like a game of Jenga, the entire mountain's worth of snow goes. But this Colorado snow was snow I had only just begun to understand.

I'd always been completely confident in my abilities as an athlete; winning was about speed, getting the right gear, visualizing, and pushing my body harder. But as our friendship grew, the lessons I had begun learning from Casey, the fascinating ideas he shared with me about how science affected sports, made me think about those sports in a whole new way. Pairing physics with physical ability began molding me into an even better athlete, and I gained even more enjoyment from it than I ever had before.

With him, I wanted to win, but for the first time, what I wanted even more than that was to learn.

Though I'd always ridden mountain bikes, I'd never participated in an actual race until Casey, a skilled rider, encouraged me to enter one in the spring semester of my first year of college.

The new sport of dual-slalom mountain bike racing was an intense side-by-side rally to the finish, around gates, over small jumps, and ending in a winner-take-all finale. As taxing as the racing action was, Casey and I opted to kick it up a notch by foolishly deciding we'd ride our bikes the eleven miles from campus to the race, then ride home afterward. Casey, a talented rider, brought the science of kinematics (the study of mechanics that describe the motion of points) and vector physics—all the reasons behind why a person wins a race—while what I brought was my competitive nature and a lot of early energy that had been destroyed by the time the first single-elimination race had started. Thanks to nothing but sheer off-the-couch physical ability, I kept winning my races, while Casey, whose ability was combined with mental awareness, was winning his, too. But I'm a fast learner. With each advancement to my next race, I was learning from my increasingly better competitors—so much so that, in the end, when Casey and I inevitably faced each other, I narrowly smoked him. He'd come to win, too, but he'd actually made me better in the process, and his pride in my win was its own reward.

The semester ended shortly afterward, and when I returned to Tahoe for summer break, I entered the mountain bike racing circuit.

I spent most of my school days in Colorado with Casey, rock-climbing, mountain biking, skiing, and talking … always talking. His studies in bioscience were going to lead him to solve big problems in the world, to really help people in substantial ways. A small part of me envied him for knowing his path so clearly, as I floundered along, partying like Van Wilder, playing baritone sax and skiing my days away. I absorbed his words like a sponge, and his passion for science and the technical side of life were infectious. We had beautiful conversations, deeply analytical and with enthusiasm of the kind that only young men with their lives before them can have. He enhanced my life, made me crave learning for maybe the first time, and inspired me to expect more from my college experience than I was getting.

I made numerous other connections through skiing as well, which gave me the opportunity to begin filming my skiing when I was just a sophomore. It was during one ski line, at Wolf Creek Pass in the San Juan Mountains of Colorado, that I broke my face.

I'd come off a cliff and hit so hard that my knee rammed into my chin on the impact, breaking my face in nine places and shattering seventeen teeth.

My chin was broken in half, my mandible broken in three places; I exploded the entire temporomandibular joint. I broke part of my maxilla, the lower part of my skull that holds my upper teeth, and I broke the jaw completely off the TMJ on the right side of my face. My face was a floating, broken mess; the only teeth remaining completely intact were my top front teeth from canine to canine.

My first thought, after my rag-doll landing and then painful drag to an awkward stop, was, *Wow, how did I get all these rocks and dirt in my mouth?* I spit them all into my glove before realizing they were teeth.

I looked down at my teeth in my glove and realized that there, down and off to my right, was my chin. *Fuck,* I thought, *I have to man up and put that back in the socket before the pain hits.* I reached up with my hand and touched my jaw, pushing it only a millimeter before the fiercest pain I'd ever known tore up through my skull like a hole being ripped through my head. I collapsed from its excruciating force and lay in a heap in the snow, grunting and moaning as I waited for ski patrol to rescue me.

Fortunately, they arrived quickly and got me off the mountain and into their shack, but not before I'd developed the early stages of hypothermia. Between putting hot packs on various parts of my body, patrol personnel worked to gather information about my health insurance. Because they couldn't be sure a helicopter ride would be covered, they instead packed me up for a five-hour ride by ambulance… five fucking hours of agonizing brutality all the way down to Durango.

Tubes reached down my throat to suck out blood and shards of teeth, so that I wouldn't swallow them, vomit, or choke. Painkillers of any kind were forbidden until doctors could verify that my spine had, thank God, not been damaged. It was here that I truly learned, for the first time, how to cope with pain. (Later, when I had obviously broken my back, this wasn't really an issue.)

I spent four months recovering in Colorado, and then, because I certainly couldn't continue school, skiing, or my medical care there, I moved home to Nevada.

My jaw was wired shut for just over three months—I was a twenty-one-year-old sipping the liquid meals that my mom made me through straws. Following that was a series of surgeries over a period of about three years, which involved implanting a false mandible and jaw joint as well as new teeth into my mouth. There were tooth recoveries, root canals, gum surgeries, and facial reconstruction.

After the final root canal surgery, about four months after my injury, I became inexplicably, irresistibly compelled to get back to my life in Colorado. My parents were concerned, believing I was dangerously rushing my recovery, and implored me to stay, calling out all the potential risks involved in overdoing it. But there was no stopping me. "I feel good, and I'm ready to get back," I told them, not quite understanding myself why I felt so rushed. But I felt confident that it was absolutely the right time to head back. Twelve hours later, I began driving.

As I pulled into downtown Gunnison, Casey spotted my truck, hopped in his, and followed me to my apartment. Over dinner—one which, thankfully, I could actually eat—and a bottle of wine to celebrate my return, Casey was unable to contain his excitement as he laid out his plans for the next day's snowmobiling trip. He and some friends of his, Matt and Andy, whom I had known from many social occasions, were headed to Cumberland Pass.

Any other day, I'd have been salivating over such a plan, maybe even inviting myself to come along. It had been such a long time since I'd done anything physical, and there had never been a day that I had been able to pass up an offer to go into the backcountry with snowmobiles. As Casey described the plans for Cumberland Pass, I felt that familiar urge.

But I was uncertain that my fragile body was quite ready for skiing, so I, to my own surprise, stayed silent. I'd also promised someone else, my girlfriend at the time, that my return to skis would be with her. And there was this other feeling, too, an unsettled feeling I couldn't quite put my finger on: It just wasn't my day to go with Casey.

The next evening at about 6 o'clock, I was in my kitchen making dinner when my apartment door burst open, and in ran our friend Peat, tears streaming down his face. He fell to his knees, and through screaming and fierce sobs cried, "Casey, gone! Matt, Andy, gone!"

I felt as if I were missing part of a broadcast, the essential parts that would lead to my understanding. I was sorting through static. "Peat, what are you saying, what about Casey?"

"Avalanche!" Peat fell to the floor, screaming and weeping.

Casey? An expert backcountry skier who had taught me everything I now knew about avalanches? Surely Peat had it wrong. He'd gotten bad information... And, he had come to me, so obviously he thought there was some immediacy, something I could do to help the situation.

I was still wrapping my mind around the swirling chaos. "Okay, it's okay, let's work this out, come on, let's go," I assured Peat, pulling him to his feet and guiding him to my truck, which I drove directly to Casey's house, where I expected to find this whole thing to be one great big misunderstanding.

A line of cars, familiar cars belonging to our many friends, surrounded the house. Only one was missing—Casey's. The looks on their faces as we burst through the door told us all we needed to know.

An avalanche had broken on Cumberland Pass—the entire pass had cut loose. Reports came in of a slide more than a thousand feet wide, with a several-foot-thick crown at the top, and it took all three of our friends with it. And, had I not listened to my gut and kept my loyalty to my girlfriend, I would have been on the back of that sled, skiing with those friends, and I would've died, too. Breaking my face had saved my life.

Was there a reason I wasn't supposed to die that day? Maybe. Maybe there was more for me to do. Maybe I needed to learn to trust myself, to listen to my heart, to trust the process that guides us all. Who knows? But maybe, just maybe, there aren't any coincidences.

With the tremendous hole that Casey's death had ripped open in my life, I felt aimless. The life I'd created for myself in Colorado no longer made any sense to me. With death hovering this closely, everything felt pointless. Taking the path of least resistance would get me nowhere, would serve no one, and would do his memory a disservice. Casey, the best man I'd ever known, had died, and here I was, alive because of a fluke decision I'd made that completely went against my character. Deep in my bones I was absolutely certain that there was a reason, and it wasn't so I could continue coasting through business classes and partying.

I had rarely felt as alive as I had on my adventures in the woods with Casey. With him, sports were no longer about the competition, winning no matter what. Because of him, and the fact that I had broken my face, I had begun to think of every little thing my body could do as miraculous and realized how important it was to savor every single moment of my life. Knowing what I knew then, how could I afford to waste another minute of my time?

On the hikes Casey and I took, we had become deeply enmeshed in and challenged by intellectual discussions about science and technology, and how they could make the world a better place. Somehow I'd gotten sidetracked on the way to my goal to become a helicopter pilot. I'd kept telling myself, because it was easy and I was having fun, that a business degree could eventually get me where I wanted to go. But when I was really honest with myself, I saw that time was slipping away and I wasn't getting any closer to my goal. As Casey's early death had proven, I couldn't afford to waste any more time than I already had. It was time for me to do something I cared about.

There was a reason I'd known him. And maybe here was my chance to explore it. I could start all over and do it right.

Within weeks, I had packed my bags, moved back home to Nevada, and enrolled at the University of Nevada, Reno. Not realizing at the time that I could simply go to a college where I could study aviation, I did what I saw as the means to create any opportunity: I majored in mechanical engineering.

When I sat down with the dean of the department, ready to plan out the courses I'd need to earn my degree, his expression looked amused.

"Well, Grant, I hate to be the one to tell you this, but after two years of college, you only have one class that will transfer: English 101. So, basically, you're going to have to start all over."

"Wow," I said, running my hands through my hair. "That's it?"

"That's it. Are you sure you're ready for this?"

"Definitely. Absolutely," I said, looking him straight in the eye. "But I was wondering… I'm not very good at math. How intense is the math?"

He laughed, a little too heartily. "You don't like math and you want to be an engineer? That may be a problem. You're going to do a lot of math here. Multi-variable integral calculus, differential equations… there's a lot of math."

I had never let difficulty prevent me from attempting things, and now that I'd moved home and uprooted my life, it wouldn't stop me here, either.

Not that I didn't struggle. In my case, it truly was 1 percent inspiration and 99 percent perspiration. In my first year as an engineering student, I went to four different math tutors on a regular basis. But because I was enthusiastic and committed to it wholeheartedly, I eventually got the hang of it. I went from struggling my way through "bonehead" math to managing a decent grade in differential equations and seeing a light at the end of the tunnel.

In the second half of my sophomore year, I took off a semester to go on an eleven-countries-in-nine-months backpacking trip around Europe. It was a trip I'd dreamed of taking throughout high school and had fully intended to take after I graduated, were it not for the fact that my parents feared such a plan would keep me from ever attending college. But now, as a college sophomore, an opportunity to take the trip came my way and I seized it, using money I'd saved up from working as a valet since the day I'd returned to Reno.

It was a great plan, except for the fact that when I returned at the end of summer 2002, I faced the prospect of starting my junior year with no internship plans—it was a requirement that most of my fellow students planned to satisfy during their junior year and which I'd somehow overlooked. If I didn't get busy lining one up, I might be the only graduating student without one.

My friend, Chris, worked for Salomon North America, a manufacturer of what is widely regarded as the finest ski equipment in the world.

Surely there had to be industrial design and engineering involved in making ski equipment. Surely they'd need an intern, I thought. I called Chris, he put me in touch with someone who put me in touch with someone else, and because fortune seemed to be smiling on me, I rather effortlessly, within days, lined up a summer internship making skis in Annecy, France.

I flew to France and arrived at the hostel that would be my home for the next three months. The next morning, I got up, showered, put on my new work clothes, and hiked to the sidewalk that would lead me to where I'd catch the surface bus, which would take me to the train station, where I'd catch a bigger bus headed toward La Clusaz, Le Grand Bornand, and finally north to an area outside Annecy. From there I caught another surface bus, then hiked to the end of the long road I had to walk in order to arrive at the front door of Salomon.

The door, so devoid of any corporate identity that I wondered if I had the right place, displayed no markers at all. In front of the door were a huge, imposing, silver gate and a few trees, which nearly obscured the small kiosk in front of the gate. And on that kiosk was a doorbell button marked with the Salomon logo—my only indication that I'd reached my destination. I pushed the bell and looked down at the paper in my hand, on which I'd written my appointment time and location. It was 10 a.m. sharp, and we'd agreed upon 10:30.

No answer. Surely I couldn't be the first to arrive, could I?

Again I rang the bell and waited, checking my paper again as I considered whether I had my dates wrong. Still no answer.

The sound of a car approaching caught my attention. A little sports car pulled up next to me. Inside sat a woman. She rolled the passenger-side window down and began speaking to me in French, a language I knew only in bits and pieces from my previous trip to Europe. I used the words "internship" and "Salomon" and showed her my paper to prove that I actually belonged there. She reached over and opened the car door. I hopped in, and she pushed a button, opening the big silver gate.

The car followed a long, winding driveway, down a hill, alongside modular buildings with floor-to-ceiling glass, through which I could see the actual foundations, could see the roots of grass growing around them, as we drove beside them and the series of intricate tunnels that connected them like some sort of home for moles or prairie dogs.

We arrived at a parking lot, and the woman escorted me into the building, to the office of the man designated to meet with me on this important first day. I entered his office, held my hand out to shake his, and introduced myself as I beamed like a child, thrilled to begin my first day of work.

"Ohhh," he said, sighing and looking crestfallen. "Oooooh, no. You didn't get the e-mail?"

"What e-mail?" I said, holding up my silly sheet of handwritten notes.

"See, we've cancelled our internships," he said. "All of them."

"All? The whole program?" I asked, incredulous. I had spoken with him just two weeks earlier. Had they waited until I was in the air to do this?

"Yes, all. I'm very sorry," he said in his masterful English, only the slightest traces of a French accent in his speech.

"But I'm here now," I insisted, unbelieving. "I'm here. I moved here. What am I supposed to do?"

"I'm sorry, there's nothing I can do," he shook his head, looking anxious to move on with his work.

"I'll work for *free*," I urged. "You don't even have to pay me. Just let me do the internship. You don't have to give me anything, I just really need to work."

"But you see," he explained, "I cannot. We've had problems with interns divulging confidential information. We can no longer have interns. I'm very sorry. Good luck to you."

And out I went, walking up the long, winding driveway, through the silver gate, down the road, which took me to the bus, then to the bigger bus, then to the train station, to another bus, to the long, pitiful walk up to my hostel where awaited... what? What on earth was I supposed to do now?

There through the trees, down the hill, sparkling in the fresh sunlight, was Lake Annecy. And it occurred to me that here I was in one of the most beautiful places on earth with an opportunity before me like few ever experience: I had three months here that were *mine*, to do with what I wanted. So I wouldn't have the internship. So what? I could see this as an opportunity or an obstacle. I could bartend, kayak, learn to paraglide in what's considered the world's premiere paragliding destination... Annecy was my oyster! *This could potentially be my best summer of all time*, I thought.

I stepped into the hostel bar, full of my usual optimism and overconfidence, marched right up to the owner as he approached the front door in answer to the bell, and introduced myself.

"Hello!" I said to him, flashing my winning (thanks to numerous surgeries) smile, "I'm your new bartender!"

He did a double-take, clearly trying to remember whether such an offer had been made during some drunken conversation, then a slow grin spread across his face.

"Non, monsieur," he said, shaking his head and chuckling.

"No, no, listen, I'm your new bartender. I'm your man!" I insisted. "I'll work for free, just let me stay here. It'll be great."

"Non, non," he shook his head vigorously, explaining that his current bartender, a French woman, had been with him for two years, and he had no intention of either cutting her loose or hiring another bartender. Plus, she had an edge on me—she spoke French like a local. "*Il n'est pas possible.*"

And with that, he excused himself and left the room. I was dismayed that he couldn't see the clear genius of my plan, which had not only fully crystallized in my mind by now, but paid off for more people than just me. I just needed to get him to see that.

The next day, with nothing else to do and nowhere to go, I decided I'd park it at the hostel bar to continue my campaign to become bartender, sure that at any moment I'd be able to demonstrate my value to the owner. I continued to do this for the next four days.

Finally, bingo. I was there only an hour when a heated conversation developed between the bartender and the owner. In French, of which I could only pick out a few understandable words, I was able to discern the gist of her argument, which went something like this: "I've been here two years, you can't treat me this way, and I'm done with this fucking job." And with that, she abruptly ripped off her apron, threw it on the bar, and stormed out.

Bar Man in Annecy, France (Photo by Whitney Waldroup)

The hostel owner's eyes went from her, to her apron, and then up, where his eyes landed squarely on me. He exhaled heavily and shook his head, a smirk on his face.

I put my arms in the air, waved them, and then pointed with both hands at my head. "Hey!" I called to him, with a huge, satisfied smile on my face. "I'm your new bartender!"

Hesitant though he was, the man had a hostel to run and a bar full of customers. He had no choice but to grudgingly give me the job, with the assurance that a) I would not be paid, and b) if I couldn't make a success of it within a few nights, he would definitely be hiring someone else.

I pulled out all the stops. Within hours I was pumping tunes that had never been heard, mixing original drinks, and even making up rudimentary snacks to serve with the drinks, in an effort to sell more booze. And because I was shameless and absolutely sure I had nothing to lose, I began practicing my terrible French on customers, making them laugh and tip me out of what was likely a mixture of amusement and pity.

It worked. The owner bought what I was selling and saw his bar numbers climb. I could stay.

I decided that I could possibly trade my way through the entire summer. I figured that in this vacationer's paradise, my athletic skills could certainly be useful in securing me paragliding lessons. From the local phone book, I made a list of every paragliding school in Annecy, and in one day, I walked from place to place and approached every one of them to pitch my plan: I would teach them kayaking if they'd teach me paragliding. But nobody bit.

I had saved the best school (and, in my opinion, the biggest long shot) on the list for last. And at the end of the day, with no successful trades in hand and nothing to lose, I went for it, pitching them my outrageous idea.

The school's owner was in, and within seconds I could see that he might be receptive. I sat and talked with him for probably twenty minutes, just bro-ing out about skiing, paragliding, kayaking, living in Tahoe, tourists… and then it hit me. I had a one-two punch up my sleeve.

I pitched my trade idea to him, and he seemed interested but hesitant. And then I pulled out my clincher: "Dude," I said, winding up my over-sell, "I bartend at one of the biggest tourist bars in the area. People ask me all the time, 'What should I do when I'm here?' I could just hand them one of your brochures and send them paragliding with you.' All you have to do is give me lessons."

He bought it.

And it worked…well. Each week, there were many people who went paragliding on my recommendation. And I was supposed to teach his clients to whitewater kayak, but before we could even start, the river dried up for the summer. So we came up with a new plan: I would send tourists on paragliding trips, and I'd get a spot in their groups.

And so went the rest of that amazing summer. I bartended all afternoon and evening, closed the bar around 3 a.m., and then would hike down the cobblestone streets with other bar patrons, who were by now friends, into the old city to visit other bartender friends at their bars, where we'd party until 5 in the morning. Then I'd hike back up the hill, back to my room where I'd sleep roughly an hour. By 7 a.m., I'd hear the horn from Daniel, my paragliding instructor, picking up his customers for the day's paragliding lesson. Many of us would have partied too hard

*Paragliding in Le Grand Bor-
nand, France, 2003 (Photo by
Whitney Waldroup)*

the night before and often still reeked of whiskey, and we'd sleep in the van
all the way to the launch site outside town.

In August 2003, I returned from this trip that already felt like I had
dreamt it, and my enthusiasm ground quickly to a halt. Here I was, entering my senior year just as I had feared—with no internship under my
belt, trailing all my classmates who had responsibly completed theirs. And
when it comes to engineering, I knew, without an internship, my degree
would pretty much be second tier. I could have a 4.0 GPA but the first thing
any employer would ask me would be, "Where did you do your internship?" I had dicked around all summer and had the time of my life, but
fuck! Now what?

The same hopelessness I had felt standing on the street above Lake Annecy three months earlier, I now felt once again. And what I'd done then
had been foolish, cocky, overconfident, and naïve. But it had worked. I had
learned that when I actually decided what I wanted, the only thing to do
was pursue it with everything I had, even if everything was against me.
What choice did I have?

I considered all my connections, analyzing every potential internship
opportunity. I immediately seized upon my friend Steven.

Grant and Steven at the LULI laser facility near Paris,
France (Photo courtesy of Grant Korgan)

Steven Malekos, a much more serious student than I, had started his degree program earlier and had taken less time off. He had already graduated in 2001 and was now working as a researcher for Dr. Jesse Adams, a young UNR nanotechnology professor who hailed from Stanford. My status as a student, my connection to Steven, and my ability to relate to other men close to my age were all points in my favor, as was my confidence in the Jedi-mind-trick approach I'd perfected in France.

So one afternoon in late August, I walked into Dr. Adams' office, introduced myself, explained that I was the friend Steven had mentioned to him, and said, a grin lighting up my face, "I'm your next intern."

And so I was.

And that's how I ended up working with Steven, flying to Stanford to use semiconductor technology in a nanotech lab to develop solutions so promising that, by the end of my senior year, the technology was patent pending, UNR had spun us off into a private entity so that it could actually use the technology, and we were getting calls from people representing the

interests of the Department of Energy and other important agencies looking to benefit from it.

I graduated from UNR with my B.S. in mechanical engineering on a
Saturday in early May 2004, and the following Monday, I began work as
president of NanoLabz.

I had clawed my way into every possible dream, turned the terrible,
life-changing injury of a face break into an extraordinary opportunity, and
foolishly, against every possible objection, managed to get what I wanted at
every turn, despite being told each time that I couldn't.

But once I decide what I want, I'm relentless about getting it, and hold
onto it with the ferocity of a bulldog. And when you're that determined and
focused on having something, when you pour every ounce of your energy
into having it, and when you're open to the unexpected possibilities that
present themselves in order to bring it to you, it's the funniest thing: You
usually get it.

So when it came to lying in a bed in inpatient rehab with a broken back
six years later, the answer, the key to my recovery, was there already, but I
was only just beginning to see it and understand it: Decide what you want,
then *go get it.*

PART TWO
FOCUS ON WHAT
WORKS

Grant taking off above Lake Tahoe's North Shore (Photo by Pam Korgan)

I FLY

Low atmospheric pressure, five-knot wind moving in a favorable direction, and clear skies. The sun has been heating the earth below me all morning and is just now starting to release this newly warmed and now-rising air skyward, forming cylinders of upward-moving, slowly cooling molecules on their way toward becoming a cloud high in the sky. Conditions are perfect for launch.

Paragliding is as human a desire as taking a deep breath. We are born to seek flight.

On my back is a thirty-pound backpack filled with high-end nylon sheets sewn into parallel ram-air induction channels, forming a curved wing with a leading edge designed to utilize both Newtonian physics and a pressure differential, as explained by the average pressure on the upper surface of the wing being lower than the average pressure on the underside to generate lift.

The wind is picking up; I can feel it on my face. If at any point the conditions become stronger than my skill level, I will find myself in a dire yet familiar environment. Once I launch, I am wholly committed to piloting myself safely to the ground. Once airborne, there will be no backing down, no pause button—only personal growth, the acquisition of new skills, mental strength, and experience.

In paragliding it has been said that you only get one big crash—failure is not an option. Many things will happen during this flight. Partial wing *collapses, turbulence, moments of freefall, and the like… none of these things will serve me or my goal of landing safely at the landing zone.*

Simply put, my life depends on focusing on what's working.

I am near the top of a mountain, hiking upward, legs burning, lungs on fire. Soon I will be airborne. Arriving at the launch zone, I drop my pack and check the conditions one more time to ask myself one simple question: Go or no go? My instructors back in Annecy, France said many times to me, "Grant, for you it will be much harder not to fly than to fly. If in doubt, walk away and fly another day."

Today is a "green light" kind of day. I lay my harness out in the direction of launch, walk my wing back until the Kevlar and Dyneema lines are semi-taut. I deliberately and reverently unfold the canopy. Helmet on, I begin strapping myself into the harness, mentally going through my pre-flight checklist.

I twist 180 degrees to face the wing, and with crossed controls, I pull extra tension on my A-line risers, allowing the wind at my back to fully inflate the approximately ten-meter flying machine. All lines in their right and perfect place, harness fully strapped, I position myself ten degrees off-line with the wind, a trick I learned so that when I inflate to kite the wing overhead, I can do it one-handed (both A-line risers in my upwind hand), all the while controlling the fastest rising edge of the wing with the brake in my downwind hand.

One step back, the wing feels the full force of the wind and flies straight up, overhead. I walk in whichever direction is needed to keep me directly at the focal point of the airfoil, kiting, playing, and controlling. When everything feels right, I un-turn the 180 degrees I used during launch to face the void. I feel the pressure in my harness, the pulling skyward, one foot in front of the other, and I am free, free to fly…

Grant and Shawna running in Yosemite's granite wonderland
(Photo by Matt Theilen)

CHAPTER 8
RUNNING SHOES

Although my cell phone had been buzzing with loving, supportive text messages and voicemails from friends and family ever since my injury, I hadn't actively initiated communication with anyone since arriving at the hospital. But the day after I arrived at inpatient rehab, I made my first call—to my godsister, Bridgette.

I've known Bridgette her whole life. Our dads, best friends since they were in kindergarten and had grown up in the same neighborhood in Oklahoma. Though college eventually separated them, they had remained best friends their whole lives, eventually even building houses in the same neighborhood back in Oklahoma. Our family photo albums contain many shots of me, a smiling toddler, holding an infant Bridgette in my lap. With parents as close as ours were with each other, Bridgette and I spent a lot of time together growing up, and I considered her, in many ways, a true sister. And I'm fortunate that my wife thinks of her this way, too.

Now that I was in one of the most difficult situations I'd ever faced, I craved that child-like feeling of connection, of safety, and of pure, unadulterated happiness. I knew Bridgette was just the person to provide it.

Which is why I was disappointed that Bridgette's first words after we exchanged hellos were, "You know, Grant, I'm expecting great things from you."

"Uhh…Mmmm-kaay," I said, completely confused. Was she referring to a conversation that happened while I was unconscious or something? To Shawna, I shook my head, furrowed my eyebrows and pointed at the phone, as if to ask whether I'd dialed the wrong number.

"I mean it," she insisted. "I'm expecting… *all of us* are expecting that you will turn this into an opportunity to do something really great in the world. Because that's who you are. You're my example of living life to the fullest every day and taking nothing for granted. *Carpe Diem,* remember? *You* taught me that. And now this is your opportunity to live that example, to seize this opportunity and turn this part of your life into something great. We wouldn't expect anything less of you. You know that, right?"

Was she kidding? Here I was, literally broken in half, in pain and exhausted, struggling even to breathe comfortably. And she's telling me what I owe the world? I mean, I didn't even know if I'd be able to go get coffee by myself when all was said and done.

At that moment, humanity and my contribution to the world were secondary to my own recovery, to just getting through the day. The crushing weight of having expectations placed on my shattered body was more than I could handle. After listening to Bridgette talk about the expectations she and my family had for me, convinced, as I'm sure she was, that this inspiration would serve me well, I backpedaled off the call quickly. "Yeah, okay, right on! Thanks, Bridgette. Love you," I said, and hung up the phone hurriedly.

And then I broke into a full-body sweat. Because I knew she was right, and I nearly hated her for it. If I played that role for Bridget, perhaps I did for other people as well. And I had asked for that role, took great joy from it, used it to push people out of their comfort zones and into doing what they knew they really wanted to do. And I didn't want to give that up.

Grant and his godsister, Bridgette,
in San Francisco (Photo courtesy
of Grant Korgan)

But more than that, more than wanting to hold onto that part of me that I had always considered fundamental to who I was, I owed a full recovery to Casey's family, I remembered.

After Casey's death, his parents had given me his old climbing gear, knowing I would use it well and keep it safe. And with it, they expressed their fondest wish: That I would use it to climb Yosemite's Half Dome for him; Casey had always wanted to go but had never made it. Now, in this bed, with Bridgette's words still ringing in my ears, the weight of this promise I had made to honor Casey fell on me, too.

❡

The day after I arrived at inpatient was a Monday and my first day of physical therapy. In order to remain at the facility, I needed to maintain a two-hours-a-day, five-days-a-week therapy schedule. If I couldn't keep that schedule, I would be transferred back to the hospital's neurology department—a move I knew would set my recovery back considerably, because it would prohibit me from doing any therapy at all. Whether I felt physically ready to tackle workouts or not, I was committed to doing them.

Despite the early hour of 7 a.m., and despite my discomfort at sitting up in bed wearing my new brace, both reggae and electronic beats blared on the portable iPod stereo Shawna had brought from home, setting an energetic, upbeat tone for my first workout.

"A room with some decent tunes. Right on!" came a bright, cheery voice at my door. We turned to find a young woman beaming at us. She had tanned, freckled skin and strawberry blonde hair in a ponytail. "Hi there, I'm Becca! I'm your physical therapist."

Her casual appearance, tanned skin in mid-March, and speech riddled with slang quickly told us that she was not only about our age, but also part of the Tahoe ski and snowboard culture that I'd grown up in. She didn't look at my brace, didn't start talking about paralysis. For a long time, we talked about the fresh powder (it had been a great weekend for it), skiing, and snowmobiles (she was a fan).

"Okay," she said, finally turning the subject to the work at hand. "So, let's talk about your goals!"

Shawna and I looked at each other. It was nice just having the subject addressed. It was the first time since my injury that anyone had seemed interested in what *we* wanted in all this.

Shoot for the stars, I thought. *What do I have to lose?* "I want to run," I said. It was the first time I'd dared to speak my dearest wish aloud. A flood of hope and optimism rushed over me just hearing my own voice speak the words.

I expected a "Well, we'll see what we can do" and a reminder about wheelchairs—the safe healthcare system routine we'd already seen a lot of in the last week.

But Becca didn't bat an eye. "Okay! Sweet!" she said brightly, smiling at me, without a trace of skepticism in her voice, and then flashing the same smile at Shawna. "But if you want to run, we've got a lot of work to do, so let's get to it, okay?"

And just like that, I was in rehab for real.

It was amazing how simply saying what I wanted infused me with energy. And as soon as I made the decision to put my energy into achieving that, instead of looking back, I felt myself gaining mental strength, which I realized would soon translate into physical strength. And that was critical, because I could quickly see that, for a while, my life would consist primarily of people pushing my body around until I was strong enough to push back. The best example of this was the rolling.

The average person gets signals all day that the body needs to move and change position; our feet fall asleep or we get fidgety after sitting for long periods of time. At first it's just irritating and uncomfortable. But when we don't listen to the signals, the blood stops moving. Do that long enough and tissues die. Of course, most people can't stay still long enough for that to happen.

But I wasn't getting those signals from my body. Without being rolled every hour, I could start developing pressure sores on my back, butt, and legs.

For the first few days, until Shawna was more accustomed to the awkward complexity of rolling me on her own, this took a few people. And the process became more complicated when I needed to put on the brace.

The custom-molded plastic brace I had endured abuse from a technician to have made needed to be worn in order to do any of my physical therapy. In fact, I'd wear it any time my body was inclined more than thirty degrees, to support the weight of my body as my spine adjusted to its new metal cage. Thinking back, I'm shocked that, while still in the ICU, I was forced to sit up on my own without its support.

Still, I hated it. The brace was composed of two solid white plastic pieces that closely fit every contour of my body's front and back, from shoulders to pelvis, and worked as a sort of clamshell. The two pieces were connected by three thick Velcro straps that could be tightened through loops on the plastic and always, ALWAYS pinched my skin when tightened.

To put it on me, the rolling process was begun—the pillow, the people at my head and feet, the gentle roll to one side. Then, the back half of the brace was laid down on the bed, its side scooped up under me as tightly as it would go, and I was then rolled onto my back again, into the cold, unforgiving turtle's shell of the back half of the brace. By now, the effort of the rolling would have already produced streams of sweat that rolled down my face and back, sweat that would only be exacerbated by the shell. Then, the front shell was laid on my chest, and the three straps were wound through the loops and tightened, corset-like, pinching my skin and pulling so tight I often thought I wouldn't be able to breathe. As a man who craved the freedom of bodily movement, being in this brace was a sort of hell for me.

Once I was in the shell, the head of the bed was raised up to put me in a seated position in order to put a little weight on my spine, to go from being

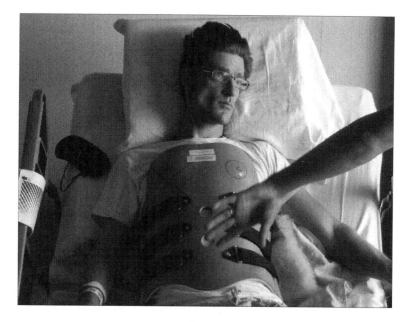

Grant experiencing the turtle shell for the first time in rehab
(Photo by Shawna Korgan)

flat, with no vertebral friction. This would force my spine and organs and muscles to adjust to being vertical again, despite the excruciating pain, because my muscles had begun to atrophy and my internal organs had shifted due to the long days of being horizontal.

In those first days of therapy, my "workouts" consisted primarily of sitting. With the brace in place and my torso upright, Becca, Shawna, and maybe another person or two—Shawna's dad, my mom, Steven, an assistant—would together help me by pulling my legs around to the side of the bed. Gradually they would help me slide so that I was eventually sitting on the edge of the bed. Then I had to sit there.

At first just 30 seconds was a success, but they kept asking for more time…a minute, then two, and could I do a full five minutes? I just sat there, acclimating to the ridiculous, burning pain of my organs shifting and my spine being upright and stacked, one vertebra on top of another, while hands hovered near my shoulders, ready to steady me. Once my goal time had been met, my team would swing my legs back up onto the bed with my back resting on the mattress. They would flatten the bed, roll me back over, remove the brace, and leave me lying there, panting and exhausted.

For at least the first half of my month in inpatient, sitting would be about as much therapy as my body could muster. And sometimes we'd simply work on elongating my muscles. Who knew that lying flat might be such hard work? But it was. After lying in a contoured hospital bed for ten days, all my muscles had shortened, tightened. Lying flat, a near impossibility for me at this point, was made an important goal, one I'd strive for, sweat and cry for, every day.

It was tremendously gratifying to see Becca involving Shawna as a necessary part of the therapy. She included Shawna in every plan, providing thorough instructions for eventually doing more once we were on our own.

At the end of our first session, our first "sit therapy," after making her notes in her chart, Becca tucked her pen behind her ear, put her chart down on my bed, and turned to Shawna.

"Okay," she said with an expectant smile, "how are you feeling about all this? Good?"

Shawna's entire face smiled, in a way I hadn't seen in what felt like months, at being so respected by Becca as to be included as a vital member of my therapy team. Shawna asked a few questions about therapies Shawna had researched, treatments she'd heard of. Becca listened without any judgment or doubt, considering Shawna's words thoughtfully, and then promised to look into those with which she was unfamiliar.

She wasn't patronizing or condescending, never suggested that Shawna get over her fantasy and get used to the idea of having a husband in a wheelchair. She, like Shawna, saw *me*, not the injury, and she was truly the first healthcare professional we'd encountered since my arrival in ICU who had done that.

"Thanks so much for believing in Grant. You have no idea how much it means to us," said Shawna, fighting tears, the weight of all we'd gone through seeming to mount in her voice.

"Oh, honey!" Becca said, reaching over for Shawna in a jovial hug. "We're going to do everything we can to give you your husband back, okay?"

Becca, who had, by the luck of the draw, just happened to be assigned to us, became the champion of my recovery. She, like Shawna, spent time at home researching therapies on her home computer or talking to other professionals for advice. She'd come to our sessions and say things like, "Hey, I was talking to one of my other physical therapist friends, and apparently this thing has worked on spinal cord injuries. I think we should try it—you up for it?"

That challenge always pushed me to work harder, to remain in a constant state of forward progression. With my music cranked, I began visualizing myself walking. The tone of her voice always told me, "This is a recovery." My injury hadn't left me with a life change I needed to get used to; it had begun a process I'd get through, to the other side.

Meanwhile, everywhere else I turned, someone was saying, "Let's get you a really nice wheelchair."

Chief among them was Dr. Abbott. The doctor in charge of my rehabilitation program had been heralded as an amazing, revolutionary doctor in the field of spinal cord injuries, and had reputedly been Christopher Reeve's doctor. The research that Shawna and my mom had done after my surgery, while I was unconscious, had uncovered information about numerous rehab facilities in the region, but all signs kept pointing to the fact that right here at this local hospital, there was this wonderful doctor with special expertise, leading a spinal research and recovery center. I was anxious to work with her, a woman who might be a pioneer in new treatments.

But the first time we met, after introducing herself to me, we spent about twenty minutes engaging in pleasantries. When we got down to business, all she said was, "Well, show me, let's see those leg muscles contract! Go ahead and move your legs. Move your legs!"

I couldn't. I just looked at her. Was she kidding?

"Mmm," she said, scribbling away in my chart. "All right." And just like that, she was gone.

The next day came, and she said the same thing: "Show me your legs."

I flexed as hard as I could to twitch a muscle, to show her something she could work with. "Look, I can almost flicker this left one!" I said, excited and completely convinced, as I searched her face, that she would be, too.

"Yeah," she said offhandedly, writing on my chart with a blank expression on her face.

What exactly was supposed to be special about her? I certainly wasn't that impressed, and I desperately wanted to be. I wanted to love her, to be filled with confidence about all I'd achieve on her watch. If she could have shown me something special, something that indicated her expertise and special interest in my condition, I was willing to follow her to the ends of the earth, to do anything and everything she asked of me, and tell everyone I knew about what an amazing doctor she was. There had to be something about her worth all the fuss. Any minute now, it would come.

But time after time, she would pull Shawna and me down with reminders about ordering my wheelchair, or she'd hand us brochures with such titles as "Yes You Can: Living with a Disability," featuring photos of smiling, happy people in wheelchairs. Getting used to my condition was the last thing on our agenda, and we resented that she seemed to think otherwise.

Though in our meeting she mentioned nothing about having been Christopher Reeve's doctor, it came to light within a few weeks of my arrival here that she had been the overseeing physiatrist at Reeve's facility, and though she technically was his doctor, she had actually been part of a much larger team of doctors who worked with Reeve. Meanwhile, this hospital's spinal therapy and recovery center, of which she was the leader, was little more than a general rehabilitation center, one which also served Alzheimer's and stroke patients, and in fact did not specialize in spinal cord injuries. In essence, Greg, my new friend here at inpatient, and I were guinea pigs.

But Becca believed in me, and cared enough to learn new things, and for the present time that was enough for us.

Grant and Shawna (Photo by Matt Theilen)

"I was thinking about decorating," said Shawna one day during my first week at inpatient rehab.

She was cooking up a plan; I could see it on her face.

"Okay..." I said, smiling with curiosity.

"I mean this room. I want to do something to make it feel really good and positive in here. Perhaps we could put some things on the walls? What would you want to see there?"

I knew immediately, without having to think. "Wedding pictures," I said. "I really want to see me jumping."

My good friend, Matt, who in my humble opinion is one of the best photographers in the world, had captured both our engagement at Yosemite and our wedding there ten months later. In one engagement photo, my favorite one, Shawna and I seem to be running, in perfect synchrony, in mid-air. In another, a wedding shot, a perfectly composed and stunning Shawna strikes a pose in her wedding dress while I frog-leaped next to her.

I wanted to see those images again, immerse myself in what we looked like as *us*, being our truest versions of ourselves. I didn't want to forget what I looked like in mid-air, unencumbered by all *this*.

That night, Matt and his wife, Tara, arrived with huge prints of these photos. With Shawna's help, they set right to work, hanging and taping photos around the room. By the time I went to sleep that night, I was surrounded by moments from the happiest days of my life.

This got the ball rolling. In another day or two, at Shawna's request, my mom arrived with a large whiteboard and some dry erase markers. "I thought we could write your goals down on this," Shawna explained, carrying the board around the room as she looked for the best place to display it.

Over the course of several days, Shawna began scribbling ideas on this "dream board" as more and more goals occurred to us. Becca was a huge fan of the board, too; she'd add goals to the board for me or bring in clippings from ski magazines that showed skiers ripping through pristine powder and write goals on those as well.

My therapy progressed well in that first week, and I was now spending time on a tilt table so that I was in a vertical position for longer periods of the day. Soon I'd be sitting in a wheelchair. Encouraged and excited about my progress, Shawna thought it was time to kick things up a notch. She went home to grab more clothes for us both and my slippers, for when I would inevitably be standing up. On the way out the door, she saw my new running shoes, the shoes I'd barely had five runs in, sitting by the door, in the same place I'd left them weeks ago after walking Obie. *He's going to need these,* she thought, and threw them in her bag as she left the house.

Unlike the first time I saw those helicopters out my window, seeing these running shoes didn't fill me with sadness by reminding me of what I didn't have. By now, I had embraced the concept of moving forward, and I'd been reaping the rewards. So when Shawna hung my shoes by their laces over the corner of the dream board, which was now propped in an arm chair at the foot of my bed, I was stoked to see them. I knew that Shawna had put them there because she believed with her entire heart that not only would I someday be wearing those shoes, but I'd be running in them. Seeing them every time I opened my eyes, I was starting to believe it, too.

The redecoration hadn't even begun the last time I had seen Dr. Abbott. So when she came in to do our next assessment, an amused expression came over her face. And, perhaps, a little exasperation.

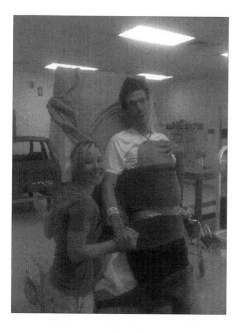

*Beginning rehab on the
tilt table (Photo by Steven
Malekos)*

"Wow," she said, scanning the walls with her eyes. "You've really turned this place into the honeymoon suite, haven't you?"

Everyone on our floor by now had heard about us, the newlyweds who never got to take their honeymoon because of my broken back. Others had actually called my room the Honeymoon Suite, and we found it refreshing to hear Dr. Abbott join in on some casual fun with us.

"Yeah, we did," we both said, exchanging smiles.

"Hmmm," she said, still scanning and leaning down to get a better look at my dream board with a puzzled expression on her face. "What's this?" she asked, pointing at the shoes.

"Uh, they're running shoes," said Shawna. *Duh.*

"Ummm. Why are they here?" she asked, looking directly at Shawna.

What did she mean by that? Should they be on my feet instead, is that what she meant? Was she finally on board with my plan to walk again? Shawna must have thought so, too.

"They're just there until he gets back on his feet," Shawna explained, reaching for the shoes as if to quickly put them on me.

Dr. Abbott sighed. "Well, I don't know if that's such a good idea."

Shawna looked confused. "Well, I just want to remind him to stay focused on his goal of running."

A patronizing smile spread across Dr. Abbott's face. *There, there, my sweet, naïve child. I hope you're enjoying Fantasyland.* "You know," she said, screwing up her mouth to form the words she meant with some sort of tact. "I just... well, we just don't want to give him any false hope right now."

What the fuck is "false hope"? I mean, isn't hope the belief or wish for something you don't have? False hope is a paradox by definition. That's the nature of hope... wishing and wanting something, believing you can have it, even though evidence tells you otherwise. And things we hope for come true *all the time.* Couldn't this, too?

Clearly, Dr. Abbott wasn't on the same page with us, and it seemed she never would be. Shawna's furrowed brow showed her frustration at this realization, and rightly so, considering how hard she always worked to be respectful of the doctors and nurses we'd encountered, and how important she knew every one of them was to my recovery.

But at the same time, there was that Bubble, that protective barrier strategically designed to protect me from just such situations.

Shawna let it pass until Dr. Abbott left, but later, after she'd had some time to collect her thoughts, although she was somewhat nervous, she set out to clear things up and found the doctor in the hallway. Standing at just enough distance from the door that I couldn't overhear, Shawna struggled to maintain a respectful tone as she told the good doctor, "Look, I want you to know that I appreciate your professional opinion and your background. I know that you've worked with other spinal cord patients in the past, and I respect that, I really do. But I think, from this point forward, I would really appreciate it if we could keep discussions, especially the ones in front of Grant, strictly to the medical stuff. Let me do what I'm going to do with my husband, and please don't ever come into his room again and tell him that he can't have hope or that he can't focus on what he wants. Okay?"

Dr. Abbott simply stared, somewhat dumbfounded by this show of opposition to her experience and knowledge.

"I understand you have parameters, and you can't tell him he's going to walk," continued Shawna, "but there's no rule saying that *I* can't tell my husband he's going to walk."

Contrite, the usually rigid doctor began to backpedal. "Well, you know, that's not really what I meant to do, I simply meant to keep him focused on his immediate goals of getting through inpatient."

"I appreciate that, I just wanted to make sure we were on the same page," said Shawna briskly. "Now that we are, and you know exactly where Grant and I stand, let's just move forward."

Minutes after excusing herself, Shawna confidently strode in, alone. The line in the sand had been drawn—anyone on the Grant-is-going-to-run-again program was welcome, but anyone who wasn't completely, wholeheartedly, on it... well, needn't bother coming in.

We knew we had Becca, and we knew our friends and family were there for us 100 percent. But even if not a single person in the world believed in my recovery but me and Shawna, that was fine. We did, and that's all that mattered. The shoes were a subtle reminder to us, to everyone who entered, of what our goal was, and their presence established that we would define our own path for recovery.

Sitting there waiting for me at the end of that first week was a landmark, something everyone around me seemed to see as a step in the right direction, but what I saw only as a big dead end: a wheelchair. In my mind, that fucking wheelchair was a jail sentence, an end, an admission that I would never walk. And by God, I would walk out of this place. If I sat in a wheelchair, I reasoned, I might as well give up, and I had no intention of doing that. I made that very clear to anyone who would listen.

"Now, what's this I hear about you not wanting to get in your wheelchair?" came Dr. Abbott's assertive voice in my door, near the end of my first week at inpatient. Skipping the niceties of a greeting altogether, the doctor breezed in, ready to tackle her problem patient, despite the conversation she'd had with Shawna just a day prior.

"Yeah, I'm really not into the wheelchair thing," I said sheepishly. She wasn't buying it.

"Look," I argued, "if I get in a wheelchair, I'm accepting this, and I don't want to accept it. I'm going to work through it and do my PT, and I'm going to walk, so I don't need that chair."

"Grant, I know you don't want to hear this, but you have a spinal cord injury," she said, in a patronizing tone, her brow furrowed and her face tight. Clearly the conversation with Shawna hadn't tempered her approach at all. "The fact is, you're paralyzed. Okay? There are a lot of things about your body that you're going to have to get used to, and you're going to have to accept the fact of the wheelchair. Now we're going to get you one very soon, and you need to accept this is how you're going to get around in the world now."

This was by no means new information to me. It seemed like all I'd heard from doctors, nurses, and well-meaning case workers. One counselor, a woman who, I'm sure, had nothing but the best of intentions, had actually said to me, "You know, sitting down for the rest of your life isn't that bad. At least you always have a chair with you wherever you go." And then she smiled at me, proud of her little joke. It took everything I had to stop myself from reaching over and grabbing her by the throat, and saying, "Really, lady? Why don't you try sitting down for the rest of your life?"

To emphasize the point, she hopped in one and began spinning it around on the floor. "Look, it's amazing, you'll see. People in wheelchairs get the best seats at concerts. And... *you'll* love this... look what it can do!" she said, elated as she popped a wheelie, seeming to expect that I'd be impressed by her daredevil moves. "You can do this everywhere you go!"

Although appointments with a counselor were part of my "rehabilitation plan," our first session, if I had anything to say about it, would be my last.

So in the middle of that first week, when a therapist wheeled in my hospital loaner, a bulky, reclining, clinical chair, I reacted much the way a toddler does to a plate of peas: I shook my head and refused.

"No. No, fuck that," I said, pointing at the offending chair. "It's not happening."

A team of medical professionals began reasoning with me, explaining to the petulant child who refused his wheelchair that it wasn't so bad, that

I would need it in order to get around, that it was essential for my therapy. But in the end, it was my wife who made the most sense.

"Babe," she said, taking my face in her hands so that I saw only her, not the chair, "If you had a broken leg, what would you do? You'd use crutches, wouldn't you?" "Yeah," I admitted, my eyes having difficulty meeting hers. "Yeah, exactly, you'd need to let your leg heal, so you'd lean on your crutches. Then when your leg was better, you'd give the crutches back. Right? And that's all this is, babe. It's temporary. Until your back heals, you just need to lean on the chair for a little while. And when you get better, you can give it back. Okay?"

It was temporary. It wasn't mine; I was borrowing it for a little while. It was just a crutch, a stop along the way. "Okay," I said grudgingly, repeating those words to myself over and over again, every time I looked at it.

For a couple days, the chair and I were in a standoff; it sat in the corner, daring me to get in it, while I stared resentfully back. But eventually, Becca broke the standoff and said, "Okay, enough. Let's transfer you to the chair."

The process began with the usual—the roll, the brace, the sitting on the edge of the bed. Then the chair, reclined about forty-five degrees, was wheeled up to the bed, which had been lowered to the height of the chair's seat. One end of a long board was placed on the seat, and the other reached across to the edge of the bed, and was wedged under my butt, forming a bridge. And then I began, ever so slowly, with lots of help and the supporting hands of Becca and Shawna, to scoot down the board to the chair.

It took almost a full day of therapy, each moment scooting a little further down the board, to finally make it into the chair. At which point, after sitting there for only seconds, I merely scooted right back up the board, got back in bed, and fell asleep for hours.

I did this a couple times a day, and on each instance, more chair time was added. Could I sit there a full minute? Five minutes? Ten? Thirty?

Although it was all so, so painful, and despite the use of the chair—perhaps even *because* of it—I could feel my strength growing by the day, which only fed my optimism about running someday. And the more I moved, the more I began to crave movement. My paralysis seemed even more intolerable.

Want to know what paralysis feels like? Do this: Fold the fingers of one hand into a light fist, and place it on a table, wrist and fingers down and all four knuckles touching the table. Leaving all the other fingers where they are, extend only the ring finger, the third one, straight out. Now try to lift it. Go ahead.

You can't. You can focus your every thought into lifting that finger, strain with every ounce of energy. Maybe, eventually, if you work at it for a while, or if you cheat and move your arm a little bit, your finger *might* leave the table. But it's maddening. It makes you cringe from the foreign strangeness of the sensation. You don't want any part of it, and it's something you immediately want to shake off. And I couldn't.

To lie in one position, in one spot, for hours and hours and hours—you wouldn't believe how uncomfortable it can be. Not being able to roll over, reach for a glass, sit up and hug my wife... hell, even walk to the bathroom—it was all so frustrating and draining. And then, in those moments when I was so fatigued from the brace or from visits from friends, all I wanted to do was fall into a deep, sound sleep—I was even being deprived of that. Despite my pain medication and the trauma my body had experienced, my inability to get comfortable meant my sleep was rarely sound, rarely satisfying, rarely restful.

Days passed like this, and those days turned into weeks. It began to eat at me, piss me off. I'd tick it off in my head, "What's it been, ten days now? Twenty days of being uncomfortable?" I counted ceiling tiles, listened for Care Flight helicopter rotor blades across the street, watched the shadows changing position on the ceiling. I could tell time by looking at those shadows on the ceiling.

Those long stretches of time between sleep felt interminable. There was the pain, the discomfort, the restlessness, and also the growing impatience. I kept telling myself, "Any day now my toes are going to turn on." Like a light switch would someday be flipped, and immediately, "Ah, *there* it is! Sensation, at last!" Shawna had to keep reminding me that with a spinal cord injury, especially one involving as much compression as I'd had, if you don't move the body and get it working, what you have is what you have. I'd have to earn it back, which meant continually increasing my levels of therapy, in order to send a message to the nerves to regenerate into the lower half of my body: *Okay, we need you again, come on over here.*

The more I worked, the more tiny little improvements I saw, the more intent I became on working even harder next time. And when my therapy with Becca was done, I'd only rest for a short while before Shawna had me doing something else, pushing just a little harder to get in a little more therapy.

While I embraced therapy wholeheartedly, and was thrilled to have Becca and Shawna guiding me in my recovery, the constant pushing and pulling, people moving me, sometimes roughly, making me do things I knew needed to be done—sitting up, turning over, flexing my legs—were still unbelievably, terrifyingly, scream-inducingly painful.

All of this was tough on Shawna, who was there for everything. She sometimes had to turn her head to hide the tears filling her eyes when she heard me screaming and yelping in pain.

Once, after watching two nurses handling me roughly, sitting me up a little too abruptly, she'd taken all she could of seeing me hurt.

"That's enough!" she yelled at the nurses, who stopped immediately and stared at her, mouths agape. "That's too much! You're done! That's it!" And they excused themselves.

After I'd been working with the chair for a few days, Becca strode into my room with a sly smile on her face. "Let's go outside today, guys," she said, grinning.

Once she and Shawna got me into the chair, where I could now sit for about a half hour at a time, the brakes were released, blankets were wrapped around me, and *whoosh*, out through the doors of the hospital and into the lawn out front we went.

Since surgery, I had been sensitive to the cold. All my body had been through had made regulating my body temperature difficult, and I spent a lot of time covered in blankets, even in my room. Here, outside on a mild winter's day, I was reminded of that day weeks ago, lying in the snow and shivering. I shivered violently, despite the warm blankets covering me, and I couldn't even see the sunny day or take a deep breath of fresh air for all the tremors wreaking havoc on my body, shaking tears from my eyes.

As the days passed, Becca, with my full consent, pushed and pushed me, forcing me to do new things and making our sessions tougher. Before I knew it, I was moving from the wheelchair to the physical therapy table, where I struggled at first to merely sit up straight with my feet on the floor, and where, eventually, I could do a few exercises—using a hand-cycle, lifting weights. And then Becca suggested parallel bars—a suggestion that, as she explained later, didn't go over so well with my doctor.

"He's not ready," Dr. Abbott told Becca when she proposed it at a meeting. "I think encouraging that would be a waste of time."

"I just think that's the way we're going to get him to walk," argued Becca. "I've been reading about this…"

Becca knew me by now, knew what I was capable of. If she could only get me on the bars, she could prove to the doctor this was a good thing. So, as we later discovered went against doctor's orders, she said to us, "I think we'll try the parallel bars today."

After wheeling me to the bars, Shawna and her dad hoisted me up with their shoulders to slowly lift me out of the chair. Becca guided me along the bars as an assistant hovered behind us, ready to catch me with the chair if I fell. As I held on for dear life to the bars, Shawna and Doug used their hands to walk my legs. I made it a foot, maybe two, before collapsing into Becca's arms. But we kept at it, trying two or three times a day, until I could "walk," with their help, two feet, then three, then four or five.

But despite my success, Becca continually struggled to get approval on therapies she had researched, things she wanted to try, that Dr. Abbott kept shooting down.

"You need to stop putting him on the parallel bars," Dr. Abbott would insist.

"But why? It's working!" Becca would argue.

"Listen, you don't have experience with spinal cord patients." With that, she would dismiss Becca out of hand.

Yet it *was* working. Thanks to Becca's innovation, her willingness to try things, despite being told not to, I could see improvement.

Having practitioners tell me not to have "false hope" may have been the best medicine. It ensured I would work my ass off, with Shawna's diligence, sometimes six to eight hours a day, getting muscles to flicker and my

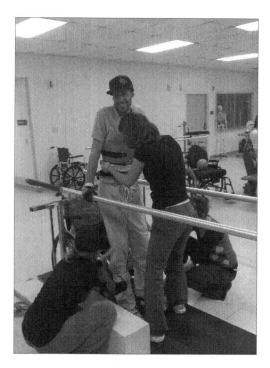

Parallel bars: 99 percent
arms, 1 percent legs
(Photo by Doug Hansen)

strength to grow dramatically. Hearing a doctor say, "No, you're not going to walk unassisted ever again" only provoked me. "Work harder," I'd think to myself as I pushed for one more rep, one more step on the parallel bars, not just to prove them wrong, but to improve my life. If everyone had said I was a shoe-in, I suppose I might not have pushed so hard. I might still be waiting for change.

So all that negativity, that fighting to recover on my own terms, was the price I paid to work with Becca, who, along with Shawna, was a hero in my eyes. And because she had minimal prior experience with a spinal cord injury, she, unlike my doctors, had no pre-set limits on my future.

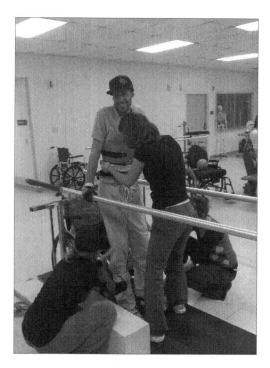

All the while, every day, I could see the tantalizing visual of Shawna wearing my wedding ring on a chain around her neck, dangling just out of reach. Every time I saw it, I felt both reassured that it was in her capable hands and reminded that I couldn't wear it, a fact I resented tremendously.

Love (Photo by Matt Theilen)

In the middle of physical therapy one day, I got fed up about it. I asked my physical therapy assistant, "Hey, can I have my ring back yet?"

"Oh, yeah! Of course!" she said. "Sorry, didn't anyone tell you that?"

Shawna and I smiled at each other. Later, after I was safely back in bed, we ceremoniously replaced the ring on my finger.

"I, Shawna, take you Grant…" she said, grinning like a child as she slipped the ring on my finger.

"I, Grant, take you, Shawna," I repeated, smiling hugely, flexing my fingers to feel it and see the band, enjoy the sensation of it tying me physically to this woman once again, just as it had on that beautiful fall day almost six months ago when we'd taken our vows. She leaned down, her forehead against mine, tears in her eyes.

"Forever," I whispered.

Laura unfolded a black pouch to reveal dozens of long needles. I was about to experience acupuncture for the first time. Laura, a dear friend of ours, who is also a fantastic bodywork practitioner, had volunteered to contribute her particular talent to my journey toward recovery, and nervous as I was about the prospect of all those needles, I was ready to embrace just about anything.

Shawna was much more familiar with the ways of Eastern medicine than I was. Her dad had been diagnosed with a terminal liver illness in 1991, when Shawna was just in middle school. Though Doug had tried every possible treatment, taken every medication recommended, nothing worked. Doctors had estimated he might have two to five years left. Having exhausted all his options, and having a strong interest in Eastern medicine and spirituality that began while serving in Japan in the Navy in his younger days, Doug followed a recommendation to see a holistic doctor, who took him through a variety of alternative therapies. It was that experience that Doug now credits with his full recovery.

Through that experience, and in her own profession, Shawna had been steeped in treatments like acupuncture, massage, yoga, Reiki, meditation, and deeply believed in their benefits. So when she came to me with Laura's offer, I didn't balk.

"We're going to do all kinds of things, whatever it takes, okay?" Shawna had proposed earlier that day. "We'll try everything under the sun. We're going to try things that might work and some things that won't. But we're on an interesting journey together now, so just be open to it. Trust me, okay?"

How our roles had reversed. It hadn't been so long ago that I had told her the same thing, on the day I made my own proposal.

Though I had never been the kind of guy who had ever imagined getting married, I had known, since I was in high school, that should I ever propose to anyone, I would do it somewhere at Yosemite. But exactly where and how, I didn't know until a couple weeks after my college graduation, when Ryan Oddo and I, along with a few other friends, took a three-day backpacking trip through Yosemite National Park.

"Want to see something really cool?" Ryan had a sort of covert and excited tone in his voice. "I'll show you, but it's super-secret, you can't show anyone, okay?"

I had heard rumors of this forgotten place to which I now hoped Ryan was taking me. He led me over fallen trees, behind rocks, and up steep switchbacks. As we hiked, he explained how, in the park's early days, a landslide had cut off the entrance to this challenging and awe-inspiring trail. It had been decommissioned, but trail builders, so satisfied with the remaining segment of the trail, had adopted it for themselves, choosing to enjoy it in secret and sharing it with only their closest, most trustworthy friends and family members, among whom were Ryan's parents.

The steep, winding trail leads to a craggy rock cliff that reveals a commanding view of at least five waterfalls as well as Glacier Point. As we approached the cliff top, a narrow space only three or four feet wide, the view nearly knocked the wind out of me. It was the most beautiful place I had ever seen in my life.

Neither of us said anything for a good minute, until I spoke up. "If I ever propose to anybody, this is where I'll do it," I said matter-of-factly. Silently, with just a nod, he seconded the notion.

So years later, a year and a half into my relationship with Shawna and with every intention of spending my life with her, there was really only one place I had in mind to pop the question. Shawna was so special to me, so rare and beautiful and unique, that every single detail of the proposal—the location, the ring, all of it—had to be worthy of her. In my plan, nothing would be left to chance.

My pursuit of a ring as unique as Shawna led me on a hunt that took months and involved a custom-made, special-order, deep blue alexandrite that would take months to receive. I planned, whenever it finally arrived, to convince Shawna to take a weekend getaway with me to Yosemite, where we would embark upon a long series of adventures leading up to the proposal. I would lead her to the cliff top Ryan had shown me, blindfold her, explain that I wanted to surprise her with the view, and instead reveal the ring while on bended knee.

But first, because I greatly respected Shawna's parents and the close relationship she had with them, it was important to me that I formally ask them for her hand. I did so at a top-secret weekday breakfast, after dropping Shawna off at work. After tears and hugs, congratulations and pats on the back, the first question was: "So, how are you going to do it?"

After I laid out my elaborate plan for them, Doug and Chris congratu-
lated me on it, knowing their daughter would be overjoyed by such a proposal.

"Just do me a favor," said Doug in his final parting words that day, "Clip
yourself into the harness before you do this, okay?"

The ring's arrival was repeatedly delayed—late October, then early November, then late November. Finally, the first week of December, it arrived.
And I couldn't help but feel smug and somehow guided by the universe to
know that, contrary to all predictable climate patterns, not a single flake of
snow had yet fallen in Yosemite. I had been dangling the idea of a Yosemite
trip before Shawna for weeks, but had always managed to find reasons at
the last minute to wait. The second I knew the ring was ready, I called her
at work: "Hey, there's no snow up at Yosemite. Why don't we get up there
this weekend? It could be our last chance."

On the drive, I described for Shawna the plan to show her *my* Yosemite.
After camping our first night, followed by a breakfast I'd cook over a camp-
fire the next morning, we would take a bike ride, have lunch at the lodge,
take a hike to see Vernal and Nevada Falls, and have dinner at the Ahwahnee Hotel that night. She was completely open to whatever I planned,
whatever I wanted to do, despite the fact that I, Mr. Off-the-Couch, never,
ever planned a camping trip like this. But her pure trust in me was a shiny,
beautiful thing.

The day remained a mystery to Shawna until we began the climb to
Vernal Falls, at the top of a fairly challenging hike. With our backpacks on,
filled with gear she believed was for a climb, we shuffled amid other park
visitors up the marked trail. A frequent climber, I would normally have
breezed up this trail, but on this day my heart was racing much more than
usual. I was overly aware of the bulging ring box in my pocket, and became
obsessed, obviously obsessed, with the passing of time on my watch. "Are
you in a hurry or something?" Shawna asked, catching me stealing a glance
at it. "Why do you keep checking your watch?"

"Oh, no, I just want to get there right when the light's perfect, that's all,"
I said, reminding myself to chill out.

As we approached the end of the Vernal trail, I stopped, waiting for a break in the crowd so that no one would see what I was about to do. Once a break came, I peeled off the path, behind a large rock, pulling Shawna with me. It was here that I explained about the secret trail.

"Okay, here's the deal. I want to take you on this secret trail Ryan showed me," I whispered, explaining what I knew about its history. "It ends up at this amazing place I want you to see. But no one can see us do this, so when I say, we have to sneak over there." I pointed at some large rocks. "You ready? You gotta be like Lara Croft, Tomb Raider, okay?"

"Okay!" she said.

We hopped from one rock to the next, dodging and weaving to avoid being spotted by other tourists, hopping from one wet log to another, then dropping into leaves. Every now and then, I glanced over my shoulder at Shawna. In our time together she had done numerous hikes with me, and was by now well-versed in climbing and repelling. And now, with utter faith in me, she was completely into the idea of playing here in this playground, which I found enormously sexy.

Forty-five minutes later, though Shawna was barely winded, I was panting heavily, almost unable to talk from the weight of my plans, but laughing at myself that I was worn out from such a hike.

"Babe, are you okay?" she asked me.

"Oh, yeah, I'm good!" I said, scanning the ground for the perfect place to drop my gear. This was the spot, about fifty feet from the top, that I had decided on a scouting trip months ago was where we should harness up. This was where I would blindfold Shawna for the remainder of the trip. I had it researched to the hilt, all the way down to how much sunlight there would be, and the approximate temperature.

"Hey, let's have a quick snack," I said, dropping my pack. She readily agreed, and while munching our Clif bars, I began pulling out the harnesses and explaining myself. "Now listen," I said, with an inviting smile, "I brought this stuff because we're going to be repelling down a drop that's about 500 feet. And we have to be quick about it. We can't hesitate. I don't want you to get up to the top and go, 'Oh my gosh, this is so big,' and get scared and hesitate. So I'm just going to blindfold you, okay?" with an inviting smile.

"Okay!" she said, curious but clearly not scared in the least.

Which is when I was reminded, again, why I wanted to marry her—she stood there, smiling and nodding. "Cool! Let's do it!" she said.

"So let's put your blindfold on," I said, grabbing for it and wrapping it around her eyes, "and I'm going to walk you all the way up and clip you in, and when I pull the blindfold off, we're just going to start repelling. Got it? I'll just put the rope in your hand, and we go. It'll be great. Trust me."

And what she said next was the most perfect response I could have hoped for: "Sweet!" If this had been a test designed to see whether she was the right girl to marry, she would by now have passed with flying colors.

But despite all my planning, I'd made one error, which up until now she hadn't noticed. I had put the ring box, which now seemed overly large and awkwardly shaped, in my pocket. So when, in her excitement, she pulled me into a huge hug, I turned my body in a way I had to hope didn't seem like avoidance. I quickly shifted gears. "Okay, you ready?" I asked, grabbing the ropes with one hand and her hand with the other.

We began tiptoeing up the narrow peninsula of rock that hung roughly 500 feet in the air but was only about twenty-five feet wide. We made our way toward the naturally carved cutout of rock that made for a sort of path scooped out of the edge of the cliff. But as we entered the narrow trail, which was just a few feet wide, I realized that simply holding her hand on a path hanging basically in mid-air might not be a safe plan. So I improvised.

"You know, why don't you just hop on my back, okay?" I said, pulling her to jump up and ride piggyback. "Just to be safe… it's a long drop."

So there I was, piggybacking the woman I love up a precarious rock overhang. Midway around the peninsula, I stopped, put her down, and hooked my protection—a perfectly sized cam I pulled from my rack of Casey's climbing gear—tightly into the rock wall we now stood beside. I harnessed Shawna in, ensuring that she was fully locked in to the rock wall. And then Doug's words echoed in my mind—despite my earlier notion that I'd be just fine, I clipped myself in as well.

The impact of what was about to happen was weakening me by the second. Shawna and I now faced each other, each of us with a rock wall on one side and a sheer drop of some 500 feet on the other. She stood there blindfolded and expectant.

*The happy girl, moments
after Grant proposed
(Photo by Grant Korgan)*

I took her left hand with mine; with my right hand, I extracted the ring. Slowly, as quietly as I possibly could, I flipped the box open. I began the movement I had practiced numerous times, lowering to one knee while keeping her hand raised so she wouldn't know. And I took a mental snapshot of this moment, telling myself, "Dude, this is the most intense moment of your life, right here. All heaven's about to break loose."

"Babe," I began, "whenever you're ready, take off your blindfold."

She casually whipped off the blindfold, and immediately burst into tears at the sight of me on one knee, now crying right along with her.

"Shawna, you are the love of my life, the queen of my universe, my true north, my soul mate," I began, fighting past the enormous lump in my throat to say the words I'd rehearsed hundreds of times, tears now pouring liberally down my cheeks, just as they were hers. "I am so unbelievably in love with you. Will you marry...?"

And before I could finish, I was interrupted by her squeals of "Yes yes yes yes yes!" and the most passionate kisses we'd ever exchanged.

Which was great until I realized that a fragile, delicate, extraordinarily rare and expensive piece of jewelry in my hand was being dangled above 500 feet of air by nothing more than a tiny satin pillow.

Without thinking, I pushed her away, checked the box to see that the ring was still in it, held my arm straight out toward her, and said, stupidly, "Do you want this?"

"Oh!" she exclaimed, laughing and crying. "Yeah! I do!"

So now, on this day nearly fifteen months later, I was being asked by Shawna to trust *her* on the journey she now planned for *me*. And if our past history had been any indication of where this would lead, it would be someplace amazing. I was in, 100 percent.

"Sweet!" I said.

And, so, in went the needles.

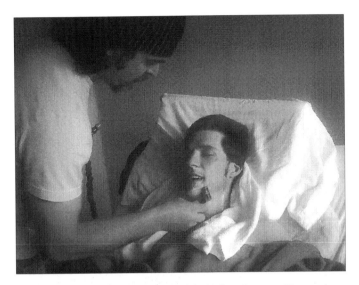

Stevo taking care of Grant (Photo by Shawna Korgan)

CHAPTER 9
HOW TO SAY THANK YOU

The Bubble persisted. Shawna's tight control of my environment, her efforts to surround me with love and support, became a force of healing for me. Throughout my weeks in rehab, the list of approved visitors, though it had grown a bit, still remained firmly in place. And now it was about much more than protecting me from nay-sayers. It was also serving new purposes: First, it kept people who loved me, who had always considered me a picture of health, from freaking out at the somewhat emaciated sight of me. By now it had happened several times, as I had dropped a good thirty pounds from my already-lean physique and my extremities had begun to atrophy from disuse.

Secondly, the Bubble preserved good vibes. Shawna's dad popped in occasionally, usually rubbing my feet in an attempt to regenerate sensation. I spent hours at a time listening to music while Shawna talked me through staying connected with my body, visualizations playing an increasing role in my recovery. Various bodywork practitioners from The Sanctuary began dropping in regularly to do treatments at no charge. Food was delivered, gifts bestowed at our door. The mood was light, upbeat, healthy, and positive, positive, positive.

But keeping that Bubble strong was tough when it seemed, all around us, that negativity ran rampant. Aside from the facility's kind director and Becca, inpatient practitioners and staff seemed downright afraid to give us any hope at all that I would ever walk unassisted again. In fact, the word "walk" seemed to be a bone of contention. In ICU, we had been told that I might have "walking legs." Then during my second week of rehab, while discussing our therapy plan, a sweet, friendly physical therapist assistant who only had the best of intentions had used the phrase again with, we noted, an odd inflection: "Well, you *do* have walking *legs*, so here's what we need to do." The word "legs" had been pronounced as if in air quotes. It was an odd enough phrase to stop us.

"What does that mean?" I interjected. "What's your definition of walking?"

"Oh, I'm sorry, I mean with KAFOs."

"KAFOs?" Shawna and I both asked together. "What are those?"

"Knee and ankle foot orthotics," she said, looking around her space, as if to find some to point to. "They're rigid braces that run from your hips to your feet. So you can walk with them, you sort of hobble like this..." and she proceeded to mimic the walk that, to me, was reminiscent of Frankenstein's monster.

As tears welled up in my eyes, Becca looked up from her equipment and paperwork and called to the assistant, "Dude! What are you doing? Jeez, don't *do* that! Stop! Bad call."

It was another moment to add to the pile of moments in which we were reminded of our goal, and that we actually had to consciously choose what we wanted, over and over and over again. From every angle came a choice: How about a wheelchair? Is that good enough? What about walking with braces? Maybe you'll be content with that? It felt like if we relaxed for even a moment, let down our guard, another choice might be made for us. The Bubble helped.

Finally, the Bubble protected me from myself. Even during rehab, I often worried too much about other people's comfort. When visitors arrived, I felt compelled to appear alert, to tell jokes, to be lighthearted, to convey a sense of, "No worries, I'm okay." I encouraged them to talk about themselves, their news, their work, their last kayak trips, rather than me and all I had going on. The cameras that were often in my face usually captured my smiles, which were mostly authentic as I was continually reminded of the amazing love and support that surrounded me.

One visiting friend, when I remarked upon the humanity that I had seen displayed since my injury, said to me, "You're getting back what you put out in the world." It was an enormous compliment, one I took pride in receiving, and I couldn't believe that what I'd put out had compared to this. From Ryan, Duncan, and Ken getting me safely off the mountain to the collective efforts of friends working at the hospital; to the dozens of friends surrounding Shawna in her moments of need; to the many doctors, nurses, and assistants working around the clock to make us comfortable; to Becca, who was going above and beyond her job duties to spearhead an aggressive therapy plan, sometimes against doctor's orders; to the massage therapists and acupuncturists and Rolfers and Reiki masters who were now taking time out of their days to give me free treatments—all of them had already contributed substantially to my recovery. We felt as if we would never be able to appropriately thank them all.

The unasked-for gestures of kindness that popped up at every turn never ceased to amaze me. With each day came more symbols of people filling us with love and wrapping their arms around us. My partner and best friend, Steven, one of the very few people to whom Shawna granted full access to me at all times, had come to ICU every day and often shaved my face while I slept, finishing just one side at a time, and waiting patiently for me to turn my head before shaving the other side. He continued to pay visits once or twice a week at inpatient, just to catch me up, help me with therapy, give me a shave, whatever I needed at the time.

My good friend, Jason Mead, who deejayed the local electronic scene as DJ Neutrino, even lent his musical gift to my recovery when he arrived one day with a brand new iPod Shuffle loaded up with tunes that would pump me up for my workouts. His girlfriend, Fairlane, presented me with the perfect gift: a blue Snuggie—only cheesy until you're in a hospital bed with a broken back—on which she'd painted "Korg Machine."

Steve Rose, a great friend of mine from college, had from the beginning taken the issue of communication out of Shawna's hands. From day one at the hospital, Steve had told Shawna that he would handle the business of reporting my status to the seemingly hundreds of people who asked for updates on a daily basis, and who even occasionally gave him flack for standing between us and them. And he did it all while remaining firmly in the background, giving us the much-needed gift of space.

On one such day, early into our stay at inpatient, while I was still nearly comatose from the heavy doses of pain medication coursing through my veins, I half-opened my eyes to find Steve silently walking in carrying a kick-ass flat screen HDTV.

Steve had seen that our room, though huge, had been designed with the intent of housing patients with traumatic brain injuries. It was comprised of vast, open spaces, empty of wires and electronics of any sort, including a television. Shawna and I aren't exactly big TV-watchers, but there were moments when it would have been nice to watch and zone out for a while. Steve had seen enough of our situation to know that.

A nurse whom Steve had signaled on his way in followed, wheeling in a small table. Without a single word, the table was placed against the wall facing my bed; the TV, a DVD player, and an X-Box were hooked up; games and movies were piled in their boxes on the table, and he was gone with nothing more than a quiet thumbs-up in my direction.

Steve's intuitive knowledge of my nature helped him to be exactly what I needed. While visitors were in the room, every ounce of my energy went to making them feel better about my situation, to continue being a force of positivity.

But then they'd leave, and because my well of energy was finite and only went so deep, I'd collapse, exhausted and often in tears, too wiped out to focus on the therapy and positive energy crucial to my recovery. The Bubble was a necessary part of keeping exhaustion to a minimum, and keeping the demands of others on the periphery.

Sometimes, even people who wanted to give Shawna or me anything we needed, people who loved us dearly and respected our wishes for positivity, would stumble unintentionally, saying clumsy things that either of us, in a tired stupor, could be easily ruffled by. Like when someone would tell me, "You know, Grant, if anyone can get through this, it's you."

And what I heard was: "If this had to happen to anyone, I'm glad it's you."

Like Bridgette, whose words meant to inspire had originally felt like an albatross around my neck, people sometimes didn't know what to say, or said things that came across the wrong way.

Of course, rationally, we knew they meant, "We know you can recover from this, we believe in your strength and abilities, we know you'll do great things following this experience, and you'll turn this into something positive." But it was something we had to constantly work to remind ourselves of in our more trying moments.

Shawna's dad, Doug, often refers to a Native American prayer that goes something like this: "May you see the beauty before you, behind you, above you, below you, all around you, and let it make your heart strong."

In this situation, one that was certainly rife with ugliness, disappointment, negativity, pain, and fear, we were nonetheless beginning to see a side of humanity that was beautiful in a way we'd never fully understood before. And we were not only choosing to draw immense strength from it, but we began fostering a desire to give some of it back, to be part of this amazing beautiful cycle that we could now see in motion all around us.

Some visitors, though, no matter how intense it was, were always allowed entrance to the room—among them were the men that saved my life.

One day at the end of my first week in inpatient, a movement at the window caught my eye and startled me, forcing Shawna to turn and look. With his feet against my window, his tongue hanging out, and his hot breath steaming the window, was my big brown dog, Obie, whom I hadn't seen since before my injury.

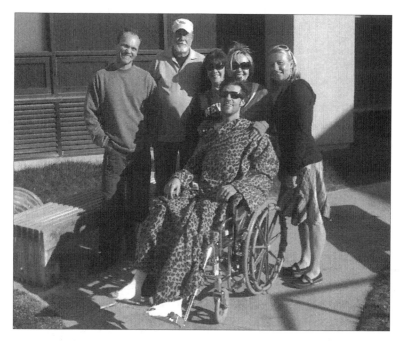

Visit from the Theilens (Photo by Pam Korgan)

A lump formed in my throat. I was emotional about seeing my dog, but more so about what it meant: Ken was here.

I'd spent many hours in the hospital and in rehab going over my rescue in my head, realizing over and over again how incredible those men were. Ryan and Duncan had been amazing in their ability to calm me, staying by my side every minute to ensure that I was alive and alert, helping me to focus and keep breathing, and alternately carving out that makeshift helipad and a groomed trail through the snow to transport me to the helicopter when it arrived, even cutting down branches to mark the giant X that signaled to the pilot that he'd found the right place.

Their efforts were incredible, but all those things would have been for naught had it not been for Ken, who undoubtedly risked his own life to ride as fast and hard as he did to save mine, eventually arriving just seconds before missing the helicopter altogether. The effort he put in that day, and the success of his task in my rescue was, in my mind, the linchpin that had determined whether or not I lived or died.

And on top of that, beyond all he'd done to facilitate my recovery, Ken and his wife had graciously taken in my dog—this happy, healthy, joyful brown bundle of energy now greeting me at my window with a wagging tail and what I could swear was a huge smile on his face. It was almost too much to take in all at once: the joy and overwhelming respect and thankfulness and love, along with the terror over what might have been were it not for Ken… all of it now competed within me.

Shawna and both our sets of parents, who had been visiting us that day, helped me to sit up as I braced myself emotionally to see this man to whom I owed my life.

Ken and his wife, Bridget, stepped cautiously into the room with anxious smiles on their faces, their eyes seeming to assess whether I was ready for this visit.

"Oh my God, guys! What's up? Come in, come in!" I called, unable to do justice with my voice to the feelings I had about seeing Ken. Shawna and her parents, along with mine, rose with anticipatory smiles.

But I was too overwhelmed with things to say and too vulnerable emotionally and physically to do the proper introductions. Words began tumbling out of me.

"Ken, bro, oh my God, I just… it's because of you that I'm… I just respect… forever, man… what you did that day…" and then words failed me completely, and a gush of tears burst out of me. Hysterical, breathless, unending tears I couldn't overcome. And all the while, Ken, Shawna, Bridget, my parents, and my in-laws stood there, watching me with worried expressions on their faces. Finally, when it became clear I needed more than a minute to recover myself, Doug said, "Hey guys, maybe we should step outside for a minute and let Grant catch his breath, okay?"

After a few minutes, with Shawna's help, I was composed enough for everyone to come back in, though the emotions that came packaged with my exhaustion wouldn't subside, and every time I tried to speak, to get out the words I wanted to say to Ken, which amounted to something like, "Thank you for risking your own life to give me mine," the words caught in my throat and the tears began to spill again. Those words seemed so inadequate. I wanted to recount every moment, to go over with him what I'd pieced together from Shawna and a few friends about the rescue. I wanted to tell him how much he had always meant, and would always mean, to me. But it was apparent that it would be a long time before I could truly say those words the way they needed to be said.

Shawna was by my side. "Easy, easy, babe," she shushed me, rubbing my arm, then turning to Ken and Bridget, who stood with my parents and in-laws: "How about you guys do the talking for a bit, okay?"

They all knew how much I yearned to connect, to entertain, to give, especially since they had all given so much to me. But with my tiny little handful of energy, I was spent, and they knew it.

"Sure! Sure, absolutely," said Ken, and then he shifted gears away from the intensity of the moment, and regaled me with stories of Obie, of people they'd seen recently, of a trip he'd taken the previous week, until a natural end to the conversation came and Shawna said, "Well, guys, I think that's all he's got right now." She stood slowly, signaling that they needed to leave me to rest.

Ken's visit had provoked within me a desire to see all my "rescue boys," and to piece together the story of what had really happened to me. The details, at this early stage of my recovery, were still foggy, and much of what had happened seemed to have blended with my dreams so that it was often impossible for me to sort out what was real and what wasn't. As exhausting as it was, I needed to talk about it, to get all the mysteries about my rescue cleared up.

It helped to have Duncan, my best friend since first grade, show up a week or so later, when I had a little more mastery of my emotions and a little more energy to see myself through the conversation.

Not that I wasn't emotional when I saw him, too. I was, in a way that I think went beyond the rescue because of our history. To thank him for his role in saving my life almost seemed trite to me.

I think Duncan perceived that. Perhaps as a way to lighten the mood, or maybe to hide his own emotions behind a mask, he had brought a video camera and a friend, Heath, with him. He was still shooting his film, *Alpine*

Grant's mom and Shawna wash his hair in the hospital
(Photo by Steven Malekos)

Assassination, the same film we'd been shooting on the day of my accident; he intended to continue documenting my story as part of the film.

Of course, his presence at the hospital while I was unconscious was by now known to me. I knew that he had not only filmed the emotional gathering of our friends in ICU, but that his information and reassurance had been invaluable to Shawna in those first moments after my injury. He and his wife had come to ICU one night, while I was still unconscious, and taken her to a quick dinner. She had felt so comforted by their presence that she had let herself cry that night—they'd been the only people to see her tears.

But until now, I hadn't actually seen Duncan, consciously, since that fateful day of my injury.

But he wouldn't let me digress into emotional territory, wouldn't let me try to thank him properly and risk more tears. With Duncan was Heath, his boss at a Tahoe-area snowmobile and wakeboard rental and tour company, as well as a dear friend of mine. Heath had broken his own back just a year and a half prior, and I had stood with him on that day. I was psyched to see him here now.

Together, the two of them, with Heath as interviewer, captured my whole story for the first time on camera. Aside from the gift of life that

Duncan had helped to give me, he was also giving me the gift of closure, the knowledge I needed to piece together the events of my accident and rescue, and the opportunity to put together the events of the weeks that had followed. For two hours we talked like this, sorting it all out, making sense of it, hammering out the details of who had done what when and how, all while Shawna listened intently, gaining, I was sure, her own sense of peace from finally knowing it all.

Late in our conversation, since I was in good hands, Shawna decided to head home for a quick shower and more supplies. A nurse entered my room and busied herself with the tubing required to draw urine from my catheter. It was here that we should have stopped. But the conversation felt so good, so *normal*, and yet so important that I couldn't bring myself to call it quits. Besides, I reasoned, Duncan and Heath were my boys; I'd known Dunc almost my whole life. Surely he'd be okay with this.

I forgot, though, about the little pills I was taking twice a day that had, among other things, the bizarre effect of turning my pee bright orange.

So I plowed on through, just chatting away, high on our conversation, until I heard Heath go, "Whoa!" I looked to see a jet of neon orange urine surging into a clear bag, and then turned to see Duncan and Heath wearing the same expression—one that was a mixture of horror, comedy, high eyebrows, and worry.

"Y'okay, man?" I asked, looking at Heath, who had known me for a lot less time and who, until now, hadn't experienced first-hand the enormity of my injury. Heath was a true veteran of broken bones, hospitals, and burly accidents himself, yet I was worried about not freaking my buddies out. "Sorry, it's these meds, no worries."

The conversation meandered then into awkward territory, but only for a short while, until we found ourselves again telling each other the stories we knew, from which we would draw comfort.

So by the time the fourth member of our crew, Ryan Oddo, arrived in my room at the beginning of our fourth week in rehab, I wanted nothing more than normalcy, a conversation that didn't revolve around my injury and the emotions associated with it.

Although Casey had introduced me to the magic of snowmobiling, it was Ryan I credited with truly showing me the ropes of the sport and fostering my love for it. And in exchange, I'd done that for him with white-water kayaking. But even before that, Ryan held a special place in my heart because of how we'd met.

While I was going to college in Colorado, a girlfriend of mine had experienced the death of her best friend, a young woman who had been killed in a car accident by a drunk driver. That woman's brother was Ryan. Connected by our losses—his sister and my friend Casey—and by our passions, we were friends who didn't always need to talk to understand each other. One of Ryan's special gifts was his ability to draw others out, to offer a pressure-free sanctuary that didn't require that I always explain myself or assure him that I was okay. It was 100 percent bullshit-free being with Ryan, and that appealed enormously to me.

In he strolled with organic sandwiches and juice from Whole Foods—some of the first *real lunches* I'd seen in a month—sat down, crossed one leg casually over his other knee, and gave me the precious gift of casual conversation. With Ryan, I wasn't an injured man whose lifesaving rescue he'd actually taken part in. I wasn't a paraplegic, some sort of invalid whom he pitied or worried about. I was just a guy eating a sandwich with him. It was a beautiful thing.

One of the first things I did once I was able to travel a bit in the wheelchair and sit for a while, as I had promised myself I would do from day one in inpatient, was to visit Greg's room. The two of us had occasionally crossed paths in the therapy room, and nurses, convinced that because of our similar injuries and similar interests we must already be best buds, would often provide status reports about him: "Greg had a good day today in therapy," or "Greg has gotten feeling back in his feet, isn't that wonderful?" I'm sure it was intended to be a source of inspiration or comfort to me, a joyful celebration of my friend's success, but its phrasing sometimes came off as competitive. Only Becca refrained from such comments, knowing as she did, and as we were coming to realize, that every spinal cord injury is different, and it was pointless and sometimes hurtful to make comparisons.

Greg and I had become great friends there in inpatient, and I cared deeply about his recovery. Our connection through this injury was brotherly, and we respected each other for all the reasons that had led us to this point in our lives. He and I had begun what had seemed to be the very same path, and now our paths of recovery seemed to be diverging. This point was made clear to me when I rolled into his room for our "first date" to watch the Supercross on TV and found him lying in bed and moving his feet. "Dude!" he called to me as I entered the room. "Check it out!"

"Fuck, yeah, that's awesome!" I said loudly, wearing an enormous smile but feeling a catch in my throat. I rolled to him and held my hand up for a high five. "Dude, that's *amazing!*"

Of course, it was wonderful. Believe me, I felt pure elation over his accomplishments. My reaction was genuine, and I was overjoyed; I truly, truly was. And in my heart, I believed that these accomplishments of his were all signs of things that would surely come for me. There was no doubt in my mind. It just made me even more impatient for the magical rejuvenation that I *knew* was coming.

But the nature of our diverging paths was somewhat unsettling for me, too. It was exhausting to continue celebrating each of his victories. Lately it was like I had strapped on a backpack, into which I tossed the weight of the burdens that were now foisted upon me: the pressure I now felt to suppress my own frustrations, to fulfill my own and everyone else's hopes, to remain positive in the face of adversity, to show everyone else that I was all right, and, increasingly, to serve as other people's cautionary tale, the person against whom every other situation paled in comparison. "Next to you, my life looks pretty good," was the subtext I began hearing in conversations, whether it was intended to sound that way or not. I made the conscious choice to shove it all in a metaphorical backpack so that I wouldn't have to internalize any of it and feel sad or resentful. Instead, I just carried it around all day in the backpack, and it kept getting heavier and harder to carry on this weakened back. It was beginning to wear me out. Just a few days earlier, a report of Greg's catheter-free urination had reached me, and I'd stuffed more weight in the backpack in order to stamp a broad, genuine smile on my face.

I knew that there wasn't any finite amount of recovery, or of good in the world. There was plenty to go around. Greg's wins did nothing to diminish mine, this I knew. But if I was really being honest with myself, this latest victory felt like a big brick on my back.

I was probably taking more than twenty pills throughout the course of the day, and at least once a day taking ten at a time—a hell of a lot considering I normally took nothing but the occasional vitamin. I couldn't keep track of them; the only one who did was Shawna. Even my nurses struggled with it. One time, a night nurse arrived with a pill we'd never seen before.

"What's this?" Chief Nurse Shawna asked, holding the offending pill up to the nurse who was bustling out. "Is this a new pill?"

"Your pills. Those are yours," he said to me, disregarding Shawna.

"No, he doesn't take this one," Shawna insisted. "You need to check your chart." He did, and, inevitably, found that he had made a grievous error.

So it was best that Shawna handled as much of my caregiving as possible, from cross-checking every pill against her "mental master list" to helping me to urinate every four hours with a catheter. But there was still something she wasn't doing—my shots, thanks to the hospital policy that forbade it.

It should be said that our day nurses were amazing, incredible, shining beacons of light and love. I'm not kidding at all when I say that many of them emanated kindness and concern for my well-being and generously gave whatever they could to provide us comfort. They offered us space when we needed it and support when we needed that.

But what the night nurses gave us was comic relief. With them we never knew what we were going to get. It was Russian Roulette, a bizarre cartoonish series of characters who said odd things and behaved strangely and almost seemed to have walked in off the streets and been asked to attend to me.

None of them, though, were as memorable as the warm, affectionate older woman from Spain, whose sparkling eyes and gorgeous, youthful face lit up to see us, and whose big bosom would press against each of us in a warm embrace at every opportunity. We don't know what her name was. We knew her as My Babies.

"Oh! My babies, my babies, you are my babies!" she said in a Spanish accent dripping with honey. "I never had babies of my own, so everyone here, you are my babies!"

Then, "I'm going to take your blood pressure, my babies; give me your arm."

She was one nurse who could be counted on to wheel the computer over to Shawna at pill time, occasionally even waking her up to discuss dosages. "Okay, my baby, I want you to see what pills I'm giving him. Okay, you see here? You see this one here? Okay, my baby, you look on the computer, you see this one? You see? Okay, now, we're taking the dosage down from two to one, okay, my baby? You see that, my baby?"

At first it was endearing and sweet, and we certainly appreciated her diligent explanations, but before very long, My Babies only elicited "oh dears" from us, because she was exhausting. All the while showering us with "my babies" and hugs, she'd completely lock eyes with us, refusing to let go until we'd memorized everything she had to show us and given her our complete and undivided attention during the whole visit, which was often way too long, while she went on and on, "Look! Look, my babies, look here, you see? You see this? Okay, my babies…"

The real problem, though, was that in her enthusiasm for her babies, she very often stopped paying attention to what she was doing.

I was completely unprepared the first night My Babies gave me Lovenox, a medication injected into my stomach to prevent blood clots. "Oh my babies, my babies!" she explained, wheeling her cart in and bubbling with too much excitement for a middle-of-the-night visit. "Okay, I give you a shot, my baby," she said, smiling as if she had a gift to give me and preparing the syringe lovingly. "Okay, my baby, lift your shirt!" She pulled the cap off the syringe, and pushed it to remove the air, squirting a little onto the floor in the process. I'd already grown used to the shot, and though I gritted my teeth the whole time, My Babies seemed loving enough to ease the process.

Holding the syringe in one hand, she vigorously rubbed my belly with an alcohol wipe, rubbing with a trembling, shaking hand roughly, as if trying to remove paint with turpentine.

Oh my God this is bad, I thought, looking worriedly at Shawna and back to that trembling hand.

But before I or Shawna could voice a word of protest, My Babies locked those eyes of hers on mine, and quick as a wink, *THUNK,* In went the needle, and out of me, as if she'd popped a bubble in my stomach, escaped a high-pitched squeal of fright and pain.

The needle stayed there, with her just squeezing, squeezing, and me squealing, and those eyes refusing to let go of mine.

And then, before removing the needle, she twisted it—*twisted it*—about twenty degrees and pulled it out, essentially slicing me with its beveled edge on the way out.

"AAAAHHHHH!" I screamed.

"Oh, my babies, my babies, I did not hurt you! Did that hurt? No, I do not ever hurt my babies, would never hurt my babies. Never! Gentle shot, gentle shot, my babies."

With that, she packed up her tray and bolted out the door. And I lay there, exhausted and in shock, staring at Shawna.

"Holy fuck," she said. "Did that just happen?"

The next night, after "the twist," Shawna and I kept one eye on the door for night rounds. Who would be our night nurse this time?

And lo and behold, as if on cue, in walked My Babies, singing and smiling. She set right to work, as usual, going through the spiel while Shawna attentively listened and suppressed the occasional laugh: "My babies, I have your pills, look here, see this pill, my baby?"

Then My Babies whipped out the shot.

"Okay," I piped up, "Hold on real quick, okay?"

My Babies leaned in toward my abdomen, seeming not to have heard me.

"No, stop. Just stop!" I said, pushing her away with one hand and holding my shirt down with the other. My Babies stood erect, slowly, with a puzzled expression on her face.

"Listen," I began, "last night you gave me that shot, but it was a little painful." I stopped, checking her expression to see whether I'd offended her.

"No, my baby, I never hurt you!"

"Yeah, but, you did! It did hurt, okay?" I insisted. I mean, she was a nurse, right? Surely she'd heard that before. Surely she could handle that truth.

"Aww, my baby!" she said as a smile broke across her face. *Shit, she thought I was messing with her.* "My baby, you not mean that! No, I did not hurt you! I did not hurt you! So gentle!" Again, she leaned down, alcohol wipe at the ready, as if the moment we'd taken to talk had dirtied that spot again.

Then the cap off, the squirt on the bed, the eyes on mine, the wipe scrubbing skin off, and then, THUNK, the needle was in.

Okay, I'm okay, I thought, exhaling. *Just don't twist it.*

"Okay, WAIT!" I said to her, staring intently into her unmovable eyes as I said this. "No, no, don't twist it, just wait!"

"Oh, my baby," she said, and then *twist.*

"SON OF A BITCH!" I screamed as the needle went *scraaape* all the way out.

I grabbed her arm and held it, staring deeply into My Babies' eyes.

"That fucking hurt! You just hurt me!" I said, hoping to convey the seriousness of what she'd just done.

"Oh, no, my babies, that would never happen," she said, with a patronizing smile and pat on my arm. Then she capped the syringe, tossed it on the tray, removed her gloves, and she was gone, instantly.

And again, Shawna and I sat there, stunned and silent, feeling like the unwitting victims of a practical joke.

Days went by after that, with no appearance from My Babies. It was only a matter of time, we knew, and the more time that went by without her, the harder I knew it would be when she showed up, which she inevitably would. I shared my concerns with the head day nurse. I confessed my fears, the pain of the bad shots, my anxiety over facing her.

"I mean, she just has this great personality, she's so sweet," I insisted, afraid to appear to be tattling. "She's just not real good at giving shots, maybe she needs to be retrained or something?"

"Okay, I'll look into it for you, okay?" she said, patting me on the arm.

But whether that conversation ever took place, we don't know.

Just when I had been lulled for days into a false sense of security, the day nurses had done their final rounds, and Shawna turned to me and said, "You know, I think she's going to come tonight. I just have this feeling."

As usual, Shawna was right. Within a few hours, in marched My Babies, wheeling her cart and those pills. Once again it was "My babies" this and "My babies" that, and I wrestled with myself. She was so kind, so sweet, so happy as she spoke of her nieces and cousins, and it was clear that she was a lonely woman who longed to share and connect to others. But then, out came that shot.

"Whoa! Okay, look, stop!" I said, pushing at her with both my hands.

"No, my baby, don't be silly, I never hurt you!" she said, one hand on her hip and the other trying to push past my hands with the syringe.

"Okay, I respectfully disagree with you," I said, and that made My Babies pause.

Emboldened, I proceeded gently. "I just want you to know that the last two times you've done this, you've really hurt me, and I would like someone else to give me the shot."

"Okay, my baby!" she said, capping the syringe. "No problem!" And she turned on her heels and left the room, leaving the cart behind her.

Seconds later, in walked an older woman with thinning, patchy hair who closely resembled Gollum from *Lord of the Rings*.

She even sounded like Gollum when she croaked, "Yesss, I'm here for the shot."

I fully expected to hear her say, "My precious."

Gollum went right for my covers—under which I was naked. She slowly lifted the covers in an attempt to look under them.

"What are you doing?" I asked, grabbing the covers to pull them out of her hands.

"I have to look..." she said, trying again to pull the covers up, until Shawna, alarmed, shot up off her chair and darted over to us, yanking the covers out of Gollum's hands.

"You don't need to see under there, he just needs a shot!" she said, tightening the covers down around my hips.

"I must see where to put the shot," Gollum croaked, confused.

"No, it's right here," I said, pointing at my abdomen.

"Ooo-kay!" said Gollum, shrugging. She turned to the cart and began uncapping the syringe, squeezing out the air with a squirt.

"I hear it's painful," said Gollum, looking at me with a gruesome, evil expression. "I do no pain."

"How are you at giving shots?" I asked, a last-ditch effort to reach out for help.

"Good. No pain," said Gollum.

And just then, Gollum underwent a bizarre change. She was no longer the croaking, slow-moving beast who had entered. *BAM!* went the syringe cap as she slammed it abruptly onto the cart. Then the alcohol wipe, rubbing it even harder, more painfully, than My Babies had.

"Whoa, whoa! Slow down!" I said, backing myself up against the bed. Shawna watched, stunned and unmoving.

Without a word, or even a flinch, Gollum went *SLAP SLAP SLAP* on my belly, expertly turned the syringe as if it were a dagger, thumb poised on the plunger, and stabbed me in the stomach, coming down fast from a distance of at least eight inches.

"WHAT THE FUCK!" I yelled.

"Okay. It's okay," said Gollum. It was over. She looked blankly at me, removing her gloves.

Then Gollum and My Babies smiled curtly at us and left the room without a word. Minutes passed before Shawna and I could even speak.

"Did you see that?"

"What was *that?* Did she really just slap you?" she asked me.

"Yeah," I breathed slowly. And then, in my best Gollum voice, I said, "Yes, my preciousssss."

And we both cracked up laughing.

Obviously, Shawna had barely been home since my injury. But it should also be said at this point that the day I broke my back was the day that Shawna and I were no longer employed. I hadn't worked since the day I triumphantly walked out of the Stanford lab, set into motion a change in my position at NanoLabz, and embraced the prospect of a new career. And Shawna hadn't taken the time to give so much as a backward glance to The Sanctuary, the business that had been the culmination of a dream she'd had since she was thirteen and years of hard work, since the rescue nurse had called her on March 5. Numerous trainer friends had generously donated their time to train Shawna's clients and teach her classes after my accident, none of them taking a dime for themselves.

Meanwhile, Shawna's business partner, Linda, had generously taken the reins of The Sanctuary without objection, despite the difficulties that the recession and double-digit unemployment rates had had on the business, which relied heavily on memberships and discretionary income. A visit to ICU on the day of my surgery had shown her that Shawna was exactly where she needed to be, and she had kindly, lovingly taken Shawna's hands to tell her so.

Since that day, Shawna had rarely spoken of, or even thought about, The Sanctuary, until Linda and her husband stepped into our room at inpatient somewhere in week two.

Shawna and I filled them in on my injury—the extent of it, the scope, the plan for recovery. "So now that you know a little bit more about the injury, what does this look like for you?" Linda asked, proceeding somewhat carefully for fear of placing undue pressure on us. "Where do you... What path do you think you'll want to take here?"

We knew that what she was really asking was, "Do you think you'll be returning to work?"

"I just don't know how that would work for us," Shawna said. "Grant's going to need constant care for a while."

"Are you looking at in-home care, a nurse or anything?" Linda asked.

This subject had already been raised several times by various friends, but the unfortunate truth was that, among the many restrictions my insurance placed on us, it required we make a choice between in-home care and outpatient therapy. We were completely unwilling to turn down therapy, so for us it was a no-brainer.

We explained this to Linda, but what painted a better picture for her was watching Shawna with me, putting on my turtle-shell brace, helping me to sit up. Linda and her husband saw how reliant I was on her to do so many little things, and how Shawna's whole focus was on me, watching how I moved and anticipating what I needed before I knew I needed it. The question hung in the air as if it had been asked out loud: *How on earth*

could we ask Shawna to come back and help people get fit, work them out and
train them, when her husband needs to learn to walk again?

"Well, we're here for two more weeks, so we won't really know what
will happen until we're home," Shawna said. "We'll assess it then?"

Linda was fine with that, pleasantries and hugs were exchanged, but
we knew, we all knew, that Shawna and I were on a path that would lead
to many things, but returning to work at the Sanctuary would likely not be
one of them, at least not in the foreseeable future. Linda saw it in our eyes
that day, and what we saw in hers was complete and total understanding
and acceptance of it.

I think what that day also did for us was force us, once again, to consciously decide what we wanted: Even if insurance was no issue, there
would be no way, in Shawna's mind, that she could pick up and go to work
until I had completely recovered. We weren't just in this to get well enough
to get out of the hospital. We were in this recovery 100 percent.

That night, Linda's visit still lingered on our minds until I finally asked
the question. "What's our plan? What *are* we going to do once I get out of
here?"

We looked at each other and, immediately, we made a conscious decision together. "We have to do everything in our power to focus entirely on
this recovery," Shawna said. I noted that she hadn't said "*your* recovery."

"Work is just… work," she went on, making a dismissive gesture with
her hands. "But we'll never have another opportunity to go back to *this*
time, when your body is most apt to heal and be influenced by therapy,
and to regenerate nerves. How would we feel later on if I just went back to
work and left you with a nurse so I could go train people at The Sanctuary?
I mean, I'd regret that for the rest of my life. There's no way... We just have
to do whatever it takes."

I could see that, for her, it was very simple. Fucked up as this whole
thing seemed to be, we believed that were exactly where we supposed to be
at that moment. Work would handle itself, and from then on my job was to
recover, and Shawna's job was to help me do that.

Shawna and Grant get down to work (Photo by Steven Malekos)

CHAPTER 10
THE BODY WILL FOLLOW

I'm standing in an elevator, one of those old elevators lined with crushed red velvet and filled with ornate, rococo-style brass fixtures, the kind you would find at an old theater or maybe an art deco building in New York City or something. The buttons are made of vividly colored gemstones embossed with silver numbers. The floors are silver panels engraved with intricate grid designs, like something from a piece of old, high-end aircraft. I might be a guest at Willy Wonka's Chocolate Factory.

The door opens, and indeed I'm at a theater, one with a grand, sweeping stage and velvet curtains, and hundreds of seats before it. But there are all these things happening—people milling about, dust flying, light fixtures littering the floor. I hear the scream of a table saw, occasional hammering in the far corner. I smell sawdust. A wire hanging from the ceiling sparks with a *bzzt*. The elevator door remains open just a few seconds, then *DING*, the door closes, and we are going up, though I haven't pushed any buttons.

On the next floor, the doors open again. Another theater here, too, much the same as the first one, but this one is finished. Red swoops of velvet hang on the walls and from the ceiling. The air feels warm; it smells of wood polish, with hints of the burning that emanates from the hot lights covered in colored gels, illuminating the actors on stage. It must be a funny show—the people filling the seats are chuckling and there are little bursts of clapping. *DING!* The doors close again.

The doors open on every floor. What is this place? Where am I going? Third floor, fourth floor, fifth floor… it's just theater after theater, all in the midst of some action, some in various stages of repair, some in use and in immaculate condition. Faster and faster I ascend; doors open and close almost instantly, revealing, in those seconds, one stage after another.

I've arrived at what I assume is the top floor, because the elevator stops, the doors open with a loud, confident *DING* and remain open. Here the lights are so dim I can hardly see. Through the fog of dust and dark I can make out wires hanging from the ceiling and shooting up through the floor, exposed ends sparking. Ducts and duct fans are visible through the ceiling beams. Dusty, woody air swirls around me. The theater seats here aren't in place; they seem to have been collected into a heap for eventual rearrangement and then abandoned. No one is in this room, but there's a lot happening, a lot left halfway done. Maybe it's just break time?

No, now I'm ascending again, but the doors are stuck, they won't close. I'm flying up, floor after floor. With my back pressed firmly against the elevator's back wall, up I go, flying past stage after stage, each beautiful and perfect. Past play after play, I hear crowds cheering, see lights shining; the doors aren't even bothering to try closing. I feel as if I'm watching a movie on fast forward. Where am I going?

Now I stop with a *VA…VA…VA…VRRMM…SHHHHT.* I'm in what appears to be a control room this time. I feel like I'm on board the Starship Enterprise. There's no stage here, no lights, no seats, just a long, wide deck covered in colorful buttons and switches and levers. Computer screens line the walls, blinking and flashing. Wires run floor to ceiling and run to every switch, screen, and keyboard in the room.

People are working feverishly here, pushing buttons, pulling switches, moving about in a beautifully choreographed dance of work. The communication here seems gloriously effective and upbeat. Workers high-five each other, greet each other with smiles as they sign papers and adjust measurements on screens. They're happy as they bustle about.

I see electrical impulses shooting down wires, end to end, resulting in lights and sounds. Things here are working perfectly, and everyone's completely oblivious to me; I'm a captive yet fascinated observer in this elevator.

The room, I come to realize, is an ellipse. I'm standing at the back end of it, and the deck, which curves outward, faces away from me. I see what it's facing: two large windows to the world. Everywhere around the room, the dozens of people working here are performing actions and then cross-checking them—"Push the button, then check that it worked; pull that switch, how'd that go? Everything good? Great, now push that button there. Check the screen. Good?"

I lean back against the elevator wall, feeling, for some reason, quite content. Everything's under control.

I awoke from my feverish nap at 2:00 in the afternoon. The room was bathed in sunlight and Shawna sat quietly in the chair in the corner, folded up into herself, cozily reading.

"Oh!" I said, feeling disoriented, and Shawna sprang out of her seat to come to my side. "Babe, I just had the craziest dream."

Shawna and I talked for a long while that day about the awesome power of the mind. I took great comfort in the message mine seemed to be sending me, but also in the idea that if my nerves could speak directly to me that way, maybe I could speak back? Maybe, through dreams and visualizations, my body and I could really communicate with each other. Maybe there was some way I could tell it what I wanted and needed—to run, to jump, to dance with my wife, to twinkle my toes, to stand up and take a piss on my own—and it could give those things to me?

I decided it was worth a shot, and we made visualizations a daily regimen. Much like a yogi or meditative guide, Shawna led me through closing my eyes, relaxing, tuning out the noise of the world, and focusing on nothing more than visualizing my toes and feet moving, the sensations and movement gradually returning, moving downward through my body, the muscles moving and making my body work. Seeing my spine working.

I'd visualize tirelessly, endlessly, always with Shawna encouraging me to create movement, to manifest that reality. Words that, to be quite honest, wouldn't have meant much to me before this injury. This was the kind of thing Shawna knew already; this was language she used regularly. I had been too busy focusing on the concrete science of reality, the measurable and precise calculations of nanotechnology and engines.

But now I knew that science wasn't everything. I knew that no matter how much practice and experience and planning I had, no matter how many calculations I could do in the air, I could still land with a broken back. And although science had put my body back together again and set me on the road to healing, that would only get me so far. No scientific opinion, despite its veracity or the intentions of the person delivering it, could convince me that my own current condition was a permanent one.

Albert Einstein is quoted as saying, "Everything is energy and that's all there is to it. Match the frequency of the reality you want and you cannot help but get that reality. It can be no other way. This is not philosophy. This is physics."

So I let my mind go wherever Shawna instructed me to send it and believed that eventually my body would follow.

Daily, I would get back on that elevator, ride it upward, explore how I felt on each floor, taking note of every sensation I felt. I was a construction worker, in my Carhartts, tool belt, and hardhat, and I'd enter the theaters, fixing things as I went. Each time, I'd say to myself something like, "Okay, today I need to connect this wire to that wire and run it up to the ceiling," or "That ducting seems off; I should fix that."

I never asked myself, in these visualizations, "How does this apply to my spine?" I didn't try to overthink it or analyze it. I just focused on attaching the wires and securing the ducts. And anytime I thought to myself, "Jeez, I need that part fixed over there, but I don't have that in my toolbox…" I was out of it. I was successful only when I focused exclusively on one thing. And when that one thing was done, I'd get on the elevator, push a button, and watch the elevator's doors slowly close. Then I'd leave the visualization, feeling the same satisfaction I'd felt that day upon waking.

Although I was only just beginning to practice visualization intention-ally, it was not my first experience with focusing tirelessly on what I wanted and then tirelessly visualizing it. It was actually something I'd done even as a child too young to understand what I was doing or name it anything. All I knew was that if I had a completely clear picture of what I wanted, and that if I asked for it in detail, and was then open to how it would come, it would, indeed, come.

When I was about eight years old and in third grade, my heart's tru-est desire was a remote control car. And not just any car. After all, engi-neering comes naturally to me; it's part of my most basic makeup. I must have maximization, optimization, every possible option at my fingertips. The car had to be the very finest piece of gear I could possibly have: the Team Associated RC10, the ultimate, professional-level remote control racer that dominated every other model that had come before it. I knew exactly what I wanted, from the deep, anodized, gold-colored frame to the multi-stage lug dirt tires to the Futaba servo motor controller to the char-ger and battery, even down to the connectors I wanted to solder onto the receiver unit—all of which were after-market parts found in catalogues that I pored over daily. In my mind, accepting anything less was simply unthinkable.

At school, we were asked to write an essay about our fondest wishes for Christmas. Mine described, in detail, every feature of the RC10, the intri-cate paint job I planned to give it, my plans for racing it. At night, tucked into bed in my pajamas with the lights out, I'd visualize my RC10, assemble the pieces, thrill over the racing victories I was sure to have. The lights would go out and I'd actually feel a shiver of excitement at the prospect of finally having time alone with thoughts about my RC10.

The problem was that my parents, having sacrificed many creature comforts just to keep us at Tahoe, were nowhere near being able to afford an RC10. The kit alone, with only basic parts, cost $225. The charger would be at least another $100, the controller an additional $100. Then there were all those other parts. I was looking at $500-$600—a totally unrealistic amount of money, I knew, for a third-grader's toy. But the idea of taking a Hornet, or some other car that was cheaper or more reasonable, was so far beneath my expectations that I wouldn't consider it. I was resolute.

In the meantime, I told everyone who would listen that this was what I wanted, *only* this. And I formulated a plan to earn the money myself.

One of the benefits—or drawbacks, depending on how you look it at— of living at Incline Village was the fact that, for a lot of household necessities, we'd have to travel down the mountain to Reno, a good forty-five-minute trip, to buy them. I say benefit because of the inevitable treats such trips would bring me.

On one such outing with my mother to a store in town, we stopped by a local casino. Inside was a bulk candy store lined with barrels of candy for sale by weight. "Pick out what you want," my mom said, feeling generous.

I left with sacks filled to the tops with Dubble Bubble, Atomic Fireballs, Fun Dip, and Bottle Caps, at first thinking of my own enjoyment, but soon realizing that what I had was a potential gold mine. After all, you couldn't get this stuff at Incline. Kids might pay some good money for it—maybe ten cents apiece to start.

That Monday, I crammed three sacks of candy into my enormous backpack, headed to school, and began rehearsing my sales pitch in my head. My instincts had been correct; I barely closed my backpack that day. I learned early that instead of offering change I could keep the dollar that most of my friends had on them and sell them ten pieces of candy—candy that, in a school, was like water in a desert.

My little enterprise took off in a hurry. At least once a week, my mom would bring me enormous bags full of candy from Reno. Her thought was, "Hey, you want to buy a $600 car? Go earn it—more power to you. And if you bring in ten or twenty bucks a day, you might just make it."

It was slow going, but I kept every penny. Weeks passed that fall, and about a week or so before Christmas, my mom found me sitting on my bed, counting my coins out, as had become my daily after-school ritual. She came into the room and said, "Listen, I got a message from Santa today."

I stopped what I was doing and looked up at her. Could this be it, the news I'd been hoping for? I had begun having doubts about Santa, but when it came to an RC10, I was willing to suspend disbelief.

"Yeah?" I said, skeptically.

She sat down gingerly at the end of the bed. "He said that if you were to trust him with the money you've earned, he *might* be able to get you that car."

I looked carefully at my money from the day, spread across my Star Wars bedspread, and then looked at the shoebox on my desk that contained the remainder of my nearly $400.

"What do you think?" my mom asked, patting me on the back.

"Umm..." I considered thoughtfully. I'd worked hard to earn all this money—could I trust Santa to give me the right thing? I would have to be very specific about what I wanted; maybe I should write it all down. But if he could make this $400 turn into my dream RC10, Santa would have proven himself to be one hell of a guy. "Okay."

"Okay?" asked my mom. I nodded. "Good! Okay, we'll put it out on Christmas Eve for him. Make sure you write down what you want, so he gets it all right."

So on Christmas Eve, I carefully laid my $400, which I'd spent months earning, next to the plate of cookies and glass of milk, along with my list of components, held my breath, and slowly backed away, fingers crossed.

And on Christmas morning, there it was, not even wrapped, just boldly sitting under the tree, with the colored lights glinting off the dreamy box I'd spent months of my life visualizing. It was an unforgettable moment.

So maybe what I'd done as a kid wasn't all that different from what I was doing now in the hospital's inpatient center. The lesson was certainly the same: Don't wait to get what you want. Just go get it; make it happen. Visualize what you want with precision, put it out there into the universe, be clear about exactly what you want, and be willing to do the work involved to get it. Then, be open to how it comes, when it comes.

Here, it was no different. I lay there, eyes closed, single-mindedly focusing, much like my eight-year-old self. But here, instead of an RC10, I saw my own feet, my own legs, my own body in motion, walking, running, jumping, skiing, biking, dancing with Shawna. I thought about every movement, every muscle needed to achieve that movement, imagined the feelings associated with it, the sensations each part of my body would experience. I was willing to do anything to get there. As with that RC10, nothing less than the perfect body I envisioned would do.

That perfect body included a working penis.

I mean, prior to this injury, I was in peak physical condition in every possible sense. I performed at my highest athletic level in *every* situation, and as newlyweds, Shawna and I had certainly put on some impressive performances. I mean, not to be indelicate, but in our own home, we were porn stars.

For a guy like me, I don't think it's exaggerating to say that I was often guided by my dick. And I wasn't the only one. Our culture is filled with references (usually admiring ones) to the wonder of male genitalia. Look at rap music—how often it's about how rad your dick works. Send a kayak sixty feet over a fall and you've got "some balls on you." Really have your eye on a new truck? You've got a "hard-on" for it. How could someone like me, someone so in tune with my body, Mr. Off-the-Couch, how could I *not* perceive this injury as somehow emasculating? Because, although I could, inexplicably, actually get a hard-on, what I could do with it was entirely out of my control at this point. Because at this moment I couldn't even stand up to take a piss by myself anymore.

And even beyond that, the fact that I couldn't evacuate by myself was dehumanizing. Some things you should never have to do without. Regardless of how much money you have or what kind of person you are, it should be a God-given, inalienable right to be able to pee and poop by yourself. Not to enter the chicken or the egg conversation, but a major engineering flaw was overlooked in the creation of the human body. Because there should be redundancies built in, back-ups to ensure that everything down there functions, no matter what. Unless you've been severed in half, that shit should work. Period.

In any spinal cord injury one of two things happens to the bladder: You either lose bladder control or you don't. I've heard it said, "T12 and up, everything's on the floor (spastic bladder); L1 and below, it's off the floor (flaccid bladder)." So with my L1 fracture, I narrowly missed having a bladder and bowel that emptied on reflex, just peeing and pooping myself all the time, which would have required me to wear a "condom catheter" twenty-four hours a day, delivering my waste to a bag that I would be forced to lug around every day strapped to my leg.

Fortunately, if you can call it fortunate, my bladder and bowel were stuck closed after my injury, and now required manual stimulation, which enabled me to retain a shred of dignity in not just soiling myself all day.

The urinary system truly, when working correctly, is the body's most sophisticated and complex system. Essentially what it's doing is contracting and relaxing at the same time, something that nothing else in your body, not even your heart, can do. When your bladder fills enough to achieve pressure of approximately 40 psi, it sends a signal to the brain that you need to pee. Sure, you hold it sometimes, like first thing in the morning when you don't want to get out of bed, until the pressure is almost too much and you're in pain. But you finally pull your pants down, stand in front of the toilet, and your sphincter releases so the urine can make its way out, while your bladder simultaneously squeezes and your urethra relaxes to allow the flow.

But me, I no longer got that all-important signal. So sure, I wasn't just urinating uncontrollably all day, but my sphincter was closed, and now I had to manually tell it to open. And the way I did this was by inserting seventeen inches of catheter tubing, 1/16 of an inch in diameter, into my penis nine times a day. Or, at least in the beginning, having my wife do this for me.

I know—that's a one-way hole, right? I mean, there's nothing in me that has ever said, "I think I'm going to put this in *there*." And though catheterization didn't hurt me physically at first, when it came to accepting this new part of my reality, it was definitely painful in a whole other way.

If, before, my life had been guided by my dick, it now seemed guided by my urethra. The only way to be sure that I didn't eventually stretch my bladder into incontinence or infection was to follow a strict, round-the-clock, every-four-hours urination schedule. There was an alarm to roll me over, and an alarm to catheterize me, and sometimes it felt like an alarm was sounding every hour. Poor Shawna would often just drift off to sleep when the alarm would sound, and she'd stagger, eyes half-closed, her body on automatic pilot, to the tray containing the synthetic tubing and gloves, while I lay there, frustrated by this new aspect of our lives.

The tubing was lubricated, then poked, poked, up and up, through the prostate and up through the sphincter to open it, and into the bladder—a long, arduous process in those early days. Once penetrated, the sphincter relaxed and enabled urine to exit the bladder.

The first time I became aware of Shawna doing this was while I was still in the ICU, in one of the few moments of lucidity I experienced during that week after my surgery. I awoke to the sound of a plastic wrapper crumpling and the wheels of a metal tray being pushed toward me. Murmurs in the corner to my right told me that my wife and my mother were in the room with me. I struggled to keep my eyes open and managed only a few blinking, blurry moments. A nurse in pink scrubs was talking as she looked down at her metal tray.

"We need to cath him so he can urinate," said the nurse, seeming unsure as to whether she should be speaking to Shawna or my mom. I strained my eyes to look down and realized that the nurse was starting to pull my sheet down.

Wait… *Mom?* Seriously, my mom was here, and this nurse was about to get in touch with the business end of my mid-section?

"Mmm," I said, trying to reach down and cover myself, but moving even a single muscle was a struggle. "What's happening?"

"Hello, Grant!" said the young, cheerful nurse in a clearly over-caffeinated state. "Grant, we need you to urinate, okay? We need to catheterize you."

Shawna appeared in my line of sight. "It's okay, babe."

My mom hesitantly stood farther to the right. "Grant, I'm here, sweetheart," she said, surely meaning it to be comforting, but I was mortified. I was a thirty-two-year-old man with my penis seconds from being prominently displayed—I had been a child the last time she'd seen me naked.

I closed my eyes, unable to form the words to argue, and listened, hoping Shawna would understand.

The nurse began describing tubing, giving directions that seemed far removed from me and far too complex from my drug-addled brain to comprehend.

To my mother, Shawna said, "Pam, I've got this. If you want to go ahead and step out, that'd be great."

"Oh! Uh, okay," my mom said, and began grabbing at things noisily before making her awkward exit.

But that had been weeks ago. Like with most things, Shawna was a quick study. By now, here at inpatient, watching my wife catheterize me was fairly unremarkable, and actually felt a bit like an out-of-body experience. After all, I couldn't feel it. Reaching over that far was still much too much for my spine to handle, but I was determined to take this "duty" on myself as soon as humanly possible.

Far more humbling was having her or a nurse manually helping out with my bowel movements, called digital stimulation, or, around the hospital, "dig stim."

"Have you dig-stimmed today?" was a frequent medical question.

It's an emotionally taxing process, and one that would take me months to be physically able to do for myself. Even a shoulder bend of fifteen or twenty degrees was beyond my abilities right now.

Sure, the loss of activity and the use of my legs and feet, on their own, that was a horrible, infuriating thing. We didn't dwell on these other ugly aspects, and going down that road of anger, we knew, would get us nowhere. But still, needing help to take a shit? No one should go through that.

Grant sits alone in Yosemite's El Cap Meadow
(Photo by Shawna Korgan)

CHAPTER 11
CLINICAL EVICTION

After a couple weeks in inpatient, I was pretty used to the idea of my hospital-issue loaner wheelchair. With all its awkward, clinical chrome, its reclining seat, and weighty frame that could support my strained, unpredictable body as it slid in and out several times a day, it was both a blessing and a curse. I was thankful for it, even as I expressed distaste for it at every turn. Still, I made peace with it because I knew we would only be temporary acquaintances. Like the hospital itself, this wheelchair was only a part of my immediate reality. Soon we would part ways.

But then there was talk about "my wheelchair," and that stone of hot anger in the pit of my stomach burned again. Even hearing Shawna's words in my mind, "It's temporary, when you're done you can give it back," it felt too permanent a thing to bring home. There was unsettling talk from the physical therapy department about our "wheelchair spot" at home.

Now I had to pick a chair for myself. Maddeningly, *this* was the gear I could buy now.

On a Friday, halfway through my stay at inpatient, when Ron, a smiling, balding, portly gentleman in a black polo shirt from the local medical supply company, wheeled in the ultra-light wheelchair that was considered top of the line, I could see the effort by all involved. Clearly knowing that in my garage there wasn't one piece of biking, sledding, climbing, or flying gear that wasn't hand-selected, and, in my mind, top of the line. Those closest to me and those on staff at the hospital who had spent time with me had given Ron input about my love of high-end equipment.

But even the name of this ultra-light titanium "Freedom Wheelchair," which Ron had brought as a loaner, seemed to mock me.

"I wanted to show you the ultra-light," said Ron, pointing to the chair's various special features—its top-shelf wheels and customizable color. "It's a great chair, one of the best out there. What do you think?"

I looked at Ron's face, its jolly kindness that made plain his care for his work and for my getting the right wheelchair. "Hey, thanks, Ron, that's really nice of you," I said, mustering all the sincerity and gratitude I could for his gift of Freedom.

Once seated in the chair, I could feel the high-endedness of it, and I resented it yet admired it.

"What do you think of this one?" he asked. "We need to order you a chair so we can make sure you get one before you get outta here."

"Well, I guess it's pretty nice." I craned my neck down the sides of the chair, surveying the wheels and feeling the low armrests. "But I'd like to do some research, if that's okay. I'm an engineer..." I said. "Can I have the weekend to decide?"

"Sure, that'd be fine. Just give me a call Monday," he said.

That weekend, seated upright in bed, I scoured the Web for every wheelchair company I could find until I came across the exact chair I could live with, the titanium frame and backing and carbon fiber accessories I wanted. All the while, I was ruefully aware that in any other situation, an online search for gear would have filled me with excitement.

The chair I chose was ordered Monday. The wheels, so to speak, were in motion.

Pre-accident hike and kayak, Upper Cherry Creek, 2003 (Photo by Brett Valle) and dirt-jumping near Reno, NV (Photo by Brooks McMullen)

We had expected it since day one of my arrival at inpatient, but it still blew us away when I got kicked out of inpatient rehab after only four weeks.

"Kicked out" is how the doctors put it, as in, "We're sorry you're being kicked out. It's not our doing, I assure you."

I knew in my gut that I wasn't ready to go, and Shawna knew it, too. As much as I wanted to go home, I was in such delicate condition that I was sure I could do damage to myself going home too soon.

But what really surprised us was that even the doctors and nurses and physical therapy staff knew it, and still, that didn't help. Dr. Abbott had written a formal letter arguing that I be allowed to stay on at least another month. A petition signed by the hospital physicians and staff was sent to the insurance company. None of it mattered. Insurance paid for a thirty-day stay, and beyond that, every additional day would have cost us $5,000. Our case worker was adamant: "There's nothing we can do." We would have to go home.

In preparation for this inevitable exile, I spent my fourth week in in-patient rehab rehearsing to leave. Once I was in my loaner wheelchair, I could work on wheeling myself one hundred feet, the minimum distance I needed to reach in order to be released, and which I reached during my fourth week in rehab, traveling up and down hallways and along the side-walks outside.

Next was getting into the car. Our assumption, mine and Shawna's, was that squeezing into her Mini Cooper was an impossibility for me. And I had, just a week before my injury, sold my enormous dream truck in order to pay for helicopter school; that money was now what we were living on. We decided that the beat-up old painter's van she and I had bought for $1,500 to take to the Burning Man festival the previous sum-mer would now be our lifesaver. Up until this point, the van had sat on our driveway, a convenient mode of transport to, and shelter on, the pla-ya at the Black Rock Desert, but otherwise rarely used. I had visions of turning this van into a shuttle for my kayak buddies, me, and our gear, driving it from river to river with little or no care for its condition. Now it looked as if the van would be getting a lot of use, starting with this, our first rehearsal.

I wheeled up side by side with the passenger seat, and Shawna opened the front door. There would be no cot for me, not even a long backseat. The front seat had the seatbelt.

One of the three therapists who had come to assist Shawna lowered my chair's left armrest and laid a long, smooth, wooden plank called a slide board, designed specifically for transferring paraplegics from one place to another, from under my butt on the wheelchair to the van's front passenger seat.

Practicing the transfer from my bed to the wheelchair day in and day out with Becca hadn't prepared me for this—not with the board's steep in-cline, the hard concrete below, a journey of this length, or the difficulty my turtle shell presented to a climb like this. Every movement on this uneven surface felt precarious. Within no time, I was falling, first forward, then backward, the board feeling ridiculously narrow and the turtle shell overly cumbersome, an anchor dragging me downward. I was a terrified, sweat-ing, miserable rag doll.

What had begun as an intricate choreography of movement planned to gracefully land me in my van's seat became a sort of train wreck. I was manhandled, manipulated, arms and legs grabbed just the second before I fell, pushed into the van in a way that made me feel like an awkward pair of skis being shoved into an over-full closet.

The experience was traumatic to me in a way I had not expected. Despite the progress I had thought I was making in physical therapy—the triumphs of sitting up in a chair or getting my quads to flex the tiniest little bit—I was still woefully unable to do much of anything, even the simple act of getting in my own fucking van, by myself. I wasn't ready. Holy shit, what was going to happen to me? How would I sit up in bed, get from room to room in our small house?

I felt imprisoned in this body, this life. Fear gripped me so tightly that bile rose in my throat and I began to hyperventilate, all the while desperately struggling to keep it together outwardly. I knew there was no sense in showing panic, that it would only worry Shawna, make the rest feel sorry for me, none of which I wanted.

Then there was getting out of the van. One PT assistant grabbed my feet and held them up while another grabbed my hips, lifting them awkwardly. The third lifted me from under my armpits, twisting my mangled back with its staples and stitches, until I was awkwardly dropped into a half-seated position, with one butt cheek falling off of the wheelchair, like a bag of sand.

I was utterly devastated. *I can't even get in my own car,* I thought miserably. *It took four people, and I couldn't even get into my own car with any level of ease. How am I going to live my life?* Tears welled in my eyes. The devastation was plain on my pale, sweating face.

The first rehearsal had been a failure as far as everyone was concerned, and so were the two that followed. The painter's van was clearly missing the mark, and the low-to-the-ground Mini Cooper was probably our best shot, at least in terms of getting into it.

All of this had been reported to Ron, who, a few days later, met us in the parking lot to show us an alternative. He pulled into the parking lot in a white adaptive Honda minivan. Before stepping out, he pushed a button and the back door slid open. With a soft hum, a large ramp rolled outward

The "Dream Truck" was a dirt-roostin' machine
(Photo by Grant Korgan)

toward me, then with a *VRRRR* the ramp lowered, stopping on the ground just in front of my chair. Ron exited the van, clearly pleased to show me such an option existed, and stepped around to greet me.

"What's all this?" I asked him genially, both amused and confused.

"Why don't you hop into the van, see how it goes?" he said.

"Whose van is this?" I asked, hesitant.

"It's mine, I just wanted to show you an option, show you what's out there," he said. "Look, you can roll right into this thing. I just wanted you to see that there *is* a car you can get into. Just something to think about. Go ahead; get in!"

"That's cool," I said, my voice conveying that it actually wasn't cool, not at all. A minivan. I stared, unmoving. From where I sat, I could see the front seat, the large, specially made hand controls that would enable a paraplegic, someone like me, to drive with his hands.

No no no no no no.

I was a guy who loved vehicles—cars, trucks, vans. I loved movement, action. Big and bold and rumbling, tearing down a dirty road for several days with kayaks strapped to the top. Throwing a muddy dirt bike in the back. Just a few months ago, I'd had my dream truck, a Chevy Duramax, four-door, short-box, diesel truck, black on black with matching black wheels. But that truck was gone now. Was this what I now had to live with? A minivan with a ramp? Were all the things I loved now totally useless to me? Just when I thought I had a grasp on what I'd lost, more seemed to be taken from me.

Ron leaned in and cranked up the stereo on the minivan. "Check this sweet stereo!"

Still I sat there. I wanted no part of the van, with or without the stereo. Shawna stood beside me, hand on my shoulder, carefully watching me.

A PT assistant slowly, cautiously pushed me up the ramp. "Uhh…" I said, protesting, unable to form words, just, "Uh-uh. Uh-uh."

Then, *VRRRR*, the ramp lifted me up, pulled me into the van like the tongue of a monster. And someone shut the door. There I sat, alone, in the minivan. *NO! This isn't me! This wasn't supposed to happen! You don't understand!*

Forget the soccer mom stigma, any question of status or image—this was about freedom, of which I now had none. I was literally and figuratively boxed in by the ramp, trapped in my own nightmare, screaming inside my own head.

Up to this point, I think my mental space had been pretty strong. I'd had my moments of misery, my internal complaints, my occasional breakdowns in the privacy of my own room, alone with Shawna. I'd loaded my backpack and carried my fair share of weight. But for the most part, I'd remained upbeat, worked hard, with Shawna's help, to maintain hope and a positive outlook. I'd smiled, attacked my physical therapy eagerly, focused entirely on my goals. I would NOT be that person, that minivan person.

I knew that there were many, many wonderful, strong people who drove minivans just like this, competent quadriplegics who had no bad associations with minivans and whom I admired to the depths of my soul. I knew it made me seem spoiled and petty. I absolutely saw it for what it was.

But for me and my life, for the choices I'd made and the life I wanted to have with Shawna, this was not for me, I knew that with every fiber of my being.

I sat there alone in the minivan, watching those outside celebrating, "He's in! Yay! He's in the car! That was so easy!" And I wept gut-wrenching tears.

Shawna saw me and said, "Get him out, get him out! Open the door, please, get him out."

What was I doing? Crying over sitting in a minivan? I had to pull it together. By the time the door had slid open and the ramp began its hum to let me out, my tears had been dried.

"Okay, man, good job," said Ron, seeing it all on my face and clearly feeling bad for me. That sweet, sweet man who helped people like me for a living. I felt ashamed. "Just let me know if you want something like this, okay? It might help, that's all."

"Okay, thanks, I appreciate it," I said, meaning it sincerely and shaking his hand.

But UGH, I couldn't do it. I knew I couldn't do that. No minivan.

Ron drove off, and just as we turned to wheel back inside, Becca walked up to join us, on her way in to start her shift.

Upon seeing my crestfallen face and the concerned looks of everyone around me, it was clear to Becca that something bad had happened. She could guess pretty quickly what it was.

The second I saw her I burst into tears. The physical and emotional exhaustion of the day had taken their toll, and I was wrecked.

"Oh, no," said Becca, and she ran to embrace me. Then, with some trepidation, she asked, "How'd it go with the van?"

"Dude, it was a minivan," I heaved pitifully into her shoulder. "That's just not my scene."

While we didn't exactly expect a going away party, we figured we might be given a little extra time to leave on check-out day, that the hospital might look kindly at our situation and be lenient. Or, at the very least, we thought we could have until 11 a.m., the normal check-out time, on our last day.

But on the morning of Friday, April 14 at nearly the crack of dawn, the door swung open violently, and what felt like six nurses, with trays of medication and a frenzy of tubing and clipboards, told us, in nearly so many words, "Get up and get out of here; we've got somebody else coming in here!"

"What?" I asked. We were still drinking our coffee. "I thought we had until 11? We've got all this stuff we have to pack up!" I scanned the room and saw the wedding pictures and whiteboard, papers and clippings taped all over the walls, comforters from home on the bed and cot, bags of clothes and books, a shelf of snacks we'd accumulated.

Our day nurse, a kind woman we'd come to think very highly of precisely because of her attentiveness, stopped her work to look at us. "We're moving you to the therapy room so you can fill out your paperwork there. We'll get some people to help you pack up, okay? Sorry about all this. We've got another patient coming for this room."

"But we have a workout this morning at 9," Shawna insisted.

"That's fine, you can do that in the therapy room," said the nurse. "No problem; you'll be fine."

The nurse handed Shawna the tray bearing the new latex catheters that would now be a part of my daily regimen out in the real world. I was catheterized, all materials were tossed away, and I was hurried into the wheelchair.

As soon as we were in the hall, Shawna began dialing phone numbers. My parents couldn't make it because my mom had a cold. Fortunately, Steven and my in-laws all said they could be there by 9 o'clock, which we thought was plenty of time and plenty of hands to pack up our belongings and get me on the road by 11.

I wheeled with Shawna into the therapy room, where all around me other patients who weren't being kicked out, were working out—using the parallel bars, lifting weights, sitting on exercise balls. I waved to Greg, who, in another stroke of luck, had such great insurance that he had been given another month of rehab.

"Hey, what's up, guys?" he said. "You leaving today?"

"Yeah, man, my 'top-of-the-line' insurance ran out today, so the hospital has to kick us out," I said jokingly, but not really joking.

Then a mound of paperwork was thrust into my hands, waivers and medical instructions, bills and insurance questionnaires, no-fault clauses and paraplegia pamphlets. I had only slogged my way through half of it when the day nurse came into the room and asked to see Shawna in the hall. She excused herself, leaving me alone to contend with the papers, and with Greg, who was by now strong enough to stand briefly with crutches.

In the hallway, the nurse told Shawna, "We need you to go ahead and start moving things out of your room." Her expression showed that she was flustered about these new instructions, and about having unintentionally misrepresented the exit situation to us earlier. "Sorry, we have a patient who's already here and waiting to get into your room."

"But we were told 11 o'clock! I don't understand..." said Shawna.

"I know, I'm sorry. But our beds are full."

"We have people coming to help us pack at 9. They aren't here yet," my wife argued, futilely.

"I'm sorry," said the nurse, at a loss for what else to offer us.

Shawna checked that I'd be okay on my own for a few minutes, the picture of calm, then excused herself and nearly ran back to the room, frantically throwing pictures and pillows, blankets and my Snuggie, and food into garbage bags. By 9, when Steven and her parents arrived, the haphazard packing was nearly done, and Shawna's worry and anger were written all over her exhausted face.

In the therapy room, I had finished up with the paperwork, and now nurses, doctors, physical therapists, PT assistants, and orderlies starting filing in, giving me hugs and saying their goodbyes. I presented Dr. Abbott with a fine bottle of Rombauer Chardonnay that my parents had given me days earlier to give her, and thanked her sincerely. In the end, despite our differences in philosophy and treatment, the doctor had bent over back-wards to argue on our behalf to the insurance company. Her concern for me was clear. She thanked me for the wine and gave me a warm hug.

But in the midst of all this good feeling and well-wishing, some-thing wasn't right. I was in pain. I'd been weaned off morphine early and, not being someone who liked the idea of any sort of crutches, pain medication included, I rarely took anything for pain unless it was par-ticularly excruciating, or what they called "breakthrough pain." But I was learning to manage pain, and, for the most part, I did okay, because it rarely changed.

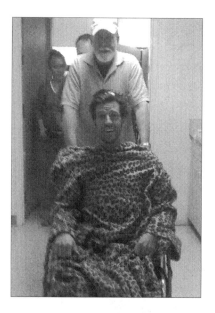

Shawna's dad, Doug, pushes
Grant, heading home
(Photo by Chris Hansen)

This, though, was a new pain, a bad one. My dick was burning. Or, more precisely, there was a fire that seemed to be coming from my urethra. The pain seemed to be building by the minute and was rising into my abdomen.

Which is what I told the small crowd that had now formed around me. "Uh, guys?" I said, beginning to white-knuckle the armrests of my wheelchair. "I think something's wrong."

"It's most likely a urinary tract infection," Dr. Abbott told me and Shawna (who had by now joined me), when I explained my symptoms. I'd already had one such infection during my stay here—a new, painful experience, yet not as bad as what I was experiencing now. "I can write a prescription for antibiotics."

The regimen of cranberry juice and antibiotics I'd done before had been effective, and I was hopeful she was right and that this by now excruciating pain would pass.

But unlike that infection, a vague internal ache deep inside my bladder, this was truly the first sensation below the belt that I'd experienced so far. On the surface, there was still no external sensation whatsoever, but here, now, there was the sensation of terrible, burning pain in the center of my penis—so painful so that it didn't occur to me to celebrate it.

Plus, there wasn't time to. The mood in the air was "Okay, move along: time to go: let's get cracking." I was already worried about what I'd deal with when I got home—leaving here with this new pain was a little too much. "Can we be sure? Do a test or something?" I asked her.

A nurse wheeled me into an exam room where a catheter was inserted, urine was taken, and the culture was sent off to the lab. Unfortunately, though the hospital had no trouble hurrying us, the lab wouldn't be rushed—it would be a day or two before we'd know the results. "I'll write you a prescription for antibiotics, and you should be fine," assured Dr. Abbott, already exchanging looks with a nurse beckoning from the doorway with questions about another patient. We were getting brushed off; I could see it.

Unsettled, I reluctantly said, "Okay," and we continued our plans to leave the hospital. Not that I had much choice in the matter.

Shawna's parents and Steven had filled their cars with our belongings, and now they anxiously greeted me with too-big smiles on their faces and eyes that revealed the depth of their concern. Doug wheeled me toward the parking lot, and the entourage of staffers that had gathered earlier began to reconvene. Through the automatic glass doors, I saw Shawna's shiny jet-black Mini Cooper sitting at the curb. With a small margin of success, we had only practiced getting into the tiny car in one rehearsal, and I hoped today's transfer would fall into the "successful" category.

Becca pulled out the slide board, using it to bridge the distance from my chair to the seat. The Cooper's small size actually made getting into it quite easy, much like moving from bed to chair in my hospital room. At last, something was going well.

Not that sitting in the car, mind you, was comfortable. My six-foot frame (or as much as a quarter inch taller since my surgery) struggled to fit in the small car anyway, but folded in there with a broken back in my turtle shell brace, together with the now-torturous fire of pain radiating through my groin—it was unbearable at best. And I knew getting out of the car would be worse, something like being birthed again. I was only slightly comforted knowing that Steven and my in-laws would be meeting us at home, with a slide board, to help.

But for now, I was in, and everyone was relieved. "So what do we do with the chair?" asked Doug, wanting to fold up the awkward wheelchair and looking at the side-by-side comparison of it to the Cooper.

Becca expertly pulled the wheels off the chair and folded the backrest down in seconds, leaned down for a brief hug, reminding me that she'd see me again soon for a therapy session, and carried it back to the trunk. I had too much to say to Becca, too much to thank her for, and the day was a blur of pain and hurried activity. I made a mental note to speak more sincerely to her when I saw her next.

Becca and Shawna pushed the chair around in the trunk, trying this way and that to make it fit until they arrived at a configuration that involved laying the back seats down and slamming the trunk shut.

While Shawna offered her hugs and thank you's to those present, I sat in the silent car experiencing mixed emotions. The pain in my groin was searing, and the fear of what it meant dampened my spirits about heading home. I was excited and terrified, comforted and anxious, all at once. This couldn't be a urinary tract infection. It was happening too quickly, too painfully. Was this what I had to look forward to? Sensation that only came with horrific pain?

Shawna got in the car, turned on the ignition, and looked at me. "Ready?"

"Yep," I replied robotically. "Let's go home."

"Okay. Let's do it."

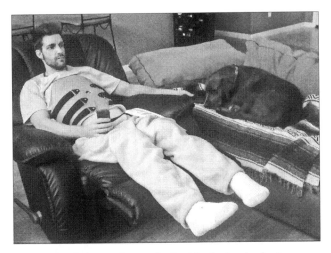

Obie helping Grant deal with the barbed wire
(Photo by Shawna Korgan)

CHAPTER 12
BARBED WIRE

We pulled into our driveway, with Shawna's parents just behind us, and I saw something that immediately pulled me up short: a ramp. I had explicitly said that I'd wanted no assistive devices in our home. At that point, I was raw to anything adaptive and had refused to let anyone mount any permanent aids to the van. I wanted nothing to make this wheelchair life too comfortable. But someone had built a ramp from the front sidewalk up the step to the front door.

"A ramp, huh?" I said, turning to Shawna with tears welling up in my eyes.

"Yeah, a thoughtful tool from Steve Rose and Cary Chisum," she replied cautiously. "Babe, you're gonna need that to get up those steps."

I knew she was right and felt enormous gratitude and love for Steve and Cary, my dear friends who had taken the time and money to enable me easy access to my home. Still, seeing that ramp hurt deeply.

"Hey," Shawna looked at me earnestly, "it's temporary." She gave me a small, reassuring smile before opening the door and heading to the trunk for the wheelchair.

Thanks to my turtle shell, which kept my torso completely rigid, extracting me from the Mini was a bit like the game of Operation—I couldn't be folded or bent, so it was about finding a way to remove me from a small, unyielding, oddly shaped hole. Add to that the fact of my pain, and you can see the task that Shawna and her parents had before them. I was anxious to get inside and lie flat, to fall into merciful sleep.

After much manhandling and manipulation, I was positioned on the slide board and moved to the wheelchair and was then headed toward the house.

Then came the front step and that ramp. As much as I was now able to wheel myself, my strength was so minimal that I couldn't even manage to get up the ramp on my own; even one step was too steep a trip for me now. I'd resented the fact of the ramp, but it was clearly necessary, and all of a sudden I was glad to have it. Shawna gave me a push, and we were up and inside the door.

Like so many other things about our life that seemed serendipitous, as if fate had been guiding us, our house seemed to have been designed for my situation. There wasn't a stitch of carpet anywhere in the one-story house, just tile in the foyer and kitchen, hardwood floors throughout, and linoleum in all the bedrooms and bathrooms. At least I would have access to everything I needed. Right inside the front door was a living/dining great room area separated only by a small bar from the kitchen. Getting around in here would actually be quite easy.

The house had obviously been cleaned; everything sparkled, and the scent of lemon cleaner combined with a vanilla candle filled the air. Shawna's parents had paid to have the entire house cleaned professionally, in preparation for our arrival.

"Hey, guys!" called our friend Jamie from the kitchen, next to an enormous bouquet of yellow flowers in a glass vase that sat on the counter. "Welcome home!"

She stood casually by the bar, hand on the back of a bar stool. She wore workout clothes and her brown hair was up in a sloppy ponytail. Her boyfriend, Cary, a friend and fellow engineer whose intellect I sincerely respected, stepped out from the hallway just at that moment.

"Hey, bro!" he said, stepping forward and leaning down to give me a delicate hug. "We were just finishing up a couple things."

"What things?" I asked, working to maintain my meager smile.

"Cary set up some automated lights for us outside, babe," explained Shawna. "For when we're getting out of the car at night." Then she turned to Cary. "Thank you so much for that; it's awesome."

"Your fridge is all stocked," said Jamie. "Is there anything else you guys need? Can we do anything for you before we get out of your hair?"

"Oh my God, you guys," I said, bowled over by their generosity. "That's amazing, truly, thank you so much."

"How are you feeling?" Jamie asked, looking at me.

"It's a tough day," I said, hesitating to dump this new pain on anyone, and barely having the energy to discuss it. "I think I just need to lie down."

"He's in a lot of pain. We need to go ahead and get him in bed," said Shawna.

"It's no problem, absolutely," Jamie said. "We'll check in on you later. Love you guys." She hugged us both warmly, and so did Cary, and the two made themselves scarce in a hurry.

Jamie and Cary had always been great friends to us, but even more so in recent weeks. Being among the very few who believed, wholeheartedly, in my full recovery, and in the power of silent, nonintrusive support, they were among the small number of friends allowed inside the Bubble. Often, they'd appear at my hospital door bearing coffees, hug us, and excuse themselves, giving nothing but love and support and needing absolutely nothing from us in return—the best gift they could have given us.

By now, the pain in my urethra had knifed its way from the tip of my penis to my bladder and radiated throughout my groin and lower abdomen. It felt like someone had inserted barbed wire all the way up my urethra and was now twisting it, incessantly, ripping and tearing my organs. Crazy, stupid, blinding pain had me gripping the armrest of the wheelchair to keep from savagely screaming. I sat in the chair in the middle of our living room, sweating and shivering, and trying to breathe through the pain, when I heard the roar of Steven's truck pull into our driveway.

"Stevo's here," I exhaled to Shawna.

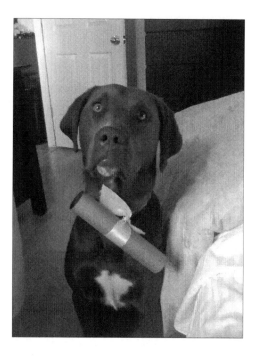

*Obie Boy bringing Grant
his birthday gift via scroll
(Photo by Grant Korgan)*

Through the front-room window, we could see Steven walk around to the back door of his fire-truck red, four-door truck. Even from where we were, we heard a frenzy of low scratching.

"Obie!" said Shawna, and we both watched, with our first amused expressions all day, as the big brown bundle of energy came bounding clumsily from the driveway toward the front door.

Shortly after my arrival at inpatient, Ken and his wife, Bridget, had needed to leave town, and it was arranged that Obie would go to live with Steven and his chocolate lab for a few weeks, until I could come home. Aside from the brief glimpse I'd gotten of him through my hospital room window, when Ken had come to the hospital weeks before, I hadn't seen Obie in five weeks. And prior to that, I'd only really known him for a few days.

Soon after our wedding, Shawna and I decided we wanted to get a dog. But as it typically does, life kept getting in the way. If it wasn't my work it was hers, or it was a pending trip that we felt would interfere with that early adjustment period any dog would require. But finally, just weeks before my injury, during one of my short weekend visits home from Stanford, Shawna got a call from one of her Sanctuary clients. "I heard you're looking for a dog," she'd said. "Are you still interested? I think I found one for you."

When we arrived at the pet food store to meet the dog a couple days later, Shawna was so excited that she jumped out of the car before I had even parked. Having lost her beloved German shepherd, Bruno, just a few years previously, Shawna was anxious to get a dog, yet pretty convinced she'd never again feel quite the same connection to one.

I parked the car and walked in to find her lying on her back, on the concrete floor, laughing as a brown Chesapeake/chocolate lab mix licked her face frantically.

When I approached, Shawna sat up, still laughing but with tears in her eyes, looked at me and said, "This is our dog!"

I braced myself as the dog bounded up, put his front paws on my stomach, and proceeded to lick my face. *I'm your dog!* he said to us.

"This is our dog," I agreed, knowing instantly that he was meant to be with us. We took him home that day, just a week and a half before my injury, and it was as if he'd always been ours.

The night I had to turn around and leave for Stanford to wrap up my work in the lab just hours after bringing Obie home, though, I felt better knowing Shawna would have him with her.

Shawna and I talked a lot on the phone about him, much like new parents do about a baby. She talked about his intuition, his seeming to know her, our house, our lifestyle, and what we needed at the moment, whether it was an energetic hug or a quiet, loving nuzzle, despite his young age of just over a year. We debated names, proposing dozens that didn't feel right, and nearly settled on Tipper because of the white tips on his feet.

Shawna brainstormed names at work with some of her Sanctuary clients. "I don't know," Shawna said. "I feel like he's so wise and so calm, it needs to be something about that."

"Oh! Star Wars!" one client blurted.

"Oh my God, Obi Wan!" Shawna squealed with excitement. After all, Obi Wan had been a great, peaceful master, one who understood the big picture and emphasized focus and discipline.

She was excited to share the idea with me later, on the phone.

"Obi Wan. That's awesome!" I said. "We could call him 'Obie One Ko-rg-nobie.'" Just then, I knew I'd struck gold.

The following weekend, I returned home from Stanford for the week that would irrevocably change my life. During that week, I'd put Obie in the back of my van and driven him to Ski Beach at Lake Tahoe to run with him for the first, and what would also be the last, time. It had been a gorgeous, clear spring day, the air bracingly cold but smelling of pine. The lake had been like glass, blue as a crystal and completely still. The two of us had run for hours with a seemingly endless pool of energy, fed by spring and happiness and the prospect of a spectacular future for our little family.

Three days later, I broke my back.

I'd been worried that Obie would forget me, though the day he'd popped up in my hospital window, he'd been just as excited as the day we'd met. Maybe he really was that wise.

Still, it had been a long five weeks, and the companionship of Stevo and his dog might have been just too much fun to leave behind. Especially with me in this condition.

And now, here he was, running up our driveway like some wild animal straight off the pages of *National Geographic*, all giant paws and teeth and spit, sniffing and peeing and wagging his entire body, his long tongue heaving with his furious pants, the power in every muscle and joint even seeming to whine with acceleration as he got closer to the door. Shawna ran to the front door to throw it open and embrace his full eighty pounds as he stood up on his hind two feet.

He jumped down, then bounded along the long front hallway and came to a dead stop the minute he saw me in the wheelchair in the middle of the room.

"Obie! Hey, buddy!" I called to him, smiling weakly at him, "Come here, boy!"

But it was as if Obie knew something was wrong, knew I was in delicate condition and that I was in pain. For a second, I thought maybe he was scared of the chair. But he didn't run away, just stood, cocked his head, got low, then ambled over, slowly, head down, tiny whines coming out with his breath. He headed right for me, past Shawna and Steven, who by now had

Obie One Korg-nobie (Photo by Eliot Drake)

reached us, past Shawna's parents. He stopped when he reached my side and gently laid his head on my lap.

"Oh my goodness, look at that," said Shawna's mom quietly.

"That's a good boy," I said, almost in a whisper, as I gently stroked his head. "Good boy, Obie."

I looked up at Shawna, smiling a big, genuine smile, and saw her eyes full of tears. When I was done petting him, he walked back to Shawna, turned a few circles, and lay down at her feet.

On top of the indignity of being kicked out of the hospital, Dr. Abbott didn't believe I needed a hospital bed at home and had refused to write a prescription for one. Despite my hatred of adaptive equipment, I was more than accepting of a temporary solution that would allow me to sleep.

"It's going to be tough, but you need to get used to sleeping in your own bed," Dr. Abbott had argued.

But the minute I could, we headed for the bedroom so I could lie down. When I saw the bed, now just a box spring and mattress that Shawna had put on the floor for ease of access, I knew I was in trouble.

Shawna's parents had carefully arranged pillows all around the far edges of the bed, anticipating their use in mimicking the hospital bed's contours as closely as possible. Shawna pulled out the slide board, and she and Steven helped me to slide down the board to the edge of the bed. Gently, very slowly, they helped to lay me flat on the bed, then rolled me to the side and began removing my brace.

Brace off, I was rolled onto my back, but lying flat was now a faint memory for me. By now, my muscles had atrophied to the point where my hip flexors were too tight to allow me to lie flat, and straightening them to any degree forced my back to painfully arch. Immediately, the four of them began shoving pillows under my knees, under my head, and under each arm, to elevate them for my comfort. I was nearly in traction. But no amount of pillows could simulate a hospital bed.

"Why don't you try to get some sleep?" Shawna said to me, and the others sneaked out of the room.

"I don't know if I *can* sleep," I told her. "I'm in so much pain right now, I don't know…"

"Okay, I'm gonna call the doctor and find out what's up with the lab work. Maybe they can prescribe some different meds or something. Try and get some rest," she said. "I'll be in a little later to check on you." Then she quietly stepped out of the room, gently closing the door behind her.

I didn't sleep. Not that afternoon, not that evening, not once the entire weekend. I watched the shapes on the ceiling, formed from the changing light as it moved across my window. I watched time changing, the day moving into night, then moving into morning again. I watched my wife curl up in a small, round chair in the corner of the room to sleep, a sleep I coveted. Afraid to move at all and risk hurting me, she opted to give me the whole bed. It didn't matter—I was too far gone to notice additional discomfort. And when she would finally drift into much-needed sleep, an alarm would sound to roll me, and if it wasn't that, it was to empty my bladder with timed precision.

I lay there, wrestling with the pain, just dealing with it the best way I knew how. I tried desperately to focus on the positive fact that I was experiencing pain of this magnitude, that it might mean that I would regain normal sensations in the lower half of my body. But as the weekend wore on, sleep deprivation and the pain, a combination of blazing razors of pain tearing up my insides and the unbelievable discomfort of being broken backed on a jury-rigged bed, kept any rational focus or perspective at bay.

The days ran together as a hallucinatory blur of raw hurt that seemed to continue its unending crescendo with each passing minute. My parents, Shawna's parents, Steven, and numerous other friends and family stopped in, each of them taking a turn to puzzle over my bed and offer a solution. Some arrived with wedge-shaped or contoured pillows, or with ideas about positioning. I felt like a bizarre science experiment. They pulled our sectional sofa apart, hoping to take advantage of its versatility in arranging some useful configuration. And nothing, not a single thing worked. It didn't matter whether I was rolled onto my side or my back, whether I was sitting upright or lying down. Sometime that weekend, Shawna suggested that I try sleeping on the black leather recliner in the living room, in the hopes that its contours and back and leg supports would help. It didn't.

Getting up from the bed was almost worse than lying in it. When we'd had the hospital bed, Shawna could put the turtle shell on me, lay me flat, then raise the head up to get me into a seated position. Without the hospital bed, we were stuck. Not like she could grab me by the arms and pull me up, not with a broken spine. So now, after the exhausting process of putting the shell on, which in these early days could take a good thirty minutes, she'd slide into the bed, just behind my head, wrap her arms under mine and around my chest, then gradually pull me up to a seated position.

And then I was stuck in the turtle shell, confined in its unyielding size and rigidity that made any position uncomfortable.

It was fucking awful.

On Sunday morning, the raggedness of insomnia and the bleary-eyed pain mounted to an unmanageable level. I was on the verge of freaking out. I found myself unable to control the screaming, savage "GRRRRRR!" issuing from my clenched teeth. With fingers clawing into the chair armrests, tearing into them, I huffed and puffed, suffering actively. This was worse, much worse, than lying in the snow with a broken back. Even the sensation of a backward-folded torso, with shards of bone tearing into muscle, had not been as excruciating or terrifying as what I was enduring now.

Unbelievably, terrifyingly, the pain in my groin continued rising, never leveling off so that I could mentally grab hold of it, make sense of it, manage it. I felt as if it might actually make me insane.

Monday morning came and Shawna announced, "I don't care if I have to pay a billion dollars, I'm getting you a hospital bed."

She began making calls, the first of which was to Dr. Abbott, who reported what I already knew: This was not a urinary tract infection. She suggested Percocet and Vicodin, both of which I'd already been taking, neither of which could touch the pain I was feeling.

The next call was to our friend and general practitioner, Dr. Pasternak. "How's he doing?" he asked.

With a voice that trembled with unacknowledged fear, she said, "He's in a lot of pain. Terrible pain, in his groin. It's not a UTI; we don't know… can you come look at him? Tell us what this is? It's really bad."

Back in the day, doctors making house calls may have been common practice, but these days, it was virtually unheard of. We were overwhelmed with gratitude when Dr. Pasternak said he would come right over that same day.

It took about sixty seconds upon his arrival for Dr. Pasternak to announce, "I will write you a prescription for a hospital bed. This is ridiculous."

Most people would sue over the bed; I knew it. But my anger over that paled when compared with the horror taking place in my urethra and bladder, which I expressed to Dr. Pasternak as reasonably as I could, through clenched teeth.

"What you're describing sounds like kidney stones," he said, and set up an ultrasound appointment for later that week.

My hopes were then pinned on kidney stones. *Please, let there be an answer to what was happening, an end to this in sight,* I thought.

It didn't take long to get an answer. But not the one I wanted. I was crushed, devastated to learn that it wasn't kidney stones. All was well in my kidneys, my bladder, my urethra.

But oh my God it wasn't, it wasn't, and I felt like I was going crazy.

The days ran together, just one big blur of unendurable pain. I couldn't sleep, and between rolling me every two hours and sleeping in a chair, Shawna didn't either.

We were dealing, one hour at a time, neither of us thinking beyond getting through the next moment, too overwhelmed to consider more than that. People came and quickly went. We might have eaten some things. I caught an hour of sleep every couple of days, after downing a few pills that did little more than cut the blinding glare of pain enough that I could close my eyes and drift away. Shawna kept the Bubble airtight, and turned people away at the door if there was even the chance that I could fall asleep.

The only bright spot of my first week home happened when the hospital bed arrived, four ridiculously long days and a couple thousand dollars after my arrival home. Four days that, despite our earlier appreciation for her talents and good intentions, we both now believed to be unconscionable on the part of Dr. Abbott.

Once the bed arrived, there was the relief of remaining in bed, sitting up without the turtle shell to watch TV or talk to friends who came to visit, distracting myself from the twisting, scorching wires slicing away at my urethra every moment of every day, day upon day upon day.

"We can't just sit around here," Shawna finally said, after we'd been home a couple weeks. She had been worried about pushing me beyond a manageable point and there seemed to be no end to the pain I was feeling. "I love you, and I know you're in pain, but there's no way we can just sit here anymore. We're setting behind your recovery with every passing day."

We had to move forward, and I needed to focus my brain on something different. I would trade any new feeling or thought for this indefinable pain.

According to the geniuses at my insurance provider, apparently, all a person like me really needed or deserved was thirty hours of physical therapy and another thirty hours of occupational therapy—basic life skills training like tying shoes or making sandwiches, that I neither wanted nor needed. I wanted PT, lots of it, months of it. Years.

After a lot of negotiation with the insurance company, we managed to arrange to trade that OT for more PT.

But let's do the math on that, shall we?

Let's see, sixty hours of physical therapy. That's per year, by the way.

At inpatient rehab, I'd done four hours per day of therapy. So, okay, I was home, maybe we'd back off that a little bit. So let's say three hours of therapy per day, at five days a week.

We're already at fifteen hours in just one week.

Okay, let's back up a bit—what if we made it one hour per day, five days a week? That's five hours a week, twenty hours a month. So now I'm at three months a year of therapy.

See where I'm going with this? It was bullshit.

I should add here that even one hour of therapy was an all-day affair. Had I slept, which was rare in the first couple months home—months of enduring intense, acute pain—it was in what Shawna and I termed "the golden hour." Usually somewhere around 5 to 6 a.m., just before the light came, pink and new, into my window. But sleep never lasted, and then we were up, more frustrated and disheartened than the day before. There was bladder and bowel time, a sponge bath for me, a shower for Shawna, and hours had passed already. Then there was the brace, the move to the wheelchair, everything still new and unpredictable and taking two or three times as long as we knew it could be. There was the slide board into the Mini Cooper, the difficulty of exiting the Mini Cooper, the trek into the outpatient facility for therapy, and all for a one-hour session, during which I would barely have accomplished anything. This was not only because I was, at first, too bleary-eyed and blindsided by pain and sleep deprivation. It was also because by the time we talked to our therapist and the assistants, let them know how I was doing and worked to ensure that everyone else felt okay about how I was, we'd eaten up a quarter of our allotted time. So twice a week simply wasn't enough time.

Still, going through the motions and focusing on the goals that existed beyond the torture I was in made the days a touch more manageable. On days when we couldn't go to therapy, Shawna would take me through movements and visualizations daily in the hospital bed at home, and I did what I could there, anything to keep the momentum going.

The story of the pain, however, overrode anything else for the first two months after my arrival home. It was a big, burly pain that terrorized me night and day and crept into my psyche. The lack of sleep, of comfort, of progress, of relief, all of it is indescribable, and words fail to do it justice. Even recounting it now, I break into a cold sweat, gripped by the fear of it, and by the anger that followed it.

One night, after a month and a half of gnarly, angry pain, I unleashed a primitive roar, and squeezed the metal rails of my hospital bed, which now resided in our living room. My fingers, now resembling animal claws, twisted and bent the rails with superhuman force as my "AAAAHHH-HHRRRRR" thundered down the hall to Shawna, who was now tortured in her own way, being helpless as she was to comfort me and forced to sit by and witness my suffering.

Even when I gave in and took the odd pain medication, grasping for the mercy of a few minutes of sleep, minutes would be all I got. I'd lie there, night after night, wrestling with demons. Fourteen hours would pass without so much as a doze, and when I'd catch an odd hour, I'd hear Shawna, in the other room, visiting with a friend who had come to call, saying, "He's asleep. Let him sleep."

She still slept without sheets. Just catching fifteen minutes here and there, on the couch, on the chair. In the hospital, her presence and involvement had felt important, but now, we thought of it as divine intervention that she'd lived there with me. To have been new to my experience, unfamiliar with my vast amount of needs or my pain, would have been a kind of hell.

It was because she had become so intimately aware of my circumstance and of health care in general that she had made call after call since we had arrived home, looking for doctors who could explain away my pain, prescribe some miracle pill. She knew what I had taken and hadn't, what I'd done when. She brainstormed night and day, alone and with others, went online, read pill bottles, desperate to do anything useful in the way of ending this nightmare.

Dr. Abbott was convinced that my spinal injury and subsequent nerve damage was causing the pain—that it was simply a product of having a spinal cord injury and something I was going to have to get used to. She recommended a visit to a neural urologist in Walnut Creek, California.

As you would imagine, getting to Walnut Creek, a trip that would take us roughly four hours, seemed a feat of insurmountable proportions. The ten-minute trip to and from the hospital in the Mini Cooper, still the only car I could get into at that time, felt too long. But we were now at the whim of necessity, and with a referral from Dr. Abbott, we made the trip, pulling over nearly every hour when my pain and discomfort reached intolerable levels, so that Shawna could recline me as much as the tiny car would allow. And after an hour of that, we'd begin again.

Then, once we arrived, we were greeted with another obstacle. Being that I was from out of state, the front office insisted that I pay up front for the exam.

Through mounting anger and tears, I argued, "Look, Dr. Abbott from Reno set this up with you weeks ago. Everything's approved. Sort it out. You have NO idea what we went through to get here. *Sort. It. Out.*"

All of which made it that much more infuriating to be told, after a day's worth of tests, "Well, I just don't know why you're in so much pain. I don't see anything."

"What?" I said. "Can't we do more tests? Let's find the answer!"

"I know; I'm sorry. I know this is frustrating for you, but everything looks fine. There's not a single test that shows me anything."

"Man, do you have any idea what it took for us to get down here?" I asked him, all restraint gone by now. Shawna and I looked at each other in discouraged disbelief. *You're a neuro-urologist,* I thought to myself. *If you can't figure out why I'm in all this pain, who on earth can?*

He wheeled his stool to the counter and took out his prescription pad. With a note of disappointment and defeat in his voice, he said, "What kind of pain pills would you like?"

He didn't get it. No one got it. Maybe this was my life now. Maybe this was all there was for me. Pain that was met with disinterest and aloofness.

I shook my head. "No. No, I don't want any pain pills. Just tell me what's wrong with me. Please," came my pitiful plea.

"Grant, I'm sure I don't have to tell you that the nerve damage resulting from a spinal cord injury is enough to create unusual or unexplained pain symptoms." The doctor's tone implied his weariness. "Bladder infections are going to happen; they're going to be an issue. So are a lot of other weird things that no one can explain, like this pain, unfortunately."

"So you're telling me you don't know," I pressed him. "I just have to accept this?"

"Yes. I'm sorry. I don't know what this is."

We left the office like two people sentenced to prison. I was in the depths of despair, lower than I'd ever been, and constantly on the brink of mania. Unable anymore to cope with the difficulty and pain of the drive, we resigned ourselves to checking into a hotel. For two people without incomes, the $90-dollar hotel bill felt crippling, but with our exhaustion and depression, neither of us could see another alternative.

In the morning, the drive home, though long, was mostly silent. Each of us wrestled with doubt, fear, worry, and a dwindling array of options.

"We'll just see another urologist," Shawna said, breaking the silence. "And if that doesn't work, we'll see another one. We'll figure this out."

But urologist after urologist just told us the same thing: "I have no idea. You've had a spinal injury. What kind of pain medication would you like?"

Seriously? Was this the best modern medicine had to offer, even while a war raged inside me, an invisible war, just swords and razors and fire in my groin, raging unchecked forever until it killed me?

More than two months of unexplained, unmanageable pain became a mask, obscuring my vision of tomorrow or next month or next year. I would try anything, *anything*, go anywhere, if someone could just take my pain seriously. More than discouraged, I was unnerved. Why was I going through this? What was I supposed to gain from this experience? I felt as if I were being punished, forced to learn some painful lesson. I needed to be working out, going to therapy. But all there was before me was more of this, more lying in bed all day, sleepless, screaming in pain.

And then Shawna mentioned Dr. Diamond, the doctor and acupuncturist who specialized in integrated medicine who had been invaluable in helping Shawna's dad overcoming his near-fatal illness the decade prior. The doctor had passed away a year ago, but his daughter, Jane, a nurse practitioner, had spent years working with her father and continued to practice in Reno.

Although traditional Western medicine had done a fantastic job with the mechanics of fixing my broken spine, it was falling short in helping me address my bladder and urethra pain. It was time to take a different approach. I literally had nothing to lose.

Jane's enormous, warm, comforting smile upon inviting us into her office one day in June conveyed a depth of concern that filled me with hope.

"So, Grant, what's going on?" she asked, taking a seat and leaning forward, looking me in the eyes as I spoke about my pain.

"Hmm," she said, continuing to look at me after I'd finished speaking. "Okay, well, the first thing I'd like to do is run a few tests, and I want to see if acupuncture helps at all."

A battery of tests, as usual, revealed nothing, and acupuncture did little to alleviate my pain. "Right now, I don't see anything," she said, an answer I'd heard numerous times already. The only thing that kept me from completely melting down in frustration was when Jane uttered five magic words I'd yet to hear: "But we'll figure this out."

We scheduled another appointment so that Jane would have time to get some ideas together, and upon our arrival, none of them worked to reveal anything.

For nearly an hour we sat in Jane's office, brainstorming, throwing out every idea that popped into our addled brains, testing the ideas and uncovering nothing, but having nowhere else to go.

And then Shawna said, "I wonder if he's allergic to latex?"

We doubted it. I'd spent years in the Stanford lab wearing latex gloves for hours at a time without a single symptom. But with no other ideas on the table, Jane said, "Well… allergies can build up over time. Why don't I just run a test, to check?"

And within minutes, sure as shit, the test indeed showed that I am ridiculously allergic to latex. And since being kicked out of the hospital more than two months prior, I had been putting seventeen inches of latex up my urethra nine times a day. The catheters I had used during my stay in the hospital were made of vinyl. All those experts, all that fucking pain and the tests and the traveling, and it's my wife who figures out I'm allergic to latex.

Without open mucous membranes, my hands weren't aggravated by latex, but the repeated exposure had built an allergy that manifested once I put latex into an open membrane, my urethra.

I had always been a man who doubted allergies, didn't believe in them, had never experienced them enough to understand them. But in my vulnerable condition, shattered and atrophied down to a slight 139 pounds, the force of the allergy was enough to pound me into submission.

Shawna called Dr. Pasternak from the car to explain what we'd learned. He phoned a prescription for vinyl catheters to the pharmacy, and by the end of the day and after just two catheterizations, the pain had already begun to subside. Within seven hours, I was pain-free. And I slept the blissful sleep of the vindicated.

In the weeks that followed, I fought every instinct of anger and retribution, choosing instead to focus on the remarkable energy and love and light that came from simply *not having pain*.

On occasion, friends and family constantly encouraged me to take legal action, one going so far as to contact an attorney friend, who strongly believed I had a valid case. Between the bed and the allergy... most people would sue, we knew that.

But as we'd seen in the last few months, the system was already broken, and another lawsuit wouldn't fix it. And it wouldn't fix me, either. All I wanted to do at this point was embark on the recovery I'd set out to do all those weeks ago, to shake off the last two months like a nightmare. I'd been mired in the misery that comes from hopelessness and anger, and it had set me back. Every time I told the story, every time I thought about the pain and despair of those months, I felt twisted in knots all over again, weakened from the memory. Could I really see living through that over and over again?

And if my intention was to make some good out of my situation, to remain positive, to uphold all the things that had come to mean so much to me, how could I preach that good word every day to everyone I met and still be dwelling on *that*? That would be a bad life, a miserable one.

And here was the other thing: It felt hypocritical. I had been a professional-level athlete with years of training and experience, and I had overshot a jump by *two feet* to break my back. Wasn't it possible that, despite the nine things any doctor might have done right to contribute to my recovery, he or she could make a mistake, an honest-to-God mistake, on the tenth one?

Here before me was another choice, a fork in the road in which I needed to decide the kind of path I wanted to take for my recovery. A lawsuit was legitimate. But it would have prolonged the negativity. I had no interest in benefitting financially from other people's mistakes, or staying rooted in the past. That day during my first week in inpatient, staring out the window at those helicopters, I'd realized the need to stop looking backward and focus on what was to come.

So Shawna and I actively chose light instead of darkness. From here on out, we'd only be focusing on the positive, on the things that were working. There had been enough of being stuck. Now it was time to move forward.

The Wedding Waltz
(Photo by Matt Theilen)

CHAPTER 13
THE DANCE

My first dance with Shawna, as her husband, was a waltz. It was the perfect choice, the only choice for us, and sort of symbolic of our relationship. The waltz is incredibly sensual and intimate, yet formal and traditional. It's physically challenging and unreservedly romantic. The couple, locked in an unbreakable embrace, remains in step with each other, each person retaining complete mastery over his or her own feet while remaining wholly in tune with the other's, never stepping outside the box that the two create for themselves. It's challenging and takes time and hard work to achieve; the symmetry and poetry of it must be earned. It is a beautiful combination of the mind, body, and spirit, the embodiment of perfection in motion, when done right.

It would be right for us. Like everything else about our relationship—and, quite frankly, everything else in my life—settling for "good enough" simply wasn't going to happen. We worked on the waltz for months, taking lessons at a local dance school.

Actually, every aspect of preparing for our wedding was approached with this same vigorous intent. It started almost immediately after we got engaged and set about looking for a wedding location. Instantly, we knew we wanted to get married outside, in fall, at the Ahwahnee Hotel at Yosemite, a now-sacred spot for us. We wanted a weekend of romance, what we called "a love retreat," where we would bask in our wedding glow and share that glow with those closest to us.

The problem was, in order to afford to get married at the Ahwahnee on a weekend in fall, even the small wedding we wanted, we'd have needed to rob a bank. When we got the hotel's estimate, we were heartbroken.

So we went back to the drawing board, looked at every option under the sun that we could see as a possible location for this love retreat. We quickly realized that if we had a wedding in Reno or even at Lake Tahoe, there would be no way we could keep this wedding small. With at least thirty family members alone, the guest count could reach into the hundreds in no time. Our best option for engineering it as a small, intimate, budget-friendly event was a destination wedding.

We found a lodge in Canada that looked promising, and we set our sights on that—until the difficulty of working with the proprietors made us question the wisdom of this choice. "It just shouldn't be this hard," I told Shawna.

Next, we formulated a plan for a beach wedding in Costa Rica. It actually would have been affordable, the guest list would have been small, and we knew it would be spectacular.

But these plans didn't feel like *us*. Though we went about the motions of making those plans come true, we knew it would feel awkward, like forcing our images into someone else's picture.

One evening, Shawna and I went to my parents' house for dinner and to discuss wedding plans.

"Okay, when's the wedding? Where are we doing this thing?" asked my dad expectantly.

"Well, we're not sure," I stammered, looking at Shawna. "I mean, we're thinking about Costa Rica, but we're still working on that. Just trying to find a destination that we can afford, and there are some things we want. Things aren't really solid for us yet, we're still looking at some options…"

"Okay, look," interrupted my dad, shaking his head and waving his hands to cut me off. "Pretend I just gave you a million dollars. Now, where would you get married? What would you do?"

Shawna and I exchanged glances, and both of us chuckled wryly. "That's easy," I said. "We want to get married at the Ahwahnee in Yosemite. We looked into that and it's just way too pricey, Dad. But if we had a million dollars, that's what we'd do."

"Okay, great," my dad said, clapping his hands with finality. "So, you're getting married at the Ahwahnee. Now, I'll take back my million dollars," he said, pulling his invisible money from my hands and placing it in his pocket. "All you have to do is figure out how to make it happen."

Of course, it was really that simple. If that was really what we wanted, why would we settle for anything less? It was our *wedding day*.

The next day, Shawna gave the Ahwahnee another call, just to see what she could work out. And as it turns out, while getting married there on a weekend costs an obscene amount of money, doing it on a Thursday wasn't obscene at all—it was right in our budget, actually. Not only that but we'd have the place to ourselves, so it could be as intimate as we hoped it would be. Once we'd stopped analyzing and worrying about money, about pleasing other people, and focused on what we wanted, the solution came. The simplest answer was the right one. As an engineer, I found a certain kind of poetry in this.

And after the wedding, when we stepped out on the rustic dance floor that October evening to do our waltz by the firelight, under the glow of dozens of candles, there was poetry in that, too.

Since my injury, I'd thought a lot about that waltz, fixated on it as a touchstone in my recovery. There were many things I knew I wanted to do when I had moved past my injury—kayaking, climbing Half Dome, hopping on a mountain bike, skiing, running a marathon. A lot of people, friends and family and nurses, spoke of these things as if they were my ultimate goal, and of course they were all goals I intended to reach. But I knew that the real marker, the true milestone I would need to reach before I knew I was fully recovered, would be to once again dance a waltz with my wife. That would be me, 100 percent, with all the elegance and grace and physical prowess it would take to sweep my wife into my unbreakable embrace and glide her across the dance floor.

Sometimes, in an effort to show me love, support, or understanding, people would say things like, "You're still the man she married." And rationally I knew that was true. I *am* still that same man who proposed on a mountaintop, who waltzed with her on the dance floor so gracefully. In my heart and soul, it was still me. But then again, it wasn't, and I wasn't okay with that. Nothing in our history as a couple, nothing since the day we met, would *ever* indicate that I was okay with giving even 2 percent less than the authentic, optimal me. Every one of my actions, from my selection of a rare, custom-designed ring that took months to receive to my ridiculously complex proposal, was the best I could give. So it wasn't okay that I couldn't do the things I used to do with her. We couldn't go jogging or biking together. I couldn't carry her on my back. We couldn't climb a mountain, take our honeymoon, run on a beach, or go dancing.

But it was the loss of a million tiny things that made me ache. I remembered when I was recovering from breaking my face, the angst I felt over two years of taking my meals through a straw, the regret of having taken chewing for granted. And now, I couldn't make Shawna a cup of coffee. I couldn't cook her pancakes, or carry my plate to the sink. I couldn't spoon her in bed at night or pinch her playfully with my cold toes. I couldn't walk by her side and hold her hand.

I knew that it was only a matter of time before she got that husband back, before I was complete. And I knew also that in her mind, I was complete already. But in my mind, I had quite a ways to go.

One day in spring, while I was still suffering from my latex allergy, as I lay in my hospital bed in the middle of the living room, the picture of misery, there was a knock at the door. Shawna opened it to find two unshaven guys in jeans and T-shirts standing on our doorstep.

The taller one, who introduced himself as Adam Baillargeon, was thin, with a long face and crooked, shy smile. The man with him was Roy Tuscany; he was shorter and quite muscular.

"I'm a friend of Steven Siig," said Roy to Shawna as she held back an over-excited Obie by the collar. "We're with the High Fives Foundation. We wanted to meet Grant."

Steven Siig, our Alpine Assassins film director and a longtime action-sports cinematographer, had long been a friend of mine and Duncan's; he had actually officiated Duncan's wedding. Friends of Steven's would be friends of mine. We immediately welcomed them into our house. They both gave Obie hearty pats on their way in.

I first began to hear of the High Fives Foundation months ago from Duncan, while lying in bed at inpatient rehab. Founded by Roy Tuscany, who had suffered a burst fracture of his T12 vertebra five years prior, and supported by Adam Baillargeon, a survivor of a rare form of cancer, the nonprofit organization helps professional athletes who have suffered life-altering injuries as they pursue their dreams in winter sports.

And now, Roy, a superstar in my opinion, was walking—*walking*—un-assisted into my house. Although he had a slight limp, he was the living, breathing example, the first one I'd seen since my injury, of what was possible for someone like me.

The two entered the house, and I called a feeble, "Right on! Hey guys, what's up?" with an exhausted smile on my face.

"Hey man," Roy said and shook my hand. Adam stood just behind him and reached around Roy to shake my hand while Roy looked around him for a place to sit. Spotting my wheelchair positioned just feet away against the wall, he said, "Hey, mind if I sit in your wheelchair? You're not gonna need it much longer, anyway."

I laughed, relieved and overjoyed to meet people who got it, who could talk to me confidently in terms of recovery, which so many others were hesitant to do.

For the next several hours, Roy shared his story with me—how he had broken his back skiing in 2006, how he had been told by doctors that he would never walk again, and how he believed with his whole heart that hard work and positivity, his own and that of those around him, were the keys to getting back on the slopes two years later.

I threw a barrage of questions at him, realizing that I had an incredible opportunity here to see a glimpse of what could be my future. I asked questions that doctors wouldn't touch: When am I going to feel my feet? When can I take a piss by myself again? When will I start to have bowel movements? When am I going to walk? Because he could do all these things.

Shawna and I told Roy of our experiences, how we had been going it alone, believing that, regardless of what anybody else said, I would recover. What a relief to find someone else who could share that with us. "But we've had nothing to back that up," I opened up to him. "We've never seen anybody with our own eyes that had recovered and could walk, so it's awesome to see you here, thank you so much."

"You guys are on the right track," he said. "Just stay with it. Don't let anybody convince you otherwise."

Sometime during our second month home, I noticed some internal sensation changing in the tips of my toes. Similar to frostbitten extremities, the feeling was tingling and burning tinged with numbness.

But I was feeling something. FEELING! Though still dealing with the ridiculous pain of the latex allergy, I now had reason to celebrate.

But within days, the feeling shifted from frostbite to red ants. Thousands of red ants, starting at my toes and gradually, week by week, swarming over my feet, up into my ankles, chewing and chewing on my skin, fire and pain. The desire to shake my feet and get them off was overpowering, yet sensation wasn't movement—I could do nothing about it. The ants were nesting on my feet, feasting for hours and hours. Within two months, the ants had pulled out razor blades, and were sliding the blades under my toenails, slowly, cruelly, all day.

It was a signpost in my new reality: Want to feel your feet? This is what you get to feel. Welcome.

Here I was feeling barbed wire twisting in my urethra, ants and razors on my feet. But could I feel my wife's hands rubbing my feet? Could I sense when I needed to pee without being told it was time to? No. Just like my dream in which only a few of the wires had been connected, my pain receptors were receiving signals, but other sensations were conspicuously absent.

It was a lesson in getting what you ask for, but also in gratitude. I was learning to be thankful for having pain in my feet. The therapists were pleased that I had pain, and I was learning to be pleased about it, too, though it was a hard lesson. I had to consciously remind myself that this was a good thing, and that if I could feel pain now, it meant that at some point in the future I would feel pleasure, too. Still, when I was awake and alone at night, watching the shadows on the ceiling, the fear that pain was all I'd feel for the rest of my life would creep into my mind, and I had to practice shooing those fears away.

The equipment implanted into my spine was working. On a cool day in early June, soon after my latex pain had subsided, we went back to see the surgeon in his office—for the first and only time since leaving the hospital in April—for an X-ray and, hopefully, my release from the turtle shell.

Surgeon Smirk had an assistant X-ray me and then performed a perfunctory exam. "Okay, you're good to go. Everything looks great, so you're done with the brace."

"Really?" I said, thrilled to be rid of the torture device I'd come to loathe the sight of, yet a little afraid to sit without it.

"Yep," he said, pulling together my file with, of course, a smirk. "The spine's all set. You're ready."

"Cool," I said, ready to embrace the next challenge and convincing myself that my back was, too. Then, before he could escape from the room, I said, "Hey, I wanted to ask you…"

Surgeon Smirk grabbed the metal, wheeling stool and took a seat.

"So, I wanted to tell you, I've been having some pain in my feet. I was wondering about when you thought I might have some feeling in my feet…" I began.

The surgeon leaned over, as if to confide a secret. With a smirk, he said, "You will never again feel your feet." Just like that. Firm and final.

"Okay, well," I began, taken aback by his frankness, "I respectfully disagree. I will feel my feet again."

The surgeon stood up, retrieved the file he had laid on the counter, put his hand on my shoulder, and said, "I'm glad you do."

So maybe he thought I was in denial and was being patronizing. Hell, some of the nurses had been that way, too. It was a tune we'd heard played

Grant and Shawna on their new journey together
(Photo by Duncan Lee)

many times. But what his voice also said, at least what I heard, was this: "I can't tell you you're going to feel your feet. I've seen your spine. I know what it looks like in there, and it's probably not going to happen. But if you think you will, then right on, kid, prove me wrong. Go get 'em."

〇

That same week, the call came to announce the arrival of my wheelchair. My own wheelchair, for which the insurance company had no problem dropping $7,000, despite their unfathomable reluctance to cover additional rehab, acupuncture, physical therapy or other treatments that might, in the end, help me to forego the chair.

MY chair. MINE, meant to stay in my life forever.

There had been a lot of progress since I'd come home. Sure, there had been the crippling allergy pain, but there had been painful feelings in my feet, losing the turtle shell brace, and making good progress on the parallel bars in my outpatient therapy sessions. The wheelchair had, at first, been simply a matter of course to me, and remained so until we pulled into the parking lot of the medical supply company and saw Ron standing on the curb next to my chair. My heart suddenly sank with the intense weight of the chair's significance.

Grant in the wheelchair
(Photo by Duncan Lee)

Outwardly, I kept it together. Shawna pulled the loaner chair out of the car and I graciously accepted the new chair with my thanks.

"What do you think, man?" Ron asked tentatively, after having seen me fall apart in the minivan the last time we'd met.

Here again, the wheelchair was messing with my head. The sense of permanence that a $7,000 piece of equipment I'd ordered and received presented to me was overwhelming. Each chair I'd used up to now was a loaner, completely temporary. My mind grasped for Shawna's long ago words, "Just like crutches, we'll pass it on to someone else when we're done with it."

Forcing the tears back, I took Ron's hand, determined to show him that I was growing stronger and appreciated all he had done for us. "Thank you so much, truly, I really appreciate it," I said, shaking and shaking his hand. And in my head, a little voice said, *Do NOT get comfortable in this chair.*

We folded it up, put it in the trunk, and pulled out of the parking lot, and I finally felt comfortable enough to let the tears flow.

My darling wife had gone without sleep for months. She had curled uncomfortably in a tiny chair and listened to me scream in pain. She had put a catheter into my penis nine times a day, inserted fingers into my ass, dried my tears, and cleaned up after me. All of it she'd done without a shudder, a tear, or even a moment's hesitation. So the universe decided to see what else she could handle.

In early July, after I'd been brace-free for a couple of weeks and was moving my torso with greater ease every day, I decided to give our bed a try again, and found that I could actually get comfortable in it. We were officially done with the hospital bed. The medical supply company sent a van to pick it up, and we watched, somewhat emotionally, as the bed that had been such a vital part of my recovery here at home was driven slowly down the street.

Three days later, I awakened to sunlight streaming into our bedroom window and across our bedspread. Shawna was curled against me, awake but with her eyes closed, savoring the last few moments before our day of rolling, catheterizing, and working out began. I had long since passed the thirty-minute window of time in which the mountain of pillows propped under me could keep me comfortable, and I was restless and anxious to be moved, as well as too warm under the covers on this sunny summer morning. But we snuggled a few minutes more, and I relished the first relatively normal morning I could remember having.

"Okay, we gotta get up," said Shawna, kissing me on the cheek and sitting up promptly to wake herself up. "I'm gonna go make some coffee, and then I'll be back."

She hopped up, threw on a pair of cut-off sweatpants she'd discarded on the floor the night before (and which I found sexy), and walked around the foot of the bed toward the door.

I threw off the covers to cool down, and saw there, on my foot, this… thing.

"What the fuck is that?" I said, firmly, calmly. I squinted, trying with all my might to sit up, even a couple inches, and get a closer look at the black spot on my foot. Was it a scab, a skin lesion, another bizarre side effect of my spinal cord injury?

Then it moved. My voice escalated. *"WHAT THE FUCK IS THAT?"*

Shawna, who hadn't heard me the first time and had made it to the kitchen, heard my shout and came bounding back into the room. My eyes, wide as saucers, stared at the thing I was pointing to.

Shawna leaned down, squinting to take a good look at it, and got within inches of the fuzzy black spot that appeared to be as wide as a silver dollar. Then it moved again.

"AAAAAHHH!" came Shawna's spine-chilling scream as she jumped, then darted back and banged clumsily against the door frame.

"That is a *huge fucking spider*," she said, panting and deadly serious.

Indeed, a giant, furry, black wolf spider was enjoying a relaxing morning on the instep of my foot.

With all we had faced together, we were now in an interesting situation. Shawna, terrified beyond all reason of any spider, had always been the one up on the table, pointing and screeching, "There's a spider over there! Get it, get it!" until I picked it up and walked it outside to release it on the front step. And now, there wasn't a thing I could do about it.

The spider then rotated his body, like a machine gun, *ch-ch-ch-chuh,* so that his bizarre, furry face—it had a *face*—full of eyes looked at me square in mine. I swear, that spider squared up to me and puffed up, as if to say, "Whatcha got? Bring it." It was doing pushups on my foot. The slightest movement, we knew, would have provoked it to jump.

I knew wolf spiders were venomous, but usually harmless unless provoked. And who knew if it had been there all night. I was concerned about my foot, but mostly I was concerned about my wife, who was a shivering, horrified, white-faced puddle of fear huddled, panting, against the wall.

I had regained quite a bit of strength in my torso of late and was propped on a good four pillows. But still, I doubted if I could do enough of a crunch to reach down and grab the spider, and I knew that the slightest misstep could force it under the bed, where it would hide for who knew how long. And Shawna, likely, would never come to bed again. The stakes were high.

I looked over at her, and watched the internal argument she was having with herself play out on her face. She closed her eyes, gradually stood up to her full height, took a deep breath, and exhaled.

"I'll be right back," she said.

She walked into the master bathroom, pulled out a long strand of toilet paper, and balled it up in her hand. She strode back into the room, deter-

mined and focused, though her shaking hands and white knuckles gave
her away.

"I can do this," she muttered under her breath.

"Shawna, look at yourself," I said, trying not to laugh. "Here, give it to
me. I got this, just help me up."

That was all it took. She gratefully handed the toilet paper to me, and
rushed to help me up gently so as not to disturb the spider's position.

"Okay, mother fucker, I got you." I leaned down, slowly, cautiously,
reached out to grab it, and missed by a long shot, my back still far too delicate for a reach of that size. The spider darted down the side of my foot, off
the side of the bed, bounced to the floor, and ran at lightning speed toward
my armoire.

"Uuuggh," I said, falling back on my pillows, frustrated.

Shawna snapped into action. She snatched the paper out of my hand,
jumped over the bed, grabbed the spider before it could reach a good hiding place, looked at it to be sure it was in the paper, and squeezed, popping
it. "A-ha!" she exclaimed proudly. "Fuck you, spider!"

And she marched triumphantly to the toilet, tossed it in and flushed.
From the bathroom I heard a shrieking, "OOooooeeeewww!" She ran out
of the bathroom, dancing as if to shake it off her body, and ran out of the
room, back to the kitchen, calling, "Eww eww eww eww..." all the way
down the hall.

Shawna's alter ego, "Salt," training Grant back on his feet
(Photo by Liz Margerum)

CHAPTER 14
SALT

One of my favorite movies is *American Beauty*. It's a painful, beautifully told story, but probably my favorite part of the whole movie is the closing monologue:

I guess I could be pretty pissed off about what happened to me, but it's hard to stay mad, when there's so much beauty in the world. Sometimes I feel like I'm seeing it all at once, and it's too much, my heart fills up like a balloon that's about to burst ... And then I remember to relax, and stop trying to hold on to it, and then it flows through me like rain and I can't feel anything but gratitude for every single moment of my stupid little life. You have no idea what I'm talking about, I'm sure. But don't worry ... you will someday.

I had lately been thinking about this monologue, and how it could have been written about me. Without the blinders of work to fill my time and thoughts, without the constant *go-go-go* that my brain and body used to live by, I was beginning to see, for the first time, the importance of truly being present. I had always been focused on moving forward: "gotta pack, gotta work, gotta finish this project, once all that's done I can think about that great 'be present' stuff you're talking about, but *not right now.*"

Now, I finally had nothing but time, vast expanses of time to sit and think. I had time to really *see* things, to look closely at them. And I realized like never before that there was beauty all around me, in the actions and words of friends, in the simple grace of my wife, and of the magic that exists in the body to heal itself, to move and create. I knew that never again would I take any of it for granted.

Emotions, even painful ones like anger and loss, were beautiful, too, and served my soul in some way. Shawna told me once, "Let it flow, don't bottle it up. If you keep it inside, it morphs and will build up illness inside you." I'd seen people in whom this had been the case—negative, grouchy people that seemed unable to find joy in anything, who always seemed to be sick and were always enduring some terrible drama, and who resented the whole world for the shitty lot in life they'd been given.

I was beginning to realize that if I let myself feel whatever I was feeling, I didn't have to be one of those negative people. If I honored my feelings instead, and let them flow through me unheeded, I could then really look at them, like a passive observer, not weighed down by their heavy burden. And I could examine how emotions served me, allowed me to move forward. If I needed to scream, rage, or cry, I did it without restraint. And each time, I could see a little balloon of negative energy floating out of me. I concentrated on visualizing it, watching it carry away all the pain and destruction in my body, leaving behind spaces for health and happiness to fill me up. I gave myself permission to cry tears, lots of them, anytime the mood struck. I embraced the tears that sprang to my eyes nearly daily, sometimes because I was overcome by the sheer beauty that life revealed to me, even through all the pain.

And when I was sad, I let that flow through me too, knowing that every emotion had a purpose, and it was to serve me for a short while, manifest, and pass through me. It was all there for a reason, and none of it was good or bad. It just *was.*

I became a vessel. I became fully present, because I had no choice but to be. I had wide-open spaces before me, time to be fully conscious of all that surrounded me. The blinds were lifted, and rather than seeing how

Birthday crew on Lake Tahoe (Photo by Jamie Schmidt)

bad off I was, I saw the opposite. All around me now was beauty, loads of it, remarkable beauty that at times became overpowering. And rather than trying to selfishly grab onto it and hoard it, while stuffing back the negative thoughts that popped into my head and suppressing the emotions that followed them, I let it all go, seeing the here and now as it all just flowed through me like water. My burden grew lighter as a result.

There were *so* many astonishingly beautiful things to see. Though I was no longer in the hospital, the acts of kindness, big and small, continued to fill me with awe. There were little gestures from people who volunteered to make phone calls or provide much-needed hugs. There were people who showed up with bags of groceries or gift cards. And there were extraordinary gestures, like Steven assisting me with a workout or taking Obie for a walk, or Becca coming to our house every week to work with me on her own time.

Another such event was my thirty-third birthday, roughly four months after my injury, on June 27. Having grown up in Incline Village, I liked celebrating my summer birthday on a boat more than just about anything else. From all-night boat parties spent visiting Tahoe's various waterfront libation-selling establishments in my twenties to sunrise floating dance parties in the middle of the lake in my early thirties, celebrating life by boat on Tahoe is something I have always cherished.

*Grant's birthday, aboard Lake Tahoe's Sierra
Cloud (Photo by Matt Theilen)*

Knowing this and knowing our friend and past neighbor was the captain of the Incline-based sailboat, *Sierra Cloud*, Shawna had worked her
magic with the help of Captain Pearlman and friends to plan a thirty-third
birthday party on Tahoe that I would never forget. It not only enabled me
and my wheelchair to be on the water with my friends, but I could do
so with all costs being waived, allowing our friends the chance to donate
their individual admission price to my recovery. This birthday gift gave me
more than much-needed financial assistance; it filled me with unconditional love.

There I was, just months after my injury, sitting in a wheelchair on the
deck of a fifty-five-foot catamaran sailboat on a gorgeous Tahoe day, once
again celebrating life on the very water I grew up in, surrounded by friends
and family, all blowing me over with the gift of friendship, the gift of experience, and the gift of beautifully unexpected humanity.

Then there was Sam Solomon, who made me a set of parallel bars.

Sam had been of great comfort to Shawna since that day in ICU when
I'd had surgery, and he had come to the hospital to offer his help to us in
any way we needed. Often, though, the only thing we needed was space to
sort out our situation, and he gave us that, too. In our last week at inpatient,
Sam had come to visit me and caught me at the tail end of a therapy session, working feverishly on the parallel bars.

Grant's first post-injury birthday, with
Adam Freeman (Photo by Jamie Cooper)

"When you get home, what are you guys going to need?" he asked Shawna.

She had already gotten a glimpse of what we'd be missing once we left for home. It would be nearly impossible to accomplish what we planned if we were struggling to fit therapy into a one-hour-a-week allotment. "Honestly?" she said, sort of joking. "More therapy. More of this. Parallel bars."

She may not have been serious, but Sam, a gearhead like me, took it seriously. He had seen enough of my therapy to know that parallel bars were the key to getting me walking. After I finished my therapy, he lingered behind to take measurements.

A week after my inauspicious return home from the hospital, while I was still was grappling with the unyielding pain of my latex allergy, Sam came knocking at our front door.

"Hey, I just wanted to show you guys something," he told Shawna when she answered the door, and beckoned for her to follow him around to the front.

Thinking he was about to point out a problem with our house, Shawna stepped outside to follow him. He walked her to the garage, pushed the code to open the door, and revealed a hand-welded, therapy-grade set of parallel bars on a wooden platform that had been adjusted based on my height. He and the mechanics at his snow-removal company in Truckee, California, had generously donated time and resources to making the bars that would be vital to me reaching my goals.

"Okay," he said, clapping his hands and rubbing them together. "Get to work!"

Though it wasn't nearly enough, the one-hour physical therapy appointment I had each week was useful to me, and we were thrilled to find that our outpatient therapist, Jen, hailed from the Becca School of Positive Thinking and Open-mindedness, and she embraced some out-of-the-box thinking when it came to letting me try new things to expand my repertoire of activities.

But the four hours of logistics involved in getting me to that one-hour appointment each week were clearly an ineffective use of my precious energy. In inpatient, we'd had three hours of therapy every day, plus the work we did on our own in my room. Sixty hours a year was ridiculous; it would take six hours a day to get what we knew I truly needed. And we needed to kick-start this recovery in a big way. So Shawna developed her own home therapy plan for me that would complement my "official" therapy. We were working out three or four hours a day, and sometimes more.

At first, there was a lot of mat work—exercises I could do lying down, in order to create nerve associations. Shawna would say, "Your nerves will remember, as long as we keep reminding them." Nerves grow each day, but we needed to tell them what to do as they grew. If we didn't tell them, "Hey, go to my big toe—that's your job," they might not be sure. They might go elsewhere, to someplace else where there are electrical impulses—someplace where I wasn't paralyzed. But if we stimulated the nerves, we'd be stimulating muscles. And stimulated muscles were stronger muscles, which provided movement and sensation.

Shawna would say, "Now, concentrate on your quads." And I would. I'd fixate on them, envision them flexing and contracting, enabling me to stand up and jump. She would take my foot in her hands, pull it up and rest it flat against her chest, and gently push toward me, forcing my knee to

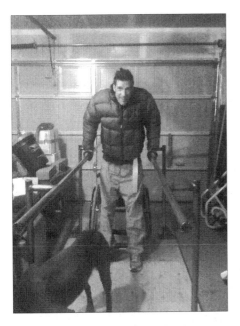

Pushing his limits on the parallel bars made by Sam Soloman (Photo by Shawna Korgan)

bend and the quadriceps to stretch. She'd rotate my legs, stretching my hip flexors, and she'd stretch out my legs, flexing my hamstrings. If I thought about my toes, she'd flex them and point them as I created the mental association, imagined doing it on my own. The goal was to keep my mind as connected to my body as possible: "My toes are pointing up now," I'd say, as she did precisely that. Sometimes she did it while I slept; she rubbed my feet, pointed my toes, massaged my legs.

During my early inpatient sessions, Shawna was tireless with me. I wanted my recovery more than anything, but Shawna, if it was possible, wanted it more. If Becca said, "Let's do two sets of ten," Shawna popped over her shoulder to say, "Three sets." And at the end of the day, completely worked and begging for mercy as I fell into bed, Shawna would say, "Let's do two more sets of that."

Because we both believe that nutrition plays a vital role in health and healing, it was crucial that everything I put into my body aided in my recovery. My diet was under strict control from the very beginning. Shawna, while chatting with the extremely helpful and supportive director of the inpatient facility, requested a refrigerator for our room, because as soon as I was eating real food again, we realized how inadequate the hospital food was. It was at times tough to swallow, actually, although their enchiladas were inexplicably delicious and were the one treat I allowed myself.

Every day, Shawna used our Magic Bullet blender to whip up miracle shakes made of protein powder, milk enhanced with Omega-3, and fresh produce. Breakfast consisted of a shake or cottage cheese with fruit. Supplements changed, large concentrations of B and D vitamins were added and amounts were always recalibrated, fish oils became a frequently featured addition, and gluten was now avoided as much as possible. Shawna consulted a nutritionist friend, holistic healers, people who worked out a lot, my acupuncturist... whoever could provide insight into what it took to create an optimal healing environment. No recommendation was off the table.

Meanwhile, as the weeks gave way to months at home, my therapy, both at outpatient and at home, got more aggressive. There were parallel bar sessions, with help from Becca (who stopped in at least once a week for my first few months home) or another friend or family member; it took two to lift me off the chair, and while one assisted my upper body to do the bulk of the work, the other person made walking motions with my legs and feet. And always, the tunes Jason Mead had put on my iPod cranked in my ears, throbbing my favorite electronic beats, which could get my heart rate up and have my whole body humming with energy.

One day in late June, just before my thirty-third birthday, I moved my own leg. I had been working for weeks, expending truckloads of concentration on lifting my leg a few inches off the bed to meet Shawna's hands for leg lifts, to push back on her hands when she pushed against my feet. And on this day, I pushed back.

"Oh my God," she said, stopping. "Did you do that?"

"I think I did," I said, breathless and panting from exhaustion.

"Do it again. Can you do it again?" Shawna said, nearly jumping out of her skin with excitement.

I channeled the force of the universe, summoned every nerve and fiber in my body into duty and every ounce of my will, and I pushed back on Shawna, with what I imagined to be the force of a stream train. I moved my leg against her so that her body, leaning into mine, was pushed erect.

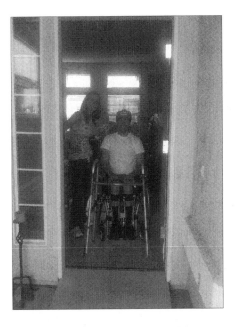

*Becca Deal doing gratis
therapy in her free time
(Photo by Shawna Korgan)*

We celebrated for hours that night. The next day, therapy kicked up a couple notches. Within days, I was lifting my legs a few inches without help, shuffling a few inches on my own on the parallel bars.

During workouts, there were no warm fuzzies from Shawna. No more of the sweet, gentle woman my friends and I called "The Naa." It was client and trainer now. This Shawna wanted some fucking results. This Shawna had no sympathy for her poor husband. This Shawna was a Viking woman, a hard, cold, demanding vixen bent on ultimate domination. There was no asking, "Oh, sweet wife, why would you ask me to do another set of this awful, painful exercise?" There were only her shouts of "More! Give me more! Do it again! Do it harder!" and my inevitable acquiescence.

Somewhere along the way, Shawna had developed this ability to switch from the Naa to this unforgiving, hard-edged Angelina Jolie-type figure, taking down anyone who stood up to her or got in her way. This Shawna wasn't my wife; she was secret agent Salt.

Salt had a look in her eye, a defiance and a hardness. She didn't pity. She didn't compromise. She could take someone down with a ruthless look. And she was gonna get my ass moving again.

Salt was a force that the universe had conspired for years to bring to me.

I know a lot of people say things like, "We were meant to be together." But Shawna had originally gone to school as a business major and had nearly earned her degree in business. Despite repeatedly teaching aerobics classes and being intrigued by the fitness industry, she had no interest in changing educational paths until she got to talking with one of the trainers heading up a leadership training program she had enrolled in. The trainer was a fitness manager at a local health club, and the conversation, which centered around opportunities in the fitness industry, had Shawna completely rethinking her path. She began working part-time as a trainer at a local gym while continuing to study business, growing more and more interested in a fitness career. Just before finishing her business degree, she jumped ship, enrolling in a health ecology program, where her studies emphasized fitness physiology. Her studies encompassed everything from anatomy and physiology to ethics and health, fitness management, chemistry, and sports psychology.

As a personal trainer, she began taking on clients ranging from the injured to professional athletes and everything in between, and always with an eye toward eventually starting a business that focused on total wellness, a place that emphasized holistic health, bringing the body into balance with the mind and spirit. That business became The Sanctuary, a center built on the philosophy of the *Seven Dimensions of Health*, based on the idea that when balance is achieved in all seven dimensions (physical, mental, social, occupational, environmental, emotional, and spiritual), optimal health and well-being are achieved.

So now tell me that Salt and I weren't made for each other.

One night after I'd first arrived home from the hospital, I was lying in bed, coping with the excruciating pain and a lack of sleep. I heard Obie's nails clicking as he walked across the hardwood floor, into our room, and across the linoleum to the bed. I stared at the ceiling until I heard a strange sound, the sound of spittle and licking. I looked down and saw Obie licking my foot. Licking and licking, as if he could somehow lick life into my feet.

The dog had never been a licker, not really. Not like this. This wasn't excited licking, the kind that comes with a jump into your arms and a wagging tail. This was slow, methodical, reverent licking. As the weeks wore on, the licking continued, for long minutes at a time, on my feet and knees and legs. When I began to experience sensations in my feet, the pain of fire ants chewing on my feet, somehow Obie knew, and he never licked my feet again. He licked until I didn't need it anymore.

So now I had two therapists living with me.

PART THREE
CHOOSE POSITIVITY

Kayaking Dead Bear Falls (Photo by Jamie Cooper)

I LIVE

Water in the face, I need to splash more water in the face.
I passed my test—a bit of a ritual, actually. When scouting a stout rapid or waterfall, a kayaker keeps an open mind until the decision to boat the drop, or begin the often-technical climb around it, has been made. But once my mind is made up to go, there is no turning back, except for my ritual: three attempts to get the Kevlar-wrapped spray skirt popped onto the kayak cockpit rim.

It happens where my head is so focused on the task at hand, my hand slips on the semi-physical task of connecting myself to the boat. My ritual is simple—if I get my skirt connected to the rim within the first three attempts, I rally, but if I miss on the third go, I walk the rapid. I have yet to walk a rapid on this technicality, and today is no different.

Water. I am floating in a calm micro eddy only feet from the entrance of the monster I plan to party with just downstream. I am splashing myself in the face to focus, to reduce the shock of the first impact, to get the contacts in my eyes ready for the war they are about to witness.

Time after time it seems to be the same. When the game is on and the stakes are high, my mind and body prepare without my consent to definitively slip into flow state. This is the magic of whitewater kayaking. I see energy. I am above the drop, on the rocks. The skirt is on, and I slide into the water. I am in the calm and stillness of that eddy, the breath before the storm.

My energy is scattered—I see it everywhere, and I rehearse, visualize my entire run from the bottom to the top and then from the top to the bottom. I am aware of my plan B lines, and the reality of their distance. I feel the energy coursing through my body, overwhelming and scattered. I hold still in waiting, and within seconds it comes.

The energy all around me plays games with my stomach, my mind, and my muscles. I feel it imploding all around me like a semi-dim colorful light falling inward, condensing into a bright ball of brilliant light. This collision of internal energy is a fire so strong it changes everything in an instant. My hearing fades to nothing, my vision fades to black and white, and my whole world slows down to a crawl. Flow state is upon me.

My mind is clear, my muscles are strong, my will is unbreakable, and I peel out to meet the monster.

One long Dufek stroke takes me to the first move, ten strokes center to left, and then a delayed water boof into freefall. Keeping the nose up I land hard on a right stroke and give it hell to fight back to center. Safety is a few feet wide and I am right on line. The exploding white room is all around me and my only exit is the horizon line I scouted from river right only moments ago.

I pull my boat onto the perfect piece of water and brace for the ride ahead. Everything is happening in slow motion—each stroke, every move, the inputs of the boat in my glutes. There is no stopping, there is no quitting, only execution. I am committed with every cell in my body to stomp my line in this black and white world of apocalyptic explosions.

Upside down... I cannot be upside down... Tucked up, face against the cockpit, I am under water, holding my breath, eyes closed. A rock hits my shoulder, and I feel the current slam me into the river right rock wall. I am floating toward the lip on a high-speed ramp of white anger. I know where I am; I've memorized this whole scene. The downside is unthinkable.

Focusing on the positive, I wait to feel the right moment and snap a roll back to the world of air and chaos. This is it, the moment. I hit the lip, lift my bow, and send it deep with the mist through the air, down to the safety of the cushiony white and green pool below. Under water, surfacing... stomped it!

Instantly and simultaneously, the color returns to my vision, I hear the roaring of the falls, and life is once again happening at normal speed, right before my eyes.

I am beyond alive, and in this moment, truly present in the knowledge that I have more than lived this life.

Grant wrote, "FOCUS and DO WERK" on his knees
(Photo by Grant Korgan)

CHAPTER 15
120 PERCENT

People were great to me, to us. I mean, *so great*. It was an awesome thing, in the truest sense of that word, to see how blessed we were with kindness from friends and family, people who constantly called and came by, wanting to do for us. It was a beautiful, beautiful thing.

People we hadn't seen in months, people who had just gotten wind of my injury and were overcome with a desire to show their love and support, would arrive with dinner, and it was wonderful and vastly appreciated by both of us. But then, they'd want to hear the story—the accident, the helicopter ride, the surgery, the weeks in the hospital, all of it. They'd ask, "So, what did the doctors say?" or "Have you tried this therapy?" And, increasingly, there was the desire to establish a connection by saying things like, "That happened to someone I know, and this is how it played out for them," or "Yeah, I know what you mean, because I had a similar experience when this other thing happened to me."

Reliving the experience was stressful, every single time. Shoving the weight of others' stories, the burden of others' success and failures, into that backpack of mine was stressful, too. More stressful, still, was the fact that, at least for the first two months after my return home, I was in breathtaking, searing pain, and I couldn't bring myself to upset others by letting it show.

So these beautiful, amazingly kind and generous people whom I wanted to see, who loved me, wanted to come over, and have barbecues to celebrate my return home, and I was *just barely* keeping it together, squeezing the rails of my bed to keep from screaming, just dealing and breathing, thinking, *Oh my God oh my God oh my God* until they went home.

And even after the symptoms of the latex allergy had passed, as much as I loved having visits from people and appreciated with my whole heart the way they reached out to me, my natural instinct to protect the feelings of others, to take care of others, often won out over my need to protect myself.

So when my friend, Reid, along with his fiancée, Logan, arrived to cook dinner one night in May, *I* was the one worried about *him*. Reid was my boy, a dear friend of mine from my college days, someone who had always had my back and whom I'd always thought was a rock. Yet here, while we toasted my health with a glass of wine and he and Logan revealed details of their upcoming nuptials, something was off. Reid seemed nervous—shaky, with a slight tremor in his voice. He wouldn't meet my eyes.

Shawna, Reid, Logan, and I (in my brace), sat around the table, eating the amazing lamb burgers with blue cheese that Reid had prepared, as an eager Obie waited for a crumb of burger to fall that he could catch. Reid had barely touched his dinner, and I caught Logan, on more than one occasion, shooting what seemed to be anxious glances at him. Something was up.

"Dude, are you okay?" I asked.

"Yeah, yeah, I'm good, really," he said, dismissing my concern with a wave of his hand. "I just had kind of a big lunch."

After dinner, the three of them carried all the empty plates to the kitchen. Then, while Reid and Logan cleaned up, I wheeled back to the hospital bed and Shawna helped get me out of the chair and removed the brace to get me fairly comfortable in bed—a process that took nearly a half hour.

Once I was settled in bed and the dishes were done, Reid and Logan made their way to my bedside, and the room grew awkwardly silent as all three of them stood in a circle around my bed. The energy of the evening had somehow shifted to something serious.

Reid looked over at Logan, grabbed her hand, and squeezed it.

"What's up, are you leaving?" I asked, confused and concerned. Then I realized what I was seeing on Reid's face. It was the same expression I had worn a year before, with my buddies, when I had gotten engaged.

The concern I had felt eroded as it dawned on me what might be about to take place, and an anticipatory smile slowly spread across my face. *He's going to ask me to be in his wedding!*

"No, no," he said. He looked at Logan, exhaled, and the two looked at me. "We want to ask you a favor."

"Oh, sweet!" I said, before he even had a chance to ask.

Through visible tears that now welled in Reid's eyes, through his trembling lips that he was trying desperately to gain control of, he said, "I would... *we* would be *so* honored if you would consider marrying Logan and me."

Marrying them? As in, being responsible for their union? I was honored, so honored, so completely stoked, and it was plain all over my face.

But then, like those mornings when you wake up and the terrible thing that happened to you, which you had temporarily forgotten, suddenly dawns on you again, and you mourn as if it were happening all over again, my smile changed. "You guys," I said, my hands instinctively touching my heart, "I am beyond touched. I'm so touched that you would ask this, nothing would give me greater joy. But, brother," I continued, thrusting my hands to gesture to my legs, "I'm broken in half. I'm shipwrecked right now. I..."

"Oh, no, oh my God, Grant," Logan said, rushing to cut me off.

"Hey," Reid said, putting his hand on my shoulder. "Stop. Shh. You're the *only* one I want there doing this for us. Please, would you *please* marry us?"

Logan leaned in, hugged me, and kissed my cheek.

I wiped the tears that were now flowing freely, and looked up to find the other three in the same shape. I laughed. "Bro, are you sure?"

"There's no other way," he said, hand still on my shoulder. "There's just no other way."

It was the first time since my injury that I had been asked to do something for someone else, the first time when my injury wasn't a factor. The first time the conversation wasn't focused on my condition, but on how I could finally really do something for somebody else. I was being asked a favor, an important favor, but really, it was a huge gift for me.

Immediately, my therapy kicked into an even higher gear. No matter what I had to do to make it happen, I *would* stand at Reid and Logan's wedding. There was no way that I would give any less of myself than that.

In addition to my weekly outpatient therapy session with Jen, I explored a series of chiropractors, all on recommendations from friends. One nearly rolled me off the table while paying an inordinate amount of attention to Shawna; another was far too rough, and then chastised me for being the "big extreme athlete" who couldn't handle a little adjustment. After some time, we did finally arrive at one we really liked, a very gentle and caring man. For a little while, this chiropractic therapy fit well with our recovery plan. However, with resources as thin as ours, Shawna and I eventually had to focus our energies on other therapies and on going to the gym.

Although we had joined the gym in order to expand my exercise repertoire, we had also done it to make my showering easier. Though the layout and flooring in our home were ideal in so many ways, there was simply no way to make showering possible. I'd managed to transition to the bedroom and could use the wheelchair to get from room to room, but the bathroom was too tight a squeeze for anything useful. I couldn't wheel into it, couldn't get into the single-person shower stall with a pull door, and couldn't fit through the opening while seated on a slide board. I managed to get by on sponge baths, but really just wanted to sit under a shower and feel the water streaming down my body, breathe in the steam.

This gym, which was on the bottom floor of a local medical center, had a family locker room with a private, lockable room, as well as a shower I could roll into and a bench I could sit on, and it enabled Shawna to come in and spot me while I transferred from chair to bench, and then to direct the water on me as I washed.

The other big benefit of this gym was that it had a NuStep, a piece of equipment that I had first used during my inpatient therapy, and which I believed would still be hugely beneficial to my recovery. The machine was a recumbent stepper, so that my arms could help my legs to step until they could eventually take on more of the movement themselves, and I could work both my upper and lower body at once.

The equipment in the gym was surrounded by a running track, so as I worked out, people milled about all around me. No matter what direction I turned, I saw people walking and running, riding stationary bikes or using the step machines. I wore a ball cap, put on the earphones to listen to the iPod mix Jason had made me, a Jefr Tale podcast, or to listen to one my favorite groups, The Glitch Mob. The music, a high-energy blend of industrial and electronic tunes, powered my workout, gave me the fuel to push harder every day on my path to standing at Reid and Logan's wedding. I pulled the brim of my cap down low, closed my eyes, listened to my pulse combined with the driving electronic beats, and visualized my energetic self standing, walking, waltzing with Shawna at the reception, climbing down to the shore in Mendocino, diving into the ocean and kicking my legs, free.

Music had fueled me in many of my past adventures. I had cranked the stereo and heard the throbbing beats on the drive up to mountain bike trails and to snowy mountaintops where we would snowmobile. The energy would fill me up and carry me all day while I killed every jump.

One day, completely immersed in a memory of these great times, and deep in The Glitch Mob's set, *Crush Mode*, a loud noise prompted me to open my eyes. I scanned the room. Someone had just dropped something, but otherwise it was business as usual. People exercising, people running. My wheelchair sat beside me. The gravity of the difference between where I was, physically, and what I'd been daydreaming about, was enough of a jarring reality to me. But to be surrounded on all sides by the normality other people were experiencing, and to hear this driving music as I struggled to pedal a stepper with my arms… the magnitude of that disparity was just too much. Tears filled my eyes quickly. A lump formed in my throat.

I pulled the brim of my cap low, nearly covered my eyes completely, and cried hard, energetic tears, the force of which fueled my workout.

Shawna, working out nearby on a treadmill and keeping a careful eye on me, spotted my breakdown, but said nothing. She knew I needed to let it out and work through it on my own. And, eventually, I did.

By June, I was strong enough that I felt ready to try sitting in the Mini for the forty-five-minute trip up to Truckee, California, to begin seeing an acupuncturist and a unique physical therapist named Ladd Williams.

"Wherever we are is where we're supposed to be," Shawna had begun telling me. In fact, this was as much her journey as it was mine, as she was constantly learning new ways to beef up my therapy and stimulate my nerve regeneration process. She became a sponge, soaking up every recommendation, every lead to a practitioner who might have something to offer us, and was open to the idea that if it landed in our laps, it was for a reason, and we should explore it. So when Roy Tuscany, who was now in frequent contact with us, said, "You *need* to see Ladd," we listened. It was Ladd's magic fingers that Roy credited with healing him, and it was so important to him that we go to see Ladd that he and the High Fives Foundation stepped up to donate money for our sessions.

Ladd was a sort of "therapist to the stars" in Truckee, an area where professional skiers and Olympians frequented. He was willing to see me two times a week for a half day each, which was an unheard-of, extraordinarily generous gift to us, one we couldn't afford to pass up, regardless of how much effort was required in getting me up there.

The office, located in a Tahoe cabin-style office building made of rustic, hewn wood, smelled of pine and lavender, and a cool breeze was enough to remind us that summer hadn't quite arrived at this little mining town in the mountains, despite the bright sunshine. On our first day, Ladd, a Native American man with short, thick-but-thinning, salt-and-pepper hair and a mustache, greeted us at the front door wearing a Hawaiian shirt. His appearance put us at ease immediately, as it was completely contrary to the medical façade we'd become used to seeing.

With a soft voice and a slow, deliberate manner of speaking, he talked to us about his experience working with former athletes and people who had a wide variety of injuries. But it was clear to us as he spoke that his tribal upbringing had heavily influenced him—spirituality, visualization, and the force of positive energy would be playing a big role here in my sessions.

Then he began the hands-on work, massaging my hips, legs, and feet. He attached electrodes to my legs and used electrical stimulation, or "e-stim," along with his magical fingers, to stimulate muscles that I didn't know I had, or which would have otherwise lain dormant. While he was releasing the long psoas muscle that runs from my lower back to my hip, I shared with him my intent to fully recover, to push past the pain and frustration of paralysis.

Ladd looked right into my face with a kind, contemplative expression and said, "During this recovery, in every moment, you need to manifest beyond what you can imagine. Not just what you can imagine now, but beyond that."

It was the first time I'd ever been encouraged to not only consider a full recovery, but to go beyond that, to imagine limitless possibilities. Right now, all I could imagine was the freedom of movement, because at the moment all I could feel was that same sensation of dead weight, like a sinking anchor pulling me to earth. But he was right, and the force of that hit me hard: I didn't just have to settle for "back to normal." Why not go beyond what I'd been before, not just stronger but wiser, more in tune with my body, my mind, and my spirit? Why not remove the limitations of math and science? Why couldn't I just plan for a recovery of 120 percent?

Each day I seemed to experience greater strength and a greater ability to manifest movement in my muscles. And each day, we would try new movements and new visualizations of movement.

One day, several weeks into my treatment, after our initial talk about how I was feeling and what I wanted to work on, he turned to Shawna. "Now, Shawna," he said, taking her hands and looking deeply into her eyes, catching her somewhat off guard, "Your hands can heal. Did you know that?"

She beamed and grew teary but said nothing.

"Today, your hands are going to do the work, okay?" he said, smiling warmly.

"I'd love that, thank you! Let's do it!" she said, clearly eager to participate in a new and important way.

"Okay!" he said, placing her hands gently back on her lap. He turned, his movements always slow and methodical, and pulled, from the corner of his desk, a mason jar containing several full sprigs of lavender. He held the jar out to Shawna, who took it carefully and then looked to Ladd with a confused expression.

"Take this lavender. Go through that door," he said, pointing through the office door toward the front door. "Go to the patio. Just take some of this lavender," he said, gently fingering the sprigs, releasing a burst of their lemony scent, "and crush some of it on the floor, just sprinkle it around. Okay? Then, lie down, just close your eyes and breathe. Just connect to the earth, get grounded. Take a few moments, just breathe, and connect to who you *know* you are. Okay? You're a healer. Connect to that healing energy inside. Prepare to be the medicine woman that I know you are. Now go." He grew silent, and stared at her, smiling and expectant. Shawna brushed a hand along my shoulder as she left the office and headed outside to the cool, sunny day.

While I continued my e-stim and focused on movements of muscles as Ladd manipulated them, Shawna stepped out the front door of the building and climbed the stairs that led from the front door up to the deck that sat amidst the trees. She did as Ladd had asked; she sprinkled the lavender and lay down on the floor, shivering slightly from the cool breeze and the excitement about what was about to be asked of her. She took a moment to connect with herself—something she hadn't done in months, I'm sure—and focused on breathing in and out, on the lemony scent of lavender and pine, on the breeze rustling her hair and the dappled sunlight kissing her skin. She became aware of an internal vibration, an electrical humming that felt warm, much warmer than the mountain breeze would seem to allow. A current was running through her, electrifying her bloodstream. Her hands grew warm and tingly, as if she'd been clapping for a long time. She held them up before her face as she squinted against the sun to see them,

Roy Tuscany empowered Grant in therapy and brotherhood
(Photo by Shawna Korgan)

pink from the warmth. She sat up, took a deep breath of lavender, grabbed the jar, and headed back to the office.

"Oh, you're ready," Ladd said when he saw a cheery, pink-faced Shawna come through the door. She held her hands up, and he touched them, then nodded his assent. "Now, do the work." He stepped aside and gestured to me, as if ushering her to the stage.

Shawna's hands, throbbing with healing warmth, did the work that Ladd communicated to her verbally. She stretched my body in ways she'd never done before, exhibiting a new level of strength and expertise. Her look of satisfaction in making this energetic, beautiful new connection to my body as a healer was doubly satisfying for me.

Also satisfying was the enormous progress I seemed to be making through a combination of physical therapy at Ladd's office, acupuncture, and home workouts on and off the parallel bars. As much as I wanted it and believed in my ability to make it happen, Ladd seemed to see what I could do before I could. During a session in late June, three or four weeks into my time with him, Ladd had me lie down on a mat, and he put a bolster pillow

under my right knee, with the left leg lying flat next to it. After wiring the
e-stim electrodes to my legs and turning on the juice, Ladd said, "Now, lift
your left leg onto the pillow."

As if I were struggling to lift a ten-ton anchor, I struggled, heaving, my
body writhing and contorting itself for lifting the dead weight. A primeval
"AAAAARRRRGGGH" came from deep in my gut as I fought, futilely at
first, to lift my leg. Over and over I attempted, and finally, on the fifth try,
the leg lifted.

Lifted!

Shawna and I called a triumphant "YEAH!" She jumped up and down,
kissed me, and, with tears of joy flowing down her cheeks, she hugged
Ladd tightly.

Progress seemed to come like dominos, each milestone more quickly
leading to the toppling of another.

At the gym, my work with the NuStep continued, and eventually, after
several weeks, I began to notice that no longer were my arms doing all the
work. Little by little, my legs were taking on the responsibility of pedaling.
About four weeks into our gym membership, which we'd taken advantage
of at least three or four days a week, Salt caught me looking at the stationary bike from my seat on the NuStep. "It's time to get on that bike," she said.
"You're ready."

I had felt ready, but her confirmation was all it took to get me to slide
into the wheelchair and roll myself over there.

Shawna helped me get my foot strapped into the pedal and the rest
of me clumsily up onto the seat, positioned to its lowermost position.
Stares from other members and staff said, "Are you crazy?" I channeled
the strength I'd pulled at Ladd's office, closed my eyes to envision myself
standing at the wedding, and feverishly pedaled three strokes. In about
sixty seconds, I'd pedaled three strokes, but for someone who was never
supposed to move my legs again… *fuck yeah!*

At home, things were just as good. My work on the parallel bars every day had progressed to the point that, by the end of June, I could actually walk myself along the bars by slowly dragging my own feet along, instead of needing Shawna or Jen or Becca to move me.

My sleep was still fitful, due to my difficulty in finding a comfortable position in our bed, the incessant fire-ant pain that had spread throughout my feet and into my ankles, and being awakened every few hours to be rolled or catheterized. I was probably getting about fifty to 60 percent of the sleep I had gotten before my injury—real, legitimate sleep. Sometimes, Shawna's alarm would awaken her, only to find me so obviously in the middle of blessed, deep, calming, restorative sleep that it pained her to wake me. In those moments, she often sat and watched me, reveling in the joy of my comfort, my not needing anything but what I had at the moment. A blissful, rejuvenating calm.

But when she rolled me, a process that simply had to occur regularly for my own safety, it certainly did wake me. If I was on my back, it involved rolling the bottom sheet up to my body, then pulling me on the sheet toward her, placing a pillow between my knees to keep my back aligned and my body stable, then gently pushing my side away from her so that I was on my side. My sleep was such a delicate thing that it took very little movement to startle me awake.

But one night in early July, Shawna actually woke up without her alarm, between rolling cycles. In an effort to save our rapidly dwindling money, we were keeping the air conditioning off, and while the open windows at night kept the room mostly cool, it was an unseasonably warm night. She stood up and moved to the window, to open it wider and take in the cool breeze.

She heard rustling and turned to check me, which was by now, for her, a second-nature response to sound. What she saw was me, in deep sleep, rolling over to my side. After more than four months of rolling me every two hours, of watching me struggle to move my body at will, my brain had gotten the impulse from my body that it was time to roll over, and my body obeyed. Shawna sat in the dark by the moonlight streaming in from the window, watching me sleep and weeping tears of joy. And soon, overcome by sleepiness again, she turned off the alarm clock, lay back down beside me, and went to sleep.

Considering the magnitude of what I was planning for—standing at the ceremony—it almost seemed too easy to get ordained. The process was shockingly simple: Fill out an online form, take some paperwork to the city clerk's office, check into the state's laws for marriage ceremonies to make sure you're compliant, and boom, you're official. And as far as I was concerned, as someone who totally gets off on talking to people, I had the easiest job of anyone there. I got to just bring love, so it couldn't have been more natural for me.

I was growing excited about the wedding, and my progress over the last month had been tremendous. But I was still nowhere near being able to stand for any longer than a few seconds. I was exhausted from working my body as hard as I'd done. And there was no way, after the work I'd been doing, that I could approach the ceremony itself in a half-assed way. I could have downloaded a prepared script off the Internet, but instead I worked with Shawna to craft the perfect words, which we'd worked on every night for days and which continued to evolve.

There were moments that month in which I was overcome with the enormous pressure that I continually put on myself to do something I wasn't sure I was ready for. How could I possibly have believed that I would be ready to stand for their wedding, which would surely last a good hour, when I could barely stand up from my wheelchair for more than a handful of seconds?

But all signs seemed to point to this happening: the progress I'd made physically, the ease of becoming ordained, and even the drive itself, which was remarkably smooth, considering my recent track record with road trips.

We opted to take the Sportsmobile. For fifteen years of my life, I had dreamt of having a van I could camp in—a tricked-out, four-wheel-drive conversion van that could act like a mobile home, something I could throw my kayak gear into and live in for days by the river. In December of 2009,

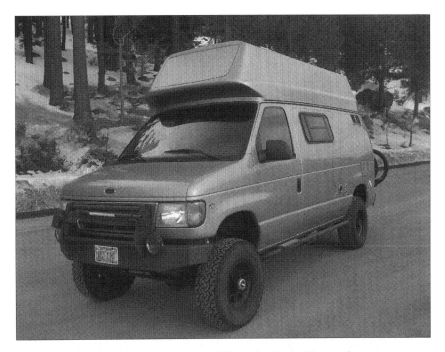

Limitless opportunity (Photo by Grant Korgan)

just four months before my injury—another moment of providence—I was surfing around on Craigslist to see what I could see, and wandered into van listings. There was a gold 2001 Ford E 350 Sportsmobile 4 x 4 camper van for sale at a ridiculously low price—not low enough for my budget, which was stretched tight until we successfully completed our NanoLabz project, but low enough that I could consider it. Despite having more than 200,000 miles on it, the van appeared to be in great shape, and the ad, which referred to it being "well taken care of," resonated with me.

I called the owner (whose name, the ad said, was John) in Colorado and explained that I was interested in his van. And in the course of the conversation, I discovered that, in fact, the van had been used for exactly what I'd envisioned, and had been outfitted with cabinets, a bed, and other amenities that would make it possible for Shawna and me to have the leisurely adventures I imagined. John, it turns out, was a renowned rock climber, a superstar in the world of boulder climbing, who had periodically lived in the van during extended climbing trips around the country.

John and I talked for hours about sports, his and mine, and afterward, he said, "Well, I want you to have this van. How much can you give me?"

I named my meager price, really an outrageously low price that I knew was roughly thirty cents on the dollar of what it was probably worth, and still he said, "I can work with that." So the deal was sealed. I bought a plane ticket and drove the van home, believing that Shawna and I would be taking it on numerous outdoor adventures. But between my time in the lab and my injury, "Gold Finger," as we christened it, had seen little but our driveway.

And now, we had a drive to Mendocino ahead of us, and the Mini Cooper, for all it had done for me when I returned from the hospital and in getting me to my various therapies, was probably the most impractical vehicle we could have had in our situation. Plus, with our savings dwindling by the day, we would need to live in whatever we drove to Mendocino. Between its height—much too tall for me to get into from my wheelchair—and its many after-market amenities making it too tight for me to reasonably be comfortable in my inflexible condition, the Sportsmobile had been impractical, and had sat unused for months. But now that I was stronger and more flexible every day, it looked like I might finally get a chance to use it to camp, albeit uncomfortably, at the beach, just as I'd dreamed of doing.

Because the trek to Mendocino would be a long one, longer than I had ever done successfully, and because it was important to me to be at my very best for the ceremony, we left a good five days before the day of the wedding. Sam Soloman's Donner Lake house, just off Interstate 80 inside the California border, made a convenient place for us to stop and rest, and we wanted to build in as much rest as possible. We pulled into Sam's driveway, and, though we visited with him that night, we slept in the van as a sort of trial run for the days to come.

Though my sleep was erratic, I did sleep, and despite the constant fire-ant sensation in my feet, I wasn't in pain. I was, however, hot. The cool breeze wasn't circulating through the van, which was still warm from the July day, and between that and my struggle to find comfortable positions on the bed, I was sweating. I tossed the plush comforter off of my body and propped my torso up with my elbows so that I could see the clock on the dashboard and the pink sunrise coming across the lake, beginning to peek through our windows. Then I looked at my body, my feet and legs. A small, cool breeze of air wafted in through the window and across my legs, rustling the hairs there. I watched them flutter, and saw, on my skin, unmistakable goose bumps on both legs. I couldn't feel the chill that usually accompanies goose bumps, but there they were, a neural response to cold air.

I lay there, watching my legs, reflecting on the huge strides I'd made in the last few weeks, things I would have, until very recently, disregarded as not such a big deal. But it was *absolutely* a big deal. My body was showing me every day what it could do, revealing little miracles to me every day. Sure, I couldn't walk yet. I couldn't urinate, couldn't even sit up on this bed without help. But when I focused on what *was* working in my body, all the little communications going on between my body and my brain that I hadn't even considered or been aware of, it was a marvelous thing. If I could accomplish this much in my three months home, why couldn't I pull off this wedding? And what more could I do in the months to come?

I took a mental picture of this moment, and decided to come back to this picture every time I got frustrated with what felt like a lack of progress. Gratitude swelled in my chest. I lay back on my pillow, gave a heavy sigh, and chuckled to myself. "Goosebumps," I said to myself. "Fucking unbelievable."

I had pushed harder than I'd thought possible, had left nearly a week ahead of schedule, and had survived a gnarly, difficult ride to Mendocino, arriving three days early in order to rest up so that I could perform at my top level for my friends.

But it was all worth it once Shawna and I arrived. Because once we arrived, scoped out where the wedding was to take place and where our friends were all staying, and parked the Sportsmobile on the enormous grassy bluff overlooking the ocean where the wedding would take place, Shawna and I (and Obie, an enthusiastic passenger) experienced a rush of freedom. We were on vacation for the first time in months, free from the constraints of my situation and the rigorous schedule we'd set for our-

Grant and Shawna moments before the wedding (Photo by Jessi LeMay)

selves. We began to understand, like we never had when we'd been regular people working jobs, the restorative value of vacation. And we discovered the power of being open to and recognizing valuable opportunities when they came along.

Still, we were broke. We'd been living off savings and the rest of the money from my truck's sale (the bulk of which we'd used to pay off the hospital). So to experience a vacation like this, on beachfront property, surrounded by the people I loved, was more than I had hoped for. Friends brought us food, and Reid outfitted me in a handmade suit the likes of what might be found at a *GQ* photo shoot. Despite having little in terms of financial resources, my heart swelled with a feeling of abundance.

From Reid and Logan right down to their friends and family and every single member of the wedding party, the collection of stunningly beautiful human beings attending this wedding was of breathtaking proportion. As much as I was thrilled and grateful to be a part of it, part of me felt ill about arriving at the ceremony in a wheelchair. It wasn't because I was vain, and though part of it was because I didn't want their pity, it was mostly because, in my mind, the guy in the wheelchair wasn't me, and it wasn't representa-

Reid and Logan's wedding, on the bluff in Mendocino, CA
(Photo by Jessi LeMay)

tive of my intent. And I didn't want my wheelchair to be the first thing they saw in their pictures years from now. Though Reid and Logan would have been upset to know I'd even considered that, and though I knew with all my heart that they wanted me there and weren't just "letting" me be there to be nice, I wanted to give them all of me, not a broken me.

But it was too late now to do anything about it. All eyes were on Reid and me as he wheeled me down the aisle to the enormous stump that would serve as the altar, with Shawna walking behind us. I wheeled to turn and face the aisle and the crowd of guests. Beyond the row of seats, several yards away from the tent that would house the reception, sat the Sportsmobile.

The bridal party approached to stand by me, and when the strains of the acoustic guitar began changing their tune, the guests knew it was their cue to stand for the bride's entrance. Logan was stunning, dressed in white, and commanded the attention of every person there.

Though Shawna and I had arrived at a good script for the ceremony, I had awakened early that morning, the exact words I wanted to say hav-

*Standing tall in Reid and
Logan's beautiful moment
(Photo by Jessi LeMay)*

ing come into my brain in a lightning flash. I had gotten up and furiously scribbled, though the sunrise had still only begun. But the lengthy script I now had in my hand, I was confident, resounded with my love for the couple and my hopes and dreams for their future together.

After months of training, manifestation, and miraculous progress, I stood, leaning on the makeshift stump altar, with Shawna waiting in the wings to catch me, as Logan made her way down the aisle. She and Reid stood together with tears in their eyes, thrilled with my accomplishment. I hastily launched into the ceremony, to quickly turn the focus back to the couple. Waves crashed down below and seagulls cried as I fought with every ounce of strength inside me to stand there, to make it all the way through the ceremony upright. I lost myself in the words, the emotion of the day, and my love for these friends of mine, and forged on, though sweat was making its way down my back and across my brow.

At the end, Reid and Logan kissed, and made their way back down the aisle, my triumph in standing rightfully taking a distant second to the purpose of our being there. As they turned to head back down the aisle, Shawna subtly joined me to quickly, smoothly get me back into my chair. I sat there watching our friends begin their marriage, and I silently congrat-

Reid and Logan's amazing wedding party (Photo by Jessi LeMay)

ulated myself for another win and gave thanks to a universe that allowed me to be there.

After the reception, Reid and Logan, Shawna, Steven, and I, along with several other friends, emerged from the reception tent to soak up the cool night air and the sound of night waves crashing down below. Someone had lit a bonfire.

Before I could even think about it or protest, several of my friends picked me up by my wheelchair and delicately carried me down to the beach. Within minutes, we were seated beside a roaring fire, drinking whiskey and swapping stories of the good old days.

It was one of the best days of my life.

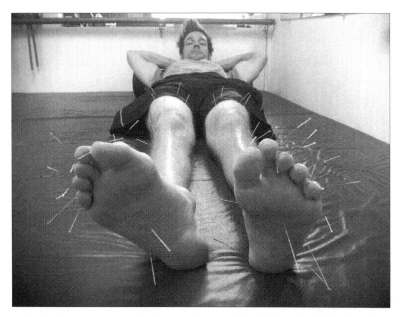

Grant meant it when he said he would do whatever it takes
(Photo by Shawna Korgan)

CHAPTER 16
NEEDLES

E arly into my recovery, while I was still in inpatient, Shawna had come to know who *the* experts were in spinal cord injury circles. Between her professional background and colleagues in fitness circles, as well as countless hours spent online, she explored dozens of spinal cord recovery practitioners and numerous therapies. Names kept coming up over and over, online and in the words of other doctors, nurses, and therapists. One name that came up over and over was Dr. Zhu.

Dr. Zhu's neuro-acupuncture practice had been hailed by many as a powerful recovery treatment. He had developed his method of scalp acupuncture in China after many years of study, and it appeared to have created dramatic improvements for spine-injured patients. Shawna couldn't let it go—we needed to get to San Jose, she thought. If it didn't work out, fine, but at least we'd know, and we wouldn't have to wonder about it, or maybe we could share what we learned with someone else. Either way, we had to try anything that came this highly recommended. So in May, while on the road to see the neuro-urologist about my urethra pain, the plan had been to head straight down to San Jose to see Dr. Zhu. But that disastrous trip couldn't have gone worse, and there was no way we could make it happen. Since then, we'd explored many options, many of them out-of-the-box, and many remarkably helpful. But still, Shawna couldn't let Dr. Zhu go. Something about what he offered piqued her curiosity so strongly—called to her—she was determined for us to go see him.

What clinched it was getting a call from the High Fives Foundation. I had been selected as an "awarded athlete," which meant I would be a regular recipient of their deep-reaching support and donated funds that would help us pay for therapies.

So before leaving for California, with me on the mend, High Fives' generous assistance, and the freedom afforded by our home on wheels, Shawna called the office and scheduled an appointment with Dr. Zhu for the week after the wedding.

When we entered the facility, I saw a large, open room that looked a lot like many other gyms and outpatient physical therapy centers I'd seen in the last few months—a wide, open room full of exercise and therapy equipment, tables, and mats. There was one teenage boy who looked to be about seventeen sitting on a chair in the corner, beside an aerobic step. Based on his movements, he appeared to have a spinal cord injury. As Shawna and I waited at the front, I watched the boy intently from my wheelchair as he awkwardly stood up and began stepping slowly, on and off the step.

He saw that I was fixated on him and smiled at me, then made his way, walking with crutches, toward us. "You here to see Dr. Zhu?" he asked.

"Yeah!" I said, with a huge, amazed expression on my face. When he approached, I extended my hand to the boy, whose eye contact and direct approach revealed an unusual maturity for a kid his age. This kind of injury will do that. He moved one crutch under his arm and extended the free hand to shake mine.

"I'm Grant, this is my wife, Shawna. Man, you are *killing* it out there, that's amazing!"

"I'm Jack," he said, smiling at me knowingly. "You keep coming here, this'll be you in a few months."

We were eventually ushered back to an exam room, where we were met by Dr. Zhu and two of his colleagues. "Hello, Mr. Grant!" said Dr. Zhu, a man who appeared to be in his seventies or eighties and had a thick Chinese accent. His huge smile made his warm eyes crinkle behind his glasses. "This Dr. Moyee and this Khan; he therapist," he said, pointing to two other men. "How you feeeeling?"

"I'm good, good!" I said, eagerly shaking the hand of the man who had helped the young man I'd just met.

"Pah-don me," he said, his quiet colleagues beaming at us wordlessly, "I not speak perfect English."

"No problem, it's fine," I said.

"So!" he said, looking expectantly at us. It took him a moment to say anything else. "Why you here?"

Shawna and I, collaboratively, shared the story of my injury, surgery, hospitalization, and subsequent recovery plan with him. Shawna explained that she'd heard many great things about his work and that we'd felt compelled to see him for a consultation.

"When this happen?" he asked.

"Well, my injury was in March, so..." I said, looking to Shawna with raised eyebrows to calculate, "about... six? Six months ago."

"Oh, no!" Dr. Zhu said despairingly. "Six months? That very long. No, you begin *now*." He gave a definitive nod, and his two colleagues began bustling around, opening cabinets, murmuring in Chinese, and wheeling me into the therapy room. And within about sixty seconds and after a confirming nod from me, there was the *Thunk* of a needle being pushed into my scalp.

"OOWWW!" I shouted, caught completely off guard and shocked by the piercing pain. Forget what you know about acupuncturists being gentle and calm, about sessions being relaxing and invigorating. Forget about the work I'd done with Laura. This was full-on *therapeutic* acupuncture.

More needles were added, and with each needle I winced, jumped, and said, "OW!"

"Paaain?" asked Dr. Zhu upon placing the fifth or sixth needle in my scalp.

What I wanted to say was, *Yeah, having needles shoved in your scalp is painful.* What I actually said was, "Uh, yeah!"

Thunk went another needle.

"Mm," said Dr. Zhu, twisting the needle.

Shawna was torn between confusion and concern over my pain, and amusement over the scene playing out before her.

The consultation we'd expected became a session that lasted roughly six hours—just needles and more needles, first on my scalp, then all over my body, in places that I thought were all bone (ankles and knees and elbows). All the while Dr. Zhu asked loudly and forcefully, "Paaain?" and encouraged me to move my legs, to stand, to flex my muscles.

I worked with Khan on the parallel bars and the recumbent bike that allowed me to use both my feet and my hands, with needles boring into my scalp for the duration of the day. All the while, the pain was so intense, so prolonged, that I'd felt like screaming for much of the session. I had foamed at the mouth, spit and rage blinding me as I desperately struggled to sustain my workout, growling like an animal the whole time.

At the end of the brutal session, when I was almost gloriously needle-free (except for the needles Dr. Zhu insisted needed to stay in my scalp day and night for the entire week), Dr. Zhu took a seat opposite me, and put his hands in his lap. "You come back tomorrow. You come every day. You need come six month ago. I hope we not too late."

Shawna and I exchanged looks. Could we even afford this? Although High Fives was covering the therapy, we still had to buy food, gas, or a hotel room so we could catch an occasional shower. Our savings seemed to be dwindling by the second. And besides that, could I even bear any more of this painful therapy?

But despite all that pain, I felt remarkably relaxed once it was over, and I knew my body had somehow transformed during the session. Shawna had been saying for months, "Wherever we are, that's where we're supposed to be." I could see that something big could come of working with Dr. Zhu, and I was open to seeing how this played out. If Jack's results, and

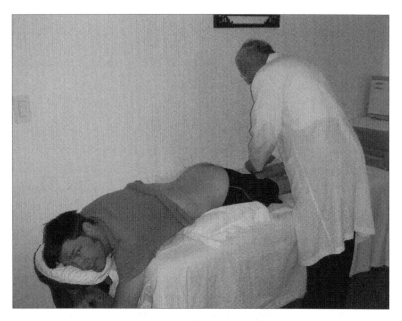

Doing whatever it takes (Photo by Shawna Korgan)

those of the many Shawna had heard about, meant anything, there was also the promise of something good. We needed to give it a real shot.

"Okay," I said, nodding my exhausted, wary agreement.

"You exercise," said Dr. Zhu, looking me earnestly in the eye. "Exercise twenty-five hour day. Exercise in your sleep. You come back tomorrow. Early. Okay?"

"Okay." I left feeling stunned as we headed to the Sportsmobile to find a parking lot to spend the night in.

◠

We spent the rest of the week in San Jose, sleeping in the Sportsmobile at night and enduring long seven- to eight-hour days at Dr. Zhu's office. Every day was much the same: We arrived between 8 and 9 a.m., and I would immediately wheel myself to the recumbent bike and work all day, leaving for the Sportsmobile exhausted, both physically and emotionally.

"How you feeeeling?" would come Dr. Zhu's cheerful greeting each morning as he approached me on the bike.

Excited about his new quad muscles (Photo by Shawna Korgan)

Whether my reply was, "I'm feeling pretty good," or "I'm not feeling so good today," Dr. Zhu's forceful reply was always the same: "Paaain?"

Which was ironic, because nothing compared to the pain he would begin to inflict on me as he inserted needle after needle deeply into my scalp.

This was no soothing "Ahhh!" as the needle was gently tapped in—the only experience I'd had with acupuncture up to that point. This was the frequent *Thunk* of a handful of needles being jammed, in a cold, business-like manner, into my head and, eventually, all over my body. Saliva would immediately pool in my mouth, collecting in the corners, as my eyes stung with tears and every nerve in my body rallied in defense.

These needles didn't just go in a few millimeters. This was a good inch or inch and a half, even into my ankle—my *ankle!* I mean, where the fuck did that needle *go?*

I would continue to bike for forty-five minutes, with needles sticking out of my head like Pinhead from *Hellraiser*. Then Khan would arrive and signal the beginning of a six- to seven-hour regimen of physical therapy that included parallel bars, sometimes including step-ups or side-stepping while I held onto the bars. There was a range of mat-work activities and a good hour, sometimes more, each day of using a standing frame. This device enables a person who relies on a wheelchair to spend time in a standing position while completely, safely supported. And most of the time, as I stood in the standing frame, more needles were poked into my spine. *Thunk thunk thunk!*

My therapy was broken only by an hour-long lunch, during which Shawna and I would seek out the healthiest, least expensive food we could find.

Then we'd return for more physical therapy and, finally, cap off the day in a treatment room—and needles, so many needles, all over my body.

It was the most indescribably intense, grueling kind of therapy, the kind that brought about a sort of hallucinatory exhaustion. At the end of each day, Shawna and I left the building in a sort of trance, shell-shocked.

After the first week of therapy with Dr. Zhu, Shawna and I realized two things: First, as tough as this therapy was, something was happening. I was gaining strength in my legs. Shawna often kicked herself about not getting us there sooner, though I knew for certain we wouldn't have been ready for this trip any earlier. "If I had known," she would muse, "I would have flown him to Reno, had him come to you at inpatient."

But I was through with looking back. Where we were, I reminded her, was where we needed to be, so there was nothing but to push forward. And this was definitely something I needed to continue.

The second thing we realized was that living in the Sportsmobile was exhausting. Yes, it was providence to have it. When Khan heard us talking and asked, "You're living in your *van?*" we explained to him that this wasn't your average van. The Sportsmobile was rad, and we were thrilled to have it. Aside from it making our lives easier, getting us to and from therapy and our camping spot, providing free shelter and a ride to lunch, and offering plenty of hardware and handles for me to grab onto in order to move around inside it, it was comfortable. And for two unemployed people with their life savings slipping away from them, it was a life raft.

But still, we couldn't shower, we didn't have nearly enough room to stretch out or dress, and having Obie with us made things a bit too close

Showing off in therapy (Photo by Shawna Korgan)

for comfort. Although Dr. Zhu's receptionist, Lisa, invited us to dinner on several occasions, even generously offering to let us stay at her house, we simply didn't want to put her out and never took her up on the offer.

The inevitable time came when we were running out of clean clothes. So we headed back to Reno that Friday for a much-needed break from the intensity of Dr. Zhu's results-driven therapy program to pick up clothes, take showers, and get a little extra sleep.

When we were home, Shawna began a campaign to find us an affordable hotel that could provide occasional respite from the van. After all, it seemed we could plan on San Jose becoming our home-away-from-home for the next couple of months. With an online bid of about $50 per night, Shawna managed to find us a room in Sunnyvale for a couple nights the following week.

We returned to San Jose on Sunday, loaded with clothes and food to last for the next week. If we were going to be staying in a hotel, we certainly couldn't afford to eat out, not even at fast food joints.

"I wonder if we could talk to the hotel manager," I said in the van, thinking aloud. "Maybe if we explain our situation, we could work out a deal with someone. I mean, we got the room so cheap, maybe they could work something out for us on a recurring basis."

From our hotel room that night, Shawna wrote an email to the hotel manager to explain our situation and how we needed to continue therapy in the area for the next month or two. She asked for some kind of affordable arrangement. Along with the email, she attached videos and photos of me in the hospital.

The manager at one hotel in Sunnyvale responded the next day. "We are touched by your story and would be happy to extend to you a sponsorship," he wrote, "and a special price on a room on our Club level."

Even with the special deal, Shawna and I were sure we couldn't afford to make this a regular thing. Not if we were still going to make rent on our house, which was already a difficulty for us. We couldn't even buy food. Fortunately, my dad stepped up and offered his credit card for an unlimited number of nights at the hotel. Once again, the stars had aligned and the universe had provided what we needed.

The hotel, just five minutes away from Dr. Zhu's office in San Jose, not only provided a big, comfortable bed for us, but it gave us unlimited access to the free breakfast and snacks in the lounge and to the gym and swimming pool and, even better, they were willing to accommodate Obie as well.

After our extended stays in San Jose, which usually lasted a week or two, we would inevitably return home for a break and to repack our suitcases. Shawna would email the hotel manager as soon as she knew when we would return and for how long, and we would be given "our room," the same large room on the hotel's first floor.

The hotel staff became our friends, calling cheerful hellos to us as we entered at the end of each exhausting therapy day, giving Obie treats, and asking how our day had been.

We had become, for all intents and purposes, local residents.

Each therapy day continued much as they had been in that first week. More needles, more awful pain, more day-long physical therapy sessions. More days that began with, "How you feeeeeling?"

"Oh man, I'm wiped out," I told Dr. Zhu at the beginning of a new day, unsure as to how I could do another eight hours.

"Pain?" he asked.

Yeah, you could say that, I thought. *How you think I'm feeeling?*

"Well, yeah, it's a little painful today," I said.

"You come here. I show you my try. This my try."

He beckoned me to wheel to the therapy table and gestured for me to lie down. With forceful hands that looked deceptively gentle, he grabbed my head and began the work of sliding needles into my scalp. Then he began working out my legs, pulling and pushing vigorously.

"How much exercise yesterday?" he asked me.

"Uh, about six hours?" I said, wincing.

"*NOT ENOUGH!*" yelled Dr. Zhu. "Twenty-five hour a day. Now, my show you my try."

Dr. Zhu helped me to sit up, and then invited me to watch as he effortlessly lifted his aged body onto the parallel bars like some sort of sprite and balanced on one arm. He jumped down, smiling, eyes crinkling, brushed his hands, and moved toward me once again. "Okay?" he asked.

Then *thunk!* Another needle. This time, he twisted it.

We sometimes thought this therapy might be too intense. I even screamed at him once, and said, "Dude! Oh my God, you're hurting me!" Occasionally, Shawna caught me looking at her like, "Really, babe? I know you said 'Trust me,' but really?" I won't lie, it was *hard-core.*

Still, there was no doubt that it was working wonders for me, and that's the reason I kept coming back. Despite the therapy stepping up in aggressiveness with every passing week, despite the (I thought) unreasonable demands being placed on my broken body, I began experiencing sensations I hadn't had since my injury. I could regularly stand with a walker, and could move fairly smoothly to it from my wheelchair. By the first week of September, I could push myself across the floor with one.

And perhaps even more exciting was that, for the first time since before my injury, I had begun to feel a need to urinate. All those needles in my spine, all that mat work, all the shouts of, "Not enough!" were worth it on that day in September when I felt an odd-yet-familiar burning sensation that told me, "I need to take a piss."

I worked for a long, long time that day, strained and squeezing muscles I had no control over, until finally two or three drops of urine trickled out. Those drops were some of the most beautiful things I had ever seen.

"All *RIGHT!*" I exclaimed, and Shawna nearly bowled me over with her exuberant hug. A cheer rose up throughout the room as the entire staff reacted to my accomplishment. Dr. Zhu wore an enormous smile, the corners of his eyes crinkling with pleasure, and patted me on the back.

I still had to use the catheter to draw out my urine, and dig-stim was the only way to empty my bowels, which still provided no warning as to when they might unload on their own (which happened on occasion). But I now *knew* when I needed to urinate. I felt it. The intensity of the challenge I was putting myself through every day, the pain and the grueling workouts, *all of it was working.*

The more progress I saw, the easier it became for me to embark upon another punishing day. I began setting goals for myself outside of therapy. I wanted to try using the walker to get the twenty feet from the van to the hotel's front entrance. And one day, about six weeks into our therapy with Dr. Zhu, although it took me almost a half hour and three separate "rest stops" on the wheelchair, which Shawna pushed slowly behind me, I made it. I entered the lobby, panting, red-faced, and sweaty, but completely exhilarated. The front desk staff of the hotel's swing shift was waiting just inside, and they cheered as I made my way through the door into the cool hotel lobby.

One day, after a long, extra-difficult day of therapy, my muscles were screaming for the hotel's hot tub, which was also the only thing that helped to alleviate the incessant, increasing burning sensation in my feet. With Shawna's help, I made the long trek down the hall, through the door to the patio outside, and along the concrete to the hot tub.

There were six steps leading down to the awaiting warm tub of bubbling bliss. I had made a lot of progress in my therapy, but steps remained a difficult challenge for me—especially these steps, made of unforgiving concrete, narrow, and covered in spider webs and grime, with no team of therapists to catch me if I fell. I dragged my weary body awkwardly along the concrete, sliding my feet gingerly to catch up with the walker just two feet in front of me.

Driven by pain, I was determined, no matter how hard it would be, to make it into that hot tub. With a moment's hesitation, I exhaled, then grabbed hold of the metal rail leading down the steps, abandoned the walker on the top step, and proceeded to climb down. With Shawna spotting me, I made my way carefully, slowly down the steps, gripping the rail for dear life with white knuckles and forearms rippling, as I leaned heavily on it.

A man, another hotel guest, wearing a bathing suit and flip-flops and carrying a towel, walked past on his way to the pool. He saw my plight and, unthinkingly, picked the walker up and wordlessly carried it down the steps to leave it by the side of the hot tub. It was such a simple gesture, and took no time at all. Yet I was overcome with gratitude. He hadn't helped out of pity, hadn't said, "Oh my God, I'm so sorry for you, how can I help?" It was just a stranger doing something nice for another human being. The difference was now apparent to me.

"That's awesome of you, thank you so much!" I said, my heart swelling. The relief and appreciation in my voice were clear.

"Sure!" he said, tossing his towel over his shoulder and hopping back up the hot tub steps to make his way to the pool, with no idea of what his gesture had meant to me.

We had gone from doing therapy three or four hours a day in midsummer to an eight- or nine-hour day by the end of September. Thanks to

Dr. Zhu (and to High Fives for helping us afford to be there), I had learned to get out of my wheelchair, regained bladder sensation, could walk at least a thousand feet with the walker, and was making steps, literally and figuratively, in getting around in life on my own power. I had accomplished more in my two months with Dr. Zhu than I had anywhere else, and had reached major milestones that filled me with a sense of excitement about what else was possible in the future.

My attitude, as I looked back over the tremendous progress I'd made in the last three months, was extraordinarily positive, and my belief in a 120 percent recovery was unquestionable. Based on what I'd been through the last two months, I knew I could handle an aggressive therapy schedule, regardless of what it involved.

Nonetheless, just as we'd learned to be open to what came our way, to the opportunities that seemed to present themselves to us, we had also learned to trust our instincts. Despite my huge progress since first arriving in San Jose, I had come to a point where I no longer felt connected to this therapy. Though it had always been hard work, I could always reach down inside myself and draw upon my deep reserves of energy and positivity to keep going. But I had lately begun to feel only exhaustion. I was tapped out, and increasingly uninterested in this form of therapy. Shawna had begun to notice my declining enthusiasm over the last couple of weeks, and she watched closely for signs that I was ready for something else.

So on a Wednesday at the end of September, after an ordinarily painful day of therapy, Shawna and I looked at each other and seemed to decide simultaneously that we were ready to move on.

The financial costs of this temporary residence in San Jose and the high cost of the therapy itself had become unsustainable. But more than that, the physical toll it took on me was insupportable. I credited Dr. Zhu and his staff for making an incredible contribution to my recovery. And if he were in Reno, we'd probably have decided to continue seeing him weekly. But if I'm being honest, I was over it. The pain was wearing on me, and I was anxious to move on to something else. No matter how fantastic the treatment, my gut was telling me it was time to go.

Shawna, knowing now that I was no longer connecting with this therapy or willing to accept that pain as part of the process, initiated a conversation about what might be the next stop on our journey, what treatment might serve me next.

So when Antonio, a friend from Reid and Logan's wedding we hadn't spoken to in months, called to say, "I want to put you in touch with my healer," that seemed as clear a sign as any. We finished our week in San Jose, and headed back to Reno for good.

Grant hiking the John Muir Trail somewhere between Yosemite
National Park and Mammoth, CA (Photo by Eliot Drake)

CHAPTER 17
FUCK STUFF

It had been more than a week since we'd been in Reno, so it was hard to know exactly how long the sign had been there. As we pulled into our driveway after leaving San Jose for the last time, we found it on the door, fastened with red tape. It read, "Public Auction Foreclosure Sale."

The house was to be sold at auction on the courthouse steps on Monday, November 1. We had a month to vacate our home.

Seriously?

We had been busting our asses to make the rent on this three-bedroom, two-bath home with the three-car garage that now contained parallel bars in addition to the remaining athletic gear I still owned. We had sold a lot of it, along with my truck and snowmobile trailer. We'd also used the money we had allocated for our honeymoon. Almost all of it had gone to paying my hospital bills. We had, while traveling back and forth to San Jose, also sold the Mini Cooper, in order to pay more of those bills as well as the additional living expenses that came with living on the road in order to see Dr. Zhu. We had cut into our now-tiny savings account each month to pay rent in order to maintain our month-to-month lease, yet it seemed to have had little consequence, because now we were being tossed out. It seemed like every time we took a step forward, we had to take two steps back.

This had to be a mistake—we'd been paying the landlord's mortgage. A landlord who knew the extent of my injury and had been very generous with us. Surely this couldn't be right.

But of course it was. It didn't matter that the landlord was an okay guy or that we'd upheld our end of the bargain and paid rent every month. The point was that he had not paid his mortgage with it, and the home was now under foreclosure.

Of course we knew that we were in the midst of a recession—in the state that had been statistically hit harder than any other. Foreclosures had become commonplace in our neighborhood. And our landlord was, to his credit, truly sorry to be putting us through this.

But how about a heads-up? How about a call to say, "Look, I can't pay the bank, but I need you to keep giving me your money. I'm not going to pay my mortgage with it, though, and chances are you'll eventually be asked to leave." At least we could have planned, started looking for a new place to live. We might not have thrown away our last dollars on this place.

Regardless, it was enter-and-deal time. We were in it now, no point rehashing what might have been. All we could do was reach way down deep inside to find understanding and forgiveness and continue moving forward.

All this we knew logically. But that doesn't mean we weren't pissed off about it, or that we weren't freaked out about the fact that, in a very short amount of time, we could be homeless.

Money was flying out the door faster than we could grab hold of it. Friends, family, and the High Fives Foundation had been extraordinarily generous with us, bringing us food and gift cards, raising money for us, giving us credit cards for hotel rooms, donating therapy… but neither Shawna nor I had worked in six months, and therapy was expensive. And even before my injury, things had been tight.

Shawna's business had been struggling, and she already had gone two years prior to my injury without taking a paycheck in order to keep her dream business afloat. A return to The Sanctuary would only have meant assisting Linda with the remaining paperwork involved in closing the business, which had happened a few months back. Meanwhile, Steven and I had completed our final project with NanoLabz by the skin of our teeth, and I had closed that chapter.

In the midst of eight-hour therapy days that week—at home, the outpatient facility, and, soon, at our new healer's office—Shawna and I also would now have to figure out where we would live. We might actually get a chance to see what living in a van really meant.

◠

It was providence that we had Free Candy.

Free Candy was a painter's van we had purchased just weeks before our wedding in a last-minute decision that Shawna and I made to go to the Burning Man festival over Labor Day weekend of 2009; this time, we were on our own. In past years, we would spend months planning for a trip to Burning Man with friends. But with our upcoming wedding, work schedules, and the time off we knew we'd need for our honeymoon, Burning Man had been looking a lot less feasible for us. But being that this event in the desert was truly important to us, we decided that we needed to make it work. With the idea of a tricked-out conversion van still a far-off dream, just a glimmer in my eye, I scoured Craigslist looking for a van we could camp in. A cheap, hollow shell of a thing that would get us there and back, something I could either resell after Burning Man or maybe even fix up later and turn into my dream Sportsmobile.

What I found was a $1,500, dented, beat-up white van with a bad engine and a coating of paint lining the interior, which implied years of sharp turns resulting in overturned paint buckets. It wasn't pretty, but mechanically, and for our purposes (driving it onto a dusty playa to party for a weekend), it was perfect. I bought it on the spot.

The windowless, white-paneled van reminded us of a second-rate ice cream truck in the ghetto, or something a creepy old man might drive into a poor neighborhood, offering kids free candy if they'd hop in. And because, for some inexplicable reason, Shawna and I had gotten into the habit of naming all our things, by the end of our weekend at Burning Man, the van was christened "Free Candy."

When we got home from Burning Man, I replaced the head gaskets on the van, cleaned it up, and put it on Craigslist to sell. But it had no takers. Meanwhile, as our plan to cart our belongings to Yosemite for our wedding the following month took shape, Free Candy was looking more and more useful to us. So we took it and had fun watching friends and family embrace Free Candy as a member of the family, delighted in hearing Shawna's grandmother say, "Oh, just throw that in Free Candy," or my godfather scratching his head and saying, "I believe I left that in Free Candy."

Free Candy began taking on its own fun personality, a rebelliousness and lack of pretension that came to represent us in many ways. I started seeing wonderful potential for it, and after the wedding, I started fixing it up. I tuned up its motor, installed a new stereo, added a tow hitch and an awesome rack to the top. Free Candy wore its ugliness with pride, declaring its humble beginnings and sitting gaudy and obvious beside my gleaming black dream truck and Shawna's beautiful Mini Cooper.

Months later, I found the Sportsmobile, with all the amenities I had always wanted, while Free Candy sat languishing on Craigslist, a Cinderella story of sorts, without a single interested buyer.

Now, in post-injury October 2010, we had shed our beautiful cars. The Sportsmobile, a fantastic convenience that had aided in my out-of-town recovery at Dr. Zhu's, was also an incredibly expensive gas-guzzler and clearly was now going to have to go under a tarp. So now we found ourselves with one drivable vehicle between the two of us: a $1,500 painter's van with character almighty, covered in dents. And we were so fortunate to have it.

We drove Free Candy to our first session with our healer, Aaron, the day after returning to Reno.

There was nothing airy-fairy about Aaron Shaw. He wasn't a guru in a robe, burning incense and chanting while he put his hands on me. No

Free Candy's first day of service (Photo by Grant Korgan)

freaky weird voodoo stuff. Because that was what we half expected to find when we scheduled our first appointment with him, on my friend Antonio's recommendation

"Our family sees him, and he's incredibly gifted," Antonio said, sharing stories with us about people Aaron had helped—final-stage cancer patients who went into remission, sufferers of chronic pain who finally found relief, people who suffered from depression finding a renewed sense of joy and peace.

What, exactly, he was gifted at, we weren't sure. He had no medical training, no letters behind his name, and he offered no "therapy," in the traditional sense. He just had a gift. A healer, as he explained, is just someone who helps people move through whatever situation or ailment they're facing. And considering all we had on our plate at the time, we were certainly up for that—and open to all the healing possibilities that seemingly came to us at all the right and perfect times.

We were hopeful, optimistic, and open-minded when we pulled Free Candy into the driveway of Aaron's 1950s-era brick home in downtown Reno for our first session that bright day in early October.

Aaron was standing on his front porch waiting for us. With his soul patch, beanie cap, jeans, and t-shirt, he looked more like a thirty-five-year-old ski bum than a healer. His hands were shoved deep into his jeans pockets, and he stood leaning against a front porch beam. His expression wasn't so much "Welcome to my home" as it was "What the fuck are you doing here?"

We opened our doors, and while Shawna hopped out of the driver's seat and walked around the back of the van, I called an ebullient "Hey, bro, what's up!" to Aaron through my open door to break the ice and make my connection to him. I hoped that his seeming lack of hospitality was because he simply hadn't known who we were when we pulled into his driveway. "I'm Grant, and this is my wife, Shawna," I said. "How's it goin'?"

"Hey," he said, tipping his chin to me with no change to his expression, and then squinting a bit as he appraised Shawna, who was now leaning into Free Candy to retrieve my walker. Then he slowly, almost reluctantly, stepped off the porch and began walking toward us, while Shawna helped me get out of the van and settled with my walker.

Meanwhile, because I couldn't stand the awkward silence between us, I proceeded to fill the silence with upbeat, inane comments, like, "Hey, great to meet you, Antonio's been singing your praises!" and "We're stoked to be here!"

Aaron approached us and held his hand out to shake Shawna's and then mine. But me, I'm all about the love. I hug. I went in for a one-armed hug and was met with a cold, uncomfortable silence as he stood there, arms at his side, and allowed me to hug him.

"Okay," he said gruffly, adjusting his body to pull away and interrupt the hug. "So tell me what happened."

I had pretty much ditched the wheelchair once I'd realized at Dr. Zhu's office that I could walk with a walker. I had built up my strength to where I could do about one hundred feet at a time in the walker without stopping, but after that one hundred feet, I needed a chair. And with the constant burning pain in my feet, aching back, and weak legs, I couldn't stand for any extended period of time, either. So Shawna kept the wheelchair with us, at the ready in case I needed a break. When it became apparent that Aaron was going to have us talking here in the driveway, maybe trying to decide whether we were legit, Shawna reached into Free Candy once again and pulled out the wheelchair.

Preparing for conversation on the broken and uneven concrete driveway, I took a seat, and pushed the walker out in front of me. I began to explain to him my predicament: "Well, I was snowmobiling and burst-fractured my L1 vertebra…"

"Are you done with this?" he cut me off, looking right at me.

I stopped to look at what he meant and saw Shawna looking at him with a quizzical, somewhat offended expression on her face. Apparently, "healer" was another word for "jackass."

"What?" I asked, not sure what "this" he was referring to.

"The wheelchair. Are you done with the wheelchair?"

I considered for a second and realized that regardless of Aaron's rude approach, he had a point. I had been saying that my goal was to get out of the wheelchair, had made my goal clear when we'd made our appointment, and had worked hard to get to the point where I could use the walker. So why did I keep this safety net?

"Actually," I paused, "Yeah. I'm done with the chair."

"Okay!" Shawna said, relieved that I seemed to be okay with this bizarre approach. Putting my hands back on the walker, bracing myself, I summoned my strength and rose to eye level in the clinical aluminum cage I had worked to use. Shawna picked the chair up, tossed it into Free Candy, and shut the door.

"So, yeah, what I was saying," I began, turning again to continue walking into the house, "I was with my buddies at Sonora, and I took this hundred-foot jump, overshot the safety zone by *two feet*…" I said, breathing heavily as I made my way to his front porch steps.

I stopped and looked at the five steps leading into the house. This was going to be fun. At this point, I still had little experience with stairs, especially not crumbling concrete ones with no railing.

Shawna said, "Here, let's do this…" and encouraged my walker close enough to the first step that I could begin to walk my hand down the contraption to the ground, which left me in a sort of yoga downward-dog pose. All fours on the concrete, I watched Shawna place the walker at the top of the stairs, where she stood at the ready to watch me climb this mountain.

Then, because there was no railing, I began the long, sketchy process of literally crawling in my downward-dog position, up the stairs, using my upper body to pull and hoist my lower body, stair by stair, up to the top. I crawled onto the entry porch and, with Shawna's help, inched my way back into the walker, back to upright, and eventually began moving toward the front door.

Aaron said nothing and made no move to help me for the whole ten-minute ordeal. Once I was comfortably moving in my walker again, he stopped us in front of the closed door.

"Okay, made it, good times," I said, sweating profusely but looking at him with a reassuring smile, as if he cared whether I'd made it safely to the top of the stairs.

"You done with all this?" he said, waving his hand at the walker, at my legs.

"Uh," I said, baffled.

I looked at Shawna, hoping she knew what he meant. She didn't. "What do you mean? Done with the walker?" she asked.

"No, *this*," he said, pointing directly at me. "Are you done hurting yourself?

"Well, clearly, I mean, I'm here, so yeah, I'm done being hurt," I floundered, not sure what he was hoping to hear. *Why, exactly, did I sign on for this?* "Yeah, I'm totally done with this." I looked down at my atrophied legs.

"No, uh-uh," he said. "I won't treat you—I won't even talk to you—unless you decide right now that you're done hurting yourself. Or maybe you're not ready to recover yet." He folded his arms, leaned his shoulder against his door, and stared at me with a sneer on his face.

Were we being filmed? Was this a joke? I had no idea what he was getting at.

"Well, that's ridiculous," I said, laughing uncomfortably. "How could I say that? I mean, I could get into a car wreck, I could fall… how do I know if I'm going to get hurt again?"

"No, no," he said, waving to cut me off. "You're widgeting. *Are you done hurting yourself?* Are you done snowmobiling? Are you done with this whole idea of extreme sports? Are you done?"

Okay, now I was pissed. I wasn't even in the house yet and I was getting this shit? Is this seriously what we'd come down here for, a lecture on
the dangers of "extreme" sports? With or without my friend's generosity, I
didn't need this. Fuck him.

"Fuck no, I'm not," I said, deadly serious and bracing myself for a fight.
And I'm the last guy to engage in fights. But vulnerable as I was, and now
backed into a corner, I was being manipulated. And I was going to come
out swinging. I looked at Shawna, and internally decided to give the guy
about another second to redeem himself before we turned right around
and left.

"Well, then, I guess you're not ready. You'd probably better get back in
the car," he said, reading my mind. He turned as if to leave us on the porch.

"Okay, dude, whatever. I'm not gonna play your little game, whatever
it is," I said, and I began to turn myself around. "Take care," I said bitterly.

There was a beat, a moment of silence.

"I'll ask you again," he said, as I began working my way back to the five-
stair mountain I fully intended to descend under my own power. Clearly,
this little stunt of his had backfired, and he was trying to save it. I smiled a
tiny smile of satisfaction and then erased it quickly before turning again to
face him as he said, "Are you done hurting yourself? Because I need you to
be able to say that you are."

I realized that I was in control here, so I took advantage. "Well, let me
ask you a question," I said. "Are you trying to get me to say that, sure, I'm
done snowmobiling? Because I'm *going* to snowmobile again. I'm going to
do a lot of those things again. I'm recovering so that I can do those things."

"No, no," he said again, realizing that I hadn't understood. He stepped
closer to meet my eyes. And with a calm, firm delivery, he said, "That's not
what I'm asking. I'm asking, 'are you done hurting yourself?' And, more
importantly, are you done not listening when that little voice in your head
tells you to stop, and you go forward anyway? Are you done not listening
and just blindly going into things and getting hurt?"

I had never been reckless. My approach, my whole life, has been about
calculated risk. I've always taken the necessary safety precautions and have
been involved in adventures my whole life. I wasn't showboating out there,
being stupid, working outside of my own limitations, when I took that

snowmobile jump. In a way, I felt that what Aaron was asking was a little like asking the victim of a drunk driving accident whether he was done being an idiot on the freeway. *You don't even know my story, you dick,* I thought, *and you're going to judge me?*

"Look, that's not me. That's not what this was about," I argued. "You don't even know... I looked at all the angles, I was *well* within my limits."

"Okay," he said, clearly not caring to hear a word I said about who I was. He turned, opened the front door, and stood inside it expectantly. "You coming in?"

I was utterly confused, and it made me angry. Here I'd come to be healed, to feel better and improve my situation. I'd been up and down about four times already, and we hadn't even gotten inside the door yet. I wasn't so sure I was all that interested in whatever he was selling.

He went inside the house, leaving the door wide open. I looked to Shawna. "What the fuck?" I mouthed to her. She shrugged and shook her head. She was as lost as I was.

"Let's just go in," she mouthed. I turned around and made my way to the door. Aaron was sitting in a chair across from a wide, pillowy, yellow couch. He watched, with his hands clasped on his lap, as Shawna helped me maneuver with my walker into the tight, antique-themed living room. "Watch out for this, babe," she directed, pointing out a rug on the floor.

"Yep, got it, thanks," I said, my head down, my lips pursed in concentration. The inviting couch beckoned to me. Shawna wrapped an arm around my waist lightly and guided me to sit. I fell into the cushions, relieved, and exhaled.

"So!" I said, looking at him expectantly, hoping he'd begin a new line of questioning. The ball was in his court.

"Okay," he said, leaning forward. "What weren't you listening to?"

"What do you mean?" I asked.

"What weren't you listening to on the day you went snowmobiling?"

I was exasperated. This was getting us nowhere. "Seriously? Nothing! I was snowmobiling, something I'd done hundreds of times before, and this time I broke my back. I mean, I can tell you my story, just let me..."

"No, listen, there's *always* something. What didn't you hear?" he pressed.

I had no idea how to talk to this guy. He asked questions but wouldn't let me answer them. No matter what I said, it was the wrong thing. Simply by being there, I felt like I was putting him out. *And he was getting paid for this.* I didn't get it. He was testing me.

Perhaps a small part of me was angry because, as I sat there in silence processing his question, I thought about the events leading to my injury. And I realized that, in a way, he was onto something. While maybe I didn't break my back recklessly, I also hadn't listened to that voice in my head saying, *Something's not right.* Just before that jump, I saw the check tree, and I knew I was moving too slowly. And I knew in that moment that on any other day I would stop, circle around, and start over. But I had been deprived, we were losing light, I was in a hurry, and I ignored that voice.

And I could own that. I had allowed my feeling of deprivation, not my head, to dictate my actions.

Aaron saw this realization dawn on my face, and took what I thought was an undue amount of credit for it. "So there was something, wasn't there?" He looked pleased with himself.

"Well, I guess…" I began, about to explain myself. But he had no interest in my explanation.

"So let me ask you again. Are you done with that?"

"Yeah," I said, nodding slowly as I said this not just to Aaron but to myself. "Yeah, I *am* done with that. For sure."

That was true. With Shawna's help, I had begun to pay much closer attention to my gut. Gut instinct was what had guided us to Dr. Zhu, after all. And though Shawna and I had both questioned Dr. Zhu's methods, we had been open to the possibilities. So we'd stuck it out, and it had done wonders for me.

Gut instinct was also what had guided us here, to Aaron. That and a friend whom Shawna and I both greatly respected. So although I was skeptical, didn't I owe it to Antonio and to myself to be open to what this, too, might bring? Didn't this kind of healing also have potential, even if it wasn't what we expected?

At the very least, the first session had given me a useful piece of information. "You know, they make walkers with seats," Aaron told me with a smirk, arms folded.

Grant at Lake Tahoe,
first outdoor hike
since injury (Photo by
Shawna Korgan)

That had solidified my resolve. When we returned home that day, I asked Shawna to put the wheelchair in storage. I *was* done with it. With High Fives once again offering to fuel my recovery by generously providing therapy-based financial backing, we could immediately make a phone call to Ron to place an order for a four-wheeled walker with a seat and hand brakes.

Ron seemed a little emotional about it when we went in a couple weeks later to pick up the new walker, which I affectionately named Blue Steel.

"Well, this is great!" Ron said, surprised and enormously pleased when he saw how much progress I'd already made since he had last seen me. "I don't usually get to see anyone's recovery. I get them the wheelchair and I don't often see what happens after that. I mean, this is just fantastic!"

From now on, I'd be walking wherever I went.

Aaron was a professional figure skater who, at age eighteen, contracted a severe case of pneumonia, spiked a fever of about 108 degrees, collapsed on the ice and was later pronounced dead in the ICU, where he stayed dead for four and a half minutes.

As he tells it, while ICU staff began bagging up his dead body, his soul went to the pearly gates, climbed a flight of stairs, and met a council that included various archangels and such luminaries as the Virgin Mary and Buddha. The council proceeded to explain to him that each human being has a sort of "life contract." His was about to expire, and he had a choice: He could either rewrite his contract and go back where he came from or move on to his next universal destination.

As you can imagine, it was at about this point in his story when Shawna and I sort of leaned back on the couch and thought, "Ooo-kaaay... had a good moment up in heaven, all-righty." Nonetheless, it was a riveting, impressive story, true or not.

Anyway, Aaron, as you've by now guessed, chose to return. He woke up, miraculously, after four and a half minutes, and took a huge breath of air the instant before they zipped him up in his body bag. Everyone freaked out, his lungs were full of puss and his temperature spiking. And he healed himself completely in two weeks and walked out of the hospital, symptom-free.

He eventually resumed his figure-skating tour, and while on the road, he started realizing, as he was meeting new people and putting his hands on his fellow skaters, that he seemed to have this gift. Because every time he would touch people, any problems or ailments they had would just go away. And even more than that, he knew how to heal himself, and knew that others could too, if only someone, like him, could show them how.

I can neither confirm nor deny any of that—the death experience, the out-of-body journey, or the healings. Maybe they were fact. Maybe they were just fantastic teaching aids. I can, however, say that Aaron looked like he was in his early thirties, despite the fact that his true age was fifty, so I suppose you can make the argument that, if he, in fact, died and was born again (or whatever) at age eighteen, the math does pencil out.

I also knew that, regardless of whether he could actually do what he said he could do, there were a lot of people, including our friend Antonio, who believed he could. In fact, Antonio and his family believed so fervently in Aaron's abilities that his loving mother insisted on paying for my unlimited sessions. So it was important, for them and for me, that I seize this opportunity, stick with it, and find out for myself whether he could indeed help me.

There was nothing at all magical about Aaron's plan for me. When I asked him, "What is it you do, exactly? What does a healer do?" he told me, "I'm not doing anything—it's you, not me. I'm just a conduit. Look, the universal constant is perfection. It *wants* to be perfect. Your body *wants* to be perfect. But we get in the way of that. I help you get out of your own way. I help create an environment for your body to heal."

Aaron, in fact, disapproved of other people calling themselves healers. He called them "wowie-zowies."

"If I can give you one piece of advice," he said, "stay far, far away from the wowie-zowies."

As Aaron explained it, our bodies have the innate ability to heal themselves. This is something we all know—if you cut your hand, your body knows what to do to fix it. Sometimes it needs assistance, so you use a Band-Aid or stitches. These are just support measures that aid your body in doing its thing. Healing work is the same. Aaron saw himself as an outside support measure that helped remind the body what it was supposed to do.

It's noble work for such an asshole.

And he'd be the first person to tell you he's an asshole, too. Truly, if a good friend hadn't already stepped up to pay for unlimited sessions, I would have said, "Thanks, bro, but no thanks." Aaron's the guy you'd least expect to become a healer. He was rude, he never listened to anything we said, never took a moment to get to know our back story, he cussed incessantly, and he leered at my wife. I didn't like the guy at all, if I'm being honest. But the more I think about it, the more I think that was part of his plan.

I think he wanted me to be pissed off, to oppose him and the process. I think he wanted me to hate those sessions so much that I'd hurry up, get better already, and be done with them.

With Aaron, there was no easing me into the process, taking it easy on the guy in the walker. I think there was a little trial by fire going on to make sure I was truly ready to make the changes I needed to make. He gave me the worst possible first experience so that he'd know, if I came back, I really was serious, that I was ready to recover.

Almost immediately we began to see him twice a day, five days a week, for about an hour each time. And every time was much the same as that first day. We'd pull up in Free Candy and wait in his driveway until he'd come out and let us know with a nod if he was ready for us to come in. Every time, I'd struggle up those stairs. But eventually, thanks to Blue Steel, it got easier. And every time, no matter how much I'd struggled or how long it took me, there Aaron would be, sitting in his chair, arms crossed, without speaking a word, just analyzing me like, "Well, that took you long enough. You done with all this yet?"

He watched and waited, observed where I was emotionally and mentally, examined how I might be different than I had been last time. Shawna and I sat on that big soft couch like patients with a psychologist, and when we were quiet and grounded, we could begin.

Most of the time, our sessions involved him presenting us with riddles to solve. The riddles were almost childish, seemed completely unrelated to the subject of my recovery, and were usually designed to remind us of basic life lessons. They were so basic, in fact, that we tended to over-complicated them; this was what Aaron called "widgeting" or "running around the tree."

For example, there was the day in week one when he laid this one on us: "Let me ask you a question. If a tree falls in the forest and nobody's there to hear it, does it make a sound?"

I'd heard this riddle a thousand times before, and knew it had no answer. But I also knew it's rhetorical nature was usually asked to spark a philosophical debate, so I played along. "Well, it depends on how you look at it."

"No. There's an answer," Aaron said.

As a man of science, I sat there rationalizing. "Well, literally, to hear means to perceive sounds with the ears, to actually interpret them as sound. So if no one's there, and no one can hear it, then the word 'sound' is no longer applicable. So no, there's no sound."

Aaron sat and looked at me, expressionless. "So you're gonna run around the tree?" he asked, folding his arms and watching me.

"Well, wait a minute," I backpedaled. "Let's take the other side of that. 'Cause I mean, sound is also defined as a sonic wave, which occurs whether or not something is there to detect it. So it's going to propagate those waves, regardless. So… there appears to be an argument in multiple directions, and…"

"Keep running around that tree," he said.

"Well…" I silently pondered what he was looking for, took into account the simple nature of the universe that his sessions were geared toward helping me to see, and piped up, "It doesn't matter… It doesn't matter if the tree makes a sound."

He smiled. A real, honest-to-God fucking smile. That was new.

"What? Why are you smiling?"

"You know, you're the first person to figure that out?" he smiled. "There's hope for you after all."

So "it doesn't matter" was the answer? What kind of answer is that? People *paid* for this?

Yes, actually. It was in this way that Aaron healed—he shined a flashlight on things we knew already, but which had been buried by the clutter, the noise, the widgeting, the accident. There were dozens of stories and riddles, all just as inane as this, and all of which, for the most part, boiled down to one basic message: Silence the noise. Slow down. Clear the decks. Quit filling your life, your mind, with all this useless analysis that amounts to nothing. Stop running around the tree. Simplify. Stop!

Aaron's point was that now the energy I expended on widgeting was detracting from my recovery. My life had taken a one-eighty, so my approach would have to do the same. What Aaron aimed to show me was that I could take all that "widget" energy, which I often expended on things that at the moment didn't matter, and turn it inward, focusing it on healing instead. Once I could turn that noise off, just be still and simply *be*, I could create a space in which my body could heal itself. What did it matter whether the tree in the forest made a sound? The point was that I should focus only on what mattered, and that was my recovery.

"Everything's a lot simpler than you want to make it. You and your widget mind," Aaron told me. "The universe is a very simple place. No matter what language you speak, two plus two is always going to equal four. You know everything you need to know, if you'd just get out of your own way. Once you're back where you want to be, you can widget yourself into oblivion. But right now, you need to *stop*."

On the drive home in Free Candy after that session, we were fairly quiet until Shawna suddenly said, "Oh my God! I just realized something," and turned to look at me with a smile of sudden realization on her face. "Analysis leads to paralysis!"

We'd both heard this phrase a dozen times, but now we actually saw firsthand what it meant in a literal sense. After all, before my injury, I had planned my life down to the second, and had laid extensive groundwork on my activities for the week leading up to my injury, even for the snow-mobile jumps we'd make that day. And my focus had been so intense and unbreakable that day that I had forgotten to just *be*, to be flexible. Stopping would have given me freedom and choice. Stopping would have given me a chance to be flexible and open to what the day would bring. Had I not been so fixated on my plan for that day, maybe I wouldn't have injured myself. In my case, analysis had actually led to paralysis.

So maybe Aaron's lessons were simple because life is simple. Maybe he had a point.

Meanwhile, we'd found no solution to our living situation or our financial quandaries. We'd had so much going on over the last several weeks, from our travels to San Jose and the intensity of my therapy there, to re-starting our in-home therapy and adding sessions with Aaron to the mix. So we still hadn't taken the time to analyze our full financial picture. This hit home for me when, about a week after our return to Reno from San Jose, I finally managed to sit down in front of the computer and look at our bank accounts online.

"Uh… babe?" I called to Shawna from the table. "Can you come here a sec?"

She came in and saw my face, a mixture of shock and, perhaps, amusement, the kind that comes when something is so bad that all you can do is laugh. "What?"

"Um, I'm online and… well, come look," I said, pointing at the screen.

According to the bank's website, the sum total of all our accounts amounted to about $300. In full. No savings, no investments to turn to in case of emergency. Everything was gone. We could probably buy food, and that was about it. All our liquid capital, our entire safety net, amounted to just $300. In about two weeks, if not sooner, we were going to be dead broke. With or without the landlord's foreclosure, we would have been kicked out of our house soon anyway, because there was no way we could have made rent.

Having grown up at Lake Tahoe, I had been used to struggling. Outwardly it may have seemed like I lived a lavish life there in that prestigious resort town. And because I ski-raced, a very expensive hobby, people generally assumed my family was well off. But the truth was that my dad had traded his mortgage banking for ski passes and gear for me. The truth was that my parents had sacrificed a lot to keep us there. The truth was that I had been raised on cans of Beenee Weenee.

Because of that, I'd been a very enterprising kid. I learned early that if I wanted things I had to work for them. I had started by selling that candy to raise money for my remote control dream car. When I got older and into BMX racing, I sold special shoelaces that I bought in Oklahoma while visiting my grandmother—shoelaces you couldn't get in Tahoe and that turned into a huge fad—for $10 a pop. Then I turned that money into a "Frankenbike," a racing bike I built myself out of used parts. When I went to college and declared my engineering major, I vowed to do well for myself so that I could buy whatever fucking gear I wanted, so I could be like James Bond, with a garage lined with shelves full of top-of-the-line gadgets. And I had finally begun to live that goal, buying myself the best gear I could find and even the spare-no-expense truck I'd always wanted to drive.

For the first time in my adult life, I was looking at two weeks of money left and nothing on the horizon to replace it, no way to enterprise my way to safety.

Even if Shawna could have gone to work the next day, The Sanctuary was gone. Starting fresh as a trainer, it would have taken her months to build up a clientele and earn enough money to support us. That didn't help our immediate situation. And as for me, returning to the lab in any capacity would require me to carry highly delicate items and pour heavy containers of chemicals all day—an impossible thing for me at this stage. I could barely sit comfortably at the computer for longer than a few minutes at a time. I really wasn't equipped for any job at this point.

Shawna leaned back on her chair, arms folded, and sighed. I ran my hands through my hair, shaggy now that I hadn't had a haircut in months. We looked at each other in silence, neither of us speaking for a few minutes as panic raged inside our brains.

After a few silent minutes, we began to go back and forth, volleying ideas that we knew wouldn't work, recalling untapped money and then remembering we had actually tapped into it after all. We once again plunged into silence.

And what I kept thinking as I sat there was this: I had just lived through the thing I had always feared most in the entire world—paralysis. I had broken my back and was fighting every day to come out the other side. Was it really possible that *money* would be the thing that finally did us in? Because, what a fucking waste.

"Well," said Shawna, all of a sudden resolute. She firmly put her hands on the table, stood up, and walked determinedly to the kitchen to fix us something to eat. "We're problem-solvers. We've gotten through this much. We'll figure something out."

I had faced a similar financial crisis before I had the accident.

In 2004, I graduated from the University of Nevada, Reno's mechanical engineering program, and, having demonstrated enthusiasm that bordered on outrageous naiveté, I had earned an incredible internship with the department's youngest professor, Dr. Jesse Adams, an upstart with a newly minted Ph.D. in nanotechnology from Stanford. Our work together involved making proprietary laser science-driven devices for high-energy, high-density, high-intensity laser oblation experiments. We made very expensive laser targets for high-end, high-powered, multi-million-dollar lasers held by such prestigious government facilities as Los Alamos National Lab, LULI in France, and the FZD in Germany.

Grant and Steven at the laser facility in Japan
(Photo by Jesse Adams)

The work we were doing held remarkable promise on a global scale, thanks to its many possible applications in the medical and renewable energy fields. So once we'd developed the science, the University of Nevada extended us the opportunity to spin out of the university into a full-fledged company, which we called NanoLabz, of which I became president. So in May of 2004, I literally graduated college on Saturday, and bright and early on Monday morning, I was taking calls as the president of a nanotechnology company.

To give you an idea of the magnitude of our work, our average contract size was generally on the order of several hundred thousand dollars, so that we could produce roughly twenty-five to fifty targets for one single experimental campaign. In order to do this, nearly the entire cost of the contract would be spent right off the bat to buy the palladium, platinum, erbium hydride, gold, silver, and other rare and semi-rare materials; purchase fabrication equipment; outsource tool time; and travel to out-of-town laboratories in order to build these things, which needed to be hand-fabricated in all three Cartesian planes at nano- and micro-resolution, or one billionth of a meter tolerance. Like a tiny game of atomic Tetris, we were manipulat-

*The NanoLabz team in Dresden, Germany (Photo courtesy of
Grant Korgan)*

ing individual atoms and their elemental combinations, stacking them up
to make something that, when finished, was usually too small to be seen
by the human eye.

All of this money and energy went into producing something that
was roughly 1/100 the width of a human hair. Contract after contract, we
were constantly throwing Hail Marys to keep our company in the black
and moving forward. But the stakes and situation were always the same:
We only had one shot to get it right and, as if it were some video game of
extraordinary risk and exposure that mimicked perfectly the athletic 80
percent of my personality, it could take a hundred steps to get from concept
to a finished product, with each of those steps compounding the difficulty
and risk of not finishing. If, at any point in the process, one of those steps
was unsuccessful, we were left with an invisible yet ridiculously expensive
piece of junk, worthless to the client, and, like that video game, we'd be
taken back to the beginning, with our hands out, asking for another six-
figure amount so that we could do it all over again.

All of this meant that nothing was left to chance. It was only through
meticulous attention to details, months of exhaustive planning, long days

Grant working at the Stanford Nanofabrication Facility
(Photo by Steven Malekos)

and nights of hands-on work with chemicals, million-dollar pieces of equipment in the Stanford nano-fabrication lab, and consultations with every possible expert at multiple junctures along the way, that we were able to prevent such a scenario from happening. And, miraculously, we had been winning for years.

But in February of 2010, just weeks before my injury, Steven and I had hit a roadblock that could have had disastrous consequences. The amount of our contract provided us with money to buy only enough materials for one shot. It was do or die, because the whole company was on the line. We spent every dollar the company had to (hopefully) produce a piece of technology that we would then sell to the Los Alamos National Lab for the cost of materials and time, plus some profit. NanoLabz was making only marginal profits on these things; we would be making enough to stay in business, but we certainly weren't getting rich. It was a whole lot of risk for very little return.

Steven and I had reached a terribly frightening moment of exposure: If what we were building didn't work, we failed. The company would be done, and that failure would be on a huge scale. We had burned through all our contract dollars. And there was no way we could even go back to the client and ask for more money to buy more materials—even on the off-chance they said yes, it would take months to procure any, and we were out of time.

After three days without sleep on a work bender, we sat with our last hope in front of us. After investing thousands of dollars in development and achieving milestones over many months, we were poised to perform the final step of this product's fabrication cycle and finally call it successfully completed. Steven and I sat in our white, head-to-toe, one-piece Tyvek suits for the clean room. We each wore two sets of gloves (latex against the skin and a sacrificial layer of vinyl on top), safety masks, and full head coverings.

In order to prove the technology was more than just theoretical, and in order to supply our clients with the devices they needed to perform this six-figure experiment themselves, this step had to work. We double-checked our numbers, our logic, and our sanity.

We had begun this entire two-month project with numerous silicon wafers, and were now down to only two. We needed to dip one of them into a highly calibrated mixture of potassium hydride and deionized water in order to finish the creation of this proprietary product. Somewhere around midnight, with everything on the line, we went for it.

Nothing. It didn't work. Our worst fear had come true.

I had been getting texts all night from friends who were partying, updating me on all the fun I was missing, and I was sitting in a lab with Steven, facing the prospect of having driven the company into ruins.

After commiserating for a long while, Steven and I hashed out what had gone wrong, explored our options, and came up with a game plan that we felt sure would work, if only we could get our hands on more of the materials we needed. But that was the problem—the money was gone. The idea of quitting broke our hearts, because the project was so important, had so many potentially groundbreaking outcomes.

"What if we just used our own money?" I proposed, unsure as to whether this was coming out of the delirium of sleep deprivation or from a place of genius. "I mean, how much do we believe this will work?"

"Oh, I really think it'll work," confirmed Steven, rubbing his chin.

"Okay, well, do we believe enough to put up our own money?" I pushed.

Grant and Steven at the Stanford Nanofabrication Facility (Photo by Jasmine Hasi)

"What do you mean?" he asked.

"I mean, we could sell our stuff. Maybe we could loan the company our own money to finish the project, and hopefully make it all back when we deliver. What do you think? Do we believe, Stevo?"

We both thought long and hard about it, alternately sighing heavily and saying, "Well... I don't know..." as we mused about what we might have to sell and weighing how important that stuff was to us when compared to the ramifications of not completing the job.

The sun had begun to rise, setting the sky ablaze with orange and pink, by the time we arrived at our triumphant conclusion: We did both believe. We believed strongly that this technology was the key to future advancements like free renewable energy or a cure for a life-threatening disease. After all, what the technology might do was more important than our stuff. As we left the lab that morning to get some coffee, determined to sell our belongings and invest in ourselves, our battle cry was "Fuck stuff."

In the span of twenty-four hours, we had both experienced a paradigm shift. Our stuff really, in the vast scheme of things, meant very little. Sure, we'd worked hard to be able to afford this stuff, but it was *just stuff*. In a wave, all at once that night, we realized that, truly, we didn't need any of it.

"Well, I could sell my snowmobile," Steven had thrown out, exploring the possibilities.

"Yeah! Fuck stuff, man. It's just stuff!" I had said to encourage him. "And I could sell my dirt bike! Fuck stuff."

"Hell, why not sell the furniture in my house?" Steven had said.

"Yeah!" I said, high-fiving him. "Fuck stuff!"

We went home to Reno and began purging our belongings, putting dozens of ads on Craigslist. I sold my dream truck, knowing that I would eventually get paid back, and I would just use the money for my helicopter rating anyway. I sold my four-stall enclosed trailer, which I used to carry my snowmobiles and dirt bikes; I sold a bicycle and cycling gear and even clothing. I returned to the lab, leaving Shawna and her dad to meet with buyer after buyer. More money was coming in, and the more I sold, the easier it got. The idea of "fuck stuff" was freeing.

My godfather had once told me, "The things you own will own you." I had never really seen the truth in that until I began shedding my things I could feel my tethers being cut with every sale. It was all replaceable, all of it. And getting rid of it all created opportunities. So fuck it.

Fueled by funds from our combined sales, Steven and I finished the project, which was a huge success. Los Alamos was not only going to pay us back what we'd spent, but we'd earn a profit to boot. It was time to celebrate.

A week later, I was in the ICU. Shawna and I didn't get to use the money I'd earned to replace my stuff, because now we needed it to pay the hospital. All that work, the two months I had sacrificed to make it happen, the things I'd loved and sold, it had all helped me to make a significant scientific contribution, and I felt good about that, but now I had nothing tangible left to show for it.

Now, eight months later, Shawna and I were on the precipice of homelessness. And just like that night with Steven months before, Shawna and I had a few sleepless nights, banging our heads against the wall, brainstorming ways to bring in enough money to live. The tension in the house was overwhelming. Our financial crisis was all we could think about. It fought with me during my workouts, hovered like a black cloud over our dinner table, sat like a stone in my stomach during my sessions with Aaron, and lay like a suffocating blanket on us in bed at night.

But then I remembered: Fuck stuff.

See, I got an unanticipated gift that day I landed in the ICU, one I didn't expect to get, and one I hadn't really wanted: perspective. Because when you break your back, you realize how truly unimportant *things* really are. All my lists of stuff I thought I needed—a new seat post and pedals for my bike, a new kayak—it all seemed so fucking trivial in the situation Shawna and I now faced eight months later. This injury had given us the opportunity to experience what it's like to lose everything and still to realize in our hearts that we were *okay*, we were still the same people, and that those things don't define us. Fuck stuff.

With vigor, Shawna and I dug into our garage, threw open the closet doors, and purged the gear we both had, which sat useless in the garage. I sold another mountain bike, snowmobiles, ski gear, clothing, and furniture. We sold things we had hung onto for far too long, things we thought it would hurt us to lose. But then they were gone, and my response, surprisingly, was, "Wow. I'm still here. I'm okay." The more we sold, the more, strangely enough, we wanted to sell, because it made us feel powerful to unload it.

We cried, "Fuck stuff!" and high-fived each other as more and more went out the door. Like our worries, we let it all go. We let go of the idea of the importance of our things, because it was just stuff and it was all replaceable. We were thrilled by this new realization that if we wanted more later, after this part of our lives was over, we could just get more. The only really important things were Shawna, me, our big brown dog, and our life together. We were still the same people and still had the same things to give to the world, even without our stuff. As long as we had us, we had what we needed.

"Fuck stuff" was not only a motivational battle cry; it now came into sharp relief as a universal principle. Whether the noise was tangible or not, it was all noise that distracted us from what was really important, and it made life way too complicated. All of it was temporary, an illusion that could come and go, that had no bearing on our lives. So fuck it, all of it. The parts of life that were important were also the simplest parts.

In the days after discovering we'd lost everything, rather than feeling bereft, robbed of our things, we felt strangely, unexpectedly liberated. We'd been given an opportunity to show ourselves that none of our things defined us, that who we were was who we were, and that was actually plenty. And as a man who had been broken in half, it was a powerful lesson for me.

Selling our things gave us a little breathing room, but it certainly didn't fix the problem. We still didn't have a place to live. And this little bit of money would be gone all too soon. Despite the smiling faces we showed the world, when we were at home alone, we worried and widgeted.

Until one day when Shawna announced, "We have to let it go."

"Let what go?" I asked.

"Being stressed out and building up all this negativity about our financial situation. It isn't helping us. I mean, look at us," she said, pointing out our anxious body language. "We have to just let it go. All we can do is put it out in the universe that we need help, and *let it go*. It'll work out."

As long as I had known Shawna, she had said things like this. "Putting it out in the universe" was a principle she had always believed strongly in, while I got caught up in my day-to-day grind, my "widgeting." I assumed I'd eventually take the time to figure out what such universal concepts meant later on, when I wasn't so busy. But this journey I'd been on had shown me her wisdom, and at this point, I had nothing to counter with. The universe seemed like our only hope.

With encouragement from Aaron, who asked us at the start of every session, "What do you want?" Shawna and I were practicing asking the universe for what we wanted. "Take your time and really think about it," he instructed. "You have to ask in full, in completion," he said. I needed to articulate what I wanted completely, specifically.

It wasn't enough to say, "I want to walk." Because he countered with, "So what if that means that you walk with a limp? Or prostheses?"

So I reconsidered it. "Okay. I want more feeling in the lower half of my body."

"Well, more feeling might only be more pain," Aaron said. "Is that really what you want?"

"Nonono," I said. This was trickier than I'd thought. "No, I don't want more pain. I want the pain to stop."

"Okay, well, if all your nerves died tonight and you couldn't feel anything, is that what you'd want?"

"Ugh," I groaned. This was like talking to a five-year-old who was waving his fingers in front of my face and yelling, "I'm not touching you!"

"Okay," I said, taking a deep breath. "Let's try again." I paused, thought for another minute. "I want… I want my body to feel normal."

"No, no," he shook his head. "The universe doesn't understand 'normal.' There is no normal. Define what normal looks like."

So what I ended up with was, "I want to move every muscle and feel every skin cell at the highest level possible for a human being on earth." Now I was getting closer.

The idea that our words had power was really hitting home for me. As I began to trace everything that had happened to me in my life, I could see the value of asking for what I wanted in full and how I had gotten the things I'd really asked for. I had wanted the RC10 as an eight-year-old, had articulated specifically the exact car I wanted and had gotten it. I had managed to work my way into every adventure I'd ever asked to have, from my summer making "Frankenbikes" in order to become a sponsored mountain biker, to skiing competitively through college, to landing the summer adventure in Europe that I'd always wanted, to my nanotech internship, all from sheer will and clear intent.

But I'd also screwed some things up when I hadn't been clear. When I had asked for a simpler life and more time with my wife, I had wound up flat on my back, unable to work and widget, and with my wife by my side every day for months. We needed to be so aware of what we asked for, because truly, in requesting a more simple life and more time with my wife, I got exactly what I asked for.

And how many times do we say what we *don't* want? How many times do we say, "I don't want this job anymore," or "I don't want to live in this house," instead of saying, "This is what I *do* want, and this is when I want it"?

Aaron pointed out that saying what we don't want puts energy to it. And that made some sense to me.

At The Sanctuary, Shawna used to meet with new clients to develop their fitness goals. Working together, trainers and clients would arrive at plans that best met those goals and brought mind, body, and spirit into balance. Clients would say, "I don't want to be a runner," or "I hate gyms, so I don't want to have that kind of experience." And Shawna would have to ask, over and over, "But what is it you *do* want? What kind of experience are you looking for?" Wherever your energy goes, even if it's on what you don't want, that's where it manifests. You have to focus your energy on what you want, in a positive way, then get out of your own way so it can happen.

So with all this in mind, Shawna and I began to ask the universe for what we wanted in full, in completion. Sometimes, they were things we decided together, and sometimes they were things I asked for privately, in those early morning hours when I lay awake, fighting through the burning pain that now radiated throughout the lower half of my body. I made it a habit, chose to act rather than being acted upon, chose pleasure instead of pain, so that this could perhaps replace the burning as my primal sunrise ritual. It was an incredibly empowering idea. If our words had such power, couldn't I ask for anything? And couldn't I have any of it? And if that was the case, who cared whether I woke up in pain? Because just look what I had to look forward to.

After a few days of this, I explained to Aaron with satisfaction that Shawna and I had been practicing this concept.

"Did you tell the universe when to start?" Aaron asked.

"What do you mean?" I looked at Shawna to see if this was something she knew. She furrowed her brow and examined him, curious.

"Well, if you don't say 'start,' the universe won't know when to give all this to you. You could get old waiting for it," he said. "Ask for what you want, and say, 'start, start.'"

"Okay, start now!" I said, looking heavenward, at what I didn't know.

"No, 'start, start.' Once for you, once for the universe," he corrected. "And when you want it to stop, say, 'cancel, cancel.'"

"Why?" I pressed. Why on earth would I ever want any good fortune to stop?

"Well… you want some hot tea?" Aaron asked, changing the subject abruptly and heading to the kitchen to get a cup. We followed behind him slowly as he talked to us over his shoulder.

"Uh, I guess," I said.

"So, if you say you want me to start pouring some tea, I'm gonna keep pouring," he said, hovering the tea pot over the empty cup Shawna held out for him. "You have to tell me when to stop, or else the tea goes everywhere and makes a mess, doesn't it?"

The universe was proving to be pretty particular.

That night, Shawna and I talked very frankly with each other, late into the night, about what we really and truly wanted and needed. We were specific and complete: "We *need* A, B, and C; we *want* D, E, and F; and it would be really cool if G came, too." It was time for us to spell out what we wanted from life, in specific terms, because that was the only thing we *could* do right now. We weren't previously in control of our financial situation, obviously, but in this, we had the empowering realization that we could at least control what we asked for, selecting the perfect words to do so. We asked in full, to completion, and then told the universe, "Start, start."

And then we made the huge, scary decision to just let it go, so the universe could start pouring the hot tea. And we went to sleep.

Make no mistake, this wasn't a half-assed, "Let's let it go, but still, in the back of our minds, we'll keep stressing about it." Because it's tempting to keep thinking about it, to try to widget a solution as you go about your day. If there was something we could *do*, we were completely willing to do it.

Committed to six to eight hours a day, six days a week of therapy, we made recovery our full-time job. But aside from selling our stuff, we had come up with no long-term resource-generating solutions. Meanwhile, the worrying had detracted from the amazing physical progress I was making. So instead, we committed full-bore to the process, and that meant articulating exactly what we wanted and choosing wholeheartedly to completely release it to the universe. Whatever will be will be, we said. We knew there had to be a solution to our problem, something we could do to fix it. And we believed that if we kept our hearts and minds open, it might just reveal itself to us in a way we didn't expect.

So we let it go. There was nothing else to be done.

Moving Day (Photo by Chris Hansen)

CHAPTER 18
SPONSORED BY LOVE

L et me say first that when Shawna and I "let it go," we didn't sit around twiddling our thumbs, expecting the universe to show up with a bag full of money.

But I'm not kidding when I say that it was only *days* after formally, completely asking the universe for what we needed that it started sending us life jackets.

First, we heard from Shawna's parents. They had recently vacated the home she had grown up in, in exchange for a two-master-bedroom house that would allow them to take care of Shawna's grandparents full time. They had decided to take the old house off the market and wanted us to live there instead, providing us a very affordable roof over our heads. By the first week of November, thanks to the efforts of about thirty friends and family members, Shawna and I were completely moved into her childhood home.

Our families and close friends had already done so much for us since my injury, and there was no end to our gratitude. But astonishingly, it kept coming. We began finding cards and checks in our mailbox. We were approached once or twice by people, total strangers, who said, "I just felt like I needed to give you this," as they handed us cash.

Duncan's film, *Alpine Assassination,* finally premiered in November and gave me two amazing gifts. First, it gave me closure on my injury, enabling me to see exactly what happened that day and in the long, difficult week that followed, while allowing me to show my friends, in person, how far I'd come since then. Second, Duncan generously gave us the $2,000 in ticket sales raised from the premiere party.

Money came in. My godparents repeatedly asked, "What do you need?" and then generously provided those things in the form of a huge donation to the High Fives Foundation.

The number of people who came out of the woodwork to help us was beyond all comprehension for us—stunning in its magnitude, absolutely appreciated, and wholly unexpected. But that night when Shawna and I had asked the universe to reveal some answers to our financial problems, one thing that presented itself turned out to have been right under our noses all along. Or, more precisely, on our arms. They were the bracelets I had made out of bike parts.

In 2002, after I had broken my face and shattered seventeen teeth, then endured a series of surgeries that included one marathon nine-root-canal day, I was at my parents' home, recuperating and in a lot of pain.

Among the many activities I had on my plate when I was in my twenties was being a mountain bike racer. And whether I had a mouth full of metal or not, I still had races to prepare for.

My mom had been a phenomenal source of strength and comfort for me in my recovery from that injury—driving me to and from my doctor's visits and surgeries and attending to my many needs, which included whipping up that disgusting liquid diet I had been on for months. So in the garage, as I finished building the wheel I needed to complete work on my bike, it occurred to me that I might make something nice to thank her with.

To build a bicycle wheel, you lace the stainless steel spoke wires from the hub to a nipple, a colored bolt that hangs from the wire and screws it into the wheel rim. You tighten the nipple by screwing it on, which pulls the spoke taut. You create uniform tension around the wheel, bringing it into perfect alignment with the hub.

When I'd finished my wheel, I had extra spokes and nipples lying on the floor beside me. I took a spoke, bent it into a semi-circular bracelet, and screwed a nipple onto it to add color. I presented it to my mom with my deepest thanks, gave her a hug, and told her I loved her. She seemed to really like it, and I went back to the garage, my creative juices now flowing.

I began experimenting with bracelet configurations, twisting one end of the spoke into a loop, creating something that the head of the spoke could fit into. I twisted the spoke around the loop once, then twice, then four times, then six. I used blue nipples, red ones, green, and pink. Prototype after prototype lay at my feet, and by the end of the day, my fingers were calloused and bloody.

But I loved the design so much I took ten back with me to UNR the next day to test out on my fellow engineering students. At a mere $12 apiece, the bracelets were a hit, and by the end of my first class, they were gone.

The next day, the people who had bought them came in with requests for more for friends who had admired them. They caught on like wildfire. I spent that next weekend in my parents' garage feverishly bending and twisting to make nearly fifty bracelets, which sold in an hour the following Monday. Orders continued coming in, and I couldn't seem to make them fast enough.

I began to wonder, what would happen if I made a couple hundred and took them to a bike race? I focused my sights on a race a few months away, and gave up entire weekends to manufacture 300 bracelets. I built a point-of-sale bracelet display out of welded neon acrylic pipe, and hit the road for the Sea Otter Classic bike race at California's Laguna Seca Raceway.

I sold bracelets like crazy. And though I didn't make a profit, I did make back all the money I'd spent on materials and travel to get there that day. I broke even, which in my eyes was an incredible feat.

Even more exciting were the connections I made. I met up with wholesalers and, fortuitously, an editor at *Velo News*, the cycling magazine. Too cocky and ambitious to know better, I pitched him on the idea of featuring my bracelets in the magazine.

"You hand-make these things?" he asked skeptically, fingering one bracelet in his hands and examining the workmanship.

"Yeah, absolutely," I said, believing this was a selling point.

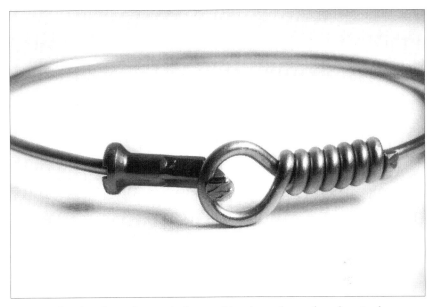

The Korg bracelet made from a bicycle spoke and spoke nipple
(Photo by Grant Korgan)

"So what if I give you an order for ten thousand of these?" he asked, handing the bracelet back to me. "What would you do? Could you even fulfill an order like that?"

"Honestly, sir, I'm not sure," I said, determined to stay positive to convey confidence, still not understanding the premise of under-promising and over-delivering. "But I can assure you that if you order ten thousand, I'll make it happen."

And, of course, weeks later, I got a call from *Velo News,* with a request for a thousand bracelets.

I spent the next weekend honing my manufacturing process, developing it to the point where I could make two or three of them at a time. I fulfilled the contract. Orders continued coming, and by my senior year, my education was being funded by the "Korg Industries" bracelet, which retailed for $14, and which was now being manufactured with the help of a plant in Los Angeles. I was big time.

I began seeing the bracelets at clubs and around campus, on total strangers. But as satisfying as that was, the experience of seeing a stranger on a train in Switzerland, during my summer in Europe, wearing a Korg

Industries twist bracelet with a green anodized nipple, was one of most satisfying engineering moments of my life.

But when I returned home from Europe, I got swept up in mechanical engineering and nanoscience and lab work at Stanford, not to mention snowmobiling and whitewater kayaking. This work-hard-play-hard mentality meant shelving the bracelets. Korg Industries went on hold, and I packed up my remaining inventory of roughly a thousand bracelets, assuming I could pull that nest egg out if I ever lost my job or something, put it all on eBay and make ten or twenty thousand to get me through.

The bracelets became a sort of salvation for me in more ways than one. After meeting Shawna at a party on the night that changed my life, she casually mentioned getting together some other time to discuss selling the bracelets at The Sanctuary. It had been a complete ruse—our meeting turned into an intimate five-hour discussion in which the bracelets never once came up. Even so, I owed it to the bracelets.

Then, when I was flat on my broken back in ICU, when flocks of people arrived to give us love and support, they would hold up their arms and show Shawna, "Look I wore my bracelet for Grant. He made this for me in 2002."

The message of solidarity conveyed through the bracelets got Shawna thinking about that leftover inventory. She thought about giving them away to visitors, a token for them to show, "I'm thinking about you and your recovery. "But when she offered them, people insisted on paying.

Before The Sanctuary's closure in July 2010, Shawna's business partner held a "Circle Up Around Grant" event, where people purchased these bracelets as an ongoing symbol of showing support and belief in my recovery. Then, eight months after my injury and going into the holiday season, when we most needed a way to earn some money, we began getting requests for bracelets, at $20 apiece. Orders big and small came rolling in, and hundreds of dollars in payment for them began arriving in our mailbox.

So there was this unbelievably advantageous money-making opportunity that had landed in our lap, something that enabled us, in return, to give back something tangible, a handcrafted item I'd made with love and which symbolized me in so many ways.

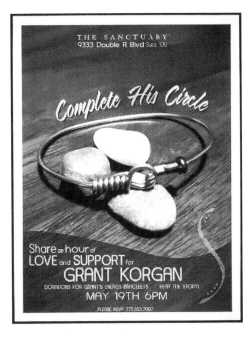

Circle Up event flier
(Design by Fairlane
Vicente)

It was the galvanizing effort of many that propelled the development of our first fundraiser that November. Because though free therapy from the extremely generous High Fives Foundation was an incredible gift, we couldn't do much without food and gas.

The idea of a fundraiser had first come up at Reid and Logan's wedding back in July, where the universe had brought us the gift of new friendships. A good many of the groomsmen were entrepreneurs and well-connected people in the Reno area. Being that they were natural go-getters, the question, "What can we do to help?" came up frequently during the course of that weekend. And over whiskeys beside the bonfire after the wedding, someone said, "What about doing a fundraiser?"

Of course, I was deeply touched and honored by the show of support from these people, but as we all know, ideas tossed around late at night while drinking whiskey don't often come to pass. But they actually intended to do something. By the end of the wedding weekend, the question of a fundraiser wasn't "if," it was "when."

Emails began flying that summer, a fundraising board was created, and between days spent with Dr. Zhu, we had made a plan to meet in August with the guys from the wedding, during one of our trips home from San Jose, so that we could get our planning underway. In a moment of genius, Shawna invited her best friend, Kerrie, to join the meeting.

An events director for a retirement home, Kerrie is a born event planner, a cross between Colin Cowie and Martha Stewart (only likeable). A beautiful, graceful, visionary woman, Kerrie has the innate ability to take any occasion and see the final result in her mind, right down to a centerpiece, a cake design, and the flow of any room. She can turn a vague idea into reality, and better yet, she has the initiative and connections to bring it together rapidly.

Twelve people attended that first meeting in August. We set our sights on a fall or winter event, and Kerrie spearheaded the planning efforts. And because she's so great at selling people on her ideas, within days she managed to get a great friend of ours, the manager of a Reno casino steakhouse involved. But time had been rapidly ticking away, and by the time we had scheduled the event for November 19 at a local casino/resort and planned a delicious menu of food, Kerrie and the fundraising board members only had about two weeks to pull the thing off.

The meetings continued, with the core group of board members being Reid, Kerrie, Shawna, and me, sitting around our dining room table. In one brainstorming session, Reid suggested producing a video telling my story, and Kerrie eagerly jumped on board. With their production help, Shawna and I took our little handicam outdoors and shot a video that would run during the event.

Someone also suggested that we find companies to sponsor the event, and it seemed worth pursuing. We certainly had enough clout in our midst to pull that off.

But it almost felt greedy to ask for more. Shawna and I felt so supported, so encouraged by friends, family, even complete strangers. "You know, I really feel like I'm already sponsored," I said, sitting back in my chair and marveling at the love surrounding me at the table. "I'm sponsored by love."

It was true, my recovery had been sponsored by the love and generous support, shown in ways big and small, from kind people who believed in me and stepped up to help in whatever way they could. Without my intending to, I'd come up with the theme for the fundraiser—Sponsored by Love.

The fundraising board members managed to round up silent auction items, assembling an impressive sponsor list of thirty or forty companies and individuals who made extraordinary contributions, including a $1,000 helicopter ride from a company in Alaska, $700 worth of snowmobile gear, free meals at local restaurants, sunglasses and goggles from a local optician, and even a $1,000 bottle of wine signed by actor Lloyd Bridges. With only two weeks to promote it, word of mouth, a YouTube video designed to solicit donations and sponsorships, and a frenzy of Facebook posts to the "Korg 3.0" page comprised the last-minute marketing efforts.

My buddy Cary Chisum had dreamed up the name *Korg 3.0* months previous, when he had come to visit me while I was still on a hospital bed in our living room. Cary was one guy I could always speak engineer with; he loves gadgets, admires technology, and has a mind that, like mine, seeks optimization and innovation. Despite the vulnerable state he found me in that day, he was impressed by the sheer magnitude of what I'd already lived through since March and the physical and emotional strides I'd made already and continued to make every day.

"Man, think about how much stronger you're going to be after all this," Cary remarked. "I mean, every time you've gone through something huge and challenging, you've come out the other side even better. Like after you broke your face?"

I shuddered, remembering that accident. But he was right, that accident had precipitated major life changes for me—my college degree, my engineering career.

"And then you married Shawna, and you, like, you kicked it up to here," he said, moving his hand up in the air to imply an increased level.

I nodded, "Oh, no doubt," I said, struggling now to imagine the man I might have been without Shawna.

"So now," Cary continued, raising his hand even higher in the air, extending his arm as high as it would reach, "you're gonna be up here, man. A broken back? Seriously? What *can't* you get through after this? They're like your three badges of honor. " He paused, looking around as if grasping for a physical representation of what he meant, "You're like, the third version of Korg... Korg 3.0."

I laughed. "Genius!"

"Yeah, I'm looking at Korg 3.0 right now. That's it," he said, and we high-fived.

In the scientific world, the "rule of three" is enormously important. There are Newton's three laws of motion, three basic principles upon which engineering and our entire understanding of the universe are based. In wilderness survival training, the number three is key. The three basic things you need to survive are food, water, and shelter. You can't survive more than three days without water, more than three weeks without food, or more than three hours exposed to extreme temperatures. And in statics, the most stable and universal object is a tripod; anything with three legs is stable on any ground. To me, the number three has special, even magical, properties. So the idea of three powerful defining moments in a life resonated with stability and survival for me. Cary was right. After surviving three significant moments of transformation, what couldn't I get through?

As the idea of "Korg 3.0" made the rounds among our friends and family, we realized that many people could name their own three defining moments, key turning points in their lives that they had survived and been transformed by. And it didn't take a broken back for them to change and become stronger. The more we shared the idea with people, the more we saw that Korg 3.0 hit a nerve. This new take on the rule of three seemed to hold tremendous significance, and before long, this wasn't just my recovery. Korg 3.0 was a movement.

The Korg 3.0 Facebook page became the sounding board, the way people could connect to us, share words of inspiration, get updates on my recovery, and, of course, participate in Sponsored by Love. We'd been blown away by the generosity of others and the gift of caring we'd gotten from people throughout my recovery. But as the fundraiser approached and Korg 3.0 grew legs, Shawna and I began to realize that maybe the path she and I were on was inspiring others and giving them a gift, too. She and I had always dreamed of helping others, giving back to the world in some way. Perhaps now, despite my injury and our current struggles, we were doing just that. And maybe, just maybe, there was a reason for all of this.

Once I'd gotten out of the wheelchair at Dr. Zhu's and begun to use the walker, my primary goal was to get better at it so I could walk away from my wheelchair for good. And I'd done it when I began working with Aaron. I had stood at Reid and Logan's wedding, and I had wanted to carry that progress forward in a big way. Now that we were planning this fundraiser, I wanted to give back to all the people who had come together to help me by walking across the stage on crutches—without my walker—at the Sponsored by Love event.

Each day I worked for hours, getting stronger as I used my clinical walker. In the beginning of my using the walker, while we were still at Dr. Zhu's, it took two people to get me up out of the chair, and I could only go about ten feet, with someone following me with the wheelchair, before I would collapse. But before long, I could make it twenty feet with relative ease and had enough upper body strength and fortitude to get myself up out of the chair. With frequent work, I could go twenty-five feet, then thirty, then fifty, then one hundred. Near the end of our time in San Jose, my goal had been one thousand feet. I would walk excruciatingly slow laps around the facility with needles hanging out of my body. By the time I finished with Dr. Zhu, I still could only make a couple hundred feet, but I knew I was getting stronger every day.

In fact, so much stronger that Shawna decided one day in October that it might finally be okay to leave me alone in the house for a little while, so that she could attend a fundraiser planning meeting.

She left me seated at the dining room table, where I had spent some time on the computer. Feeling invigorated by this moment of independence and feeling somewhat over-confident, I decided to get up, and use my walker to scoot over to the couch, where I could sit and relax for a while until Shawna got home.

But the reach to my walker, as it turns out, was too precarious, and my body wasn't as strong as I'd thought it was. The four-wheeled walker, sitting against the wall to my left, was just slightly too far away from me, and its awkward size and shape didn't enable me to grab it easily. I leaned over, grabbed hold of it, and felt my body moving in slow motion down to the floor. I wrestled with gravity and lost, pulling the walker down on top of me. It, in turn, slammed into my stationary bike, which was positioned just next to the couch, and it came crashing down, scratching the side table as it fell.

I cracked my head as I fell on my still-healing back, onto a hardwood floor, and lay an achy, sweating, miserable mess under my walker.

"AAARRGGGG! FUCK!" I yelled, and I pounded my fist hard onto the floor in frustration.

Really?! I mean, Shawna had only been gone twenty minutes Was I really this fucking helpless?

I panted for a few moments, exhausted from the fall, and then struggled to regain my composure. I hadn't been hurt; I was okay. I had to pull it together and get myself back up. And after a couple minutes passed, I actually chuckled as I considered what I must have looked like covered in equipment on the floor.

In my mind, I began running through calculated scenarios for getting myself up. I took a minute to recall where my phone was—maybe I could call Shawna and have her come help me. It was too far away to reach. I considered pulling the walker closer to me and using it to propel myself up with my arms. But this would take strength I didn't have, and the walker's wheels and large size made it too awkward to be helpful. I simply couldn't sit up; my weakened abdomen and spine made a sit-up impossible, and though I'd begun rolling slightly on my own in bed, a 180-degree flip was not in my wheelhouse, and neither was lying on my stomach. I was a like a giant turtle, stuck on his back.

I reached back to feel my head, sure it was bleeding from the fall; it wasn't. Waving my arms as if making snow angels, I started pushing things away, sliding the bike and the walker away from me, to make room to slide across the floor to the couch. Once I had some room to move, I used the palms of my hands to create traction on the floor, and pushed myself across the floor, inch by inch, on my back.

After an agonizingly slow twenty minutes I reached the couch. I began pulling cushions down to the floor, and slowly sliding them under my back until I was propped up enough to sit up. I then created a makeshift slide board of cushions, elevating myself pillow by pillow until I could pull myself onto the couch.

It was here, dangling halfway off the couch, red-faced and bathed in sweat that made my rangy, uncut hair cling to my forehead, that Shawna found me. Surrounding me was utter chaos.

"Oh my God! What happened?" she cried as she dropped her purse and a binder full of papers and ran to help me.

"I wanted to sit on the couch," I said between pants.

She pulled my arm up and positioned her body under it, then used her body to lift me to a comfortable seated position in the crook of our L-shaped couch.

She sat at the end, next to my feet, and examined my face for signs of distress. "Are you okay? Did you hurt yourself?"

I exhaled and looked down to do a quick physical examination. "I think I'm okay."

I looked back at her and blinked. And then the two of us burst into laughter.

Even as early as June, in preparation for standing at the wedding, I started working with crutches. When Jen first suggested that I try it, I appreciated her progressive attitude and eagerly went for it. But then, once she and Shawna picked me up and put my arms in the crutches' cuffs, my eagerness turned to anxiety. Down I went, over and over—forward and backward and sideways. I'd take a step and collapse clumsily into their arms.

But my progress in the walker helped my progress with the crutches, and I was driven to walk at Sponsored by Love. One of the benefits of our new home was that it had stairs—it was additional, built-in therapy. Every day, I did laps up and down the stairs, first with my walker and then with crutches—whatever I could do to squeeze in more time on my feet.

Nonetheless, people frequently offered to help move our bed downstairs so I wouldn't have to contend with climbing. And while I thanked them for their kind offers, internally I responded with, "Fuck that." Because there was no way I wasn't going to sleep upstairs in my bed, with my wife, in our bedroom.

So by the time our November move rolled around, I had worked hard enough that I was ready to practice walking a long stretch of our uneven, patchy lawn with the crutches. My mom captured the moment on video while Steven, my godsister, Bridgette, and Shawna were spotters. I fell repeatedly, barely knowing how to move the crutches so that walking would even be possible. But after practicing for a good hour, I had begun to figure out what to do.

By November 19, I *was going to walk across that stage.*

"What do you want?" Aaron said at the beginning of another session.

"I want to walk across the stage at Sponsored by Love," I said boldly.

"So do it," he said matter-of-factly.

"Well, I'm trying!" I said proudly, with a broad smile. "I've been working every day…"

"What did you just say?" he asked, his interest piqued. As if I'd slapped him in the face, he sat up, his eyes wide.

I'd heard it as soon as it had escaped my mouth. "Try."

In the late nineties, while Shawna was still in college, she'd gotten wind of a leadership class that many people she admired and respected had completed. She enrolled and spent a year exploring the principles of powerful communication. She had gotten so much from it that in 2008, I enrolled in the same program, on her recommendation.

Among the many things I got out of that class was the power of choosing the right words, and the word "try" was definitely not one of them.

It's like Yoda says: "Do or do not. There is no try."

As kids, our parents tell us, "Give it a try. Try this food. Just try it. Keep on trying. If at first you don't succeed, try, try again." But the more I think

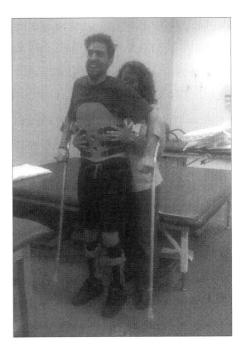

First time in the arm crutches (Photo by Shawna Korgan)

about it, the more I realize that our parents had it all wrong. Because the word "try" is nothing but a way to flake out.

If a friend invites you to a party, you might really want to go, in which case you'll say, "I'll be there!" But maybe you don't want to go, and maybe you don't have the balls to just say, "No, I'm not coming," so you say, "I'll try to be there," because it seems nicer. But you know you won't be there. So really, "try" is a sort of disease of a word. We use it all the time. We say, "I'm going to try to work out. I'm going to try to get better. I'm going to try to learn that skill." The "try" gets us off the hook. It keeps us from committing fully. "I'm going to try that food" means you have no intention of actually eating it. It keeps one foot outside the circle. Why wouldn't I just say, "I'm going to work out" or "I'm going to eat that food"? Don't *try* to be better, just *be better*.

I'm not *trying* to recover, I'm recovering. End of story.

Everywhere I turned, there was "try," a big roadblock to any actual doing. Everywhere, people would say they'd try to help, try to get back to me, try to fix this or that.

But what really blew me away, after first addressing this concept in my 2008 leadership class, was watching Supercross, where guys on two wheels do battle with no cage around their bodies, hucking hundreds of feet through the air, lap after lap, man versus machine, the ultimate test of physical performance and mental strength. Race after race, the only way to succeed is with endless mental toughness, unshakable confidence, and an everyday commitment to training and preparedness that's unmatched in any other sport. These dudes are warriors, and I admire them completely. So it consistently broke my heart to hear, in the post-race interviews, all the top racers say, every time, "Next week, I'm going to try to get back on that podium." There was Bubba Stewart, thanking sponsors and fans for helping him to completely dominate on the course, and his goal for next week is to *try*?

Sure, humility forces them to hold back; who likes the guy who says, "I guarantee domination next week"? But the thing was, Bubba didn't always win the next week. "Try" was a self-fulfilling prophecy.

What an opportunity it would be, I thought, to sit down for ten minutes with Bubba and explain to him, "Look, you don't have to be cocky, but maybe instead of saying 'try' and shooting yourself in the foot, you could say something else? I've got this secret weapon…"

But even though I was aware of it, even though I came to embrace the "no-try rule," here I was in Aaron's office, struggling with one of the greatest difficulties of my life, and I was saying "try." It was so deeply embedded into my consciousness, my manner of speaking, that it had slipped out, seemingly without my control.

"You're going to *what?*" Aaron said.

"Oh, wow, I cannot believe I just said that," covering my face with my hands.

"Did you really just use the word *try?* Are you fucking kidding me?" He shook his head at me.

It happened more than once in my sessions with Aaron. Sometimes I'd catch it on its way out: "I'm gonna tr-aaaaah," I'd blabber, then laugh at my mistake.

And Shawna would bust me now, too. "I'm going to try to pedal for five minutes today," I'd tell her as I hopped aboard the NuStep.

"No, you're not *trying*, you're *doing* it," she'd say.

"Oh, shit! You're right! Sorry," I'd say.

And "sorry" was another one. "Sorry" was pathetic, pitiful, depressing. Are you sorry, or do you apologize? Do you just feel bad, or do you own the mistake and intend to rectify it?

The more conscious I became of my words, thanks to the constant reminders from Shawna and Aaron about the importance of choosing them correctly, the more powerful I felt in my recovery. My words were spoken with intention, with the full force of my actions behind them. Taking "try" out of my vocabulary helped me clear the decks, forced me to be in the moment and to stop putting off the inevitable. It helped me get out of my own way, to stop "doing laps around the tree." I was no longer trying, I was doing. It was energizing, and it was a small change that, interestingly, made a big impact.

Shawna once told me that there are two kinds of people: There are the "Have-Do-Be" people and the "Be-Do-Have" people.

The Have-Do-Bes think like this: "Once I have this, then I can do that, and then I'll be happy." They rely on the material, the external, for their internal peace or happiness. These people say things like, "Once I have that job, then I can buy a better car, and then I'll be happy."

But the Be-Do-Haves think this way: "I am this way, therefore I can do this, and I can have that." The Be-Do-Haves are fewer and farther between. The Be-Do-Haves decide to be happy first. They can choose to be joyful, to be positive. They choose to *be*. They are completely present, in the moment. And that presence affords them extraordinary clarity and contentment that's wholly internal and relies on nothing but a state of mind. Ironically, although they focus on the having *last*, it's the Be-Do-Haves who actually *do* and *have*, because that presence and clarity of mind allows them to truly see the gifts that happen to be right in front of them.

Shawna is a Be-Do-Have person. And I was well on my way to becoming one as well.

For example, when I was in middle school, I had this friend who never seemed content with anything. When we were in middle school, she'd say, "It'll be so much better in high school because we'll be able to do this." In high school, she said, "I can't wait until I'm in college so I can do that." I remember how miserable she always seemed, how she never seemed happy with where she was or who she was with.

I ran into her a few years back and learned that she'd eventually become the nurse she had always said she wanted to be. She was married, had a family and a great job with a hospital. And she was still as miserable as ever, still seemed to be grasping at something beyond her reach, while entirely missing all the things that were right in front of her. After we parted ways that day, I felt really sad. She had wasted her life. She had wasted so much time thinking the grass was greener, relying on so many material possessions, so many things that were out of her control, in order to achieve contentment.

My decision all those months ago in the hospital to stop looking back and only look forward had been a critical piece of my recovery. Had I not made that decision, I might not have made the progress I had made. It was why Aaron told me, at the end of our very first session, "Don't ever tell that accident story again. Forget about it. Stop reliving it." Because if I kept dwelling on the past, kept talking about it, I gave it power. Then I was putting energy there instead of into the present moment. If I kept remembering the pain and difficulty of that day, if I still attached such emotional significance to that day, it would always be the reason I couldn't get up and walk on my own. It would define me. That would be the energy I was surrounding myself with.

But the other part of this is that when you're only focused on the destination, you forget to notice the scenery. You get so used to saying, "This is where I'm going," that you forget to say, "This is where I am."

"When I can walk," I'd begin to say to Aaron, and he would cut me off to say, "You're already walking."

I was. I was walking several hundred feet at a time. I was walking with adaptive equipment, but I was walking.

"So what are you focusing on? Are you looking for a problem or looking for a solution?" he'd ask me. "Are you recovering, or aren't you?"

And that's the real trick, isn't it? To be present, to appreciate the moment you're in right now. It's not so hard when we're young; that's our natural state. We simply are happy, joyful, aware, and immersed in the moment. No one needs to tell a child "Hey, be present." That's all kids know how to be; it's instinctual. It's when we get older and fill our lives with noise, when our minds begin to widget, that we begin to lose this instinct. We're born balanced, and it's only when we clear away the clutter, strip away all the analysis that paralyzes us, that we regain that balance and open our eyes and realize, "Hey, I *am* happy. I am healthy. I am where I need to be." And it doesn't depend on doing anything or having anything. The haves and the dos are always going to change, but I can be whatever I choose to be, and that remains constant.

I can choose to be whatever I want.

Shawna and I had nothing, and we could do nothing about it. We'd gotten rid of our stuff. I'd lost my ability to walk under my own steam. We couldn't work, buy things, go anywhere. But as I realized the power of my words, the power of statements like, "I am recovering" instead of "I will recover," I realized that I was inherently making a choice every time I opened my mouth. I was steering my own ship.

It's not easy to simply decide to *be* anything. It takes practice, lots of practice. Fortunately, we now had the time to practice. And it was because of that time, that forced stillness, that I got clarity I didn't have before.

"What do you want?

We were in Aaron's office again.

I knew instantly what I wanted. "I want to get back on a snowmobile."

Aaron considered this and nodded his head once. "Why?"

"What do you mean, 'why?'" I asked.

"I mean, why do you want that?"

I looked at him sideways, exasperated. Aaron had never let me share my passions with him, never let me explain why sports were so important to me. On that very first day, I had felt him accusing me of being "a stupid extreme sports guy," but I had never gotten a chance to dissuade him of that idea. After seeing him for several weeks, here we were again. Why did I need to justify this desire to him?

"There he goes, taking some more laps around the tree," he said, looking at Shawna. He chuckled, shook his head, and then leaned in toward me. "Okay, look. It's like your wife's fake boobs."

Shawna, who sat at the end of the couch deep in thought, was startled out of her reverie. She widened her eyes in shock and disbelief. "I'm sorry, *what* did you say?"

"What the fuck?" I said angrily. He had always checked Shawna out, appraised her body in a lewd, obvious way, despite my standing just feet away.

Shawna sat there with her mouth hanging open, not sure how to respond. She stared at Aaron, waiting for an apology or a clarification.

"Okay, Shawna, why did you get fake boobs?" he leaned in toward her, and looked pointedly, unapologetically at her.

The impulse in me to reach out and wrap my hands around his scrawny fucking neck was so strong that I began to shake. But Shawna, interestingly, seemed almost amused.

"No one's ever asked me that, actually," she said, surprisingly not seeming offended anymore.

"Seriously," he said, clasping his hands, still looking at her intently. "What brought you to the place in your life where you chose to do that?"

Shawna looked thoughtfully at him, looked sideways at me, and then smiled and shrugged. "Because I wanted to."

"Why?" he pressed.

"Because that's an experience I wanted to have. I'd never had them, and I wanted to see what it would be like," she said, completely unashamed. I beamed with pride. Good for her.

"Beautiful!" said Aaron, beaming as well. "Perfect. See?"

"See what?" I said, baffled and mildly irritated.

"Life is about experiences," he said. "Shawna just chose an experience she wanted to have. That's all there is to it. No deep answer, no psychology. People always want to make life this complicated, deep thing, attach all this meaning and energy to every decision we make. But for pretty much everything in life, the answer is the same: 'Because I want to. I want that experience.' Beautiful."

Aaron looked at Shawna appreciatively, seeing in her now a newfound wisdom, a sense that she got it.

"So what does that have to do with anything?

"It means, decide what experience you want, and stand in it," he said, turning his attention to me. "Life is about experiences. You're the master of your universe."

This was, of course, something I'd always known without thinking about it. This was the truth I'd always stood in, and it was why I had skied, snowmobiled, kayaked, all the things I loved doing. I just wanted those experiences, plain and simple. Aaron wasn't teaching me anything new. He was just forcing me to solidify my beliefs, to decide what I stood for and stand in it.

I was beginning to see that my experience was simply cause and effect. I had chosen an experience that had given me a particular result—a spinal cord injury. My injury wasn't good or bad, and there was no sense beating myself up about it, because I wasn't a victim of my circumstances.

My godfather has always said, "You are the sum total of every thought you've ever had in your life." I finally understood what that meant. In a strange way, every choice I'd made had led me to paralysis. And standing in my truth had given me a whole new set of experiences to choose from. There was no good or bad in that, just cause and effect. I wasn't a victim of circumstances, I was actually the master of them.

Because of my injury, a life-altering thing, I had put it into its own category, thought of it as an exception, a situation with its own rules. But in truth, it had the same rules as everything else. Standing in my truth had consequences, and presented me with a new set of choices. I wanted to snowmobile again, and I had complete control over setting that into motion.

*

For me, this was a sort of epiphany, but for Shawna, it was more like, "Oh, yeah! I forgot about that!" It was the truth she'd always lived in until she landed in the position of spending twenty-four hours a day helping me survive, and she lost sight of the forest for all the trees. Aaron, he was just reminding her of the forest, and it was miraculous for me to watch her see it again. She had always been told, ever since she was a child, that she was an old soul. I saw that in her the first time we spoke, and now I was proud to see that Aaron was beginning to know it, too.

So although I was getting powerful reminders from Aaron every day, it was through Shawna that I could see how those old principles applied to me in my new life, and how to put those abstract lessons into practice for my recovery. She was my true teacher; she was my guidebook. Circumstantially, I'd been operating on the bottom tiers of Maslow's Hierarchy of Needs, focused on the day-by-day details that helped me survive, got me through the day, worked to overcome pain, and moved me forward. Shawna had operated at the top of the pyramid, and was in fact highly self-actualized. It was because, all those months ago, that she'd said "trust me" and had encouraged me to operate on that higher plane with her, to take a path that was unpredictable, challenging, out-of-the-box, and, admittedly, sometimes uncomfortable, that I had actually been able to learn those lessons.

I was glad to see that Aaron understood this about Shawna. With every riddle, every story with a moral, he would now turn to Shawna and say, "You already know this. Do I really need to tell you this?" And the light bulb would inevitably turn on—Shawna did know, seemed even to think in a different way.

"What's your job?" Aaron asked her one day, early on in our time with him. "What do you think your role is with Grant right now?"

"I feel like I'm a warrior," she said, somewhat shyly, looking at me to be sure I was okay with this terminology.

"Totally," I said encouragingly.

"Yeah, it's like, it's my job to protect and embrace Grant, to hold him up here, to his highest place," she said, spreading her hand and holding it above her head. "That's what he's always done for me. We help each other be the highest version of ourselves."

Early on the morning of the Sponsored by Love event, there came a knock on our door. Shawna was delighted to open it and find our great

Free Candy with the fresh graphics from Boost Creative USA
(Photo by Grant Korgan)

friend, Ronnie Parker, standing on our front porch. Ronnie, the owner of a local graphic design and advertising firm, had been helping Kerrie to make the fundraiser a huge event with his vast array of marketing talents.

"Hey, Shawna," he said somewhat slyly. "I'm here to borrow Free Candy."

"Um..." Shawna said, confused, her eyes narrowing to puzzle him out. "Did you... need something?"

"I can't tell you, I just need to borrow it for a little bit. I promise it'll be in good hands. I'm gonna leave my wife's truck here for you to use until I'm done with it. 'Kay?" He casually gestured at the luxurious, tricked-out, all-white 2008 Chevy Tahoe sitting on twenty-two-inch wheels, with a stereo so complex I didn't even feel comfortable touching it.

"Use it all day, okay?" Ronnie instructed, handing over the keys. "When you come tonight to the event, just park it in valet. We'll see you over there."

In the last few weeks, Shawna and I had come to expect the unexpected. Every time we thought we'd had all the surprises there could possibly be, there were more. We were living in a strange, alternate reality in which we could now open the door and find things like this. Confused and somewhat humbled, we got into the SUV and decided to just enjoy this experience for a few hours until the mystery resolved itself.

That afternoon, dressed in our finest clothes, we drove to the valet entrance at the hotel and found a new and improved Free Candy waiting there for us. Ronnie and friends, who had lent their professional artistic talents, had worked all day to have the van custom wrapped with graphics representing me, Sponsored by Love, and the Korg 3.0 movement—a photo of me atop Mount Whitney, logos of various sponsors that had stepped up to be part of this fundraiser, and a new Korg 3.0 logo.

Free Candy had been given new life. Saved from the junkyard, it had been a salvation for us and had become a new and improved version of itself. Like me, Free Candy wasn't expected to make it, but it had come back. Now, just like me, it too was sponsored by love. Free Candy and I, we were birds of a feather.

I sat on stage, on my walker's seat, behind a curtain. Beside me, leaning against a large plywood cube among an assortment of backstage props, were my arm crutches. My heart was in my throat. My own voice strangely boomed around me, telling my story: *"We were having one of the best sled days of our lives."*

I was hidden, preparing for my big moment. As the video now rolling would soon show, I had walked with my crutches for my longest distance the previous week, on a day full of firsts. We had shot that portion of the video just minutes after I had exited a Beechcraft Sundowner c23.

Before breaking my back, I had been part-owner of this plane and was working on getting my flight ratings in it, in preparation for my eventual career as a helicopter pilot. Rent on a plane is usually about $100 an hour, not to mention the cost of gas and an instructor's time, so it would have cost me about $4,000 just to finish the process of getting my license. After which, I still wouldn't have had a plane to fly. So instead, I had called my buddy, Matt, a certified flight instructor, and proposed a buy-in on his personal plane, which he had kept at the Stead, Nevada, airport very close to

Sponsored by Love Event flier (Design by Jason Mead)

my NanoLabz Nevada office. Anxious to split some of the costs and to see me licensed, he agreed. I'd go early in the morning to the airfield, go flying, practice my budding aviation skills, then walk over to my office to start the workday.

Always with my endgame in mind, I jumped at any and all chances that came my way to fly, ride along, or experience helicopters. My desire for aviation had been very strong since I was a young child, and since becoming more conscious and clear of my desire to become a pilot, the opportunities seemed to emerge all around me.

I'd done nearly everything but my final check flight, the flight that would have seen me licensed as a pilot. "Quit flying for fun and focus on your check ride, already!" Matt kept nagging me, and I honestly don't know what I was waiting for. We talked about scheduling my check ride for mid-March of 2010—the week after my injury. After my injury, Matt bought back my half of the plane, just handled it so that I didn't have that on my plate, too.

In early November, with Sponsored by Love just weeks away, I called Matt and told him I was ready to fly again. He was all for it, so I got to fly before I could even drive.

We met at the runway at the Reno-Stead Airport. I walked on crutches toward Shawna, who recorded every moment.

Matt had brought several friends so that we could fly in formation. Getting me in the plane from my walker was the most difficult part. Once in, I began experimenting with the rudder pedals; without sensation in my feet, I had no sense of pressure or direction. Fortunately, Matt had a second set of pedals that enabled him to correct any of my mistakes. Still, it was the worst takeoff I had ever done. I violated one of the two taboos in flying (bad takeoffs and bad landings) when I bounced off the ground before making it into the air. I had forgotten all the numbers, including the speed I needed to reach before takeoff.

But once in the air, working the controls to feel the freedom of flight, I knew I was back. Barring costs (which were still an issue), there was nothing to prohibit me from pursuing my dream.

In our three planes, we touched down at the Sierraville, California airstrip, where I walked the runway toward a camera that filmed the concluding moments of this Sponsored by Love video.

And now, in this moment, I would live another dream. I would walk again, across a stage, surrounded by the people I loved, who had come to give generously to me.

"My goal is 120 percent recovery," came my voice from the video. The moment was approaching fast. The ten-minute video of my story was almost over. I needed about half that time to transition comfortably and stably to my crutches and make my way to the wings at the edge of the stage.

"I hope. I focus. I rally. I live. I progress. I love. I thrive. I rise. I am sponsored by love," my voice said.

The electronic music, the video's soundtrack to my first walk, abruptly stopped, and the room plunged into silence. The house lights came up, and applause and whistles rang out.

With my eyes fixed to the floor, to ensure I didn't ruin the whole show by tripping on one of the dozens of cables lying in my way, I ambled slowly,

Ready for takeoff at the
Stead, NV airfield (Photo
by Shawna Korgan)

awkwardly, just working it out as I began the long, gnarly trek across the stage on my crutches.

Suddenly, the applause turned thunderous. For the first time, I looked up, confused as to why the fifty or so people I expected to see would sound so loud. I nearly toppled over when I realized that there were roughly 400 people filling the room, just wall to wall people. And all of them, even manly men I dirt bike with, crying.

Fueled by adrenaline and the outrageous show of support, wearing a smile from ear to ear, I made it across the stage, where an emcee reached out to hand me the microphone.

Weeks before, I had come up with a quote, a zinger that I knew I'd whip out at the end of my talk. But beyond that, I had no idea what I was going to do when I began to talk.

But just as I had done at the wedding in Mendocino, I reached down deep inside myself and found a reservoir of energy and accomplishment that even I didn't know I had. Because not only did I manage to walk across the stage, but I handed the emcee a crutch so that I could take his microphone and thank from the bottom of my heart the group of people assembled. Shawna was waiting in the wings, at the ready in case I collapsed and needed her to catch me. From where I stood, I could see her chest heaving with sobs, her eyes sparkling with tears that were streaming down her cheeks, despite the warm, encouraging smile on her face.

This victory of mine was every bit hers, too. Now was my chance to share it with her. While Ryan, Ken, and Duncan had saved my life that fateful day, Shawna had been saving it every day since.

"Right now, I want to invite the person up who helped me stand in a time when I couldn't stand for myself," I said, my eyes on her. "Shawna, could you please come help me stand now?"

She sobbed again and tried discreetly to wipe the tears from her face as she made her way across the stage to hold me.

She hugged me tightly, in one of the first true, full-body hugs we had had since my injury, and kissed me. Looking me in the eyes, she said, "I love you." Then she inserted herself under my arm to be my second crutch as I held the microphone to speak. I had prepared nothing but a sentence, but I was overcome by the need to talk.

"This amazing, gorgeous woman, Shawna, my soul mate, my true north," I gushed, overwhelmed with love for her. "This wonderful woman has stood by my side every minute of every day. I just want to thank her for sharing in this amazing moment, and for walking this path with me. I literally would not be here without her."

More applause and whistles rang out as Shawna and I embraced and kissed again.

I was so overwhelmed with gratitude, my words felt hollow, inadequate. Yet, having nothing else to work with, I stumbled my way through thank-you's and appreciation for love and support and favors large and small, for every kind word and thought, even for the sheer existence of the many people I loved. I rambled for fifteen or twenty minutes as I tried to grab hold of enough of the right words to appropriately express my emotions. I told my story, described the past months of recovery, the astonishing progress I'd made, the struggles Shawna and I continued to overcome, and my unwavering goal.

*Grant and Shawna holding
each other up (Photo courtesy
of* Reno Gazette-Journal)

*Sponsored by Love (Photo by
Angelo Anastassatos)*

"My intention is not only to completely recover, but to pay it forward to the world, to share what I'm learning about spinal cord injuries and to help others to recover, too. And I intend to recover 120 percent."

I paused dramatically and pulled the zinger out of my pocket. I said with heart-felt conviction: "It's not about what I've done. It's about what I'm going to do!"

Blown away by the applause that once again filled the room, Shawna took the microphone from me and handed it back to the emcee in exchange for my crutch. And then I walked back to where I'd started, this time with my wife at my side.

The next four hours were a blur of hugs, people crushing me with the weight of their love and well wishes, so appreciated but *so painful.* Shawna's dad was on hand to remind the over-excited huggers to be gentle each time they went in for another hug. But I didn't care about the pain. I just soaked in the love.

Grant gives Roy Tuscany
a gratitude-filled shout-out
at SBL
(Photo by Jesse Hon)

Sponsored By Love had proven to me that nothing is impossible, nothing's out of reach for people with heart, ambition, and positivity. Because with two weeks of marketing and only a little longer than that to plan the entire event, we managed to raise an unbelievable $25,000 that night.

Instantly, everyone involved with the event knew it would be an annual thing. And it wouldn't just be about me—it would raise awareness about spinal cord injuries, even help others struggling with them. Someday there would be no recovery costs for me, and perhaps, we thought, the event could give back to the High Fives Foundation in the way it had given to us, and they could sponsor another athlete, even ten athletes, and help them like I had been helped.

That first event, along with funds raised by High Fives, paid off the remaining medical bills. We had a roof over our heads and just enough left over to buy food and gas, to keep the lights on and the water running.

I was flat-out blown away by all this. Humanity was raining positivity all around us, and we couldn't be more grateful. Just when we'd think we were barely keeping our heads above water, we'd get another call from High Fives to announce plans to do another fundraising event, or from Alpine Assassins saying they were going to do an event in my honor to raise more money.

Free Candy's message made the local rounds, its graphics proudly, even audaciously, boasting its message of hope and positivity. Text messages rolled in most every day from friends who had seen it around town and had been reminded by it of the idea of survival, of simplifying and being grateful.

And the life rafts kept coming. One day in early December, we heard a knock at the door. We opened it to find a courier hand-delivering a piece of certified mail. Inside we found two letters: The first was from Tom Jacobs, an attorney and long-time family friend, who had written, "You're doing great—hang in there. We're behind you 100 percent."

The other letter was from a neurosurgeon named Dr. Liam Ryan, who wrote, "I heard your story through Tom and have been inspired by your drive to recover. I'm a neurosurgeon and I want to help you out. Enclosed, please find a check to assist you with your continued recovery. I would also like to extend to you full access to all the resources I have available, including unlimited physical therapy in our office."

Miraculously, we would stay afloat.

Grant and Shawna walking around Virginia Lake (Photo by Pam Korgan)

CHAPTER 19
ONE FOOT IN FRONT OF
THE OTHER

Outside the two hours a day we spent with Aaron, the rest of the day, pretty much, was devoted to working out at home, distance walking outside and, indoors, and doing constant visualization and manifestation rituals I had come to perform daily. Between our move to a new house with a more navigable shower and my transition out of the wheelchair and into more time spent standing each day, I no longer needed (nor could we afford) the gym.

It helped that we had secured some incredibly useful equipment. Thanks to a combination of funds raised at Sponsored by Love and donations from the High Fives Foundation, we were able to purchase some used equipment from The Sanctuary, which Shawna had previously used to train her clients. So in addition to the parallel bars and some weights we already had, I could add a Pilates reformer and a Power Plate to my routine.

The reformer was something Ladd had introduced me to months prior. The bed-like frame with the movable carriage and foot straps was designed to provide resistance during stretches, and could be used in dozens of ways. Working with the reformer, I was able to strengthen my core, enhance my flexibility, and improve my balance, and I could work numerous parts of my body with this one piece of equipment. The Power Plate was a little like something you'd see on *The Jetsons*—a vibrating platform with a handlebar. I could do exercise while on the plate, and its vibration would provide ten times the workout of what the exercise alone could do. A push-up on the Power Plate was the equivalent of ten regular push-ups. At first, I could only stand on the thing for a few seconds before the intense shaking wore me out, but I kept at it every day. And I could immediately feel the results of the workout in my aching muscles, and within a few weeks I could hold on for almost a minute. All of a sudden, our time and efficiency were maximized ten-fold. And this gave us time to begin work with Dr. Ryan.

The office of Dr. Liam Ryan, M.D., F.R.C.S.I., was a hive of activity when we arrived for our first appointment in early December. Physicians, physician assistants, and physical therapists buzzed about, consulting with patients about X-rays, performing diagnostics, guiding patients in stretches and therapy techniques—the space was akin to a high-end professional office space. Clean, clinical, and decorated with dark blue and silver accents, its energy was both welcoming and warm, and it bustled with the business of all things spinal. How had we never found this place before?

We were welcomed like family and ushered directly into Dr. Ryan's private office. As we waited to meet the doctor in person, we read the awards, accolades, and articles about him and his spine treatment center that lined the walls. From what we could gather, Dr. Ryan had misrepresented himself to us. He wasn't just a neurosurgeon. He was a superhero rock star neurosurgeon, one of the top fifty in the country and certainly the best in our area, who had an unbelievable three fellowships and gave lectures in this country and abroad.

"Hello!" came a happy voice from the doorway of the office. Though the certificates and awards lined the walls, for some reason we felt as if we had been caught snooping as we pored over them, looking for a sign as to who this man was who had, without meeting us, graciously offered the full force of his recovery resources to us free of charge.

He was a handsome, thin man with an oblong face, a mouth that naturally smiled, and a head of thick brown hair. "Good to meet ya!" he said in a musical Irish accent and extended his hand to Shawna. I had taken the seat farthest from the door, and set my crutches on the floor behind me and to my left. Feeling bowled over by both his talent and his generosity, using his desk and the arm of the chair, I pushed to my feet, and opened my arms to hug him with gratitude. "It's fantastic to meet you, Dr. Ryan, thank you so much for all you've given us, and for seeing us today!" I said, beaming at him.

Unlike Aaron, who was put off by my huggable nature, Dr. Ryan, a true professional with the distinguished charisma of James Bond, was also a hugger at heart.

"Not at all! Liam. Call me Liam," he said, patting my back and withdrawing briskly but in a friendly way, then looking from me to Shawna and back again. "How are you two feelin'? Thirsty? Can we get ya some water or anythin'?"

"No, no, we're good, thanks," I said, taking my seat. "We were just taking in your achievements here," I said, gesturing to the walls. "Really impressive!"

"Ah, well," he said, dismissing it with his hand. "So shall we get started, then? I've taken a look at your digital charts through the hospital's database."

Shawna pulled out our file, the information she'd been gathering and keeping. My body in a file. She handed it to him, and he opened it to reveal several X-rays, CT scans, and MRI pictures.

"I've also read your surgery reports," he said.

"Really? Wow, we haven't even seen surgery reports," said Shawna wryly. "We haven't seen any of that."

"Well, let's just go through it then, shall we?" Dr. Ryan said cheerfully.

For the next two hours, every incision and every nerve, every decision that had been made that day in surgery was explained to us in careful, exacting detail. For the first time since my injury, someone was explaining what exactly had been done to my body, and why. "He went in here, because of this," Dr. Ryan pointed to an image, "and see this nerve here and

In-home Pilates with superstar Laura Hirsch
(Photo by Shawna Korgan)

how it runs? That's why you have numbness there." On and on he went, explaining every line, every shadow.

And then, leaning back in his chair, he said, "He did a beautiful job, really, decompressing your spine. Absolutely beautiful."

During our last visit to Surgeon Smirk, the day I said goodbye to my turtle shell, the extent of the information we got was, "Looks good." So it was good to know that although his bedside manner was shitty, his surgical skills were exceptional.

Dr. Ryan picked up an X-ray of the rod and cage now connecting my T12 and L2 vertebrae, and examined the workmanship involved.

"Fantastic, yeah?" Dr. Ryan said, seeing my interest. "Want to see what's in there?" He walked over to the cabinet and opened a deep drawer, then rifled through it a bit. "I think I have it… well, not exactly, but a little bit like this." He triumphantly held up a hunk of sophisticated metal hardware and handed it to me. "That's about 90 Gs, that," he said.

I caressed the small metal rod, the tiny yet indestructible screws like those holding my body together.

"Ask any questions, any at all," he invited. "Let's have a look around, shall we?"

He promptly stood up, grabbed my file, and beckoned us to follow him as we took a look around the cutting edge facility. We met doctors and therapists and office staff and had each room and each piece of therapy equipment explained in detail.

"Thaïs!" Dr. Ryan called, beckoning to a young therapist who had chin-length, straight blonde hair and an enormous, white smile. She placed her file in a pocket on the wall and made her way to us. "Thaïs, this is Grant and Shawna Korgan. Thaïs is our lead physical therapist," Dr. Ryan said proudly. "She has been apprised of your injury and will be working with you on your therapy plan. She and all of us are at your disposal. All right?"

"This is amazing, oh my God, I can't begin to tell you," I said humbly, bringing my hands together as if to pray, a gesture of supplication and gratitude. "Thank you. Thank you."

"Thank you so much," Shawna said, embracing Dr. Ryan. He had warmed up already—he hugged Shawna back. As they parted, Shawna brushed a tear from the corner of her eye.

"Ah, fuck," Dr. Ryan said, smiling at her and patting her shoulder. "Don't you start!"

Let me be clear: It was never us against the doctors. We didn't like the way some things went down at the hospital and with some healthcare practitioners, but I think it's important to say here that I know I wouldn't be here if it weren't for all these experts who have dedicated their lives to treating people like me.

But more than that, I also think that when people like Surgeon Smirk, or our physiatrist, or any of the people along the way who doubted that I would ever walk, actually said, "You're not going to walk unassisted ever again," they were giving me a sort of gift. Because if a doctor would have said to me, "You have a real shot at it, and you're going to walk again," I might still be sitting around waiting for it to start.

The media loves to make heroes of the injured; they love comeback stories. They love to say things like, "Doctors said he would never walk again, but he proved them wrong." It's sexy, and it makes good copy.

And people have asked me, "Don't you just want to walk into that surgeon's office and say, 'How ya like me now, dude? I showed you, didn't I?'" But I don't. I think I have had the greatest doctors that money can buy—my visit with Dr. Ryan that day solidified that even more for me. We're in the best country for medicine, and I have had access to the best care. And given my injury, I think the prognosis I was given, based only on statistics, was fair. I think the doctors were right to say, "You're probably not going to walk the way you used to ever again." Not only could they be sued for offering any hope that didn't come to fruition, but because I was undersold, every bit of my recovery has been a blessing.

As I had learned through my experience in business, it's better to under-promise and over-deliver. If I had been told, "You'll probably walk," then the sensations I was feeling, the ability to roll over, the goose bumps, all of it would likely have felt anticlimactic. But it was so undersold to me that I celebrated everything. I found joy. I got a greater perceived value simply by expecting nothing. The fact that I was stripped of hope actually helped me to reap more reward, and in that, the doctors, I believe, did something heroic for me.

And here's another thing: When I woke up in ICU, I lay there expecting that anytime I might be able to wiggle my toes. I might get it all back at any moment, because that's just how nerves work sometimes. And if one single nurse or doctor had said, "You could very well get it all back, you never know, but hang in there!" I very well could have lain there thinking, "Well, the doctor said I'll eventually feel stuff, so I'm just waiting for it to happen." They didn't know me; they didn't know how hard I'd work. Even with an injury less severe than mine, it takes work to recover. And had I not given my all at every moment, I might not have made the progress I'd made. So, essentially, what they'd given me was the incredible gift of motivation and drive. I'd focused so hard on passing the naysayers by in the other lanes that I had, as a result, won the race.

I can think of many tough teachers and coaches from my childhood, people who never let up on me. They pushed me, and I respected them and feared letting them down, so I worked harder, pushed myself to the extreme to meet their expectations. I'd take the gratitude I felt for a hard C in any of those classes over an easy A any day. They made me better, and it's those people whom I feel played the greatest role in my becoming the man I am now. I would also add my doctors to this list.

Our bond with Dr. Ryan had been instant, and the connection we forged with Thaïs was no less immediate or strong. She had heard about us, had seen our videos online, was thrilled to see in person an example of someone with a spinal cord injury like mine who had made such strides, and, as an avid cyclist and outdoors-lover herself, she was just as passionate as we were about a 120 percent recovery. And she didn't just want it or hope for it. Outwardly, in every interaction with us, she conveyed utter conviction that I would absolutely reach it.

She honored and respected the therapy I'd done to this point. The plan we worked out together was meant to complement, not replace, what we already had in place. If our work at the time focused on strengthening larger muscles, she concentrated on activating smaller muscle groups. If I was focusing heavily on my lower body, she spent time working on the upper body. She wanted to add to the mix, to round out a full therapy regimen. Occasionally, like Becca, she assessed my workouts at home, bringing her own dog along with her to keep Obie company.

But honestly, our favorite thing about her was the laughing. Thaïs's huge smile and deep belly laugh were contagious, and no matter what had happened that day, our spirits lifted to see her.

In fact, Dr. Ryan's entire office had begun to feel like a home away from home. Though we worked out much of the time at home and spent hours each day at Aaron's house, it was here at the spine center that we felt truly like we were where we belonged. Dr. Ryan (or Liam, as we now called him), who rarely had a minute to spare as he attended to dozens of patients each day, could still manage to have coffees with us at the café next door. Here, Shawna would bounce ideas off him, share research she had just done, or ask about equipment she'd stumbled across or heard about and whether it would be useful for me. He appreciated, even admired her fortitude, and spoke to us casually, liberally sprinkling curse words in everything he said, addressing us not as patients but as friends. Sometimes, his beautiful wife, Caroline, a lovely Irish woman with an intoxicating accent, would join us as well.

At one such get-together, Liam asked, "I was hoping you would give a talk to my staff? Tell your story? I'd like them to know you better."

Me? Interested in speaking?

"Absolutely. Anything, anything for you," I said.

The idea that I might have anything to say that a room full of spine experts might need to hear struck me as odd and somewhat intimidating. But as Liam reminded me, I had dealt with my circumstances in a unique fashion. The combination of an activity-based recovery plan and the choice to remain positive in the face of adversity had been powerful, and he believed that power could carry a strong message to his staff.

As I prepared notes for my talk that following Wednesday, I considered the very real possibility that I could be perceived as preachy or somehow as if I knew all the answers. I knew better than most that every spinal injury and every recovery was different, so who was I to presume that our choices were right for everyone? I needed to choose my words carefully. The approach Shawna and I had taken—foregoing regular jobs, visiting acupuncturists and healers, using visualizations, day-long therapy sessions—was certainly unorthodox. But as I made my notes, it also occurred to me that what I really needed to say didn't just apply to those with spine injuries.

Everyone is surviving something. Some people have cancer. Some people are experiencing divorce, poverty, a struggle to find work, the loss of a loved one, war, or atrocity, or abuse, chronic pain, or crippling depression. Some people are overworked and coping with extraordinary levels of stress or unmanageable conflicts on their jobs. A lot of people lost millions of dollars in the recession. Even my situation was by no means even the worst of what could result from a spinal injury. In fact, many things, namely Shawna, made me spectacularly fortunate.

We all have difficult challenges that make us survivors. And many of us feel like we're alone in our struggles. But no matter how big or small you may think your troubles are, it's all survival, and for that, none of us is alone. We're all in it together. And if we're together on a sinking ship, struggling to survive, we can either sit around staring at the hole as we watch the boat fill up with water, and be pissed off about whatever caused the hole or we can work together to plug the hole so we can get to shore. Survivors like us, we have a choice: We can dwell on how tough we have it, going over it and over it in our heads, beating ourselves up over what went wrong and grieving for what's been lost or changed. Or we can focus on what's working and make the choice to be positive in the face of all that adversity, to push through it even if water's filling the boat.

I chose positivity, and all I can say is that, for me, that made all the difference.

Which is what I told a room full of staff members at the spine center that day. They seemed appreciative of what I had to say and were extremely generous with their comments afterward. But to have a room full of professionals of this caliber consider anything I had to say as important and valuable was a remarkable gift to me.

That day, Dr. Ryan and his staff enthusiastically made Wednesday "Korg Day." On that day each week, they all wore blue t-shirts depicting a spine on the back, with a heart emblazoned where the L1 vertebrae would be. Across the top were my own words: "It's not about what I've done; it's about what I'm going to do."

The choice for positivity was something Shawna and I made actively over and over again. Every day, we had to choose it. And we believe that this choice has rewarded us with countless opportunities and wonderful experiences. Because we didn't complain, because we have always focused on the bright side, few people actually saw or understood how gnarly our lives got. And in our opinion, that's great, because the last thing we wanted was to make people feel sorry. I never wanted people to feel sorry about me or to see me differently than they did before.

Physical therapy with Thaïs Mollet and Jen Mavis
(Photo by Shawna Korgan)

The danger of that, though, is that people get pretty careless with the things they say. We've been given gifts and money and experiences, had therapy and equipment donated, and no, we don't work in traditional jobs. And people say things like, "Dude, you're *killing* it, I'd give anything to have that!" But really? Would they give up the opportunity to drive? To stand up and take a shower? To piss or take a shit?

On a party boat at Tahoe with some friends, I had seen numerous people stand on the back of the boat or hang off the edge if they needed to pee. But me, I'd have needed to ask the twelve people there with me, "Hey everybody, can you hand me my catheter and some lube so I can stick it up my dick real quick?" People would lose their minds. So I had to find myself a private spot, which wasn't easy, and I hated every second of it because I knew it might diminish how they saw me and make them uncomfortable.

My friends talked that day about doing their girlfriends doggie-style in the shower, and one of them turned to me and said, "You know what I mean?" And I thought, "Yeah, sure, I know exactly what you mean—you mean that thing I can't do with my wife anymore." I shoved that into my metaphorical backpack, put a smile on my face, and high-fived my friend for his good luck. I don't begrudge him his good fortune, but it doesn't make me miss it any less.

People talk about not getting sleep, but they have no idea. I mean, almost a year after my injury, sleeping still didn't come easy to me. It wears a person out to not ever get a great night's rest. I hadn't slept a full, restful night since before my injury. I experienced burning pain in the lower half of my body twenty-four hours a day. I probably only got 60 percent of the legitimate sleep I would get pre-injury.

All of this and more was what I lived with. So yes, life had been pretty fucking good to us, but would I trade all of it, all the free stuff, the jobless days, the amazing friendships and opportunities we'd received and would continue to receive, just to have what I had before, and to be able to walk down the street hand in hand with my wife? You fucking bet I would—in a second.

It tormented me sometimes, the loss of this simple pleasure. And it tormented Shawna, too. As we approached the new year and thought about our intentions for 2011, this topped Shawna's list of goals. She shared this with Thaïs. "Okay, that's our goal," she said. "We're going to make that happen. This is what you need to focus on in every therapy session."

It struck me then how my life was an odd reversal. In the previous year, I'd learned so much about life and the universe, principles of self-actualization that I hadn't even thought about before. I had grown aware of myself, forged an even deeper connection with my wife than I'd ever thought possible, and had gotten an opportunity to realize my life's ambition to help others. But ironically, this year, my big goal would be to simply walk and hold hands with Shawna.

By now I had been seeing Aaron for a couple of months, and while the lights were turning on in my body as my physical therapy took on an added dimension, lights were turning on mentally and emotionally through my work with Aaron.

But despite a budding friendship that he seemed to begrudgingly bestow on Shawna and me, Aaron was still just as much of a jackass as ever.

Every day, he'd stand there with his arms folded, just watching me struggle up those fucking stairs, without speaking a word. He looked at me scornfully, like, "Well, I'm waiting, motherfucker." No matter what I said or how jovially I greeted him, he would only nod and watch me, silent. He scrutinized my every move from the moment I got out of Free Candy until the moment I sat on his couch. We would then, for the rest of the session, be greeted with the full force of his observations.

One day I fell. I missed the last step and down I went. I would have fallen flat on my face had not Shawna been right there. She lurched over to catch me, pulled me up, and helped me as I fumbled to get hold of my crutches again and pull myself upright.

Aaron stood there watching, not a bit uncomfortable with the fact that I'd just fallen clumsily on his front porch, and he hadn't made a move to help.

With Shawna's help, I awkwardly, resentfully, made my way to the couch. Again, I struggled around the coffee table and awkwardly teetered above the comfort of the yellow cushion and backrest.

"Don't move," he ordered Shawna, halting her abruptly as she attempted to guide me to safety. She stopped where she was and looked at him, confused.

I made my way, slowly but surely, to the couch, where I collapsed and exhaled deeply.

Aaron crossed one leg over the other, and clasped his hands, gathering his thoughts before speaking.

"Why'd you do that?" he asked Shawna.

"What, help my husband?" she asked, with annoyance in her voice.

"Yes," he said, unmoved. "Why did you help him?"

"Because I don't want him to be hurt. Because that's what you do in a marriage, you catch the other person when he falls," she said, as if explaining the obvious to a bratty kid.

"Well, if you're always there, you're giving him a safety net. You're telling him to go ahead and fall," he said to her. "You're sending energy that conveys that he's going to fail."

Her expression changed as she considered this.

Aaron turned to me for his daily greeting: "What do you want?"

And I thought about it, as I'd now gotten into the habit of doing. I thought about what he'd just told Shawna. Did I really want someone to come to my aid?"

"I want to be able to stand on my own and to walk up those stairs on my own," I said to him.

"Good," Aaron said. And it occurred to me that him treating me as if I *should* be standing and walking up those stairs was maybe the most helpful thing he could do for me.

As for Shawna, while what Aaron said made good sense to her, it was hard to stand back and watch, just say, "Oops. Down you go." She would do that as long as it made sense, and often it did. But she would never stand by and let me hurt myself or get into a situation that would actually set back my recovery.

It was a little tough for me too, at first. Especially because the world seemed to be a minefield. Everywhere, people were clamoring to get past me, just "Out of my way, bro!" as they blew by me and often kicked my crutches out from under me. Even well-intentioned people got so focused on their own stuff that it was like they couldn't even see my crutches. The walker had been stable, large enough to part a crowd. The crutches made life precarious.

As we went out into the world, Shawna had developed a sort of Spidey-sense. During a concert we attended with some friends, I struggled to maneuver through a crowd and failed to get my crutch moved in order to catch myself. I was headed straight for the concrete. But Shawna, whose back was to me, was so innately in tune with me that I simply had to say, "Baby, falling," and, in a sort of super-human display of skill, Salt emerged. She leapt to my side, *HI-YA-YA!*, like a martial arts move from a comic book, and caught me without missing a beat.

Nonetheless, I didn't want to fail, and knowing she was always there to catch me was, in a way, setting myself up for failure. So if I went down, it was okay. I'd just keep getting myself back up until I didn't fall anymore.

For months, I had set a goal for myself to walk the one-mile loop trail around Virginia Lake, a small lake set in an old residential area in the middle of Reno. The trail was relatively flat, but old, with numerous cracks and pits in the asphalt, not to mention dozens of joggers, at all times of day, passing us as they went around and around the circle—all of which made navigating the trail tricky. But despite the difficulty, I practiced every day in order to achieve a full lap.

The first time, moving at a snail's pace in my walker, we spent four hours, I made it about one-eighth of the distance around the loop and found myself in the dark, waiting it out while Shawna went to get Free Candy and come pick me up. A few days later, I made it twice that far, to approximately one-quarter of the way around.

Eventually, I could amble cautiously around on my crutches, enjoying the sounds of ducks and kids playing on the playground across the street, breathing deeply the fresh, cold winter air, and watching the windblown peaks in the water as they sparkled in the sunshine. I saw the same people pass me over and over, four or five times. Shawna and I became fixtures at Virginia Lake, the couple who took an afternoon constitutional every day.

One day, I felt a strange hand on my shoulder. I looked up to see an elderly man in a blue satin track suit. "Oh, cerebral palsy," he said to me. "That's too bad—hang in there, fella."

It was astounding, actually, the number of people who said things like this. "Oh my Gosh, I'm so *SOR-ry!*" was a familiar refrain and one I bitterly resented.

Shawna and I talked about this during the ride home in Free Candy after one such occasion. What was it about me, I wondered aloud, that seemed to invite such comments and such pity? Just as Aaron had reminded us that our words are immensely powerful, he also opened our eyes to the idea that the same might be true, in an energetic sense, about the way we view ourselves. If I viewed myself as whole, healed, and complete, perhaps the world would follow suit.

"Let's think about the energy we're putting out there," Shawna said, as a sort of brainstorm. "In those moments, how are you feeling?"

"Well, I mean, it's a struggle," I said frankly. "I guess maybe that seems obvious." I pictured myself in my head, considered what I must look like, huffing and puffing, frustrated by my fellow walkers and dreading every stranger's approach. As much as I worked to maintain an attitude of positivity, I conceded that in those moments, I could have appeared to be in worse shape than I was.

"It's not an uphill battle," I affirmed to myself as much as to Shawna. "This is just a bump in the road."

"Yes! Exactly! You just get out there tomorrow and put one foot in front of the other with that in mind," she said.

That day, just like every other, we set out for a cold winter's trek around the lake. But this day, we did it with new intent, new energy. "This is just a bump in the road," I said again to myself, remembering the power that words have over our circumstances as I put my feet on the path at Virginia Lake that afternoon.

And as if manifesting this truth on our very skin, we now projected this outwardly. Strangers, who otherwise might have come at us with pity, now came with encouragement. A middle-aged man taking a stroll, hands in his pockets and whistling, turned with a smile to face me. "You're doing fantastic," he said. "One foot in front of the other!"

You know how, when you buy a car, all of a sudden you start seeing the same car everywhere? You may never have noticed that model before, but now you see it everywhere? It was eerie like that. Strangers were speaking my truth now at every turn, mirroring what was going on with me internally. What I asked the universe for, I was getting. Likely that truth had always been there, but now it was in the spotlight, and because we remained open and conscious to that truth, we could now hear it and see it for what it was. We began to realize that if we really listened, we might hear what we needed.

We were no longer in the space of, "Uggh, I can't wait until I recover, this is so burly"; now I was recovered. I was walking. Within a matter of a month or two, I had made it around Virginia Lake.

But the winter weather worked against us. Despite my best efforts, ice and snow often made the trail impassable for me, and on those days, we became mall-walkers, joining the legions of elderly folks getting their exercise inside, on flat, safe surfaces. On those days, I put on my gloves and braced myself for a test of endurance.

On one such day, Shawna used the opportunity to exchange sizes on a shirt she'd gotten for Christmas. "Hey why don't you hang out here for a minute and rest?" she said, pointing to a bench just outside the store. "I'll just be a minute."

I sank gratefully onto the bench and swiped at my sweaty forehead with my sleeve. I was joined a moment later by a man who looked to be in his late 60s, although he appeared to have been treated roughly by life, and so maybe looked older than he was. His unkempt gray hair, longish despite the receding hairline, hung below the trucker hat sitting askew on his head. He wore a flannel button-down shirt and jeans worn thin with the layers of filth and grease that stained them.

"Hey," I said, just to be polite, when he sat down. I didn't expect an answer. I scanned the store for Shawna.

"How you doin'?" he asked, sounding breathless. "Whew! Hot in here, huh?"

"Yeah, I guess," I shrugged.

"You know, I saw you crutchin' back there," he said. "Doin' real good."

"Thanks," I said, truly thankful but dreading what might next come out of his mouth.

"Yeah, I know what it's like," he said.

Now I'd heard this a hundred times from well-meaning people who thought they knew, but didn't. I braced myself and said, "Oh yeah?"

"Yeah, I got hit by a semi-truck few years back," he said, taking off his hat and scratching his dirty head. "They said I'd never walk again."

Now he had my full attention. "Seriously?"

"Yep," he replaced his cap and turned to look at me. "But now look at me!" He spread his arms in the air and smiled, revealing holes where teeth should be.

"Oh my God! When was this?"

"Oh, 'bout five, six years ago, I guess." His face, despite his dirty, unshaven complexion, revealed a certain contentedness. "I just wanted to say to you," and with this, he leaned forward, and put his hand on my shoulder, "you will recover. You hear? Just keep putting one foot in front of the other."

Grant at the LULI laser facility near Paris, France
(Photo by Steven Malekos)

CHAPTER 20
STOP TO START

In 2004, around the same time in which the technology of NanoLabz was forming, Dr. Jesse Adams, along with Steven and I, joined forces with two other scientists, Ben Rogers and Ralph Whitten, who were deep in the development of a project utilizing cantilever-based sensors for terrorist threat detection, which would be the beginning of Nevada Nanotech Systems (NNTS). As an engineer at NNTS, I got an opportunity to work on contracts with the Department of Defense and the Department of Homeland Security.

To get a sense of what we were doing, imagine a little cantilever, like a diving board about the size of a human hair. Imagine it's hanging over open space, and it's coated in a specific polymer that has an affinity for a certain atom so that it will attract only that kind of atom and it will repel all others. This means that the atom the diving board has attracted will land directly on that plastic-coated diving board's tip.

Everything on this planet vibrates. All the atoms around us—your chair, the cells in your body, the steel making up a building—at the elemental level, it's all vibrating at what's called a natural frequency (the cycles per second, measured in hertz, at which everything in the universe vibrates normally). So if that cantilever coated in polymer is vibrating at its natural frequency and along comes a molecule of explosive TNT, for example, to which it is attracted, that TNT will land on the cantilever and change its natural frequency.

Through pattern-recognition software, and by simply monitoring the frequency of that cantilever, one could, in theory, detect a single molecule of TNT. And one could do this with any material desired for detection— explosives, Anthrax, viruses, anything. The potential for use by the Department of Homeland Security was, as you can imagine, extremely intriguing.

Nevada Nanotech Systems had received government appropriations to pursue testing on this idea to ensure its viability. It was crucial to vet the science and strategies before investing the months, perhaps even years, of our time, not to mention multiple millions of dollars, necessary to its development and roll-out. We needed to bring in an expert, give him the royal treatment, ask him to sign a non-disclosure agreement, run the concepts past him, and find out what pitfalls might await us before endeavoring any further. Just as we'd become used to at NanoLabz, exhaustive research and planning were the order of the day for NNTS as well, and were the only way to ensure that we would see success at the end of each day.

Our president, Ralph, and Jesse knew that Timothy Chambers, head of the Nanoscale Science and Devices group at the Oak Ridge National Lab, was the nation's leading expert in cantilever physics. We saw it as essential that our ideas pass muster with him. We began in earnest to put together a flawless presentation, double- and triple-checking our facts, seeing to every remarkable detail of his visit, during which we would show him a wonderful time at Lake Tahoe. We stayed up nights laboring to ensure against every possible objection.

NNTS bought Dr. Chambers a ticket to Reno, had a car pick him up and escort him to the spectacular Hyatt Regency on the north shore of Lake Tahoe, and reserved an enormous, round, corner table overlooking the lake at the four-star Lone Eagle Grill. To all of this, though appearing pleased, Dr. Chambers remained steadfastly quiet, and we anxiously observed his every movement and gesture for signs of doubt or disapproval.

We sat around the table—Jesse was there, Ben, Ralph, me, and our principle investor, Stuart Feigen—and began looking expectantly at Dr. Chambers. After enjoying our delicious meals, basking in and remarking upon the view, and engaging in some nervous small talk, we cleared our throats and began our lengthy presentation.

It was a perfectly choreographed song and dance in which we revealed the theme of the project, the mountain of theoretical data we'd collected, the feasibility study we had conducted, and our strategy for rolling out the technology, for real, as partners with two very strong government arms of support. All the while we expected, even hoped, that Chambers would disprove our theories, interject with comments like, "Because of the Van der Waals' force, you can't do this," or "Because of the Bernoulli equation, the math won't scale," or "It's not reasonable to find this result by the given time." We expected Dr. Chambers to blow our idea apart, so we pulled out all the stops, cited numerous results, and just kept pitching and pitching and pitching.

When it was finished, he sat there watching us, a contented smile on his face. Each of us having been a presenter, we exchanged congratulatory glances, and now sat at the edges of our seats, waiting for this man to pass judgment on our revolutionary project. A long hush fell over the table.

Dr. Chambers leaned forward, and we all held our breaths. A somewhat uncertain grin appeared on his face. He surveyed the table, looking first at Jesse, then me, then Ben, and Ralph, and Stuart, seconds ticking by in ridiculous silence. We braced ourselves, leaned in toward him, awaiting our verdict. He then sheepishly shrugged his shoulders, leaned forward even further, and said, "Start."

Five faces glared, expressionless, at Dr. Chambers for a moment. Then, riotous, anxious laughter erupted around the table.

He continued to look around the table at us, somewhat bemused, clearly having no idea what was so funny.

"Okay," we said to him and each other. "Let's get started. Please, go ahead and tell us what you think."

"No," he insisted. "Start."

We were confused. What did he mean? Start where? Start explaining ourselves? Start saying more things? Start justifying our reason for taking on this huge project? Start what?

"Looks like you've thought it through. You've covered everything. Just start," he said. Then, shrugging, he took his fork, stabbed a piece of his dessert, and put it in his mouth.

The five of us sat there, clearly the most befuddled, unprepared bunch of scientists ever to be collected in one room. We'd spent three months researching, doing beta tests, preparing for this presentation, anticipating every possible objection, and seeing to every minute detail of Chambers' pricey corporate suite and the fine dining experience we were now enjoying. There was only one thing we hadn't anticipated: a green light.

We'd done the work, considered all the variables, mapped out our future perfectly on paper, so what were we waiting for?

I was a man who had spent his whole life anticipating obstacles and strategizing every movement that it would take me to overcome them. My widget mind could analyze something forever. But, again, analysis can lead to paralysis. You can only research and plan and map for so long. There's never going to be that perfect moment, the lightning bolt that sorts it all out for you. At some point, you have to have the courage and the gall to *do something*, to make things happen for yourself, to jump in even if you aren't completely sure what's going to happen. You have to stop waiting for external validation or for the stars to align. You have to *start* already.

This business of starting and stopping had been on my mind a lot lately. "The universe is a ridiculously simple place," Aaron liked to say. First, I had to stop widgeting and analyzing. I had to stop, decide what I wanted, and then just start getting it.

As a scientist, I was actually enormously pleased by this concept. It's basic, something primitive that animals instinctively know. Animals don't multitask the way we do. Animals eat, then they play, then they sleep, then they shit. And some hibernate, the biggest stop of them all, in order to start eating, playing, and shitting again in spring. Animals are completely present at every moment.

Life moves so fast for us people that it's hard to stop sometimes. It's hard to shut your brain off when you're asked to engage it fully at all times. And all that noise keeps us from doing the really hard work of beginning something new and from having the presence of mind enough to recognize when it's time. But I had to stop the noise of nanoscience, the ridiculous travel schedule, and the frantic "I've only got the money to finish the rest of this project, and I sure hope it works out so we can all have endless free energy." I mean, you can't live under that kind of stress. It's unhealthy.

My life ground to a halt with this injury, but now, ten months afterward, I could see that it was a sort of blessing—not one I would have asked for, but one I could recognize in hindsight. It shut all the noise off for me, so that I had time to decide my next course of action and to become fully aware of what I really wanted out of life. And I had the courage, and, frankly, the time, to go after it. Dr. Chambers reminded me that my colleagues and I had been spinning our wheels when we could have begun the race. With one word, Dr. Chambers had sucked the wind from my sails that day. But now, as I reflected back, that one word filled my sails with wind, and although I haven't talked to my colleagues about it since that day, I hope it did the same for them, too.

Now, being stopped offered great yawning expanses of time to think about my next move, to enjoy being present and conscious of all the stuff that was right in front of me that I never saw before. So that when it was time to start, I could see opportunities for what they were and have the strength to seize them, undistracted and open to where they might lead.

A lot of people think of stopping as a bad thing, like being stuck. A lot of stops are forced upon us, against our will, like losing a job. But it doesn't have to be an ending, because every time you stop, you get to start again. It's always the beginning of something... a new job, more time with family, or something completely unexpected that you might never have seen otherwise. All of those things that stopped you were opportunities to start getting exactly what you wanted in life. Just as I was beginning to get now.

$$\langle\rangle$$

I never set out to spearhead a movement that revolved around the power of three. But like I said, there's something almost supernatural about that number. The Korg 3.0 movement evolved naturally, completely independent of forethought. And yet the importance of three kept revealing itself to Shawna and me in unexpected ways.

Korg 3.0 had been based on the idea of a life's three defining moments. But while the movement gathered momentum, three takeaway points had also begun to emerge for me, which Shawna and I were now calling the Three Points of Possibility. They were the three points of progression that I had used to get through my injury, which I shared with others through the Korg 3.0 movement: Decide what you want (and be open to how it comes), focus only on what works, and then choose positivity in the face of adversity.

And when I began doing speaking engagements regularly, these three points became the foundation of my message.

The effort was born out of the tremendous amount of gratitude I felt for the people who surrounded me every day, the friends and family who had come together to help Shawna and me in so many ways, the therapies of all kinds that contributed so much to my progress. I wanted to express that gratitude, to pay it forward, to show others the power they actually had within themselves to get them through the hard times.

Shawna and I practiced gratitude every night and had done so since those early days in the hospital. The first time was in inpatient rehab. I was wracked by pain and could hardly bring myself to think about anything else. Shawna sat down beside me, leaned forward and spoke right into my ear, "Okay, babe, I want you to tell me three things you're grateful for."

The question caught me off guard, and my pain was so intense at the moment, so hard to navigate past that all I could say was, "You. You. And you."

She chuckled. But the next night, as I once again grappled with the pain that seemed to double in its vigor in the quiet evening hours, Shawna again leaned over to speak in my ear, "Tell me three things you're grateful for."

"You," I began, turning my head to smile at her. I rolled my head to face the ceiling and think some more.

"And?" she prompted me.

"Nurses. And coffee."

What I found was that this exercise took me out of whatever gnarly pain or challenge that came at me, and forced me to focus on something else in a positive way. I channeled my thoughts into gratitude, and in turn felt better.

Soon Shawna and I were observing a nightly ritual, one we observe to this day. Each night, before going to sleep, we both get a chance to share what we are grateful for. As my recovery has progressed, I've been grateful for Obie, friends, therapists, love, sunshine, family, good food, Dr. Ryan, increasing sensation, my crutches, the High Fives Foundation, Free Candy... And always Shawna.

This is how powerful gratitude can be. It hits a pause button on whatever we're struggling with, and allows us to focus on what works. Even when things are really bad, I can be grateful for my wife, my dog, and my cat. And there's enormous comfort in that kind of positivity.

I wanted to share the idea of gratitude as a tool. That was really what Korg 3.0 was all about for me. My injury had changed the course of my life in a way I hadn't wanted, and it's hard to understand sometimes why obstacles get thrown at us. But the universe has a way of achieving balance. Look at nature—if you dam a river, the water inevitably overflows somewhere else. The water will always move and flow to find balance. Coyotes only breed to carrying capacity. The number of new pups born won't exceed what the area can provide. Wildfires eventually decimate overly forested areas. New plants grow where the sunlight was once blocked by trees.

So it's easy to say that what happened to me was bad, but then again, I had been given tremendous gifts. I realized that, despite my fears on the day of my injury, breaking my back had indeed not been a tragedy. I was now being given a chance to experience and understand gratitude, to meet wonderful people and have life-altering experiences. And I was being asked to speak to others and share that with other people. And I knew that if even one person could be affected in a positive way by hearing my story and the lessons I'd learned along the way, then what I'd really been given was an opportunity. My life has been achieving a balance, and this is how I've chosen to see it.

If there's one thing I have learned in the course of my recovery, it is that life presents lessons at every turn, but only if you learn to recognize them.

We had come to a new juncture. Just as our time with Dr. Zhu had naturally, instinctively drawn to a close, so did our time with Aaron. The work I was doing in Dr. Ryan's spine center was taking up more of my time—time that I felt was extremely well-spent. Meanwhile, I no longer connected to the work I was doing with Aaron and felt I had progressed in my recovery beyond the point where what he offered was something I needed. It was time for Shawna and me to embark on the next phase of our journey. It was the High Fives Foundation that helped bring it to us.

The first High Fives-sponsored athlete, Steve Wallace, a ski racer, burst-fractured his T9 vertebra while skiing at Squaw Valley in 2008. Paralyzed and told he wouldn't walk again, he embarked on a serious journey of recovery that I was also very familiar with. Part of his recovery involved five months in Atlanta working on the unweighted treadmill at The Shepherd Center, one of the nation's premiere spinal cord recovery centers. The machine is designed to harness a person into a cage, making him or her essentially weightless in order to assist with relearning to walk. Without needing to support the weight of your entire body on your legs, you're actually able to walk, unimpeded, for long periods of time. This, in turn, opens and strengthens neural pathways that are critical for walking, which, over time, becomes a more natural process for the body.

Now, Steve Wallace was walking again, unassisted. So when Roy Tuscany told me that High Fives wanted to send Shawna and me to Atlanta for a week so I could use this thing myself, we knew it was an incredible, potentially life-changing opportunity.

But it meant my getting on a commercial airplane for the first time since my injury, the difficulty of which we vastly underestimated.

We knew it would be gnarly, sitting for the length of an entire six-hour cross-country flight. It's tough for someone without a spinal cord in-

Grant in LocoMotor Training at
Atlanta's Shepherd Center
(Photo by Shawna Korgan)

jury. But knowing I'd need to sleep, knowing I'd need room on the plane to stretch out, we opted for a red-eye flight, thinking it would be less full, certainly less expensive, and maybe easier for me to sleep.

I didn't sleep at all. It was painful, exhausting, uncomfortable, and seemed to take an eternity. I honestly didn't think I would make it, and internally a war was raging in my brain My mouth actually opened, preparing to scream out, "Land this plane! We have to land this plane now!" But at that moment, a voice interrupted my thoughts: "We are making our final descent into the Atlanta area," it said, and I felt myself relax for the first time.

When our flight landed, it was early morning, and we were completely worked over, raw, bitter and tired right down to our bones, so we were thrilled to be back on terra firma.

Unfortunately, though, the Hartsfield-Jackson International Airport is the busiest in the world and certainly one of the largest. I mean, seriously, it just goes on and on and on, and for a man on crutches it's just about the cruelest place on earth. There's a train, certainly, but then there's the vastness of each terminal, the interminable moving sidewalks that run on for

LocoMotor Training at the
Shepherd Center
(Photo by Shawna Korgan)

miles, the sheer square footage of the baggage claim and ticketing desks and parking lot, not to mention the crowds pushing past at all times. Occasionally, we could hop aboard a cart hastily making its way from place to place, but eventually we'd have to hop off, and then begin again the long, laborious trek to what felt like the end of the earth.

A wheelchair would have made things easier. But I had jettisoned the wheelchair months previous and had no intention of using one ever again. I had made the decision in October to say goodbye to the wheelchair, knowing that if I kept it around as a safety net, I was sending a message to my body that I wasn't healed yet, as Aaron had pointed out months ago. And that wasn't a message I had any intention of sending.

The problem was, when we arrived at The Shepherd Center for our 11:00 appointment, I was so completely done in and in pain that I had almost nothing left for my workout. In fact, though the work we did that week at The Shepherd Center was beneficial and exciting, it took days, weeks even, to recover from our trip through the airport, before I felt like myself again or had enough energy to bring my workouts back up to where they'd been before. Instead of propelling my recovery forward, I'd actually set myself back.

The week after we returned to Reno, Shawna enlisted a series of body-work practitioners to help me recover from the trip. I got massages, sat in Jacuzzis, once again returned to acupuncture, and began a holistic therapy system designed to realign the body, called Rolfing.

Kim, the quiet, mild-mannered Rolfer who had, off and on, provided bodywork services to me in the hospital, wanted to talk to me before our session, to find out what areas I wanted to concentrate on and where I needed the most healing. I shared the story of our trip to Atlanta and how I'd suffered as a result.

"They have wheelchairs at the airport; why didn't you use one?" he asked.

"I'm done with the wheelchair," I said proudly. "I ditched that a few months ago. I'm crutchin' it now."

"Well, there are times you still need it," Kim said. "You could have really hurt yourself." It was a simple concept, really, but for some reason it hadn't dawned on me or Shawna. We'd been so concerned about sending mes-sages of weakness to my body that we had actually made it a self-fulfilling prophecy. My utter aversion to the wheelchair had made it more important than it was and had told my body that it was actually better to suffer than to rely on the evil chair. If I'd had a broken leg, I would have used it.

Avoiding the chair had actually sent a message that my injury, and sub-sequently the chair, were bigger or more important than they were, which was the last thing I wanted to do. That impossibly, ridiculously long hike through the airport had set me back enormously.

There was no weakness in admitting to myself that using the tools didn't always make me weak; a wheelchair was just a wheelchair. And it was just that—a tool. There wasn't anything cursed about it, no reason that I could name why touching the thing would set me back. I had needed it, and I'd made things harder on myself than they needed to be—out of sheer stubbornness.

It was a powerful lesson but a hard one for me to learn, particularly since my time in Atlanta had not been maximized because of what I'd done to myself in the airport. The unweighted treadmill couldn't be found any-where even near Reno, and I'd really missed out.

When Liam called, curious as to why I hadn't come in for a while, I explained the generous gift from High Fives and the benefits of the un-weighted treadmill. "How was it?" he asked, sounding excited about this innovative piece of equipment and its potential to help me. He was disap-pointed to hear that, although my work on the machine had been great, it had been very brief, and that perhaps I hadn't been able to use it to its greatest advantage.

"Aah, fuck," he said, sounding as if he didn't understand my dismay. "There should be one here, why don't I just buy the thing?" Which is how there ended up being an unweighted treadmill just minutes from our house, to which I now had unlimited access and which could now provide vital therapy to other spinal cord patients in the area.

My recovery program was constantly evolving as my abilities grew. I was now developing core strength and could do activities such as play catch as I worked on standing independently. Every morning began with a concoction mixed up in the juicer that usually included things like carrots, kale, and apples.

My work on the elliptical had progressed from my early days to where I could now stay on for about five to ten minutes with very little assistance from Shawna in terms of her holding me up. I was building up to being able to ride the stationary bike, which was my cross-country mountain bike (one I fully intend to ride again) mounted to a static indoor bike trainer. Three times a week I was doing Pilates on the reformer. And every day, at least twice a day, I did exercises on the Power Plate. I could now stay on for two or three minutes, with more time being added to that every day. And at least twice a week, we headed to Liam's facility, for additional therapy. Meanwhile, we would still squeeze in chiropractic, massage, acupuncture, and the visualizations, always the visualizations, which I saw as a keystone element of my recovery plan.

I would hang upside down on a tilt table, wear my headphones, and in my mind I'd go mountain biking in the sunshine at Tahoe or kayak down a waterfall in the high granite wonderland of California's Sierra Nevada mountains. In my sights was the next phase on my journey to a 120 percent recovery: walking with a cane.

Shawna's role, which had used to be providing basic stability and facilitating my movement, was now more about fine-tuning, adjusting my alignment, and forever pushing me to challenge myself, despite the milestones I reached—new sensations, new movements, longer periods of time on the equipment, or more reps on each. "Yesterday's record is *yesterday's* record," Salt would tell me. "What are you going to do today?"

But we did celebrate those milestones. It kept us out of mere survival mode. Focusing on the things that worked was what kept me going. Especially because still, through all this, I experienced burning pain in my feet twenty-four hours a day. I could have taken Vicodin, but it did little more than help me care about the pain less. And I could be really pissed off about that, but I've never really been that guy.

That pain, that burning that never seemed to subside, was a beautiful thing, a gift. Because I was experiencing sensations—something I was told would never happen—and every single day I felt more and more of them. And it meant that now I was aware of where my feet were. Pain is a neural response. Nerves were regenerating. How could that be a bad thing?

My mom would occasionally call me and ask, "How are your feet feeling today? How's the pain?" And I wouldn't have even thought about it until she asked. It's not that she wanted to bring me down, and it wasn't me just being the tough guy. I'm just always focusing on the fact that my feet are recovered, and that any second they're going to give me more of what they're already giving me.

I don't disregard the pain or ignore it. Everyone experiences pain to some degree, and it would be a lie if I sat here and said, "Oh, pain's nothing. I barely notice it." I just happened to have gotten some good lessons

Grant mountain bikes indoors, supported by his biggest fan (Photo by Shawna Korgan)

in dealing with it from breaking my face more than a decade earlier. And that's good, because it kept me from being so consumed by it, giving it so much of my bandwidth, that I shut down.

Here's how I look at pain: If you let it, like any negative emotion, it can fill your whole brain and blur your vision. So if I'm in pain, I allow my vision to go blurry, and I close my eyes, and I say to myself, "Okay, I want to find all this pain in my body, locate everything that's sending me pain signals." Once it's all in my sights, I mentally take my hands into the center of my vision, and part the pain like a curtain. I pull it to the side, and imagine my vision becoming perfect again. I have clear vision when I open my eyes, and the fog of pain is lifted. That curtain is pulled to the side. In my mind, I know I'm managing it, putting it somewhere, and that I'm in control of it. It can no longer affect my vision. I don't focus on it. I acknowledge it, accept it, put it where it belongs, and move past it. Like a heated debate in which your opponent says, "I completely understand all the feelings you're having, and your opinion is valid," the argument falls away. The armor comes off, the weapons are laid down, and the positivity can once more rush in.

Of course that doesn't mean I never got frustrated. I mean, sometimes it took me ten minutes to brush my teeth, and if I dropped my toothbrush, you wouldn't believe the time and effort it took to pick it up and clean it.

But look at it this way: If my recovery is a marathon, positivity is forward movement, and negativity is backward movement. Say I'm at the starting line and the gun goes off and I begin running, just positive and full of energy. But five miles in, I realize I'm kind of bummed out because my shoe's untied or I didn't get enough to eat that morning or someone else is passing me by on the road. Would I just say, "Fuck it," turn around and run the five miles back? No way. Because as soon as I go back the five miles, I would realize I just took all that energy only to go backward, so at that point, I'm done. I'm not going to start all over, am I? I would have burned up too much energy on a ten-mile race that got me nowhere.

So at no point in all this did it ever make sense to me to go backward. Even one step backward expended energy, meaning I probably wouldn't win the race.

Sure I vented. Venting is legitimate; it's human. Venting would be like pulling off to the curb during the marathon, tying my shoe, cursing, and taking a few deep calming breaths before I got back in the race.

And sometimes I cried. I let it out, let it flow through me, and then I'd be right back to the positive. I've never, not once, spent a day feeling sorry for myself. Because as I saw it, I didn't have that kind of time. I simply couldn't afford to give up a day in this marathon. There was no time for backsliding. That negativity wouldn't serve me. Succumbing to it wouldn't get me anywhere on this journey, would it? I couldn't afford to say, "Well, being positive is for someone else. My situation's too gnarly to stay positive. I deserve to wallow a little bit." Wallowing and negativity would deprive me of precious energy, which I need to move forward.

I'm in control of how I feel, how I react to situations. I get to choose. Just knowing that is empowering, and it helps me to push through the frustrations that confront me on a near daily basis.

Like this one time I was in the shower, seated on my shower bench, scrubbing my armpits and breathing deep the refreshing citrusy scent of some body wash or another that Shawna had purchased. I grabbed hold of the handheld shower head I used to rinse parts of my body I couldn't get to on my own.

Like most men, I've been a witness to my beautiful wife's multitudinous assortment of soaps, shampoos, conditioners, body washes, body scrubs, bubble baths, bath oils, and who knows what else, two or three of each thing, primarily purchased because of their appealing, unique scents, like cucumber mango melon or lavender vanilla. The bottles and jars were collected on a rack propped up in the wide corner ledge of the bathtub.

As I turned the shower head to rinse my nether regions, I became aware that, because I couldn't feel my butt cheeks, they were now sliding off the bench in what felt like slow-motion, just back and down, slamming my head and delicate back, still tender almost a year after surgery, hard against the shower wall and, finally, down to the floor of the tub, shooting the bench out to the other side of the tub.

I lay there thinking I must be concussed and bleeding. Water cascaded onto my belly, and I felt a steady torrent of women's spa products pelt me on the head and face. Exfoliation brushes, a shampoo bottle, a tub of sugar scrub, all pounding me in the nose and bruising me on the eyebrows, and I held my arms up over my face to shield it from the falling debris that was now raining upon me. A razor fell and hit my thigh, nearly cutting it as it made its way to the floor.

There was a brief moment of silence during which I moved my arms away from my face and opened my eyes, just in time to see the rack itself fall down, right before it cracked me on the skull.

In that moment, instinctively, I wanted to thrash around, hurl a few "fucks" and "shits" around and belt out a mighty *"ROOAAAAARRR!"* But instead, I stopped, for just a second. I thought to myself, "I have a choice." Because while I could absolutely do those things, and it would make perfect sense, I was also an evolved, civilized man who had grown quite aware of himself over the past eleven months. I could choose a different approach. I could step outside myself and see my situation from another vantage point. I could choose to be positive. I could choose to laugh. I mean, I lay there covered in bottles and weird products, and water was shooting into my face and pooling in an odd mixture of colors all around me, and that was *pretty fucking funny!*

Either way, it wouldn't change my situation. I'd still be lying there, whether I freaked out and hurled expletives or laughed and moved on. But once you get yourself into that negative space, it's pretty easy to stay there. It would have made the situation seem bigger and worse than it was, would have made Shawna feel bad for me, and would have gotten me nowhere. So Shawna, having heard the commotion, ran in and found me laughing in a tub full of pink and blue water, and she laughed too. She got me up, rinsed me off, and we high-fived and moved on. I went to bed happy that night.

So yeah, shit happens, and bad things exist, and I had opportunities to get frustrated or angry or sad all the time. But I wouldn't succumb to it. When someone came at me with negativity, told me how sorry they were for me, or when Shawna and I were at a restaurant and a server asked, out of nowhere, if we thought we'd ever be able to have kids, I could say, "You know what? We're good, thanks." And I could brush it off as easily as snow on a jacket.

Adversity was just a bump in the road. I got to choose what level of light or dark got into my space. No one got to make me feel any particular way, and no one got to affect my reactions. With Shawna's constant help, I created for myself a bubble of positivity, and, with lots of practice, made it impermeable.

If you measure distance in feet (or meters, depending on where you live), you measure energy in joules, and you measure pressure in pascals, I like to think that you can measure life's experiences in a known quantity, too. I think of this quantity as units of joy.

Everything, from this table I'm writing on to the cells making up your body to the food we eat, is made up of combinations of basic elements from the Periodic Table. You can break it all down to the same 118 elements, and reconstitute it into something else, anything you want. You can turn something you hate or fear—maybe a bomb or Brussels sprouts—into something you love, like a tree or a motorcycle.

So maybe basic life experiences can be broken down scientifically like that, too. Maybe combinations of variants of joy are what make up life. And if that is the case, you can, theoretically, reconstitute any experience you don't want or that doesn't give you pleasure into one that gives you great joy. So you can take any situation and break it down to find joy in it. If joy is the measurable quantity that allows me to be happy and positive, and if I'm actively seeking joy in all things, I'm truly present at all times, engaged in the positive.

So when people ask me, "How can you be positive *all the time?*" I just know it's because I'm finding all the beauty that surrounds me at all times, locking on to every piece of joy that exists in my world. And if I can find joy in all things, I can make the joy pile up, and therefore I can always, always be positive.

There was so much in my life to be positive about. Shawna and I had developed important, life-altering friendships with generous people who gave of themselves and their resources. Since Sponsored by Love, the Korg 3.0 movement had grown wings and was flying high as people began donating to High Fives, benefitting not just me but other recipients of their generosity. Awareness of spinal cord injury was growing in our area as I began giving talks and spreading the word through various fundraising events and YouTube videos. Local newspapers began telling my story as the one-year anniversary of my injury approached. It was all so beautiful.

I found joy in the smallest moments. At a restaurant, Shawna left my side for just a moment to go to the counter and order food. My crutch slipped out from under me and I hit the deck, collapsing in a heap on the floor. Before Shawna could even make it back to me, a stranger hopped out of his booth, swept me up and, almost effortlessly, got me back up on my crutches. Then he just jumped back in his booth, and continued his conversation. No, "Hey, bro, are you okay?" He knew I was embarrassed and upset and that I didn't need a conversation about it. Just got me back on my feet and went back to his table. I turned to him, smiled, and mouthed "thank you." Meeting my eyes, he smiled, gave me a thumbs up, and returned to his conversation.

At the end of the day, the humanity we continued to see was so big, so pure, so beautiful, that there was plenty of joy to be found everywhere. How could I *not* be positive?

That's not to say it always came so easily. Greg called me. My old buddy from inpatient wanted to get together for coffee and catch up. I was elated to hear from him, so excited about the progress he and I had both made since we'd left the hospital.

But what I'd done didn't seem to mean much to him. At coffee that day, Shawna and I sat and listened to him talk, almost without stopping, about his numerous triumphs. He was now walking independently, with a slight limp. His business was taking off, he had plans to go mountain biking, and he and his wife seemed to be back to life as usual. Things were pretty great for Greg.

More weight went into my backpack, which I had nearly forgotten about carrying until my old friend reminded me it was there. It was a constant weight that most people I'd met along this journey who'd had a spinal cord injury had gotten full use all back. Of course I was beyond stoked that Greg had progressed to this point, and I found it inspiring and hopeful. But still, there was the exhaustion of being the mirror on which Greg's reflection shined all the more brightly. He was highly aware of our contrasting situations and openly championed my recovery to close the gap between us.

People yearned to connect with me, to compare experiences, and it was a weight, because, I realized later, I instinctively felt that others' successes were robbing me of mine. Like there was a finite amount of it in a bag somewhere and Greg had grabbed up my share. He obviously felt this, too. But when I considered this, I realized that was fear talking, not reality. Because there *is* enough.

Wars have started over fear of not having enough. People hoard, become greedy, battle over who owns what. The fear that there won't be enough is instinctive. And actions sponsored by fear are never rational. The gas shortages of the seventies resulted in fights at the pump, flat-out riots. Next time you're at a party, note what happens when a new person enters the room. The balance changes, the tenor of conversation alters because many people will now wonder if some of their attention has just been taken away.

But you know what? There's enough in the universe. There is *always* enough. After one party at a wealthy friend's home, Shawna and I talked in the car on the way home about how it seemed like people who had a lot of money didn't have a lot of things. In fact, their rooms were uncluttered, with very few accessories or furnishings. They didn't seem to collect knick-knacks. Wealth seemed almost to equal a sparseness. We reasoned that this made sense; if you're rich, you rarely worry that there won't be enough. You could get what you want at any time. But people with little hoard, they hang onto things. During our low financial period when Shawna and I were purging our belongings, our battle cry of "fuck stuff!" was followed with this reminder to ourselves: "There is enough."

There is enough recovery. There is enough movement. There is enough joy. There is enough money. There is enough happiness. There's enough of everything we want. Maybe, by repeatedly sharing his accomplishments with me, Greg was staking his claim on what he perceived as a dwindling supply. And maybe the fact that I was equally thrilled for him and discouraged for myself when I was with him meant that I was struggling with that same thing.

I made two decisions after leaving Greg that day: The first was that I would put some distance between myself and Greg for the short term, in order to avoid those unsettling feelings of comparison and focus only on the positive nature of my own recovery. The second was that I would never allow my actions, or my interactions with others, to be sponsored by fear—fear that there wasn't enough for us all. Instead I would surround myself with that which was sponsored by love.

Grant's friendships with his "Rescue Boyz" will last forever (Photo by Liz Margerum)

CHAPTER 21
REDEMPTION

On New Year's Eve, Shawna and I turned down invitations to go out. Instead, I helped Shawna in whatever way I could as she prepared a delicious dinner for the two of us. She lit a fire in the fireplace, and I took a seat on the couch.

She went upstairs and grabbed colored markers and a large square of frosted glass she had bought at Ikea months previous. She propped it up on the floor, leaning against the recliner, sat herself on the floor, uncapped a marker, and said, "Okay. What do we want to create in 2011?"

The dream board was something Shawna had done with her Sanctuary clients, and it was something she had wanted us to do as a couple even before my injury. And, like a lot of other things, we'd never made time for it. We'd told ourselves, "Oh, we know what we want, and that's what we're working toward," as we hurried off to work or to any of the other distractions we busied ourselves with. But now, Shawna felt it was imperative that we do this on New Year's Eve. For her now, the overwhelming feeling was no longer, "We should do this"; it was, "We have to do this *now.*"

For me, it was a beautiful place to be in—to ask ourselves not just what we wanted, but what we wanted to *create.* Because there's no mysticism in asking the universe for what you want. It's not that you could expect the universe to hand down gifts wrapped in ribbons. You manifest what you want. You create it. You begin to wear it on your skin, until, like those cantilevers, the things you want become attracted to you. The process is powerful and empowering and unlimited.

And while the board was a great way to solidify our desires, it also kept us accountable to each other and ourselves. It was something we could frequently glance at as we made our way through the house, and be reminded of how, with each simple keyword or phrase Shawna scribed, it signified a wealth of specifics, the complete desires we had for ourselves and our future together.

With each thing we wanted, the follow-up question was "*How* do we want it?" We articulated, in full, what we wanted that to look like, and used a word or two to encapsulate the idea for us on the board.

Some of it, things we'd talked about before, came easy—like "honeymoon," which we still had never taken, or "road trip in SM (Sportsmobile)." And because we knew Free Candy didn't have much more life left in her, we added "4wd SUV" to the board. We added "Hawaii" and "Carmel" to the list, knowing these were places we wanted to visit. And because I'd always been intrigued, "stand-up paddle board" made its way on there, too.

"Walk hand in hand on beach," "fly helicopters," "acupuncture," and "skiing" were others. So were "photography and cinematography," interests Shawna and I, respectively, had always had and wanted to investigate in the coming year. "Documentary" and "public speaking" wound up on the board, too.

Some represented less specific, but no less important, goals: "inner peace" and "joy," for instance.

Dozens of things—toys we wanted, destinations we wanted to visit, experiences we wanted to have—covered the square of glass. We didn't censor, didn't put doubt or conditions on our desires, and didn't widget solutions; in that case, we might as well tell the universe "cancel cancel." We clearly, without inhibition, named our desires and turned them loose with a "start start."

We sipped champagne, spent a couple hours on the board, and then propped it up on the floor in the corner of our dining room, a silent but insistent reminder of its contents.

And then we let it go, toasted the New Year, and vowed that we would be open to how these things came to us.

As Shawna's parents tell us, when she was six years old, they asked her what she wanted to be when she grew up. Her precocious response was, "I don't know, I just want to make a difference." When she was just thirteen, she conceived of The Sanctuary, a place where people could go to improve their overall health and well-being, not just get physically fit but really allow themselves to be in that space of harmony, creating the lives they truly loved by being in good physical shape as well as emotionally healthy. That, she believed, was her path to making a difference in the world.

Even though balance was the goal, ironically, finding balance in this new career she had created was terribly hard—hard to make it work, hard to maintain a clientele in an unstable economy, hard to balance the various personalities, hard to be both the boss and the practitioner.

For myself, I had similarly wanted to make an impact on the world, and since knowing Casey, I had believed that engineering was the way in which I would do that—especially once the mission and potential of NanoLabz emerged. But scrounging for dollars and putting our reputations and personal assets on the line for each project, giving up our time and our lives to hide away in labs, that too was a hard, insupportable, unsustainable way of life. It was that life that had landed me in my current circumstances.

So now Shawna and I were on a different path, and yes, it was more challenging in so many ways, not just for me but for her, too. But in our new roles throughout this recovery, we had asked for what we wanted, had been open to how we got those things, and things had actually begun to come. It seemed to us that when you're honoring your truth and are on the right path, when you stop "trying" to make things happen in the way you expect them to, and when you're willing to do your part to bring them to fruition, things, ironically, start to seem effortless.

That doesn't mean it was easy. As Liam once told me, "I'm proud of you, the way you could have so easily gone back to the comfort and safety of engineering." The easy thing *would* be to go back to what's safe, to put my recovery on hold, go back to NanoLabz and start accumulating money again. By doing so, I could give Shawna and myself some security, the ability to know exactly what I'd be doing next year and the year after that. But I would have been denying myself the one critical time in my life in which I could actually recover completely, and that would have solidified my recovery for the rest of my life. It was the one time in my life to completely, wholeheartedly fight for it. And I was willing to do that at whatever cost. And I have reaped huge rewards from taking that risk, which tells me that, despite the hard work, I have been on the right path.

So instead of the stable choice, Shawna and I were crawling out on life's skinny branches, risking our future career security and financial stability, and saying, "We want to help people," and though we didn't quite know what that looked like yet, we had a pretty good idea how it would feel. And it didn't involve me working in a lab all day.

It was astounding the things we wrote on the board on New Year's Eve 2010 that manifested almost immediately. We had written "Korg Industries," our name for the entity we believed would allow us to pay my recovery forward by sharing the lessons I'd learned, raising funds, and giving to others who would need it; this had morphed into the Korg 3.0 movement, from which stemmed the "public speaking" that we had also written on the board.

Then there was "photography." Shawna's grandparents asked us, sometime after New Year's, whether we had a good high-resolution picture of the two of us taken during my recovery. "Well, we have iPhones?" we told them, by way of saying, "Well, that's the best quality we have." Which is how we ended up receiving from them the extraordinary gift of new, top-of-the-line photography equipment, which became our way to document every moment of our journey going forward, and to share those moments with the world.

We had written "Locomotor," which was the name of a program at The Shepherd Center in Atlanta—where we ended up just two months later.

In early spring, "fly helicopters" became relevant when I bumped into a pilot friend at a downtown Reno event. He suggested that we get started on my ground school training for my pilot's license. And the certified flight instructor I had planned, last year, to complete my ratings with, indicated to me that, whenever I was ready, I could get started.

On February 28, the day before Shawna's birthday, Thaïs and her fellow physical therapists conspired to help give her the birthday gift she really wanted, a gift we had asked the universe for many times. My therapy began that day with stretches, as it typically did, with Thaïs taking a long time to be sure I was warmed up, limber, and ready to work.

"Okay, Grant, go ahead and sit up," she said. I looked up and saw her eyeing others on the therapy team, who nodded and made their way to me. "It's Shawna's birthday tomorrow. Are you ready to walk and hold hands with your wife for her birthday?" She smiled a mischievous smile at me.

My own smile spread from ear to ear and my eyes opened wide with surprise. I looked at Shawna, her face registering that she hadn't expected this development either. We looked at each other as if we'd just been given a free pass. I didn't know how Thaïs planned to do this, but I would be eternally grateful to her for giving it a shot.

I stood up and used my crutches, with Thaïs pointing the way, to walk to the center of the room. From the corner of the room, Thaïs pulled out a large metal cane, and exchanged it with me for my left crutch. A PT assistant named Jen silently emerged from the small crowd that now formed around us, and stood behind me to spot me.

"Okay, Shawna, are you ready?" Thaïs asked.

She clearly was—she was bouncing with joy. "Absolutely!" she beamed. "What do I do?"

"Stand right…" and she positioned Shawna to my right, "here." Taking Shawna's left hand, she moved my right crutch and put Shawna's hand in mind. "Off you go!" she said.

And for the first time in almost exactly a year, with tears spilling over our eyelids, my love and I got to walk hand in hand. And we got "joy" too.

*Shots for the news about Grant's first time back on his
sled (Photo by Shawna Korgan)*

I sat astride my snowmobile, consciously acknowledging every sensation I felt—the comfortable pressure on my lower back that came from sitting upright with my legs apart; the cold air surging through my throat and
sinuses as I breathed deep the cold morning air, scented by pine and gaso-
line fumes; the biting cold stinging my cheeks and nose; the warmth inside
my yellow coat; the steam from my breath inside my helmet; the sounds of
my anxious breath; and the feeling of having my hands, wrapped in thick
black and white gloves, curled once around the black rubber handlebar
grips. I stretched all ten fingers out, then once again curled them tightly
around the grips, to emphasize their solid grasp on the machine. I cranked
the throttle, feeling the sled's angry engine purr beneath me.

It was the first time I'd touched a snowmobile since being dragged off
this exact sled by Ryan and Duncan exactly one year earlier. This was the
one toy we hadn't sold. We'd known, even then, that we would need this
day. This was my redemption day.

Before me lay a hilly stretch of Gold Lakes Road, from which perfectly
groomed snowmobile trails branched like arteries throughout the Lakes
Basin. Tall conifers seemed to brush the rapidly clouding sky and part on

Grant in his natural environment once again (Photo by Ken Evans)

the horizon, providing a view of the base of the cloud-covered, craggy, snow-capped Sierra Buttes. Flanking me on both sides, on sleds of their own, were nearly forty of my closest friends and a few reporters who'd been following my progress as a local-boy-makes-good story. Shawna and family, brothers from Alpine Assassins, Roy and High Fives, and dozens more, all smiled, cheering me on, propelling me forward with their love.

A series of late-season snowstorms had blanketed the northern Sierra with layer upon layer of deep, powdery snow, making for spectacular, almost poetic, snowmobiling conditions. We were itching to get into it. After a series of short on-camera interviews, preliminary talk of the wheres and whens for the day, all looked to me, the leader of this ride, for a sign that I was ready. I revved the throttle, heard the familiar rattling whine, and tore off, covering ground as if on a quest to carve snow.

I was a child now, traveling by instinct, the territory as familiar to me as the back of my hand, but now with the newfound freedom of again, finally, being given free rein to point my sled in any direction, drop down any hill, climb any ridge. I played with the gas, experimenting with velocity, savoring the sensation of slow, leisurely travel at first, testing out my

One year since the accident and happiness was through the roof
(Photo by Nik Sullivan)

spine and feeling good. There was no fear, no flashing back to that terrible moment a year ago. Just a glorious sense of possibility. Then, suddenly, craving speed, I hurtled forward like a pouncing cat.

There it was. There was that freedom, that deep-bone freedom that I could only experience at the moment when I was truly at my highest level, but even more powerful because it was infused with memories of the past year. This was my first moment in many, many months of complete and utter freedom, the first time I had been able to go wherever my gut directed me, to let my mind go and follow with my body.

That morning, I'd wanted to deliver my empty coffee cup to the kitchen sink, had even stood up and positioned myself in crutches, before realizing that, in fact, I couldn't carry the cup, couldn't do what I'd set out to. But now I could conquer mountains, blow past trees, leave a wake of powdery mist behind me as I twisted and turned through the forest, dropped down chutes, executed challenging pow-turns, masterfully in control and utterly free as a bird.

Six hours later, as the afternoon clouds sank into the basin and the electrifying scent of an impending snowstorm filled the air, the small remain-

The fantastic foursome back on the snow one year later
(Photo by Duncan Lee)

ing group of riders mounted the top of a commanding rocky cliff. Though several riders had by now peeled off from our group to make the drive home, the dozen or so of us who remained sent up whoops and cheers, meeting me as I pumped my fist in the air and called out a triumphant, "YEAAHHHHH!!"

I was back. Shawna and six or seven people jumped off their sleds and ran to me, piling on me with hugs, helmets banging against each other, and high fives until our palms tingled, their love for me a warm glow radiating from the mountaintop down to the basin spread out below us.

Roughly two hours later, my face frozen and aching from smiling, we pulled our sleds back into the icy, muddy lot and onto Oddo's truck, which would take Shawna and me home. And though every fiber and muscle in my body cried out for rest, my smile persisted, and my tongue flapped for the entire ninety-minute drive home. You couldn't have shut me up to save your life, so high was I on the happiness coursing through me.

And once safely at home, with redemption securely wrapped up in the palm of my hand, I curled up and slept for the better part of three days.

Grant in hyperbaric chamber surrounded by family (Photo courtesy of Grant Korgan)

"Have you tried hyperbaric?" Roy Tuscany had asked me, when he'd called the day after my triumphant snowmobile ride to check on how I was feeling.

This was the second time in under a week that someone had suggested hyperbaric to me. Our Pilates instructor had first mentioned this to Shawna, and we could not ignore its repeated mention. The idea of lying in a glass tube for an hour like some sort of space traveler had seemed odd to me, but the pressurized oxygen was said by many to have remarkable healing properties when used for a number of conditions, ranging from autism to wound care and traumatic brain injury.

Shawna was by now actively engaged in following developments at California's Reeve-Irvine Research Center at UC Irvine, where recent studies in nerve regeneration through the use of an enzyme called PTEN had yielded encouraging results. In the course of her research, she had come across a list of hyperbaric oxygenation therapy (HBOT) providers from the Christopher and Dana Reeve Foundation's Paralysis Resource Center and had read several articles about the promise that hyperbaric showed for spinal cord-injured patients. The signs pointed to the fact that we needed to give it a shot.

With a recommendation for a local hyperbaric treatment center, Monday morning, we made an appointment, and by the end of the week had a plan for five weekly sessions of an hour and a half each.

At the end of an appointment in early March, Shawna and I exited the building to find it had grown nearly dark outside. Shawna had parked Free Candy in the parking garage across the street and left me alone for a moment to go get it. I watched her dart across the street and disappear into the garage, and it was then that I looked around me and realized that there was a man who appeared to be both drunk and homeless loitering just outside the door of the hyperbaric center.

"Hey, bro," he mumbled to me in a ragged voice. "This mm mphh, my man," he seemed to say.

This sort of incomprehensible conversation had begun happening to me regularly, as strangers emerged seemingly from nowhere, almost always delivering some sort of message to me in an unworldly manner—like the man who had approached me at the mall that day. The messages, which usually reverberated with both truth and compassion, had become so intriguing and desirable to me that I remained open at all times for them, often welcoming situations like the one I found myself in, despite the fact that I was somewhat concerned for my safety, too.

"Hey man, what's up?" I said warily, looking sideways at him in case he had something positive to share.

"You buh mmph mm," he said to me.

Okay, so maybe this was nothing but a guy in a deep, challenging space of his own.

"Okay, well, have a nice evening," I said, adjusting my crutches and beginning to head toward the street to get a little closer to Shawna. I had gone only a few feet when the man called to my back, "I broke my back awhile ago."

I've often heard of very religious people speaking in tongues as the "spirit" moved through them, and it was this idea that now occurred to me as this strange drunk man who just seconds before had been unintelligible spoke clear as a bell, as if something had possessed him in order to speak to me.

"What?" I stopped and turned to look at him.

"I broke my back a few years ago," he said, pulling himself up from his crouched position on the curb and slowly making his way toward me. "My brothers, they took me out on this boat. We went miles off shore, and then they threw me off the back of the boat and said 'sink or swim' and drove back to shore." At this, he loudly coughed up a wad of phlegm and spit it on the ground, then wiped his hand across his nose and mouth. "I swam back." By now he was standing directly in front of me, close enough that I could see the dirt on his face and on his dirty sweatshirt, and smell the sour liquor on his breath. I wrinkled my nose despite myself, but stared deeply into his light blue eyes, my own eyes now as wide as saucers. He put his hand on my shoulder. "Swimming will heal you," he said, patting me once, then turning and walking away.

As I watched him recede, aware of goose bumps running all the way down my body, I could hear the rattling muffler of Free Candy as it approached.

Shawna pulled the van up to the curb and hopped out, walking around to get me. I still stood there, watching the man swerve and stumble away. "Who's that? What's his deal?" she asked, opening the van's passenger door.

"Um, I think I just had an encounter with the universe," I said, watching him turn the corner and disappear.

One morning in early March 2011, the phone rang.

"Mornin'!" said Liam in his cheerful Irish accent. "I wanted to ask ya somethin."

"Good morning!" I said to him, pleased to hear his voice. "What's up?"

"Well, I'm terrible at surprises, so I'm just goin' to tell ya, I need you to give me some dates when you might be available to leave town."

Leave town? What on earth? This man had moved mountains to help us out; surely he couldn't be planning to send us somewhere for a therapy, on top of everything he'd already done for us.

"Why? What's going on?"

"Well, you know how I told ya we go to that resort in Kauai?" he began, sounding a little hesitant.

"Yeeaahh…" I said, remembering that the Ryans had just returned from their anniversary trip to their favorite vacation spot in Kauai.

"Well, see, one of my patients has a house there."

At this point he'd lost me. I just smiled and said "uh-huh," shooting a confused look at Shawna.

"Well, it's just, I hope you don't mind but, well, Caroline and I had dinner with him and his wife and got to tellin' him about your story."

"Oh!" The pieces were starting to come together. "That's fine, Liam, of course!"

"Well, see, I told 'em how you and Shawna hadn't had a honeymoon and all, and, well, they want ya' to come stay at their house. You know, for a honeymoon."

The color drained from my face.

"Uh…" I stammered. Shawna heard me from the kitchen, where she had just gone to begin blending up our morning juice, and came to find out why the tone in my voice had just shifted.

"Um… what? His house?"

"I know, but listen, this man, he's an elderly man, very wealthy, philanthropist, extremely generous. He insists."

"Who is it?" I pressed.

"I can't say; I'm sorry. But trust me, it's a serious offer. He won't take no for an answer. So Caroline and I want to book you a flight."

As much as Shawna and I had been overwhelmed by generous gestures, including those by Liam himself and his center's team, this felt all out of proportion considering the donor was anonymous. Though my instincts were all shouting, "Take it, dummy!" I didn't feel right about accepting a gesture of this size.

"Oh my gosh, Liam, that is so amazing, truly, wow, we are just…" I stumbled trying to find the right words. "We're just blown away. Please, please, pass along our endless gratitude from the bottom of both our hearts, I mean, wow. But I just, I don't, I just don't think…"

"Look, just receive, okay?" Liam interrupted. "Listen, *take* your honeymoon already! You've been through enough, both of ya. He won't take no for an answer, and frankly, neither will I. Now, how 'bout those dates? Figure a couple weeks."

I asked him to hold on while I filled Shawna in on the basics and we searched our calendars for available dates. The end of March and early April looked pretty wide open for us.

"All right, we'll take care of it. You'll love it—a humble 3,000-square-foot, three-bedroom home next to the ocean. How does that sound?" I could hear the devilish grin in his voice.

I just smiled and shook my head, rubbing my eyes in disbelief. Surely this wouldn't really come to fruition. As kind and well-intentioned as this man and the Ryans were, we knew having a place to stay in Hawaii, even having the flights booked, were only half the battle. At this point, we couldn't afford a car, food, and sightseeing for two weeks in Kauai... And telling him this would only make them feel obligated to pay for those, too.

I just said, "Sounds amazing, thank you, and please, please, send our deepest, most heartfelt thank you's to your friend. I just... I don't even know what to say."

I reasoned that a lot of people say, "Hey, you can stay in my house next time you're out this way," but you'd never actually take them up on it. I wondered if that's what this kind stranger had been thinking, and cringed inwardly that the two of us would actually show up there to make good on a casual, off-handed offer from a stranger. I hung up, and shared both my elation and this newfound anxiety with Shawna.

"Let's just wait and see what happens, babe," she said. "I'm sure they wouldn't have offered if it was a problem. And Liam, he wouldn't be doing this if he thought it wasn't a real offer, right?" Still, she bit her lip and looked at me, eyes wide with curiosity.

A few hours passed, and no more calls came. Even though Shawna and I intentionally avoided the subject, inside we each vacillated between excitement and anticipation over the invite.

Then late that afternoon, the phone rang again. It was Liam.

"So we're all set," he said. "You're booked. You leave March 27," he said.

"Liam, seriously, thank you, thanks to your friend, this is beyond amazing, but we can't afford this," I argued.

"Afford what? It's all paid for," he said. "I'm sending you the itinerary now. Your flight's booked, you have a place to stay... it's done. Leave it to us."

I hung up the phone with a, "Holy shit, thank you!" and within the hour, our United Airlines itinerary for first class seats to Kauai arrived in my email.

"Well, babe, we're going on our honeymoon!" I beamed to Shawna.

We still had no idea how we would afford a car or any of the costs of living in Kauai for two weeks, but because we trusted the Ryans so completely and hated to turn down such selfless, kind gestures from them and their generous friends, we just accepted, as Liam had requested. We'd figure out a way to make it work, because this was a once-in-a-lifetime opportunity.

A few days before leaving Reno, during my last therapy session with Thaïs before leaving town, Liam pulled me into his office and handed me a full envelope.

"You have some wonderful friends," he said, pressing the envelope into my hand. I opened it to find a wad of bills. Confused, I looked up at Liam. "What's this?"

"Let's just say a few anonymous donors wanted to give you two a little somethin' to enjoy your honeymoon."

Having already received so much from our loved ones over the past year, neither Shawna nor I felt comfortable indicating that we needed money for this trip. We had simply said that our loving friends, Liam and Caroline, and their good friend had put this trip together for us. Still, they had all come together to ensure that Shawna and I had the honeymoon we had dreamed of.

How could two people feel more loved?

We stepped outside Lihue Airport to wait for the four-door Jeep we had rented to meet us at the curb. What a difference flying first class had made to my comfort. Despite the length of the flight, I was remarkably energized, as different as could be from my condition in Atlanta after the last time I'd flown. And though I'd remained open to the possibility that I might need a wheelchair, I was thrilled to realize that I didn't.

The air, mild and humid and floral-scented, enveloped us like a loving hug. Back home, we would be enduring battering winds and another round

Princeville fountains (Photo by Grant Korgan)

of snow and rain, part of the coldest, gloomiest spring either of us could recall.

Settled in our silver Jeep, we pulled out the map Liam had provided us of the island. He'd marked the route to Princeville, the community where we'd find the home of our kind benefactor, the "humble" abode that would be our home for the next two weeks.

The wide, grand entrance to Princeville was marked most notably by a wide pool surrounded by a line of trees. At the far end of the pool was a fountain of water cascading down a series of steps.

"Okay, the map says turn that way," I pointed, unsure at this point whether this could possibly be right. My uncertainty grew as an elaborate fountain portraying a nude Prince Albert on some sort of seashell spraying water into the air came into view. "Uh, do you think we could get, like, arrested for coming down here?" I asked, half joking.

"Babe, I'm sure it's fine. Liam wouldn't send us down here without arranging everything," Shawna reassured me, craning her neck to take in the lush scenery surrounding us.

"Okay, we go through this gate," I said, pointing straight ahead.

The kind woman at the gate knew at once who we were. She handed us a gate pass and a parking permit and waved us through.

The contemporary home, situated on a ridge at the end of a long drive, was all angles and rooftops, with large windows that reflected the sun and the sparkling Hawaiian waters below. Palm trees waved in the breeze, marking the edges of the home that seemed to vanish into the otherwise unbroken horizon of green mountains and blue waters. The driveway led us to the edge of an infinity pool, which seemed to drop clear into the ocean, despite its fair distance from the shoreline.

Shawna pulled to the end of the driveway without saying a word. She turned off the ignition, turned to me, and said, "Uh... seriously?" and then began to laugh.

"Oh, my..." I said, holding my hand to my mouth in disbelief.

The home's interior was no less impressive. Marble flooring, granite countertops, palace-sized rooms, vaulted ceilings, and expansive, heavenly views of the ocean and sparkling green, mountainous shoreline greeted us.

Shawna and I stood in the foyer, breathing in the ocean air and absorbing our dream-like surroundings.

All I could stammer out was, "Oh... my..."

"Oh, look!" Shawna said, jogging over to the kitchen counter on the other side of the enormous living room, where a vase of fresh flowers, a bucket of champagne, and an envelope propped against the vase had been left. "Unbelievable," Shawna said, leaning over to smell the flowers. Then she took the envelope and looked at me questioningly. "What is this?"

"I don't know," I said, my eyes wide open and my head shaking.

The envelope contained a two-page handwritten note. "Welcome to our home, Grant and Shawna!" Shawna read. "We hope you'll be very comfortable here. It's our great pleasure to have you! I've enclosed a list of restaurants, as well as the items we want you to order. Trust me, you won't be sorry! Have fun and relax!"

"Oh my God," Shawna said, looking at me, then pulling numerous $100 bills out of the envelope. "I can't believe they did this."

I crutched my way over to meet her at the kitchen counter. We stood there staring out the window for a long, incredulous, silent minute.

"Oh my God!" Shawna said, her grasp of what was happening just now really sinking in. A huge smile spread across her face, and she began jumping up and down, giddy with excitement. "LOOK AT THIS PLACE! Grant, this is our honeymoon!" With that she sprang at me, hugging me around the neck and kissing my face.

Honeymoon breakfast has never tasted so good (Photo courtesy of Grant Korgan)

A year and a half into our marriage we were getting our honeymoon. But by the looks of it, it would be worth the wait. With one arm I held my wife, and then I kissed her passionately on the mouth.

The surreal nature of the trip began to be something we took in stride after a few days. At first, everything astounded us, from the royal treatment we received from the people who worked at this home—groundskeepers, a housekeeper—all of whom knew us by name, to the dining recommendations that must have taken a full day to put together. On our first morning in Kauai, we ate a brunch that I could only describe as miraculous. My pineapple juice, squeezed by hand, was the most delicately sweet liquid I had ever put into my mouth, and the bacon, crisp yet chewy and cooked to perfection, was made all the more delicious by the view. Seated outdoors on a restaurant patio perched high over Hanalei Bay, we overlooked surfers, one of whom, we later discovered, was pro Laird Hamilton, getting in a little tow-in practice on a hydrofoil surfboard.

Our other dining experiences were no less incredible. We don't tend to consider ourselves religious, but the truffle reduction scallops at Bar Acuda were about as close as we had ever come to a religious experience.

Honeymoon coffee on the beach of Hanalei Bay
(Photo by Shawna Korgan)

But perhaps more remarkable, more special to us, was that it was the first time in more months than we could remember in which we truly allowed ourselves to simply *be.* There was no waking up with an agenda, no "Today for therapy we get up and do an hour of Pilates, then hang upside down, then do our visualizations until our hyperbaric appointment at 1." Salt did not come on our honeymoon.

Now, we just asked each other, "What do you feel like doing today?" Now, we woke up and said, "Let's go get a cup of coffee and go to the beach." And here I could literally crutch right into the water and begin swimming in the healing waters, just as my homeless messenger had suggested I do. He had been right.

While packing for the trip, Shawna and I had talked about our concerns that a two-week vacation would slow down my recovery. We earnestly intended to visit the gym, to do as much therapy as possible while honeymooning in paradise. But the ironic thing was, within days, I knew I was making far greater strides here, by simply being still.

Yet, without actively seeking healing opportunities, they came out of the woodwork anyway, at restaurants, on the beach—there was a massage therapist, a Pilates instructor, the owner of a therapy retreat facility with a hyperbaric chamber, and a reflexologist who gave us great insights into the benefits of a raw diet.

Find the super-stoked kid in this photo
(Photo by Shawna Korgan)

But the healing came in other ways, too. Thanks to arrangements Liam had made with his personal friends, we were provided with snorkeling gear and a guide. Four hours in the warm, clear waters went by in a blink, and when Shawna tapped me and said, "I think we should probably get going," I said, "No, no, I'm good, I'm having a blast right now." I now felt as if my energy had no limits.

A neighbor of the Ryans had received a call from Liam because of the man's connection to a touring plane pilot. Before we knew it, arrangements were made to fly Shawna and I, for free, anywhere we wanted to go. This dreamy experience began as we took off from the Lihue Airport, where the pilot turned over the controls to me and said, "It's your plane." I got to fly and maneuver, even circle over the bay to check out a whale just surfacing. For two hours, I was given freedom to explore the air above Kauai.

The pilot brought the plane down to land, and I tried to hand him money, even offered to buy him dinner, knowing that fuel alone for such a trip was several hundred dollars. He wouldn't take a dime.

Another call Liam had made was to a friend named Dylan Thomas, a superstar waterman, and long-distance surfski paddler, to tell him what a lover I am of kayaking. Dylan called out of the blue a couple days after our arrival and offered a wealth of resources and contacts to us, including stand-up paddle boards and a day of paddling his tandem surfski with him in Hanalei Bay.

Seconds from island flight with Dylan and Jim
(Photo courtesy of Grant Korgan)

I was intoxicated by the experience, because, for the first time since my injury, I was not just an *adaptive* athlete doing what he could to work around his perceived abilities in order to participate in a way that approximated the original. I was simply an athlete, participating in a real way, in a real sport. I wasn't an injured guy first. I was just a guy out paddling in the ocean.

We pulled up on the beach, where Shawna ran out into the water to greet me. Her tears and hugs told me she wasn't just proud of me for overcoming obstacles, for having recovered to this point. Because, before, she'd been watching me recover. Now she was just enjoying watching me *live*.

Our connection with Dylan not only resulted in my getting athletic experiences I'd dreamed of (and actually asked for)—like stand-up paddle boarding and sit-surfing—but in a friendship we found precious. We were honored with invitations to Dylan's home, where he, his wife, and baby hosted barbecues attended by like-minded, adventuresome, down-to-earth people who also kayaked and who invited us to join in further activities like practicing Pilates in a treehouse-like studio.

Mentally, we took note of item after item that we could check off our dream board—"Hawaii," "honeymoon," "stand-up paddle board," and even "aviation." Then there was "inner peace" and "joy," with which our cups now overflowed.

*Sit down SUP (stand-up paddle boarding) in Kauai
(Photo courtesy of Grant Korgan)*

*Shawna enjoying paddle boarding through Jurassic Park
(Photo courtesy of Grant Korgan)*

Shawna and Grant on the sands of Hanalei Bay
(Photo courtesy of Grant Korgan)

So maybe there are no coincidences. Maybe everything Shawna and I had been through in the last year had happened for a reason, to give us an opportunity to learn lessons about ourselves and the world, and to share those lessons with others. Maybe when I broke my back, I was merely setting into action a whole chain of events that had been predestined for us. I mean, here we were, in one of the most beautiful places in the world, enjoying a honeymoon that we had only dreamed about. We had met people on this trip, and in the course of this past year, who filled us with joy and love, made us better people, and helped us to also touch a few people along the way. Maybe the words I've written here will set something else in motion for those who read them. Because here's what I know about the universe: It wants to give us what we ask for.

Finally, Shawna and I had figured out how to ask.

On our last night in Kauai, fueled by the energy and love that came from an evening with friends we knew we'd keep forever, Shawna and I walked out onto the stretch of beach we'd now come to think of as ours. I lay my crutch down on the soft white sand. Shawna stood in its place, took my hand, and we walked hand in hand on the beach, into our own perfect sunset.

Honeymoon in Hawaii (Photo by Jamie Cooper)

EPILOGUE
ICE AND FIRE

Ten months later, I'm back in the snow.
I'm in Antarctica on the Polar Plateau, getting ready to push out toward the South Pole. Me, two guides, a film crew, the gear and supplies we need to carry, and snow and ice as far as I can see.

It's taken months of intense training to get here. Still, the numbers I'm looking at are daunting: 200,000 strokes with ski poles to push myself across the ice; eighty-plus miles before we will see other people; twelve days of sunlight, with night being nothing more than when we've scheduled rest.

I will be the first spinal cord-injured athlete to ski to the Pole. (And if we're going to call any sport "extreme," this is it.)

The pain is worse now than it's been in weeks. It's new. The burning sometimes eclipses everything else. It travels up my legs to my hips, wakes me every twenty minutes. My legs are waking up. It's going to be a painful awakening.

I wouldn't trade it for the world. The last ten months have been a lightning-fast succession of triumphs, challenges, and the kind of serendipity that keeps my head spinning. Every time I think I've received everything there is to receive, something new comes along. Every time I think I'm over some new (or old) step in recovery, there's some new development. For the longest time, my life was two feet back for each one foot forward. Now it's two feet forward, one foot back. Shawna is always quick to remind me that forward motion is forward motion.

The push to the South Pole is all about forward motion. Forward motion is my mantra with every stroke.

Just getting here has been exhausting. Two full days of travel from Reno, Nevada to Punta Arenas, Chile. Hours upon hours of filming. Interviews. Cinematographic plans. The repetition of small moments just for the camera. Planning big moments still to come. Then rest. Gathering final supplies. Arranging gear.

The lead guide of our expedition joined us in Punta Arenas and immediately began pulling stuff out of bags while the rest of the team I argued we needed that gear. The whole production team ;pushed for every piece of clothing, every gadget, every roll of tape. But he kept reminding us we can not physically carry everything on the ice that we've been lugging through cushy airports.

A dinner of steak and water marked the true beginning of our expedition to the bottom of the world.

We flew out on an Ilyushin 76—a massive jet with four engines and a glass nosecone. It was a big and burly jet—153 feet long, forty-eight feet high, with a wingspan of nearly 170 feet—perfect for landing on an off-airport, solid-ice runway with no brakes.

It was probably twenty-below on the Union Glacier, where we spent roughly twenty-four hours acclimating, testing gear, and camping in the snow. But there was really nothing to prepare us for the savage cold of the Polar Plateau.

A twin-engine Basler turbo-converted DC-3 airplane on skis took us to the Plateau. It was nothing compared to the Ilyushin; it was an agile, payload-hauling, mid-century, puddle-jumping airframe rather than a goliath, late-seventies Soviet throwback to the Cold War era. We came in for a landing on its skis, on open ice, the sastrugi snow formations on the surface of the ice being so unpredictable, the plane hitting so hard, there was nothing to do but firewall the throttle, take to the sky once more, and go at it again.

Once we hit the ground, there were no big goodbyes. Our accomplished pilot did little more than slow down, shove the gear out, and yell, "Good luck!" before taking off.

The cold takes my breath away.

The sound of the engine fading into the sky is the last sound of technology we will hear for nearly two weeks. There is nothing to see on this open expanse of high flat cold. Just ice, snow, sky—all varying shades of white. An introspective think tank where everything is so white, devoid of color, contrast, shape, or limits. There is only texture, only each other, and everything feels possible. There is nowhere to go but the Pole, nothing to do but pack up, strap in, and move forward.

The absolute altitude on the Plateau is 9,000 feet above sea level, but because of the polar circulation vortex, and as far as the body is concerned, we're at around 12,000 feet above sea level. It's called *effective* altitude, and I can see why. The altitude stands only behind the cold in defining this frozen world. I know I am in for the shock of my life. All my training suddenly seems laughable.

It's negative fifty degrees Fahrenheit—that's eighty-two degrees below freezing, without accounting for wind chill—which is so cold that exposed flesh will almost instantly become frostbitten. Without current ability to feel or move from my knees down, my circulation is not what it once was, especially in my feet. Hypothermia will be a constant threat. Unless I'm in the tent, I won't be able to hold still for more than two minutes at a time without my body temperature dropping dangerously low.

The constant daylight will help us find comfort in the tents. I'll be able to strip off the layers of protective clothing and make sure my toes are still healthy. Since the accident, my feet are always on fire. But during our last training session in Alaska, I learned that when my body temperature drops dangerously low, the pain blissfully disappears. It is hard to remind myself that this lack of pain is a bad thing.

I'm sitting on my sit-ski (a sort of chair bolted to a set of skis), poles in hand. A pair of electronically heated liner socks, then outer socks, then chemical heater packs, and boots rated to minus-one hundred degrees protect my feet. There are digital thermometers taped to each of my big toes so I can constantly and accurately monitor their temperature, in real time, on the fly.

My entire body is covered in the best cold-weather expedition gear available on the planet. Two layers of Smartwool underlayers, combined with 800-fill down pants are like having sleeping bags strapped to my body. Two layers of mid and heavy-weight Smartwool and polypro shirts are tucked beneath a shell jacket with five pockets equipped to the nines with expedition snacks and pee supplies. A thin fleece balaclava topped with a thick beanie cap covers my head. The fur-trimmed hood of the jacket will be my primary mode of temperature control while I'm moving. But when

I stop, I will instantly huddle into an absolute-zero 800-fill puffy down jacket. Three sets of gloves—liner, subliner, and full down mittens—cover my hands. Goggles protect my eyes. A beard, face mask, and the balaclava ensure no skin is exposed to the elements.

Connected to the sit-ski is all my gear on a trailer that looks like a six-foot-long duffel bag with a hard bottom like a ski. I will pull all this eighty-plus miles to the Pole.

Every step of my recovery has been activity-based. Shawna and I have sought out opportunities that would keep me in motion. The reason we accepted this challenge was simply because it fit with our goals, my recovery, and our mission to have a positive impact on the world by our efforts. But this trek is more than we expected. More than I expected. At the beginning of our expedition just outside the final degree of latitude, this challenge meant there were at least eighty-plus miles of cold ice between me and Shawna, I could feel every mile in my bones before I even started.

The decision to take on the Pole required thinking big. A triathlon, an off-road race, my return to whitewater kayaking… Every activity I've taken on was with this undertaking in mind. Every time I got in a kayak or strapped into a roaring off-road truck or just climbed on the exercise bike, I thought, *If I can do this I'm one step closer to the Pole.* But right now, the Pole is eighty miles away. Shawna is thousands of miles away, back in the southern tip of Chile.

This training has taken me far north of Norway (the small Arctic island of Spitsbergen in the Archipelago of Svalbard), to northern Patagonia, and to the interior of Alaska. I've gone around the world, struggling for each step, earning each foot I traveled. But I took each step with Shawna. Through everything, she's been there.

When we first started talking about the idea of a South Pole expedition, the goal was to do some of it standing up. I wanted to at least ski the last bit, my two feet back under me, carrying me. But during the training, when we realized how quickly and dangerously my body temperature dropped, it became obvious that the circulation increase that comes from standing would be integral to the success of the journey. A goal became a necessity, just as it has so many times since the accident.

Grant pushing into the unknown, Antarctica 2012
(Photo by Keoki Flagg)

I'm strapped in, bundled up, ready to push on out. I know that this will not be a gentle glide over powder. Every stroke will be a full pull, a full push over ice like sand. The scraping of the skis across that ice will be loud—a struggling sound of grit and groan. The very first stroke will make me ask, "Are you serious?!" it will be so hard. And it won't get easier. Every stroke will be full effort. It will require every ounce of my concentration, every ounce of my being.

I slip easily into flow state as I bring all my focus to bear. My breathing is heavy. The world slips into black and white, slows, slows, slows. For the moment, it is silent as my mind flashes through the math and physics of what I'm doing, where I'm going, how I will get there.

But I know I will find my rhythm and the world will return to normal. The ice will regain its shades of gray and blue, my arms will move at what will pass as a normal speed, my feet will burn, and the sound of my scraping across the ice will fill the air. Every frozen hour will be much like its predecessor and the sound will be the same, the terrain the same, the sunlight the same. The burning in my feet will be the same.

Push. Pull.

A full effort of my heart, body, and mind. Exhaustion will be a constant specter, but it's a familiar one.

Twelve days and 200,000 strokes will bring me more than eighty miles across the ice to the South Pole, where Shawna waits with the rest of my life.

ACKNOWLEDGEMENTS

To say "thank you" is in my nature. I remember a moment when my godfather, Mike, was in town for my high school graduation in Incline Village, Nevada, where he said to me, "Grant, you can never say thank you too many times." This sentiment stayed with me, became my modus operandi, and was the first of three moments my godfather would place heavy wisdom deep in my psyche.

Fast-forward to the day I earned my degree in mechanical engineering from the University of Nevada, Reno. As you can imagine, I spared no detail in celebrating this well-earned milestone, and during the party my parents were more than excited to throw, again my godfather's words rang out: "Grant, to whom much is given, much is expected."

Then there I was, gripped with a lower body encased in an invisible layer of concrete, horizontal in a hospital bed, when once again my godfather would enter stage right, to lay upon me the third leg to life's long and fantastic trilogy of sound guidance. Mike approached my bed, fully grasping the gravity of my situation, and said to me, "Grant, the mind always quits long before the body."

My godfather is spot on. Like doing a backflip on skis, lead with your head and the body will follow. With ferocious mental strength and a clear understanding of my goals, I will reach 120 percent recovery. And with my burning, gratitude-filled desire to thank every single person who has kept me on my path of love, light, feeling, function, happiness, achievement, and recovery, this is for you. So whether you are listed by name or fall into the Unknown Soldier category, thank you. Thank you for your support, your courage, you heart, your fire, and above all, your unwavering belief in me.

MadLuv

~ G

To my beautiful wife, Shawna. You are the keeper of my whole heart, the center of my world, my soul's mate. Shawna, you are the essence of my inspiration, the passion behind my every push, and the reason I am the man I am today.

We began this journey together, walking hand in hand, blissfully sharing our lives, and I was the lucky one chosen to dance with you. Shawna, we have indeed been through one of life's many storms. And sheltered by your grace, empowered by your beauty, and protected by your might, I have once again regained my ability to walk, to stand by your side, and I promise it will not be long until I again embrace your infinite elegance as we waltz together, arm in arm, down the path of life forever. Thank you for your blissful love; thank you for being my wife. With every cell of my being, I adore you.

To the heroes who saved my life:

Ryan Oddo, you, my friend, are a warrior of light. Your never-ending smile is forever a part of my mental hard drive. Our many journeys together have been and always will be epic. I remember a toast you gave in which you fought tears in order to recount the story of my first time back to mountain biking after I broke my face in Colorado. You told the crowd what it meant to you when you got the call to go riding with me again, and riding we went. My friend, stay by your phone because it won't be long until you get that call again.

To the mighty Ken Evans. I remember stabilizing your neck, waiting for the paramedics after a dirt bike crash. I followed the ambulance with your truck to the ICU and stood by your bed as you worked your way through a series of broken bones. When I think of what you did to stand by me years later on that fateful day in Sonora, it still brings me to tears. To risk your life for the life of a brother is a noble thing to do. You, my friend, gave your all, and I have everything to show for it.

To my best friend, Duncan Lee, thank you. Thank you for twenty-nine years of family—you have always been the brother I never had. From a lifetime of always encouraging each other to standing in one another's weddings (holy supermodel brides!) to my staring into your deep blue eyes when I lay in the snow with a shattered spine at the very beginning of our latest journey, we have always been there for each other. You gave a toast at my wedding that went something like this: "No matter the situation, when things get intense for all of us, Grant has this saying he sprinkles on us, and somehow things feel a lot less intense. I don't know if Grant even knows he says it, but when the game is on, Grant says three simple words: 'You got this.'" Dunc, you ended the speech by talking about love, life, and marriage. And at the very end you turned to me and said, "Grant, YOU GOT THIS." I want you to know that since then, when times get tough for me, I hear your words. I love you, Dunc, and I will never forget all that you've done for Shawna and me in our lifetime of friendship.

Being the modest heroes that you are, the silent giants that I see you to be, I've watched you selflessly explain your actions on that fateful day with comments like, "You would do the same thing for me," or "It's no problem." The three of you made every decision correctly and without hesitation. Trading credit for compassion is a thing of beauty, and another reason I will forever think so highly of you all. Thank you for saving my life; you boyz will always be welcome at my fire.

To Lucky Bat Books: My unending gratitude for your belief and support in helping me capture this year of my life in the pages of this book! You guys made a dream come true, as my process of putting pen to paper (or fingers to buttons) was, at all points, unconditionally supported by the superstars on your team!

To my managing editor, Jessica Santina... (big breath) YOU ARE A F***ING ROCKSTAR!!! I can say with certainty that this book is what it is today because of your flawless input, literary talent, and your fantastic ability to see the forest through the trees. Thank you for walking this journey with me, thank you for holding my hand through the process, and thank you for always sharing your brilliance with the team and me.

Cindie Geddes, I am hugging you right now. You always believed, you always inspired, and you always had the smallest computer at the table! Your vision, ability to achieve, and excellent talent in offering editorial suggestion were key in the writing process—thank you.

Judith Harlan, thank you for all the attention to detail, your beautiful knowledge base, your willingness to Skype into last-minute meetings, and for your ability to succeed in every task you oversaw.

From the bottom of my heart, thank you, Lucky Bat Books.

To my amazing Mom and Dad, thank you for everything. To the people who made me, raised me, and provided for me every day of my life until I was able to go it on my own, my deepest gratitude! As financially difficult as it often was, you chose to raise me in the recreational paradise of Lake Tahoe's Incline Village, and I want you both to know I am forever grateful! Your kindness, your support, and your forever love is a place in which I've walked for all my years. For this reason and a million more, thank you—all my love!

To my fantastic mother- and father-in-law, Doug and Chris: Doug, we knew it from the moment we first met. You've encouraged me to see the beauty, you rubbed the life back into my feet before I was even awake, you've given us shelter from the storm! Chris, your love, your care, and your motherly gift of unconditional support shines every day. Thank you for making Shawna, and thank you for loving me!

Roy Tuscany, you fought the good fight—a battle to return, a battle to feel, and you won. You walked into my house and into my life. Positivity shines through everything you do, and like the glow Clark Kent always had without a mask, you, my friend, beam like the sun. I watch you live each day with the heart and fire of a shooting star. Thank you for sharing your super powers with the world; thank you for sharing your brilliance with me!

I am in love with the High Fives Foundation! Roy Tuscany and his crew of walking miracles are all heroes in my eyes. This Truckee, California-based 501(c)3 has taken on the mission to high five athletes who have sustained life-altering injuries while pursing their dreams in the winter sports community, with the ultimate goal of returning those people back to the athletic realities they lived in the first place. The High Fives Foundation has been one of the most supporting, encouraging, empowering cornerstones to my recovery and twenty-plus others! Adam Baillargeon, you are pure light, my friend. I love you, Steve Wallace. Ryan Linquist, forever my respect. And to Dana Greenwood, the highest of fives. The High Fives Foundation has been a powerful support to both Shawna and me, and is a worthy organization highly deserving of all our fantastic support!

To doctors James and Caroline Lynch: Beautiful Caroline, your grace, intoxicating accent, and unconditional ability to warm the hearts of all who know you has filled our world with pure gratitude, laughter, heart, and fire. Jim, it is human nature to recognize greatness, to be moved both elementally and fundamentally by a rare force. To just call you rare or great would be a dilution of your truth—from the beginning I have seen a friend, a mentor, a doctor, and soldier of positivity in you, moving forward and holding up the delicate realities of my recovery and that of others. In my opinion, your gift to the world is not in the multitudes you've helped, the realities you've enhanced for the better, or the well-deserved accolades of a life's noble work—it's the love you give, and I am forever honored to know your light.

In December of 2010, Spine Nevada became the nerve center for my continuous and ongoing physical rehabilitation. Dr. James Lynch and his team are, in my opinion, the yardstick by which back, neck, and spinal care in our area are measured. Words can do little to express the overwhelming gratitude that I feel for this group of medical superstars. To Thaïs Mollet, for your healing hands, your endless smile, and your beautifully genuine desire to see the human form as perfect. Jen Mavis, for believing in the booty—I'm bringin' J Lo back! Chantel Koppelman, I know you've got my back. From the bottom of my heart, a fantastically huge thank you to the entire Spine Nevada team!

To my brother, Steven Malekos. From around-the-world science expeditions to battle in the global boardroom to our finest engineering moments together to summit meetings on our sleds and bikes to back in college when you said yes to that epic spring break trip down the Grand Canyon, one thing was certain: We would be friends till the day our hearts stopped beating. You stood with me on the day of my wedding, by my side in the ICU, and I know you will be there the day I put the crutches down and walk free once again! MadLuv to you, your beautiful wife, Tamara, and your baby girl, Mykenna!

To the illustrious Sir Eliot Drake, our friendship means the world to me. You, good sir, elevate the game, enhance all your surroundings, and always force me to spellcheck my five-syllable words.

What would the world be without Ronnie Parker? Black, white, semi-creative, and devoid of epic style—you, my friend, are genius, and although you prefer to rock the backstage, your light shines up front and dead center wherever you go. Thank you for sharing your brilliance with all of us.

To my godsister, Bridgette, and her awesome husband, Matt Meinhold: We love you guys! Bridgette, thank you for being Shawna's long-lost sister, an unconditional source of love and support, and, most of all, the best of friends for as long as I can remember. We are hugging you both right now, can you feel us?

To Mike and Kathy Steffen, the best godparents a kid could ever hope to have: In a million ways you both have influenced, encouraged, and guided my life. I respect you both on high, and am forever grateful to have you in my life.

To Kerrie and Jesse Hon, for your constant commitment to blowing minds wherever you go. Your genuine love, desire, and compassion for Shawna's happiness and my progression is beyond unreal, and I want you both to know how loved you are—Boom.

DJ Neutrino (a.k.a. Jason Mead): You give, and you give, and you give some more. Since our early college days, our creative sparks always seemed to end up in the same fire. You not only have the world's best calves, but one of the world's biggest hearts, and I am honored to know you. Thank you for everything!

To Steve Schroeder, for all your hours of conversation, your desire to connect the dots and see the message of positivity shine, and for truly supporting us with heart and fire!

SSSSSSAAAAAAMMMMMAAAAYYYY! Sam Solomon, you are king, and I am forever grateful to know all the ways you had my back, in a time when my new journey was beginning to take shape.

Randy, Stacey, Kobe, and Cooper Sugihara: Your family is a lighthouse to the world. Your support has always been felt, and we look forward to the day we all go ride together. And Randy, thanks for letting me crush your hand in the ICU—you are a samurai!

Reid and Logan Hamilton, thank you for sharing your beautiful fire with Shawna and me. You've left an indelible mark on our hearts. Some gifts unspoken last a lifetime.

To the beautiful and always incredible Mel Lee, you rock our worlds! Thank you, Duncan, for giving us the gift of Mel—we are the lucky ones!

Mrs. Bridgette Evans, for your unconditional support, your always epic hugs, and for giving Obie a loving home in the weeks I was initially "man down," thank you.

To Becca Deal: I want to say, again, this time with raised glass in my hand, "Becca, I do not believe in coincidences, so therefore I believe we were meant to meet. I was meant to feel your support, your protection, and your bad-ass ability to make the world a better place! We love you, and we are forever thankful." Cheers!

Lisa Mukavitz, your care, concern, and unmatched professionalism has and always will have a place in our hearts that's reserved for your grace. Thank you. Thank you for believing in my recovery, in my wife, and in my smile.

Trent Murrieta, although our paths seldom cross, when they do, I see our childhood friendship in your eyes. When I think of all you did to watch over me in my greatest time of need, I am gripped with an overwhelming sense of gratitude for your awesomeness. Thanks, Trenton!

To my big brown man, Obie OneKorgNobie: Obie, you have been a true friend, a powerful confidant, and an every-moment supporter of my smile. You gave us things to laugh at when there was nothing funny about my situation, you snuggled me with your heart in times when all I could do was lie there, and your safe amber eyes accepted my secret admissions of pain and frustration without judgment. Simple unending adoration you give. May I someday be half as cool as you think I am.

I like to sign off most calls, texts, and emails with the simple term "MadLuv." I do it because it has all the makings of the Heart Fire (love and light) Korg 3.0 Movement icon I associate with my positivity, my mindset, and my overflowing gratitude. I believe it illustrates with words (and a symbol) the passion I have for life, the passion I have for recovery, and the passion I have to express my undying gratitude to every single one of you who has stood by my side through the gift of friendship we all share together! For your endless love, beautiful support, and your unwavering belief, I wish to thank the following people from the bottom of my heart. You are the essence of MadLuv. Forever my respect and admiration:

MadLuv, hugs, and high fives to my Aunt Debby and her family; my sister and her family; Dick and LaVonne Colon; Bob and Patricia Colon; Erik and Kurt Hansen; and to all my extended family across the country for all their love and support. Jeff Ross for having it all covered!

To Cody Knight for living in Technicolor and making dreams come true! The incredible Parker family: Deanna, Zach, Montana, and my "merchandise business manager," Bella for their late nights and incredible support!

To Cherie Cook for styling my world. Sara Cheek for making the Naa shine! The always beautiful and encouraging Chocolate (Ethel Murphy). Cary Chisum and Jamie Schmidt for filling our hearts. Steve and Naomi Rose—Team Rose is a force to be reckoned with, and I've always been so blessed to have you guys in my corner! Jerry Klopf, for eating all the organic cookies (so I didn't have to). The beautiful soldier of light that is Galen Gifford and his amazing family—S2G348!

To Fairlane for making the Korg Machine. To Johno Laz, I'm gunnin' for those hammies! Jamie Laz—Coops, I see Upper Cherry Creek in my crystal ball; purple soda pop, you two! Heath, Janene and the entire Spencer family, I still feel the high fives!

To Jesse Adams for the opportunity of a lifetime. To Ralph Whitten for believing in my talent and encouraging me to find more of it! To Ben Rogers for allowing me to experience the world's most intelligent and wittiest man—you impress me. Stuart Feigin for always seeing the dream.

To Ladd Williams for your connection, your power, and your heart—thank you for choosing to be a healer. To Kim Mynatt, Sean McIntire, and the Tahoe Forrest staff for your desire to see me rise and your effort to make it so. To Bird Lew, for all the healing hours you focused on my recovery. To Gale Ferruccio, your passion and genuine desire to see me heal was and is beautifully apparent—thank you for all the hours you put into my body.

To Doctor Andy Pasternak and his wife, Joann, for being the best family medicine doctor of all time! To Amber Meyers for all the luv. To The FreeBird, a.k.a. Adam Freeman, for inventing The Freebird (pint glass, whiskey over rocks, add soda and a grip-ton of limes), and for being that grounded force of stoke and positivity that fuels the world—KaKaaaa!

To Norm and Dianna Malekos for their love, support, belief in my recovery, and for making Steven! Justin and Natalie Cassinelli, thank you for loving me like I'm a Malekos. To Aaron Baker, for showing us all the way—you walk the walk, my brother, and I am beyond honored to know you. To Aaron's beautiful, loving, strong, and world-inspiring mother, Laquita Stovall-Conway, you are a great gift to all who have the privilege of knowing you.

To Taylor-Kevin Isaaks for empowering our workouts before we ever met—we have a lot of work to do! To Doctor Nightingale, for your compassionate touch, and your zest for recovery! To Laura Hirsch, for your strength, elegance, and brilliance—may even 1 percent of it continue to rub off on me! To Steven Siig and the whole Family Siigo for their love, support, and constant desire to see me fly. To Adam Miller, for sharing his story, his wisdom, and his understanding of things unspoken. To Barbara Schaefer, for going on a hike.

To the Carasali family, for all their incredible support, love, and friendship. To Daryl Drake, for being one of the coolest guys I know. To Matt and Tara Theilen, for giving love, capturing the light of our love, and every day reminding me to climb. To Laura Oglesby, for giving me my first acupuncture experience and rocking the party that rocks the party—TORONTO!

To Ralph and Linda Hartmann for "Circling Up" around us. To James Lowey—you are a force of positivity! To Ro Lazzarone, for always waving the flag of recovery. To Justin Meckley, for the fountain of youth! To Jasmine Hasi, for being the Dogs Bollocks, reaching out to heroes, and the hours of laughter before and after my injury! To the entire Stanford Nano-Fabrication Facility, you guys have always been amazing, full of support, and on track to change the world—high five, everyone!

To J-Dub for fusing metal when it needed to be fused. Dennis Troy, damn I miss your smile—you wanna go on another road trip soon? (Huge luv to BigGuy and Family!) Eric Strasser, for the steeziest set of wheels a walker could ever hope to see. Kurt at HMK for continuing to sponsor a rider that was just learning to walk again—it means more than I can say to feel that athletic support—we ride soon! Logan Knutznen, for shooting lightning bolts. Dr. Jane Diamond for ending the latex-induced reign of pain.

To Dr. Zhu, Dr. Moyee, Kahn, and the entire staff at Zhu's Neuro-Acupuncture Center: Your work has helped and empowered my recovery in more ways than I can mention. I will always and forever be grateful for every second you gave toward my journey. Ashley McDermid, for sponsoring me with love. Kelly Anderson, for standing in the elevator. To Kim McIntire, for every session's progress.

To Jason Craig and the whole Craig family, for love, support, and the beautiful inspiration on many levels. Tom and Liz Burton, for having my back for nearly thirty years, amazing introductions, and a belief I could see from the stage at Sponsored by Love 2010. Dylan Thomas, for the biggest wave of my life, your endless aloha, and the fierce desire to wear a Speedo! Matt and Andy Peek, my brothers, it is because of your friendship, your belief in me, that I have soared the open skies—aviation is more than a goal to me, it's a dream. Thanks to you both, I've been given beautiful opportunities to touch the void! Chris Tiller, for opening the door. Ryan Croke, for selflessly telling the story. Jason Hale (I'm gonna cry when I type this, I can already feel the tears), for saying to me in a time when I needed it, "Man down, not out."

To Rick and Pam Lee, for making me a best friend, a partner in crime, and a man who would eventually save my life. The Spacecraft Collective boyz, for flossin' a kid. Mike Gardner, for sharing your genius. To Dan and Kristen Scurlock, for your love, light, and every-moment awesomeness. Joel Giandalia, for making me feel like a rock star, and supporting unconditionally. Adam Henrichsen, for sponsoring me with love—high five, Frodie. Trey Demarest, I know you came to the hospital, thank you.

To Jeff Taylor, for blowing my mind, stoking my world, and reminding me that standing in my truth means dancing on a speaker box next to you—big love, my friend! Jason Petrin, your visit left an indelible mark on my heart—respect. Brandon Blackburn, for your belief, support, and selfless desire to see the world party! To Kristine Jackson, Ruth Gordon, and the entire Jackson family, thank you for everything. Abigail Trucano, for hooking up AK heli time for the cause. Lee and Sharisse Coulter, for setting hearts on fire with your beautiful love. Mark and Katie Watson, for the Apple empowerment. Justin Boreta, Josh Mayer, and Ed Ma for reaching out, filling the tank with fire, and empowering my recovery with your brilliance—hugs and high fives, gents. Nik Sullivan and Greg Martin, for the animal feelings! To Kim Anastassatos for spreading the good word and for your unending support. To the University of Nevada cheer team, for sharing your stage.

To Liz Margerum and Siobhan McAndrew, for capturing the heart of our journey and spreading a message of positivity! Mike Shirley, for seeing the vision and supporting the muscles. To Robby Nelson, I miss dirt church with you. Kelsen Thompson, for the always-contagious smile. To Brook and Cindy Renslow, for infinite love and gratitude!

To Mike, Carol, and Jim in Kauai for all the fun. Travis Humphreys, you always braced me for the big picture. Rick at Medtech, for wheels when I needed them. Bill Hane, don't think I didn't notice those bike gloves. The Tahoe Trampers, for all their support. Aaron Pearlman and his amazing wife for raising funds and birthday stoke on a cloud. John Sherman, for the therapy-enabling Sportsmobile.

I want to give a massive shout out to the March 5, 2010 CalStar heli crew (pilot and two flight nurses) who flew me safely from the backcountry to the Renown ICU. Thank you, Renown (ICU/inpatient rehab) doctors and staff for all your care, desire to see me rise, and support!

To Patrick Rivelli, Tal Fletcher, Doug Stoup, John Davis, Keoki Flagg, Tom Day, and Petter Nyquist, thank you for a year of adventure, stoke, unforgettable experiences, and the honor of sharing a powerful message with humanity in the coming year!

To every single one of you who donated to the incredible High Fives Foundation, all who've financially and emotionally supported my recovery, each and every one of you who came to, and supported from afar, the Sponsored by Love 2010 event, and to anyone and everyone out there right now on the front lines of bringing light and progress to spinal cord injury awareness and betterment, I give to you my deepest thanks.

This book is ending, but my gratitude is not. For those of you I met in the second year of this injury and beyond, please stay tuned…

RESOURCES

The following is a list of resources and modalities that have been help-ful and beneficial to Grant Korgan and his recovery. This information is in no way offered as medical advice. You should always consult your physi-cian before beginning any new treatment or exercise program.

Korg 3.0 Movement: www.korgmovement.com
High Fives Foundation: www.highfivesfoundation.org
Body Wellness Hawaii: www.bodywellnesshawaii.com
Zhu's Neuro-Acupuncture Center: www.scalpacupuncture.org
Northern Nevada Hyperbarics, Inc.: http://nevadahyperbarics.com
Spine Nevada: www.spinenevada.com
Center of Restorative Exercise (C.O.R.E.): http://www.corecenters.info
Christopher & Dana Reeve Foundation: www.christopherreeve.org

KEYNOTE SPEAKER

"Possibility through Positivity"
– KORG

A nanoscientist and professional athlete, Grant Korgan has never shied away from a challenge. When he found himself lying in the snow with a broken back from a snowmobile injury, deep in the Sonora backcountry of the Sierra Nevada, he knew he had met the biggest challenge of his life, and he didn't shy away from that either.

With a "glass-half-full" mentality, a rock-solid determination to overcome the challenge before him, and the constant support and love of his wife, Shawna, Grant began an extraordinary journey of recovery, the first year of which inspired his first book, *Two Feet Back*. Fueled by a lifelong desire to make a positive impact on the world, Grant now shares his inspiring words of empowerment and unflagging positivity to audiences around the country.

Grant's extraordinary achievements and universal message of survival have helped him to become a renowned and sought-after keynote speaker. While his own story is one of overcoming a significant challenge, Grant's message isn't about obstacles. It's about Deciding What You Want in life, Focusing on What IS Working, and at all points Choosing Positivity Through Adversity—these are Grant's 3 Points of Possibility, the keys to meeting adversity head-on and overcoming it joyfully.

"I believe that humanity's natural state is one of positivity, greatness, and, ultimately, love," begins Grant as he shares with others what he knows about the power of positivity, achieving goals regardless of circumstance, and the importance of remembering that life is happening right now, in this moment, with or without our permission.

Teams and corporations across the nation find Grant's outlook and inspiring words invaluable in achieving focus, endless drive, and motivation. With an emotional, uplifting presentation style that is at once inspirational and grounding, Grant Korgan's words will leave an impact on listeners on many levels. Audiences will appreciate his choice to turn physical and emotional adversity into positivity at every turn, and his words will have incredible impact on individuals and teams as they strive to meet their own challenges.
As Grant says, "It's not about what I've done... It's about what I'm going to do."

Contact info for booking - info@korgmovement.com